How Teamwork Works

How Teamwork Works

The dynamics of effective team development

John Syer and Christopher Connolly

The McGraw-Hill Companies

London · New York · St Louis · San Francisco · Auckland
Bogotá · Caracas · Lisbon · Madrid · Mexico · Milan
Montreal · New Delhi · Panama · Paris · San Juan · São Paulo
Singapore · Sydney · Tokyo · Toronto

Published by
McGRAW-HILL Publishing Company
Shoppenhangers Road, Maidenhead, Berkshire, SL6 2QL, England
Telephone 01628 23432
Fax 01628 770224

British Library Cataloguing in Publication Data

Syer, John D. (John David)
    How teamwork works: the dynamics of effective team development
    1. Interpersonal relations   2. Social groups   3. Work groups
    I. Title   II. Connolly, Christopher
    158.2

    ISBN 0-07-707942-6

Library of Congress Cataloging-in-Publication Data

Syer, John
    How teamwork works: the dynamics of effective team development / John Syer
    and Christopher Connolly.
        p.   cm.
    Includes bibliographical references and index.
    ISBN 0-07-707942-6 (alk. paper)
    1. Work groups.   I. Connolly, Christopher.   II. Title.
HD66.S94   1996
658.4′036—dc20
                                                                    96–8814
                                                                       CIP

McGraw-Hill

A Division of The McGraw-Hill Companies

12345CUP 99876

Typeset by Paston Press Limited, Loddon, Norfolk
and printed and bound in Great Britain at the University Press, Cambridge

Printed on permanent paper in compliance with ISO Standard 9706

To Margaret Connolly

Contents

Acknowledgements   **xiii**

Introduction   **1**
Relationships   1
Process   3
Performance   4

PART I   TEAM SYSTEMS   **5**

1   Team systems   **7**
The team as a system   7
The team as a process   8
Systems theory   9
Boundaries   18
Feedback: control or influence   21
Conclusion   25

2   The CORE team   **27**
Team regulation through feedback   27
The consistent team   30
The optimal team   32
The robust team   35
The evolving team   37
Summary   43

3   Team task cycle   **45**
Introduction   45
The five-stage model   46
Other models   54
Stepping down: from vision to action   56

Transition barriers   56
Travelling through the team task cycle   60

PART II   TEAM DEVELOPMENT   **63**

4   The team experience   **65**
        Individual identity and team membership   65
        Withdrawal and presence   66
        Response and disclosure   68
        Trying to change inhibits change   69
        Relinquish control and gain control   70
        Help by not helping   71
        Your problem is your solution   72
        Polarities and being stuck   72
        Summary   76

5   Team development   **77**
        Awareness   78
        Contact and communication   91
        Team spirit   102

6   Resistance   **109**
        Conflict   110
        Resistance seen as healthy defence   118
        Supporting resistance   124

7   Team identity   **127**
        Discovery   128
        Attunement   130
        Vision   133
        Norms   136
        Leadership   141
        Qualities and skills   145
        Membership   148
        Boundaries   152
        Resistance   158
        Projection   159
        The team system   159

PART III   TEAM MEETINGS   **163**

8   **Warming up**   **165**
        The place   167
        Oneself   170
        Others   172
        The team   175
        Purpose   176
        Agenda   178

9   **Task, maintenance and process**   **180**
        Task   180
        Maintenance   187
        Process   195
        The relationship between task, maintenance and process   198
        Team meeting roles   199

10 **Feedback on performance**   **205**
        Evaluative feedback   206
        Descriptive feedback   206
        Feelings   215
        Past, present and future   219
        Attitudes   222
        Interpretations   224
        Advice   227

11 **Speaking skills**   **228**
        Interaction and contact   228
        Talks, presentations and content   243
        Conclusion   244

12 **Questioning skills**   **246**
        Unsupportive questioning   246
        Supportive questioning   255
        . . . And answering   264
        Conclusion   265

13 **Listening skills**   **266**
        Poor listening   267
        Good listening   272
        Synergistic listening   275

14   Warming down   **283**
    Agenda   284
    Purpose   285
    The team   286
    Other team members   287
    Oneself   294
    The place   295

PART IV   TEAM TASK   **297**

15   Recognition   **299**
    The project team   299
    Forming a team system   303
    Inputs to the team system   306
    Outputs from the system   307
    System feedback and team regulation   309
    Insight barrier   310
    Objectives of the recognition stage   313

16   Understanding   **314**
    Understanding the situation   314
    Team regulation   325
    Mobilization barrier   329
    Objectives of the understanding stage   330

17   Decision   **331**
    Establish the inputs and outputs of the system 331
    Establish a decision process   335
    Choosing the best course of action   345
    Commitment barrier   350
    Objectives of the decision stage   353

18   Implementation   **355**
    Set-up   355
    Design   356
    Pilot   360
    Implement   360
    Integration barrier   364
    Objectives of the implementation stage   366

19   **Completion**   **368**

The completion process   368

Interpersonal skills   373

Withdrawal barrier   373

Objectives of the completion stage   375

Addendum: The team audit   **376**

Systems mapping   377

Team development   377

Team meetings   377

Team task effectiveness   378

References and bibliography   **380**

Index   **384**

Acknowledgements

Our first acknowledgement is offered to all our clients but particularly to those in the Ford Motor Company and British Petroleum who have been with us from the beginning of our organizational work. Tony Lewis introduced us to Ford Motor Company in 1987. Ed Henshall, Andy Bern and Rob Brittle have been consistently supportive as we have developed our model of the CORE team. At BP, Steve Percy pushed us to create our first team development programmes while Bernie Bulkin has been a constant source of insight, ideas and good humour. More recently, Bob Dover and Nick Barter of the Jaguar X100 and X200 teams have helped us discover what is possible to achieve with teams of 30 and more.

The influence of our teachers, colleagues and friends is immeasurable. Our unique approach owes much to our friends Drs George I. Brown and Judith R. Brown. Two of the first generation of Gestalt therapists, they have greatly influenced our development and figure prominently in Parts II and III of this book. Margo Russell and Karina Kaldeway have helped us to deepen our understanding of Psychosynthesis through constant dialogue. Ed Nevis—whose book *Organizational Consulting* is a prime test for consultants who wish to adopt a Gestalt approach—and his Cleveland Gestalt Institute colleagues have all prompted new insights.

Our Sporting Bodymind team has supported us throughout. Debbie Shepherd, our administrator, held the fort while we travelled the planet both to work and to write. We could not have succeeded without her. Jonathan Males provided unflappable good humour and goodwill as he dealt with whatever was thrown in his direction. He was also instrumental in developing the materials on the team system. Gail Taylor provided quiet reassurance and developed some of the original material which evolved into the team task cycle.

Bill Risso-Gill, old friend and co-director, ensured that business continued to grow despite our absences. He, his wife Jean and the Connolly clan back in Michigan have been prime sources of laughter and moral support throughout. We thank them and all those other good friends who, tolerating our unsocial commitment to 'the book', have encouraged us to see it to completion.

Introduction

There is a Greek myth about an innkeeper, called Procrustes, whose rooms all had the same size of bed. If guests were too short, he stretched them to fit the bed; if guests were too tall, he chopped off legs or feet to squeeze them in. Like Procrustes, companies are stretching and chopping their employees to fit each new organizational model, particularly if it is marketed as the most up-to-date structure for the 'forward looking' manager.

Three concepts captured corporate attention over the last decade: 'customer', 'competition' and 'change'. We have heard stirring litanies on customer orientation; we have seen organizations frantically re-engineering themselves to maintain their competitive edge while unparalleled changes have occurred in the corporate world at a truly unprecedented rate. These herald a new paradigm of organizational life.

Yet the paradigm shift is incomplete and, because of its incompleteness, a new dilemma is emerging: the more one attempts to grasp and quantify the new forms and structures, the more elusive they become. Organizations are living organisms characterized by their processes, not their structures. The flawed assumption is that, through building a structure, through fixing a procedure and through mechanizing a process, a viable organization will emerge. This does not happen and such a spurious platform has perpetuated the fundamental mistake of considering people as things to be measured, fixed overheads in the budget, objects to be re-engineered to fit into the re-engineered organization. We challenge this relic of the days of 'scientific management'. This book seeks to bring teams to life by honouring what is unique and special about their members, so as to enhance performance beyond the bounds of past limitations.

RELATIONSHIPS

People work in teams because together they have the potential to create something they cannot create alone. By maximizing the quality of the relationship between team members, teams maximize their performance. Let us now introduce another three words beginning with 'c' to add a human dimension to the 'customer/competition/change' paradigm: *contact, complexity* and *contribution*.

Contact

People achieve varying degrees of contact: good contact is deeply gratifying while lack of contact is deeply frustrating. The quality of contact between team members affects all aspects of their relationship and the team's performance. Without contact, people misunderstand each other, information and opportunities are lost and relationships fail to express their potential. With contact, communication is meaningful, understanding of others is increased, insights are shared and the abilities of people are acknowledged. Trust takes root.

Complexity

People are complex systems and so are the teams of which they are a part. The relationship between two individuals in a partnership, marriage or friendship is a complex system. A team (or a family) of four individuals has six relationships. A project team of 20 has 190 relationships and is a system so complex that it is unlikely ever to discover its full potential. These teams are embedded in organizational 'ecologies' whose complexities exponentially increase those of team life. Team systems are not machines; they do not operate in mechanical, linear ways; and when they stop growing or evolving, they begin to stagnate and die. Nor can teams be built to order and their performances are seldom predictable. It is unreasonable, indeed unacceptable, to expect them to fit into a 'Procrustean' bed of fixed roles, functions and structures. Teams are most predictable—and limited—when their potential is most constrained by their past. Teams which surprise or innovate and delight with their innovations, are teams which are fulfilling their potential, not living off their past.

Contribution

People also have an innate need to contribute. They want their community to grow and thrive; they want their network of friends and colleagues to have meaningful work; and they want the personal and extended family to be happy and to prosper. This book presents a model of teamwork and describes an environment in which team members may make their greatest contributions to enable the team to achieve its potential. Without the ability to contribute, people slowly lose touch with their essence and become as artificial as those genetically modified tomatoes which are perfectly round, unbruised and uniformly red but have skins like leather and taste like cardboard. People have to express what is inside themselves, the juice of their creative energy, the savour of their unique personality and experience.

Our model of teamwork creates the 'user friendly' environment or organizational ecology in which teams can thrive. We believe that teams and their members are desperate to excel. If they are told what they must achieve and how they must achieve it—and are bound by structures, managed by commands and limited by controls—they will eventually lose the ability to achieve their potential.

PROCESS

A word which does not fit into our 'c' list is *process*. Teams evolve and their nature cannot be categorized. We shift the emphasis from outcome to process. The statistician, George Box, somewhat surprisingly said: 'All models are wrong but some are useful.' Yet vendors of change management want to mount processes on slides and capture them in structures and procedures. The flaw lies in thinking that if we change the structure, the process will change. But that is a spurious concept. We tend to assume that if we change the structures, people will adapt; if we change the organization, people will adjust; and if we re-engineer the organization, people will re-engineer their relationships. It may work but it works badly. Such thinking has put the cart firmly before the horse. It is the process of speaking, interacting and relating which shapes the norms and generates the structures of group life. The team in action creates the structures in which it lives.

The best teams manage their own relationships and processes. They perform consistently *and* continue to optimize their performance. They have leaders, roles, goals and measures but they continually re-invent themselves.

PERFORMANCE

This book is for leaders, coaches, facilitators, consultants and team members—indeed, for anyone who wants to help a team build its relationships, discover its identity and perform at the outer edge of its potential.

Part I (Team Systems) describes how a team operates as a complex system with an organic life cycle and identifies a team's CORE competencies. Part II (Team Development) describes the team experience, showing how teams develop and discover their identity, while confronting resistance to change. Part III (Team Meetings) gives an account of communication skills that both support the task of a team meeting and develop the team. It contains chapters on warming up, finding the right balance of task, maintenance and process, giving feedback, using non-judgemental speaking, questioning and listening skills and warming down. Finally, Part IV (Team Task) shows how the process skills and the team task cycle apply to the archetypal project team. Each stage of the cycle is explored in turn: recognition, understanding, decision, implementation and completion. This part also gives details of how organizations can conduct a team audit. The Addendum will be of interest to managers and Human Resources people who want to know how Sporting Bodymind conducts a team audit. It establishes how we map and develop team systems as well as how teams can manage meetings and improve overall effectiveness.

This is a book about *how* teams excel, not *why*. Effective teams have discovered who they are, having ceased to worry about who they should be. As teams develop, they learn to self-regulate, to self-govern and to self-direct. Their identity is not something that can be given; and, once discovered, it cannot be taken away. It is in the doing and being that their discovery is made.

While the book is mainly a compilation by both authors, certain chapters contain individual experiences. To assist identification for those readers who are interested, John Syer has related a few of his experiences in Chapters 4–14 and Christopher Connolly has stated some individual events in Chapters 1–3 and 15–19.

PART I

Team Systems

1

Team systems

THE TEAM AS A SYSTEM

A team is a system, but a group of people huddling in a doorway sheltering from the rain is not a team. Nor, in normal circumstances, are regulars chatting together in a pub or bar. We reserve the word 'team' for those groups that constitute a system whose parts interrelate and whose members share a common goal. Some groups can easily be viewed according to this criterion. The manager and players of a football club constitute a set of parts necessary to the functioning of the whole—the common aim being to win matches. At what point then does a newly established group become a team and a team become effective?

Traditional performance measurements

There have been two traditional ways to evaluate team performance. The first has been to use a developmental model which aims to trace the different phases of a team's life cycle. A popular example of this is the forming, storming, norming, performing model of team development. The second model has emphasized structural patterns of a team. These may be construed in terms of gender, seniority, length of experience of roles. The structural approach attempts to fit team members into 'roles'—for instance, the 'peacemaker', the 'aggressor', the 'blocker' and the 'help-seeker' or Belbin's categories such as 'plant', 'resource investigator' and 'co-ordinator'. Although each of these models can be used to categorize the experiences of some teams and the overt behaviour of some team members some of the time, we find them insufficient. The problem is that they impose a structure on a dynamic process which is in fact much more complex, fluid and fraught with potential. This gives a false impression of control.

THE TEAM AS A PROCESS

Traditional performance measures which are used to quantify the above categories do not indicate how or in fact even whether, a team can produce consistent, high-level, predictable results. They do not help teams to weather revised corporate policies or changing membership or new leadership or takeovers. Nor do they identify interruptions of interpersonal contact within the team when members engage in territorial wars or withhold their expertise, particularly if they are unable to agree or seldom see each other. The only form of improvement offered by these models is to replace members who fail to show a certain ability with others who appear to have it. Senior managers often replace a member in a key executive function, only to find that the carefully selected replacement does not perform as well as expected. This is a frustrating and expensive phenomenon but it gives rise to the thought that perhaps it is not wholly the individual's character that determines how he or she operates in the team. It is probable that the team also exerts an influence on the individual's performance.

We believe that teams can work effectively with their chosen individuals and present resources, objectives and environment. However, this requires the opportunity and a method to determine whether the team process can operate consistently to a required standard over time and whether it can meet objectives when the group is working at less than optimum. It would be more productive to determine how the team failed to integrate a new member than to attribute failure to that member.

A further shortcoming would seem to be that as long as the team is operating within 'acceptable' parameters, there is either no apparent need to improve its performance or no readily discernible way to make the improvement. This, however, *is* possible through the appropriate use of a systems approach to team performance.

The fact that the team is a complex system in which relationships between the members play a prominent role requires the team to be self-managed. And nowhere is this more true than in the current business arena. As technological developments rapidly turn yesterday's solutions into today's problems and cross-cultural and multinational representatives produce constant flux in attendance and membership, a systems approach to team development has considerable advantages for the team which seeks to discover its identity and potential.

SYSTEMS THEORY

General systems theory as a discipline was developed after the Second World War, as scientists of numerous disciplines gradually recognized that their work had common threads. Rules and relationships in biology, for instance, were found to have their counterparts in the behavioural and social sciences, mathematics and engineering. As general principles were extracted from these points of intersection, a theory took shape that transcended the specialization of these separate disciplines.

Previously, the two best established approaches towards understanding everyday phenomena had been mechanics and statistics. The mechanical approach, using exhaustive detailed linear analysis and modelling, worked well if the subject matter did not have too many parts, if the parts did not interact too intricately or if the parts did not significantly change their attributes. If there were many parts, the statistical method could be used, which assumed that the parts were independent, were not organized and behaved randomly. Thus mechanics dealt with organized simplicity while statistics dealt with disorganized complexity. They are still both cornerstones to understanding how things work as well as to gathering and interpreting data. However, as they both assume static characteristics and ignore the dynamic nature of most systems, these approaches lack a means for dealing with organized complexity.

Most systems, including the human body, families and teams, fall into this 'complexity' category. In its simplest form a system is any process with a boundary. Most systems have inputs and outputs and receive structured feedback. This becomes identified as a pattern which creates forms or structures to sustain the system's process and extend its life. The systems view does not attempt to explain wholes by reducing them to simpler parts; rather, it understands parts by the functions they serve in the whole. Since even the simplest teams are complex and yet organized, it is difficult to explore them properly without using a systems approach. A comparison of the three approaches can be seen in Table 1.1.

Table 1.1 From simple to complex systems

Organized simplicity (the mechanical approach)	Disorganized complexity (the statistical approach)	Organized complexity (the systems approach)
Linear	Assumes independence	Structure
Detailed	Behaves randomly	Process
Exhaustive	Normally distributed	Input/Output
		Feedback
		Circular causality
		Self-sustaining

Origins

Early approaches to the application of systems thinking have origins in the works of engineers and physicists. In 1867, Scottish physicist James Clark Maxwell published a paper on feedback as a control mechanism entitled *On Governors*. Asked to predict how new machines would perform, Maxwell discovered that they exhibited random behaviours—oscillations, runaway behaviours or gradually slowing down—that were out of control and unpredictable. To solve the problem, he produced a series of equations which traced not only the relationship between the variables involved but also the machine's operation over time. When time was built into the equations the impact that 'feedback' had on the processes of the machines enabled him to predict their performance better. For many years, the main developments in systems thinking came from engineering applications and these models now form .the basis for many sophisticated approaches to engineering design.

The broader implications of systems thinking were already being explored before the Second World War. In the United States, the Bell Laboratories was developing ways to improve the transmission of information over telephone lines, by regulating positive and negative feedback and, in Vienna, research in biology and ecosystems was examining the growth of human and animal populations. After the Second World War, such research evolved into two main schools of thought. The first was cybernetics, derived from the Greek word *kubernetes* ('steersman' or 'helmsman') and developed by Norbert Weiner (Weiner 1948). This explored the nature of feedback mechanisms used by systems to regulate or steer their performance over time. The other was the school of general systems theory, stemming from the work of Ludwig von Bertalanffy who published his *General Systems Theory* in 1968 (von Bertalanffy 1968). Much of the subsequent work in systems approaches derived from this uses his terminology.* Some of the basic concepts of systems theory are discussed below.

Circular causality

The systems approach differs most obviously from traditional methods in its concept of circular causality. In the non-systems view, every event is caused by preceding events and the scientist seeks the cause or the real reason. Using the linear method of causality, ultimate causes are sought by tracing back through proximate causes (Figure 1.1).

However, many phenomena do not fit the linear method. A system is a set of elements that have relationships between themselves and between their attributes or characteristics. There are comparatively stable relationships between these elements which can be called its structure and the different parts of the system are causally linked which are its processes. To account for the multi-faceted relationships, systems theory employs the concept of 'circular causality'.

According to this concept, a cause produces an effect which, in turn, has many repercussions, some of which have an impact on the original cause. Since any observation of a system takes place at a particular point in time,

*The field soon mushroomed as scientists and researchers in a wide range of disciplines began to apply systems theory to their work: Gregory Bateson to ecology and anthropology, Kenneth Boulding at the University of Michigan to economics and political science, Virginia Satir to family theory, Paul Watslawiak of Palo Alto to therapy and language, J. von Neuman and O. Morgenstern to game theory and economics, Eric Trist at the Tavistock Institute to social psychology, Kurt Lewin and his Field Theory approach to Social Science and Jay Forrester at the (renamed) Alfred B. Sloan School of Management at MIT to management and organizations. More recently systems thinking has also been applied to extremely complex systems. The work of the Club of Rome examines the impact of humanity on the planet Earth's resources and identifies limits to the utilization of natural resources; chaos theory utilizes the topological mathematical work of Mandelbrot fractals to characterize self-organising systems that are so complexly interactive that it is not possible to predict their outcomes, only the unpredictable recurrence of patterns; and the work of the Santa Fe Institute has brought together cross-disciplinary convocations to examine the nature of hugely complex adaptive systems in economics, physics and related disciplines.

CAUSE⇒EFFECT

⇓

CAUSE⇒EFFECT

⇓

CAUSE⇒EFFECT

Figure 1.1 Linear causality.

any identifiable effect will already have produced changes in whatever is recognized as the cause of that effect. The process of observation imposes a degree of 'stasis' on a system that is in reality highly dynamic and interactive. Although causes produce effects, the connection between observed causes and effects are often *circular* rather than linear, even though, at any particular moment in time, this may not be apparent.

One design team we worked with had to submit a proposal for the redevelopment of an office block. There was an ambitious deadline which the team leader had promised to meet on the team's behalf. A junior team member responsible for filling in much of the detail on the proposed design, started to make mistakes. The number of mistakes gradually increased, creating a trend. The first response was to blame Thomas, the young architect: there was a direct causal relationship between him and his mistakes, which could have been blamed on youth or inexperience. However, linear causality thinking ignores the *circular* interaction between factors (Figure 1.2), which might have accounted for a far greater degree of the total variance.

Asked to repeat a single function in which there was very little creativity or differentiation, Thomas became bored and inattentive. This attribute of the task influenced his attention and he made mistakes which produced defects.

However, Thomas was part of a larger system in which his immediate team leader played a role. Having identified that there were defects in Thomas's drawings, the team leader began to pay closer attention to Thomas's work. This made Thomas even more nervous and resulted in more rather than fewer mistakes.

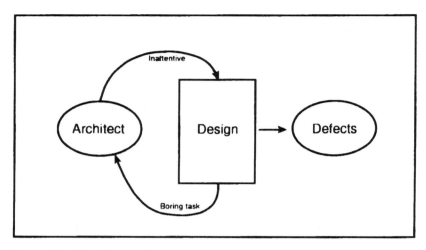

Figure 1.2 Circular causality (1).

It is inexact to say there is a linear relationship between the designer and the number of defects produced when he or she performs a task. The designer, the task and the team leader are elements of a system in which each is influenced by the others. There are circular relationships between all three (Figure 1.3).

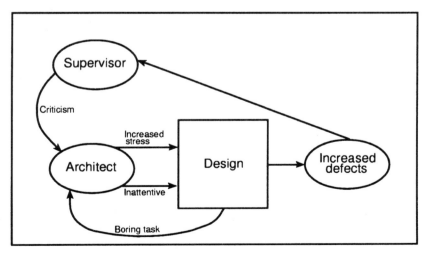

Figure 1.3 Circular causality (2).

Open systems and closed systems

A system that affects and is affected by its environment is called an open system. A closed system is one that works in isolation but is relatively rare. Some machines are almost closed systems but even they have inputs in the form of fuel and outputs in the form of product. A company that actively canvasses feedback from its customers and attempts to meet their requirements is operating an open system. All teams, to the extent that they utilize any resources, communicate outside of themselves or produce any outputs, are open systems. A cross-functional project team will be a particularly open system.

Understanding system boundaries is essential because team members can only gauge their customers' requirements by meeting and interacting with them at the boundary between them.

Four systems laws

The composition law

This defines the concept of synergy, stating that the whole is greater than the sum of its parts. Elements of the system relate to each other, showing attributes, qualities and performance that can only be observed in terms of those relationships. The relationships generate energy that is otherwise only a potential.

The comprehension law

An examination of its parts or subsystems is not enough to understand an entire system. Systems are dynamic. If the parts or subsystems are taken out of relationship with each other, they will no longer demonstrate the qualities of the relationship and will therefore not explain their attributes as part of the system.

The decomposition law

The third law states that the part is more than a fraction of the whole: the components of a system have an existence of their own. Put them in another system and they may demonstrate qualities that were not evident in the previous system. In this respect, team members have qualities and skills not evoked in the context of the team and may perform very differently elsewhere.

The complementarity law

When we view something from various perspectives it is often seen differently. The team experience does not look the same from different aspects and the system cannot be envisaged completely from within. As consultants, we seek a *metaperspective*. This allows us to appreciate the perspective of each team member as the team gets drawn into some complicated conflict, although we are inevitably influenced by and influence, what is happening.

Energy transfer

All open systems transfer energy. At the simplest level, the *raison d'être* of a system is to transfer energy while it maintains its existence (Figure 1.4). If an open system does not transfer energy, it eventually ceases to exist. Teams, similarly, can be seen as systems for the transfer of energy. They are formed to produce something from the resources, time, energy and information they receive.

Input

Energy entering the system—information or resources—is an input. This is transformed through its structures and processes. For a team the broad spectrum of inputs might include management objectives, research data, production materials, communication from other teams, problems given to the team to solve or even new members.

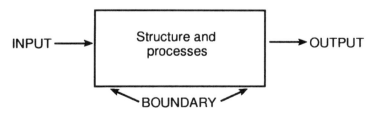

Figure 1.4 System elements.

Output

Output is whatever the system transforms, produces or expresses as a consequence of its method of processing the input. For example, a solution is the output of a problem-solving team.

When a systems approach is applied to teamwork, performance is the 'output' of the team's process. The way in which the team's input is transformed by this process determines the success of the system. The more quickly the team solves the problem and puts into place a permanent corrective action, the more effectively will the team system perform.

Mechanical teams that have rigid structures and functions are unable to perform effectively in today's chaotic world. Consciously self-regulating teams are complex and multi-functional by nature. They cannot and should not be formed to produce a single type of response: faced with the unpredictable, they need the flexibility of many options. 'Equipotentiality'—an ability to maintain a wide range of responses to a changing environment—is an essential attribute of effective team members and is cultivated as a team norm by today's finest teams. Such teams are more than adaptable; they are rapidly evolving, complex systems that keep pace with the ever-changing environment.

Structure and process

The *structure* of a team system comprises those aspects that are relatively static or enduring. *Process*, on the other hand, refers to the team system's behaviour—to those relatively dynamic or transient factors by virtue of change or instability.* A new team will frequently, though not always, have various elements built into its structure and a number of processes established to transform input energy into outputs, with minimal error and waste of resources. Structures might include specifications for the size and shape of the team, team membership, a place and time to meet and team roles. Processes will be norms that include methods of problem solving, decision making and planning.

In traditional models, the system acts to transform energy from input to output through its process. Once established, this process is subject to

---

*'Process' is also a term used to describe that part of a meeting where its dynamics as opposed to its content is considered.

deviation from target values, owing to internal and external factors that produce 'error states'—that is, outputs other than the desired output. Such outputs may just be wasted energy or may actually reduce the functional ability of the system itself.

If a particular team has to solve a problem, we can consider it to be a system with inputs, outputs and a transformation process. Team process can be defined as an activity (meetings) which utilizes resources (the team) to transform inputs (ideas, skills and qualities of team members) into outputs (discoveries, solutions, proposals, actions, design ideas and products) while being subjected to specific controls (speaking skills, the agenda, time management, descriptive feedback, warming up and the task methodology). The parameters that should be optimized are those that will have the strongest effect on the ability of the team system to transform energy effectively.

It would be simple if we could say that structure determines process—that is, that a team's membership, agenda, roles and task methodologies will determine how it operates. And in numerous situations, different people placed in the same situation do tend to act in surprisingly similar ways. In the famous Milgram experiments of the 1960s (Milgram 1965), a wide range of 'volunteers' were instructed to induce other experimental subjects to 'learn' through *negative reinforcement*—which involved giving electrical shocks to the subjects if they did not perform correctly. In fact, the electrical shocks were not real and the recipients were other researchers who only pretended to experience pain. Despite the subjects 'pleading' to be released from this form of punishment, the 'volunteers' continued to administer increasingly large shocks, at the insistence of the researchers, 'to advance scientific knowledge'. The study was finally discontinued because of the emotional trauma experienced not only by the 'volunteers' but also by the researchers as they realized that the volunteers were willing to administer 'life threatening' doses of electricity. Hence trial pleas by concentration camp guards often claimed that the social structure influenced their behaviour.

Kenwyn Smith describes structure as 'frozen process'. Structures and processes are circular in their relationship: while structures determine processes, processes eventually shape structures. Process can be frozen into a structure or a structure can be unfrozen into a process. The best and most organic way to change from one structure to another is to unfreeze the structure, mould it into a new process and let it 'refreeze' into a new structure. Similarly, the most effective teams are those which play with the relationship between structure and process, calling it 'co-operating', 'going with the flow' or 'choosing what you've got'. The frozen/melted dichotomy is paralleled in quantum physics, which allows scientists to observe the same subatomic phenomenon operating as either a wave or a particle. In this respect, the team process and structure are equally malleable in the adaptive team.

When teams insist on maintaining their structures—i.e. their 'frozen processes' and their fixed identities—their performance deteriorates. As mentioned previously, James Clark Maxwell identified this, in noting that the process of a machine running eventually influences the machine's performance. This circular relationship between structure and process becomes obvious when we examine the performance of teams over time. Intervention in the team system can be made at the level of structures and form (the roles of team members, their agendas, etc.) or via process (communication, the nature and quality of contact, etc.).

Today's constant, rapid, unpredictable changes in all aspects of a team member's work undercut an organization's ability to depend upon structure to optimize team and corporate success. Mechanical and structurally based approaches are no longer viable ways of adapting to a complex and chaotic environment. Process orientation is now the vehicle for maintaining flexibility and responsiveness in a world in which change is the only constant. Team members who participate with awareness in their system allow the team to self-regulate and increasing their competence as individuals increases the team's ability to do this.

BOUNDARIES

Depending upon the perspective one selects, the boundaries drawn around the system can be more or less inclusive. Boundaries indicate the nature of a system's interaction with its environment. Team boundaries range from rigid at one extreme to diffuse at the other. Rigid boundaries exist when a team receives little feedback from customers, suppliers or its environment. A rigidly imposed hierarchy within the organization creates a largely impermeable barrier between the workforce and management or between different teams within the organization. On the other hand, organizations with boundaries that are too permeable are unable to filter and digest

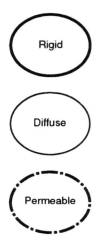

Figure 1.5 System boundaries.

information. Decision making and direction then become confused or ambiguous (Figure 1.5).

It takes energy to cross any boundary and it is almost always easier to cross in one direction than in another. When we first began to work with Ford Motor Company in 1987, design and manufacturing engineering teams working on the same vehicle rarely spoke to each other. Because of rigid organizational boundaries and highly territorial power bases, they engaged in what was called 'over the wall engineering'. One team designed the component or subsystem and then 'threw it over the wall' to the next team. This team then had to decide how to interface the new component with the system they were working on or design new manufacturing processes. Rigid boundaries blocked opportunities for communication and drastically reduced the circular feedback essential for developing the different elements of a total system concurrently. Without circular feedback, there are no just-in-time processes or simultaneous engineering. Three-, four- or even five-year development targets for a new vehicle were extremely difficult to meet.

Eight years later, in 1995, as part of Ford 2000's initiative for globalization, we have been working with the Joint Vehicle Development project team for the new X200 Jaguar based in Coventry and the DEW98 Lincoln based in Detroit. They will share common parts and processes and yet produce two very different vehicles. They have design, process and manufacturing engineers in the same teams, meeting cross-functionally and cross-nationally on phones, video conferences and face to face. They have separate and joint identities and the most flexible boundaries possible. The members of these teams say that life has rarely been so complex, unpredictable, demanding, enjoyable or exciting.

At the simplest level, boundaries can be put around almost anything, thereby defining it as a system. A team forms boundaries as it establishes its identity: it will fix regular times to meet; it will establish its membership; it will gain authority over materials, resources, finance and equipment; it will invite non-members to join the team for a period of time and it will arrange its own workplace and environment. These factors become aspects of the team's identity, so that members know that 'this is our workplace', 'these are our tasks' and 'X is a member of our team'. The first task in any systems analysis is to identify such boundaries.

The boundary may be defined to include more or fewer of the factors that impact on the system. The advantage of setting less inclusive boundaries and identifying more of the factors is that the structure and process of the system is easier to understand, monitor and control. Many factors are perceived and experienced as being subject to other forces in the organization or as being so variable that the team is unable to control them. These are best identified as external inputs to the system, characterized by a large element of 'noise'.

The advantage of including a wide range of factors is that input is tightly defined. This allows energy to be easily tracked through the system. It also minimizes possible interaction between a large number of inputs. For example, by including environment, resources and information in the system (as well as team members) and identifying only the champion's directive or the imposed monthly target as input, most of these factors can be controlled as internal noise (see below). However, the inclusion of so many environmental factors in a team's internal system can make it difficult to observe and map its process.

Different boundaries constrain observation of the system in different ways—a fact that can prove useful. For example, very different pictures of the team's system will emerge if team members are included inside the system (thereby narrowing input) rather than considered as input but *information* is identified as inside the system. Changing the boundaries to include or exclude different elements of the larger environment can allow the team to be more robust to a wide range of circumstances and thereby reduce error states. At the same time, simply playing with the boundary definition of the team will not do anything unless the team changes its process and structure to take advantage of the redefinition. Finding ways in which teams can sustain their performance or even thrive in a hostile corporate environment is easier said than done.

Team life and team process are rooted in their interactive relationships. The system improves its capacity for self-management as members enhance their personal competencies, the quality of their contact with other team members and the free flow of information and energy between them. Renewed self-management continually redefines the team's identity as it reorganizes its structures and processes. These, in turn, redefine the team identity which, in turn, is reflected in the nature of the team's boundaries.

FEEDBACK: CONTROL OR INFLUENCE

The continuity of a team system is maintained by ensuring that feedback loops prevent it from deviating unconsciously from its desired performance targets. These loops form circular interrelationships which feed information from output back into input. Feedback can monitor any deviation from prescribed limits, which represent the 'desired' behaviour of the system. An example of how such feedback loops operate can be found in the nearest bathroom. In the tank at the back of nearly every modern lavatory is a mechanism that ensures that the correct amount of water will always be available for the next flush. The feedback loop consists of water level, float, valve and water inflow. The capacity for such control is engineered into many mechanical systems—the cooling fan on a car radiator is another example—and occurs naturally in all biological and social systems. All efficient systems, including team systems, use feedback loops to maintain their critical factors at a constant level.

In this context there are two kinds of feedback—'positive' and 'negative'.* *Positive feedback* or *reinforcing loops*, reinforce the trend or direction of a factor in a system and can generate growth; *negative feedback*

*The use of the terms 'positive' and 'negative' feedback in our discussion of team systems does not mean good or bad. They are not evaluative descriptions. They identify the two major forces which operate on a factor in a system. 'Positive' feedback means that the particular factor is reinforced or augmented. 'Negative' feedback means the factor is restrained or reduced.

or *balancing loops* seek to counterbalance growing trends and maintain stability or resist change. Feedback is essential, as it provides information about the stability and performance of a system.

Positive feedback or reinforcing loops

Growth is the product of positive feedback. If a factor continues to grow without the system providing any compensating or balancing factors, it will reach exponential levels. This, however, may be construed as desirable. All investment funds show graphs of their monetary value growth over one-, five- and ten-year periods. Even a savings account will show an exponential growth curve, the rate of accumulation accelerating (Figure 1.6).

In the case of animal populations, unchecked growth can lead to unacceptable levels. This often happens when animals are introduced into an ecosystem where there is no natural predator. For example, the prolific breeding rate of rabbits in Australia resulted in an infestation. This was only checked by the introduction of myxomatosis which operated as negative feedback or a balancing influence in the ecosystem.

Negative feedback or balancing loops

Negative feedback allows a system to maintain stability (Figure 1.7). The most frequently used example of negative feedback is the thermostat, which

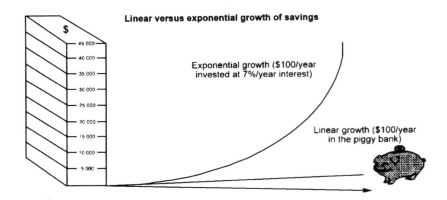

Figure 1.6 Positive feedback or reinforcing loop.

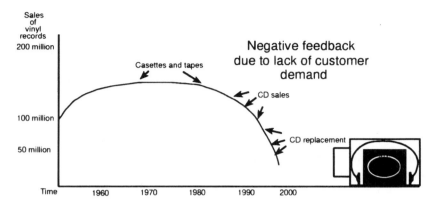

Figure 1.7 Negative feedback or reinforcing loop.

switches off the heating when the temperature reaches a certain level and switches it on again when the temperature decreases to a lower level. The word 'negative' is used because every time the system's output deviates from the target value, the mechanisms pushing it towards the new values are reversed. This process of maintaining stability is called 'homeostasis'. A thermostat with a positive feedback loop would respond to high temperature by raising the temperature further.

Continuous negative feedback can result in the decline and eventual extinction of a particular factor or phenomenon. For example, the development of the tape cassette, then the compact disc and now the joint Sony/Phillips/Mitsubishi replacement for the CD has produced a continual downturn of sales of vinyl records.

Homeostasis: system stability

Threats to the stability of a system will be countered by a powerful attempt to maintain homeostasis. If furious arguments between the parents threaten a family's survival, a child may distract attention from the parental subsystem by developing poor health or unusual behaviour. Since this 'symptom' helps the family system survive, it is important to the family that the symptom is maintained. Family therapists have noticed that when one member's mental health improves, there is often a negative reaction from other members of the family. Recovery threatens the system's stability and is therefore challenged.

In fact, 'homeostasis' is something of a misnomer. Put technically, a 'variable' is said to 'hunt' (vary) around a 'control' value. Deviations from these values are used to regulate the members of, for example, a family or team. When one family visits another, all the children are sent to play in another room. After a while, the visiting mother turns to her husband and says: 'Dear, the children are getting awfully noisy.' The father goes across to the door, opens it and shouts 'Hey kids! Keep the noise down! We're trying to have a conversation in here.' The level of noise diminishes and the adults continue talking. A bit later the woman interrupts her husband. 'Things are pretty quiet in there. I wonder what the children are doing?' Once more the husband goes to the door of the adjacent room and, without opening it, calls out: 'Hey, what's going on in there, what are you kids up to?' This causes much giggling and an answering chorus from the children of 'Nothing!' The noise level rises again and the adults continue their conversation.

Some time ago, we were invited to help a design team that was developing a new voice command feature for its portable telephone. The team had been spiralling into disagreements over every point and was unable to reach consensus. The project's champion eventually sat in on a meeting and made a pronouncement: 'I'm tired of all this squabbling. Can't you sort out your priorities and agree on some action?' Somewhat chastened, the team members took their champion's request to heart and developed a strategy for compromising on their differences. The next time the champion attended, the discussion was sober and consensus was easily reached. At the end of the meeting the champion was uneasy. 'This all looks fine,' she said, 'but I haven't heard any counter-arguments. I wonder if you've really considered this fully enough. Can't you generate a little bit of passion for this product?'

A team may well seek to maintain certain factors—dialogue, for instance—at a certain level. Too much differentiation can lead to difficulties in reaching consensus; too little differentiation can stunt new ideas. The team has to balance its amount of dialogue with other factors in its process, such as deadlines, costs, inclusion of expertise and customer requirements. Yet this issue needs to be considered in the broader dilemma of group life: does a team stress shared values, processes and norms or does it allow team members to fully self-actualize in the team environment? The answer, as discussed at length in Part II of this book is 'both/and'.

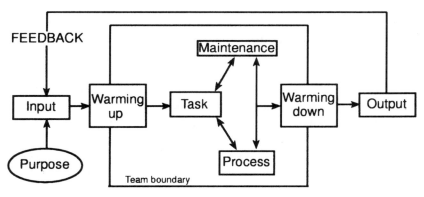

Figure 1.8 Team meeting with feedback loop.

The team system

The critical link between the team's structure and its process is found in feedback loops. Feedback loops feed information from output back to input—from a team's past performance into its future performance. A team gradually establishes patterns of operation that transform the inputs to its system into desirable outputs. Feedback ensures that this success is constantly repeated. The system 'learns' which are successful patterns of behaviour and which are not.

An effective team will build into its structure mechanisms which will both maintain effective performance through balancing (negative) feedback loops and improve the performance through reinforcing (positive) feedback loops. Feedback loops influence the way in which structure determines process and (more importantly for us) the way that process determines structure. Information is transmitted within the system and is used to maintain stability, to bring about structural changes and to facilitate interaction with other systems. A simple model for one way to structure team meetings includes the concept of feedback loops presented in Figure 1.8.

CONCLUSION

A little learning is a dangerous thing. Knowing that teams are systems is not the same as knowing how they should be structured, the boundaries that are appropriate, the processes they should cultivate or the norms they should embody. It shows neither the feedback that is appropriate nor indeed the team processes that should have feedback. It indicates neither the levels of process or procedure the team should seek to maintain nor the levels that different types of team should seek to maintain. There are no hard and fast rules about the structures, processes, boundaries, target values of feedback mechanisms that teams should use.

There *are* guidelines for achieving the team system you want but their application means discovering more about the way team self-regulation is achieved and managed. To quote Dr Moshe Feldenkrais, an old friend of ours: 'If you know what you are doing you can do what you want.'

2

The CORE team

The Greek myth of the innkeeper Procrustes, who either stretched or truncated his clients' limbs so they might fit the beds he provided, has its twentieth-century parallels. Henry Ford's concern with customer satisfaction was summed up in his much quoted statement: 'They can have any colour they like as long as it is black.' He was the archetypal 'Procrustean' manufacturer of his day and, until the 1960s, the Ford product development and marketing approach—'we know what you want, we'll design it, you'll buy it and you'll like it'—was typical of its time. Then Ford was hit by the Edsel débâcle and woke up.

During the last few decades, the financial officers and statisticians have become the Procrustean innkeepers of their day. They study the output of a process and develop tests to determine whether a system is in control (according to their client's chosen limits) and, if it is not, they pinpoint the nature of the problem. Unfortunately statisticians—and, to be fair, frequently their clients—can and often do make flawed assumptions about their statistical data: (i) because it is mathematical it is true; (ii) something is only valid if it can be measured; and (iii) financial profit is the only measure of success.

TEAM REGULATION THROUGH FEEDBACK

In a similar way, psychometrics and personality models have supported a mechanical/statistical approach to a team's process, fitting the behaviour of team members into behavioural roles that are predetermined. Through a 'Procrustean' fitting of identity and function into Belbin, Myers-Briggs or Bion personality models, employees and team members are selected for

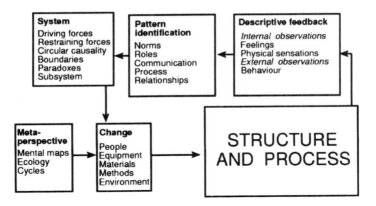

Figure 2.1   Team feedback loop in detail.

their jobs and functions and are often typecast for their career. These and other ways of squeezing people, teams and their process into fixed pigeon holes is no longer appropriate. 'Procrusteanism' is rife when old norms are not challenged regularly and when personality models are used to avoid genuine contact or cultivation of an individual's full potential.

Teams are systems with inputs, outputs, boundaries, structures and processes. But systems also employ mechanisms for collecting information about their performance to enable them to maintain their existence. The key to monitoring and regulating those aspects of team performance that are observable is to gather 'the voice of the process' through descriptive feedback loops (Figure 2.1). Descriptive feedback, as described at length in subsequent sections of this book, allows such monitoring to be done without judgement. It provides four basic functions:

1 It makes the team process—behaviour, relationships and feelings—explicit.
2 It allows team members, by describing their process, to notice when the team's level of performance 'veers out of control' or changes. (This could be when the team drops below its expectations, thereby inhibiting potential or when it exceeds expectations and sets examples that the team may want to reinforce.)
3 It prompts awareness of what could be changed to allow the team process to improve continually.

4 It avoids the trap of 'reifying' the team—turning it into a thing rather than exploring its evolving potential and the relationship of its members.

Some team behaviours are the product of cause and effect relationships that are time-related; others are not. Interventions by a time-keeper may help the team to keep to its agenda but other factors have a more circular link. For example, replacing a long table with a round one would result in more eye contact among members of a problem-solving team. This could lead to an enhanced exchange of information and a clearer description of the situation, which in turn would create a more targeted search for relevant data and eventually produce a root cause identification for the problem. The new seating arrangement may produce a root cause more quickly but the cause and effect chain is intricate.

Team behaviours require an intervention when they become part of a pattern which affects the team's performance. One-off incidents that impact performance adversely need to be avoided but dealing with them will not in itself necessarily improve performance over time. They are 'special cause' events and ad-hocism does not constitute a strategy for achieving excellence. If the interventions that need to be made from a systems perspective are to be identified, the greater picture or the 'ecology' of the whole system must be taken into consideration. We need a method of regulating team performance that goes beyond old categories, typologies and static measures.

The team's processes are the life blood of its performance. Structure no longer determines process. It is process that determines both structure and output. Maximize your team process and you will maximize your team performance. CORE teamwork as identified in this chapter involves the use of feedback. It moves beyond data collection to the identification of ways in which 'positive' and 'negative' feedback can modify the team process. What people notice and how they feel can be observed to identify emerging patterns. The patterns specify the nature and performance variability of the team's processes. This allows the team to establish performance-based targets which help regulate its process and identify opportunities for improvement.

There are four characteristics of a CORE team process. It is:

1 consistent in its performance over time;
2 optimal for the task it has to perform;

3 robust* to all the uncontrollable and unpredictable events it encounters;
4 evolving as it continuously discovers its full potential.

THE CONSISTENT TEAM

Every team acquires a set of shared norms and beliefs that orient the
behaviours of its members but they are mostly unstated and have some
degree of variability. Fluctuations of mood, differences in task demands,
attendance and time-keeping are all common cause variations within the
team process and, while there are 'normalized' limits regarding conflict,
clothes, language and moral standards, variation is tolerated here too.

Statisticians and psychometricians seem to categorize behaviours princi-
pally so that they may (dubiously) predict them but, that said, there is an
advantage in identifying targets for team performance. Rather than fitting
people (or teams) into categories, a team is helped to identify key aspects of
its performance so that it may determine an ideal performance level for
each. How much time the team spends in discussion, the kinds of questions
that are asked, the level of interaction between team members, the length of
meetings, the time spent on each agenda item are examples of such aspects.

Different types of team will require different aspects and different target
levels. At different stages of a project cycle these targets will vary. All teams
utilize brainstorming at some stage in their project cycle but brainstorming
for a creative team in the generative stage of its cycle could go on for weeks,
whereas in the problem profile stage of a problem-solving team there is little
room for it. Once targets are identified and clear mechanisms for generating
feedback and identifying patterns are in place, the team can focus on those
factors which cause it to deviate from its performance targets.

Team performance variation

Causes of unwanted variation in team performance that may be identified
through feedback can fall into one of two general categories: specific causes
and common causes.

*The use of the term 'robust' to describe a team attribute draws upon an
approach to the development of design as expounded by Dr G. Taguchi, the
Japanese statistician.

Specific causes

These may be such events as changes in membership, changes in task assignment, changes in budget and resources, illness, changes in deadlines and equipment breakdown. They occur frequently and usually cause the team to deviate from its performance targets. Because of their relatively discrete nature, specific causes can usually be identified but rarely predicted. If they cause anxiety or frustration and disrupt the consistency of the team's performance for any length of time, the team has to minimize their impact.

Many specific cause variations are the result of the organization of which the team is a part. A culture that fosters mistrust, a lack of awareness of members' needs or poor contact is bound to affect team performance. The challenge to team members—particularly to the leader—is to eliminate specific cause variation within the team process, so that the process becomes consistent again. One of the main ways of reducing specific cause variations is to enhance the competencies of team members so that they are less likely to be its source (for instance through burnout) and are able to respond creatively to causes of variation outside their control.

Common causes

These are inherent in the team as it is and represent the greatest opportunity for long-term improvement in team performance. The tennis player whose concentration is always fluctuating or the manager who responds inconsistently to resistance, are examples of common cause variation. Common causes are often more difficult to identify, are embedded in the system and can take much more effort to change. Changing deviations from ideal performance that are due to common cause variation may require the identification of strong leverage interventions or heavily resourced input.

A good team not only devotes enough time and energy to its task; it also attends to feelings and relationships within the group and observes its own dynamics. The balance of these phases of interaction will vary but the team will never completely lose sight of its task nor totally ignore the feelings and relationships of its members. To do so risks deterioration of its performance.

A team minimizes common cause variation by establishing both minimum and preferred standards of performance that it can use as criteria to monitor and improve its process. The criteria can prompt effective action in 'out-of-control' conditions. However, unforeseen changes or continued unusual behaviour of any team member suggests that the cause of such variations is specific rather than common. Though the particular events may not be predictable, it is always possible to have containment measures in place.

Typical common cause variations include:

1 The team's performance is consistently below its target for a particular attribute. Process observation can then help identify failure modes and target new objectives. Where the same failure modes recur, the team may need to dedicate time to further maintenance or a team development session to identify the underlying attributes of its performance that need to be addressed. This may lead to further training and development of team skills.

2 The team's performance is above its target—for instance, it completes a project ahead of time. Then work habits, structures, methodologies or personal performance of team members may suggest how the entire team system could be improved. Peak performance can be used as a model to enhance performance.

3 When several team members are outside the parameters of the team target or there is too much variation in the measurements of the team's performance, something may be wrong with the chosen targets or the team system—particularly its structures, processes and norms—may have major flaws and require modification. Alternatively, the measures may be flawed and need to be re-evaluated.

The CORE team audit outlined later in the book monitors variation in team performance and helps identify whether its causes are common or specific. It also suggests how a highly consistent team performance may be obtained.

THE OPTIMAL TEAM

Although it can be difficult to eradicate specific cause variations of performance—each event is unique and therefore unpredictable—if the team is to maintain control over its process it needs to identify them and at least minimize or isolate their impact. If the team knows the reasons for the deterioration in its recent performance, it can take some remedial action.

However, the teams we work with want to do more than maintain consistency of performance. Some teams are consistently good, some are consistently mediocre and some are consistently poor in their performance. Consistency is not a virtue in itself. Most organizations want to make certain that their teams are consistently the best or the *optimal* teams for the tasks they have to perform. Most good teams have this as a long-term objective. Neurotic conflict, misunderstanding and poorly run meetings may be consistent but are certainly not indicative of optimal team performance. The parameters of its behaviour may show too wide a variation to allow it to reach its objective or it may be consistently hitting a level of performance below or above the optimal level. The optimal team's performance moves not only towards increased consistency but also towards perfection.

More is not necessarily better,

The optimal team is the one best suited for the job. An optimal team is one with the right skills and a clear understanding of its task. It has the necessary resources in terms of office space, telephones, computers and logistical support. It has access to the information it requires and knows how to apply this information to the task. It is not overstaffed and carries the appropriate level of expertise.

An optimal team spends sufficient time warming up and warming down. It knows how to use communication skills to clarify information and maintain good contact among team members. It has action planning methodologies to implement its decisions. Optimal teams dedicate the right proportion of their time to getting the task done, maintaining the quality of their relationships and observing their team process for ways in which it might be enhanced. From a systems point of view, more is not better. A team which does not regulate the time it spends improving its relationships may never complete its task properly. Similarly, a team which does not regulate the time it spends on task may find its performance deteriorating; as personal relationships break down, conflicts are left unresolved.

Consistency, when it is the result of over-control or manipulation, constrains behaviour, reducing the range of possibilities open to team members. Their diversity of experience and opportunity to creatively adapt to changing circumstances is stifled. The leader who over-controls or manipulates is usually perceived as autocratic. However, when we talk of a team being consistent, we mean that variation from targets for behaviours, processes and structures which facilitate or enhance performance is reduced. The nature of these factors are discussed at greater length in Part II of this book but would typically include the assignment and performance of roles, warming up and warming down, the use of communication skills as required by each stage of the task, the translation of ideas into actions and the utilization of specific methodologies.

For teams to perform optimally, consistency needs to be maintained in certain but not all, factors of the team's performance. Variations such as dispensing with warming up or speaking about rather than to people during team meetings need to be reduced by narrowing the acceptability of variation in such issues. In these areas the team needs to become more consistent. However, there are a large number of factors that must have very wide parameters for their target values: speaking one's mind, time allowed for reflection, discussion targeted at underlying purpose and motivation and opportunity for enjoyment all need to range from minimal to maximal variation. Paradoxically, the greater the range of perspectives, behaviours and feelings a team can support, the better the team performance. Also, the most effective teams are those which create ways to develop the potential of each team member.

Focus on process

This is why we focus feedback on factors that regulate the team process and can be achieved consistently over time. Ideally, the team identifies critical factors in its performance and sets initial targets for these factors early on. The process may then be stabilized by monitoring them, so that adjustments can be made to realign until the team is performing at or around its targets consistently. Once it can do this, it can range wide in terms of talent, creativity, uniqueness and spontaneity. Such consistency also allows inputs to the team's process to be efficiently transformed into ideal outputs—there is little waste of team energy and resources on unnecessary argument, distraction, misunderstanding or delays. When these process-oriented factors have been stabilized, the team can determine those that need to be adjusted or changed to make them more appropriate for the current task.

THE ROBUST TEAM

Ideally, the team process should transfer all input energy into the best possible outputs. But this rarely happens. There are unscheduled changes of direction, unanticipated resistance, unforeseen mistakes, surprise conflicts, etc., which detract from the optimal performance and contribute to *error states*. These are outputs from the team process which sidetrack its energy into behaviours or performance which, at best, simply waste the team's energy but, at worst, reduce the perceived quality of its output. CORE teams develop attributes and processes which minimize the impact of such factors on their performance—they become more robust.

Noise in the system

There are factors both inside and outside the system which detract from the team's ideal output. They are not under the team's control even when the team knows they exist. Using the terminology of the Japanese statistician, Genichi Taguchi, these are called external and internal 'noise' factors.

External noise

External noise factors impact on the team from outside its boundaries. They may include a change in its membership dictated by senior management, aspects of its working environment, corporate culture, company norms and resistance to change. Team goals—defined as output—vary according to the task. Many of them are determined outside the team boundaries and are subject to change, as management redefines its objectives and corrects its corporate course. These, too, affect the team's performance and the behaviour of individual team members.

Most teams develop ways to minimize the effect of these factors (resistance can be *overtly* healthy). A problem-solving team finds a champion to back its search for a root cause in order to avoid being pressed into a quick fix by line managers; a design team considers the optimization of a particular system under all kinds of weather conditions; a marketing team seeks the exact details of customer requirements before signing off a design it will have to sell a year later; and a sports team scouts its opponents before a big match. These and other strategies are ways of developing robustness against external noise.

Internal noise

This relates to factors within the team system itself—its membership, its internal processes and interactions. For example, members may bring predetermined ideas as the correct design solution; they may have biases towards other team members, based on race, gender, function or grade; or some members may not trust or respect others and may impede performance with ill-timed questioning, challenging or contradictions. The team may lack time management skills and never start meetings on time or end them satisfactorily. Team members may not know how to ask open questions to access new avenues of information. Closed questions may be used to no purpose and lead to familiar non-productive and previously rejected ideas. Team members may not know how to build on the ideas of each other and good ideas may be lost. Teams can attempt to minimize the impact of such behaviour by controlling team norms and communication practices, setting purposeful agendas, perfecting time management, minuting meetings correctly, attending awareness sessions and team development workshops that improve its ability to manage its process.

Figure 2.2 shows the team system with its inputs and outputs.

Robustness

The traditional approach to building teams is to select team members with the required skills and knowledge, to establish roles and to impose codes of behaviour. Performance is assessed and, if the team then fails to perform within these parameters, it is adjusted and redesigned: team members are changed, roles are redefined and codes of behaviour are more strictly enforced.

A robust team explores and adopts ways of working together which ensure that it operates effectively, *despite* internal difficulties or awkward external influences.

- It gradually develops norms that sustain and support its performance under stress.
- It builds an environment which supports its membership, stabilizes its processes and shares its roles.
- It continues to enhance the competencies of its membership so that it has internal resources to respond to the widest range of possible events.

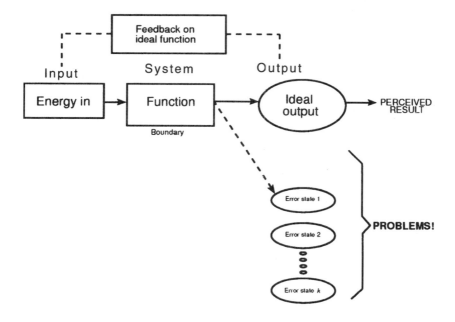

Figure 2.2   The team system with its inputs and outputs and error states.

Some aspects of the team's performance are particularly susceptible to noise. As the team finds ways to continue working well when influenced by these factors, its process becomes *robust*. This requires a judicious mix of tight control over some variables and latitude with others and is part of the team development process. The team then gets both consistency of performance and a robust response to noise.

THE EVOLVING TEAM

At first, systems are governed by the dynamic interaction of their components. Later on, fixed arrangements and conditions of constraints are established which render the system and its parts more efficient but also gradually diminish and eventually abolish its equipotentiality. Thus, dynamics is the broader aspect, since we can always arrive from general system laws to machinelike function by introducing suitable conditions of constraint, but the opposite is not possible.

(von Bertalanffy 1968: 44)

The fourth critical CORE characteristic of a team is its capacity to evolve into its future potential—and in so doing to ensure the ability of its membership to do likewise. Since potential, by definition, is not fully expressed, the best teams are constantly improving and discovering more about their identity. Unfortunately, most teams are hemmed in by the structures, rules and boundaries, by their compulsion as a system to maintain homeostasis and by the culture and bureaucracy of the organization of which they are a part. Teams live in a corporate and commercial 'ecosystem'. Many assume that their growth can only be haphazard, reactive or at best adaptive. This is a mistake and they must overcome the conservatism of corporate systems if they are to evolve. There are four key aspects of the team's capacity to evolve:

1 A team can be *self-governed* and self-regulated.
2 A team through its members can *steer* towards its purpose.
3 The *competency* of team members is continually enhanced through team development.
4 Great teams continue to *explore* new territories, looking for challenges that inspire them and draw out their potential.

Governability

It is easy to mistake those who govern as being 'the government'. As a country or organization moves towards autocracy, more and more of the system's 'government' resides in the hands of those who have taken control rather than in its members. The response is usually rebellion, as forces for diversity emerge under even the most repressive regimes. On the other hand, a chaotic system will generate internal structures which begin to regulate and govern its performance. The co-existence of these two extremes is demonstrated in the recent history of Russia. In the 1990s Russia emerged from the totalitarianism of Stalin whose gulags could not suppress the spontaneous emergence of human rights activism. The post 'cold war' era has seen the disintegration of centralized government into chaos while a clear, albeit criminal, internal structure has emerged to regulate commerce and trade.

A colleague has been developing a telecommunications network in Russia over the last decade. As his company grew in importance, he was approached by an 'agency' representative offering protection against criminals. Not knowing what to do, he spoke discretely to his Russian bankers. He was told not to worry: they would handle it. His bankers brought in their own corporate, subcontracted, 'protection agency' which negotiated an understanding with the other agencies. All of this was completely 'non-legal' but had the contractual force of law, as far as the banks and 'protection agencies' were concerned. Business proceeded as usual.

A team must build into its structures and processes the capacity to be governed in a way which allows for as wide a range of personal competencies and expression as possible, while pursuing its objective. It has to establish its governability by developing a team system that uses descriptive feedback and maintains growth and development congruent with its values and aspirations.

Feedback on output gives the team information about itself that it can use to regulate its internal systems. This kind of feedback helps maintain or modify internal process and structure, ensuring that the system continues to attain its goals: it transforms the energy input into the system, utilizing the resources it needs to sustain its structures and maintain an appropriate output. (We described earlier how this reduces error states and optimizes output.) Teams are designed to be self-maintaining and to produce output deemed useful or valuable by the greater system of which they are a part.

Descriptive feedback, operating as a mirror to the team's process, provides self-regulation. It gives a 'metaperspective', as if from outside the team system.

A *process check* invites members to describe any aspects of the team's internal characteristics, including structure, process, boundaries, norms and behaviours that stand out for them at that moment. Their comments highlight recurring behaviour and underlying systemic patterns. They can then place these in the 'ecology' of their team—how it operates as an interlocking and self-sustaining system—and choose interventions in their own processes to create change. As these processes change, so will the structures which sustain them. As the structure melts, change occurs. For a system which supports a high degree of competency and equipotentiality (the capacity for team members to respond in a variety of ways to changing circumstances) this change gradually becomes self-maintaining and self-regulating. Eventually, with a clear understanding of its goals and objectives and the opportunity to explore them, the team moves from self-regulation to self-steering.

Steering

'Governance' is a concept which encompasses vision, values and the embodiment of those values by those who lead. It involves taking personal responsibility for the well-being of the team or system over which one has governance and steering it towards its best possible expression. Governance, at its best, is characterized by the system's capacity to be governed in line with its basic values and its responsiveness to being steered by those who are so empowered. The Greek word *kubernetes*—meaning 'steersman' or 'helmsman'—was taken by Norbert Weiner (1948) as a title for his revolutionary book *Cybernetics*. Thirty years later novelist William Gibson used the same Greek root in *Neuromancer*, to coin the phrase 'Cyberspace'— that computer-accessed, non-tangible, global, digital information network. 'Cybernauts' now sail or 'surf' the cyberspace 'net' in search of information in any field they choose.

Teams used to be heavily directed by autocratic managers, within the constraints of rigid structures, which reduced participation of members to tightly defined functions. That time has largely passed but as teams move towards self-regulation and self-steering, they need discrimination. Feedback must be clear and relevant to the task, uncovering obstacles to the team's purpose and enhancing its ability to perform. At the same time, the team's potential derives from the inner capacity of its members and the quality of their relationships. Dictating what members should do and how they should do it pushes the team back into restrictive models that block synergistic innovation.

The effective team gains confidence in its ability to steer its own process using ongoing feedback. Positive feedback is targeted at factors that reinforce desirable patterns; negative feedback maintains a certain desired level of performance by inhibiting its further growth. The conscious regulations of this feedback process by the team allow it to establish levels of homeostasis in which both the team and the individual can move from mere survival to self-actualization, as described by Abraham Maslow (1954). The team does this by cultivating increasingly high levels of competency among its members. As it does so its homeostasis is in constant flux because the team is continually modifying its processes to support the emergence of its potential to meet unfolding challenges.

Increasing member competency

A team may create a system or context in which its members can operate synergistically, but success depends on the actual performance of its members. To this end, any good team works to enhance the 'competency' of each team member. This includes improving communication abilities, time management, project management, expert knowledge and other skills—but, if members are to be part of a self-regulating and self-steering team, such skills must be integrated. In this context, competency is empowerment: it reflects the system's capacity to create a supportive environment that allows team members to discover their unique approach and potential.

Team members are empowered by encouragement to *research* and *explore* rather than simply deliver acceptable, measurable answers. Research (net surfing is a form of research) increases the possibilities open to them, allows them to make contact with their inner creativity and leads to new or reinvented solutions. A team of such members has enormous potential. With increased self-awareness and the opportunity to choose their own route, team members are competent to address whatever situation may emerge: they have the kind of equipotentiality of which Bertalanffy spoke earlier. Such teams have the capacity to evolve and have members who are adept at acquiring competency amid constant change.

To be empowered—to move from being weak to strong players—both team and team members need structural support. Teams do best when *all* team members are supported, their competency and power reinforced—not just those who know how to play the bureaucratic game or who are interested in attaining power in order to control others. This may seem obvious but many teams absorb bureaucratic traits from their surrounding culture. Ritualization, symbolization and cultural objects in general maintain the status quo, embedding factors in the corporate structure which are often used to sustain rigid hierarchies of control. If members are to contribute their divergent, creative and multiple perceptions, they need to be free of such constraints. Hierarchies must be levelled and new artefacts developed to symbolize an emergent culture of empowerment.

Empowerment, self-steering and self-actualization are experiences that Mihaly Csikszentmiyalsi (1990) has called flow. He found that very similar descriptions of the experience were made by a diverse range of subjects: a swimmer crossing the English channel, a chess master and a climber on a difficult rock face. He discovered that these individuals, whom he calls *autotelic* personalities (Greek *auto* meaning self and *telos* meaning goal), develop optimal performance in the following circumstances:

- The task can be completed with the skills the individual has at hand and allows optimal control over the actions required to complete it.
- There are clear goals and feedback on results.
- The individual can concentrate on the task—mentally, physically and emotionally—with minimal distraction from other events or situations.
- The task is worth doing for its own sake.
- The rules and the goal are clear, even if the goal is not fully defined.
- The individual can identify fully with the task. At the end of the process, the sense of self returns with enhanced wellbeing.
- The individual experiences a greatly expanded subjective sense of time.

Self-steering, self-actualizing team members are more likely to experience flow. Helping them to discover these qualities increases enjoyment, job satisfaction and a sense of personal empowerment. Using them as criteria for success leads the team towards enhanced performance and increased output.

Explore

The economist Fritz Schumacher once described a train journey he made somewhere in England.

I found myself in a compartment with three gentlemen who were having a heated debate. One was a surgeon, one was an architect and the third was an economist. Finally the surgeon said: 'Look here, come off it! I mean, there's no doubt: if you know Genesis, the Lord took a rib out of Adam to make Eve and that was a surgical operation.' But, unabashed, the architect said: 'Well, long before he did this He had created the whole universe out of chaos: that was an architectural job.' And the economist said merely: 'And who created Chaos?'

(Schumacher 1979: 5–6)

In today's world, as defined by the new science of Chaos, it is no longer possible to have the predictable 'right' answers. The team must use its capacity to experiment and explore to keep discovering new ways of operating, new solutions to old problems and new ways of organizing itself. Bertalanffy's concept of a dynamic system maintains equipotentiality for its elements and open boundaries. It continues to explore outside itself while developing the full range of internal interactions between its different elements. Machine-like efficiency is sufficient for some tasks but most of these tasks are now performed by machines. Rigid structures, reporting hierarchies and imposed team norms reduce the equipotentiality of team members. They become more mechanical and less responsive to change.

Teams that evolve have and enjoy the capacity to explore new areas, to discover new abilities and (in 'Star Trek' language) 'boldly go where no man has gone before'. Exploration draws unexpressed traits and untried abilities from team members as they encounter the challenges of new regions. The team evolves as it moves from situation to situation and learns to apply its new found expertise. As the competency of its members increases, new solutions are found for old problems.

SUMMARY

A CORE team is a system that transforms energy. It has a structure and boundaries that support or create a process to transfer the energy of its inputs into outputs. Feedback loops provide it with information about the process. Ideal teams will transfer all (or as much as possible) of the energy of their inputs into ideal outputs. They do this by (i) maintaining consistent performance over time, (ii) enhancing attributes which are optimal for their task and purpose and (iii) maintaining their level of performance by being robust to factors over which they have no control. In addition they (iv) grow and evolve over time, continually expanding their potential.

Feedback loops are the key to process improvement and self-regulation, reflecting to the team its process and performance characteristics in a non-judgemental, descriptive manner. The ability to self-steer is achieved by building a foundation of competent and self-actualizing members, while the development of self-regulation and self-awareness establishes the basis for self-government. Team members then steer the team towards its potential.

Some 40 years after Weiner's systems classic *Cybernetics* and a decade after Gibson's *Neuromancer*, teams are breaking down old linear hierarchical structures and regulating themselves. As they emerge from their own inner relationship 'net', they find they can steer their own processes. As individual competencies increase and the quality of contact between team members improves, all members can direct the team's capacity to self-steer. They observe their process, describe patterns of behaviour and feed essential information back into the system. This helps to realign its processes with its purpose. The capacity to achieve its potential through exploring the unknown is the hallmark of an excellent team.

3

Team task cycle

INTRODUCTION

When I was 14 years old and in the ninth grade at the Cranbrook School for Boys in Bloomfield Hills, Michigan, my English teacher, John Bailey Lloyd, was new, young and an enthusiast. His enthusiasm and his joy in discovery and learning made a lasting impact upon me.

In an attempt to help his somewhat uninformed Midwest American students understand the plays of Shakespeare, Mr Lloyd presented us with a simple model. He suggested that the unfolding drama followed a five-stage progression. These stages did not necessarily coincide with the different acts but traced the internal structure, from the unfolding of initial premises to their final denouement.

- *Stage 1* The scene is set. The characters are introduced and their positions, relationships and personalities are profiled. We do not know how the story will unfold: the direction of the drama is still unclear.
- *Stage 2* The conflict is defined. The makings of the drama are revealed in the dynamics of the situation and in the souls and personalities of the protagonists. The stage is set.
- *Stage 3* Decisions are taken. The die is cast. The protagonists are propelled along the lines of their destiny. Action may or may not be taken but its direction is fixed.
- *Stage 4* The consequences of the decision and their full implications unfold. If commitment has been made to a course of action, it is fulfilled.
- *Stage 5* The denouement makes everything explicit. We see the impact of the inner workings of the human soul on the world at large.

Mr Lloyd used the example of Shakespeare's tragedy, *Othello*:

1 The stage is set. The successful Moor returns from his conquests to be fêted and reunited with his beloved Desdemona.

2 The conflict is revealed. Othello is a jealous husband. Desdemona is an innocent but proud wife. Desdemona has idle conversations with Cassio which reveal her love for Othello but also her naiveté. Iago sows the seeds of distrust between Othello and his wife.

3 The fatal decision is taken. Iago uses a concatenation of events to convince Othello that Desdemona is unfaithful. Othello decides that he must kill Desdemona to maintain his sense of pride.

4 The plan for Desdemona's death is initiated. Othello collects further evidence that Desdemona is guilty. Iago pours fuel on the fire of jealousy. Desdemona mixes innocence with pride and an inability to communicate with her husband.

5 The consequences are made manifest. Othello suffocates Desdemona and then discovers her innocence. His horror at what he has done overwhelms him. Further deaths follow as inevitable consequences of the event.

While this model, presented by a gifted teacher of English literature, is a scholarly basis for the interpretation of Shakespearean drama it is not a suggestion that Shakespeare utilized this model in his approach to writing. While few teams seem to enact tragedies or comedies, members may sometimes feel caught in an unfolding drama with little hope of escape— the main protagonists locked in deadly battle—or caught in a comedy of errors, where any effort to untangle the confusion inevitably makes things worse. On the other hand, many teams work through a complex tissue of events and emerge successful, complete and satisfied. These are the teams we seek to model.

THE FIVE-STAGE MODEL

We suggest that teams progress through five basic stages in the life cycle of a particular task. These are (Figure 3.1):

1 Recognition
2 Understanding
3 Decision
4 Implementation
5 Completion.

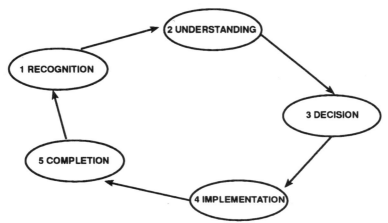

Figure 3.1. The team task cycle.

Depending upon which book you read, which organization you visit or which consultant you consult, you will encounter different models for the same methodology. Problem solving has eight-stage and seven-stage models; decision making has six-stage and twelve-stage models; process improvement has seven-stage and ten-stage models; while project planning can have as many stages as you can tolerate. Almost without exemption, the teams we meet do not fully understand the complicated procedures they are meant to follow and universally neglect or omit stages at the first opportunity. Why spend fortunes developing processes and dedicate innumerable employee work days on training courses, if the end result is a methodology that is too difficult to comprehend and too complicated to implement?

This model provides a consistent and simple template that can be used to monitor almost every type of team's progress through its task and chart the development and implementation of its strategies. When used as a process benchmark, it not only enhances performance but enables a team to discover its identity.

The five-stage model has four clear advantages:

1 It is simple. Each stage has its distinct orientation in terms of conceptualization, resources required and the type of actions that result.
2 The model has symmetry, pivoting as it does on the third stage of the process. Decision is the third and culminating stage of the first half of the

process (unfolding the situation) that moves from recognition to under-standing to deciding. It is also the first stage of the *second* half of the process (implementing the solution) that moves from deciding to implementation to completion.

3 Each stage of the team task cycle can include subcategories if the task becomes unexpectedly complex or diffuse. These will differ depending upon the nature of the task. There are a multitude of additional methodologies that can be applied at each stage and although each of these more detailed models has its place, no one model meets every situation. At the decision stage, for instance, some situations will call for prioritizing in a decision analysis mode, others will call for a SWOT analysis and still others may need a concept selection methodology. Having clear demarcations for transition from one major stage to the other, it is possible to contain the substages or methodologies in a manageable and appropriate way.

4 It works. More complex models may cover all possible contingencies and may demonstrate a certain erudition on the part of the model builder but those who attempt to use them in their workplace find them difficult to apply. Key stages are often omitted or ignored and frequently, even when a complex process is followed, it is performed in a cursory manner out of obligation.

Stage 1: Recognition

The recognition stage of the team task cycle describes the team's initial contact with a situation and early impressions may determine the ultimate success or failure of the ensuing process. An executive team may learn what has happened soon after their Monday meeting starts—a competitor has just launched a new product or the monthly financial report shows an unforeseen increase in expenditure on a project that was already over cost. A problem-solving team meeting may be called to deal with a sudden surge in warranty returns. A marketing team may be formed to discuss the development of a new model or product.

The essence of this stage is identification of the circumstances—not making a response. Nothing useful can be done until the team has gained full awareness and a clear definition of the circumstances. Many teams jump to conclusions and base actions on hasty decisions, targeted at mythical situations. The first stage—whether the issue is a new four-year product development cycle in the auto manufacturing industry or a green-field site development for new chip manufacturing facility—is to identify and define the task or purpose the particular situation presents. This also means recognizing and accounting for any biases, assumptions and constraints, as well as the ideal outcome and possible measures for success. It is about establishing the objective for this particular team operation. There is usually an additional need to establish confidence in the process that will be utilized to lead the team through its task.

Process

- *The team is formed.* If the team has a champion and stakeholders, they will make sure it has the right membership and expertise. If the team already exists, membership is reviewed once the project is clearly understood. Roles are established, interpersonal skills identified and the team warms up.
- *The team system is identified.* The team decides on its structures and processes and clarifies its boundaries. This gives a first glimpse of its identity.
- *The situation is identified.* The team takes note of background information, the context in which it is to work, time allotment, materials and resources available. These are all inputs to the team system. It then clarifies the first ideas of the desired output—what it is expected to achieve, what success will look like.
- *The team regulates its process.* The team decides how to develop its CORE attributes, focusing particularly on the first two: its needs for consistency and how it will optimize its performance. Identifying noise factors against which it has to become robust will help refine its processes. Members will probably put out first ideas as to how they want the team to evolve over the course of the project.

Stage 2: Understanding

Here the team has three primary tasks. Firstly, to make certain that the issue identified at stage 1 is really the one to address; secondly, to collect data which clarify and amplify the nature of the situation; and, thirdly, to prepare an analysis of the data that will show how to deal with the situation. The first two often proceed circularly—the first directing the second, the second informing and modifying the first.

Process

- *Widen and deepen understanding.* A systems approach asks the team to keep looking beyond the immediate details of its task to the context and system in which it is embedded. The team can then recommend courses of action, which will include a systemic perspective for change.
- *Observe, generate information and collect data.* Data are accumulated through research skills, data collection tools and process observation.
- *Analyse data.* A team needs good analytical skills and tools to organize and understand the data. If the analysis includes a systemic perspective, the team can identify limiting factors in the system which have produced the current situation and which may inhibit change. Based upon this multi-level approach, the team can prepare a report on the findings and recommendations for action.
- *Team regulation.* As relationships improve, the team begins to move from maintaining consistency to identifying how it may optimize its performance. If they have time to refine their process to increase their robustness to noise (external or internal), most teams benefit from the reduction in their error states. At this stage most teams are too engaged in their task to consider their development and too fixed on the present to consider their future!

Stage 3: Decision

Traditionally, decision making is a rational, linear process comprising a series of discrete events. These events are considered to be relatively simple and easy to achieve, with the implicit assumption that as long as each stage is carried out correctly the end result is an effective decision. According to this framework, movement through each stage is due to recognition of a required action and subsequent choices motivated by a need to produce the greatest benefit at the least cost. Unfortunately, this simple logical model often does not work in practice. It fails for two main reasons.

Firstly, it does not take into account the interaction of the various elements involved in the overall process. For example, the way a situation is defined is dependent on a host of factors, including the experience and capabilities of the team tackling it. A team may identify an issue and go on to clarify goals, generate options and so forth, based upon the definition of the situation— only to find out too late that its decision, while logical, is at best ineffective and at worst presents a bigger problem than the original issue.

Secondly, such models are insufficient because of their assumption that people behave in a logical manner, motivated by economically based rationalism. From an academic stance, where the variables involved can be tightly controlled, this may be the case but human behaviour is far less predictable. The context within which the decision is required, the information relating to the choices and the mind-set brought to the issue by the decision maker all influence the perceptions of team members.

Decision making, therefore, is as much an art as it is a science and all decision makers should recognize that the processes they go through only lead to a recommendation of one option over another based upon the subjective criteria they have chosen. As long as the team does not forget this, it can start on what can often be the briefest of the five stages. The 'understanding', if performed effectively, will have included the framework for making a decision on the likely options and possibly some initial criteria for success. The 'decision' stage finalizes the criteria for success, aligns them with the initial objectives, generates options for action (if these have not already emerged from the second stage), and decides on the best course of action. The team takes time to ensure that every member can support the decision.

Process

- *Map the system.* The 'decision' stage ensures that there is a systems map for the entire decision-making process. This will include the inputs where it has to be verified that the information is useful, has a context and has no bias or distortion.
- *Agree on desired outputs.* The team clarifies what success will look like.
- *Establish process.* The team agrees on a decision-making process that will vary according to the nature of the decision. Since decisions involve choice from different options, prioritization criteria (both quantitative and qualitative) have to be established. The team also needs to settle the methodology for prioritizing.
- *Finalize options.* The team identifies the best leverage points to create change. This may require adding loops to reinforce a process, breaking

links which block the process, shortening delays, encouraging certain factors to grow, curbing others and relieving limitations of resources.

- *Decide.* The team applies its methodologies to decide on the best option. Its process may at different times include unilateral decision making, polling, compromise or consensus seeking. It ensures that feedback mechanisms for the outcome of its recommended actions are in place.

Stage 4: Implementation

At the 'implementation' stage the team moves on to project management. It has already designed, developed and implemented the process for translating the idea into action. This may be a small-scale project managed at one team meeting with a simple agenda or it may be a large, long-term project requiring Gantt charts, Critical Path Analysis and strategic planning.

Task responsibility is closely re-examined and often changed at this stage. The strategic planning and implementation of certain projects (a new product launch for instance) will involve the entire team but, where the team holds the focus for a number of projects simultaneously, it now appoints or reconfirms a project owner or subgroup to co-ordinate the implementation of its decision. In fact, it is rare for all team members to be directly involved in strategic planning. Usually one member takes charge while the others are engaged in the various aspects of implementation. Alternatively, if the team retains responsibility for implementation, it may require new members to join the team and support the process. Sometimes the team may hand over the entire responsibility for implementation to another agency, ensuring that tactics for successful implementation are pursued in line with the team's vision.

This stage begins with excitement and ends with hard work. Completing the 'decision' stage frees the team to act but, after the initial excitement, action is not always glamorous or simple. Planning involves great attention to detail and should include all the criteria for success that emerged in previous stages. Team members need to concentrate on a specific part of the plan and then expand outwards to check the big picture.

Implementation makes the plan work, putting it into practice. The steps in this stage may reflect the Plan–Do–Study–Act process of Shewart and the more well known Dr Deming (Deming: 1988).

Process

- *Set up and prepare.* The team assembles all necessary support resources, people and logistics.
- *Design the strategy.* The team designs, plans and develops the actual strategy.
- *Pilot the strategy.* Where necessary, the team pilots the implementation strategy.
- *Implement the strategy.* The team implements the strategy. During implementation it continues to think systemically, identifying limiting forces that it needs to reduce. It avoids short-term fixes, negative synergies, ad hocism, sabotage and power blocks. It continues to seek out and replenish any resources that have become scarce.
- *Monitor progress.* The team establishes feedback mechanisms which monitor the ongoing progress of the implementation strategy.

Stage 5: Completion

Completion includes (i) setting up processes for assessment, follow-up and support; (ii) empowerment of process owners to take charge; and (iii) release of authority to others. It allows the project team to move on to other things. Completion also includes maintenance factors (see Chapter 9)— appreciations and concerns, congratulations, sometimes acknowledgement that the team's life span is over and assurance that all the effort will be sustained in the workplace after the team concerned has moved on. At this stage, the team establishes structures and processes that will support the new system and, at a later date, checks that it is working well. Skills specific to this stage include analysis and logic to develop procedures, organizational understanding to set up monitoring processes and interpersonal skills to handle issues arising from the review.

Process

- *Refine further.* The team refines the new procedures, product or system— based upon observation of its operation.
- *Hand over ownership.* It empowers those who will be maintaining and operating the new system in the future with all the knowledge and expertise necessary to operate with complete confidence.

- *Improve continuously.* It follows up on the project to see if there are ways in which the process can be further improved.
- *Continually enrich the systems capacity to embrace change.* It re-examines its own purpose and direction so that it operates as a source of motivation and inspiration. It puts into place feedback mechanisms which support auto-correction. It ensures that the change reaches critical mass without escalating out of control and becoming a problem in itself. It sees that the system continues to develop variety through empowering others and increasing their competencies.

OTHER MODELS

Gestalt cycle

We developed our model for task completion through our experience with a wide range of teams but it has parallels with other models. The Gestalt Cycle of Awareness, developed by Fritz Perls and Paul Goodman, follows the experience of the individual achieving his or her objective but may also be applied to the team experience. Some key points on the cycle are:

1 *Awareness.* The process starts with awareness of some lack or need that translates into an objective—I am thirsty: I need water. A team's objective—a new initiative or an analysis of an existing situation—arises from a perceived need.
2 *Mobilization of energy.* The individual makes an effort to satisfy his or her perceived need. Having clarified its need, the team searches for the required data and information necessary to understand and achieve its goal.
3 *Contact.* The third stage is connecting with the lack or need that began the cycle. Team members return to the meeting room, discuss and assess the data they have. They reach a choice—an appropriate course of action that is based on the data, their purpose as a team and their priorities for success.
4 *Assimilation.* Until what was lacking, and has now been found, is properly absorbed, the original need is not met. The team implements its decision. The impact of the decision is experienced by and integrated into the greater organization.
5 *Withdrawal.* Assimilation allows closure and withdrawal from the experience. New needs can then come into focus and the cycle of needs

awareness recommences. The team confirms that the action it took achieved the result it wanted. It now disperses and redeploys its resources or maintains its identity and moves on to new items on the agenda that have become figural. The organization is still integrating the team's solution but the team itself is free to move on.

Innovation decision process

Everett Rogers' (Rogers 1983) five-stage innovation decision process also parallels the team task cycle we observed when watching successful team processes. Rogers' 'change agent' can influence the possibility of innovation to a greater or lesser extent at each stage.

1 *Knowledge.* The more change agents know about their customers and their customers' needs, the more likely they are to be understood, to be perceived as being compatible and to be seen as understanding these needs. They will also learn who are the early and late adopters and be able to support the early adopters first.
2 *Persuasion.* While we have reservations about the 'ethical' issues associated with the word 'persuasion', we take it, in this case, to mean that the potential adopter of an innovation seeks to understand how he or she will benefit. In this context the change agent presents the innovation to the client in a way that will be readily received.
3 *Decision.* At this stage, the change agent sustains support and information for the client. If the first two stages have been completed correctly, there will be a favourable context for change. The client will adopt or reject the idea on the basis of the foregoing.
4 *Implementation.* The change agent continues to provide knowledge, support, information and the actual product, idea or service. As far as possible, the agent meets all requests for the innovation, providing the best combination of technical and personal skills to support and facilitate a smooth and effective implementation.
5 *Confirmation.* The client gives feedback. The change agent uses this to ensure that the innovation continues to evolve to meet the client's developing needs. Early adopters may re-invent the innovation, to adapt it to their special needs and develop some ownership. The early majority adopt following the lead of the early adopters. The late majority and those who initially rejected the new idea eventually follow.

STEPPING DOWN: FROM VISION TO ACTION

This team task cycle does not always progress in a linear fashion. Each of its stages may be revisited several times. The team also needs to be aware that the transition from a vision to a way of life is not an automatic process—the wrecks of visioning processes on the way to cultural change are numerous. Stepping vision down to observable changes in the team or organization's output asks the team to act as a transformer, turning its inputs (including the conceptual, often abstract vision) into concrete measurable outcomes. The levels of the step-down process are defined below.

Vision or mission   The pre-eminent premise for the team's existence, congruent with the values and expectations of stakeholders and customers.

Purpose   A statement of a team's aim: its direction and intention.

Objective   More precise definition of purpose including desired outcomes which include measurements.

Strategies   The plan of action to be followed to achieve objectives.

Tactics or actions   Precise steps taken to implement the strategy, including individual and operational issues and actions.

Controls   The means for regulating the process, including targets and regular measures against the targets. This allows modification of the team process via feedback, when required.

Outcomes or outputs   The final product of the team's effort. These can be subject to measures and final qualification.

While the team does not move through the 'step-down process' in a completely linear fashion, any more than it does through the team's five-stage cycle, stepping down from abstract vision into concrete outcomes often parallels progression through the team task cycle. As the team moves through the cycle, on a specific project, its work becomes increasingly tangible and measurable.

TRANSITION BARRIERS

Teams are systems in and of themselves, wherein members form complex system dynamics. As such they are subject to circular causality, interdependence and some of the dynamics of systems that Peter Senge (1990) has identified—for instance, 'the harder you push, the harder the system pushes back' and 'the easy way out leads back in'. Consequently, teams do not

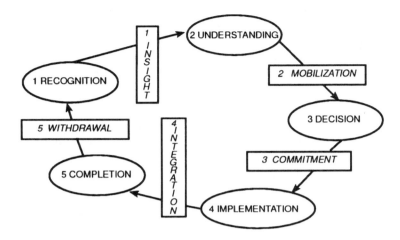

Figure 3.2. The team task cycle with transition barriers.

always move straight through the cycle; they often go back and forth from one stage to another, ignoring unfinished business as they move on or waiting for elements of a much earlier stage to be completed before advancing further.

Some teams will get stuck at a particular stage every time. In fact, each stage of the cycle has a *transition barrier* (Figure 3.2) to moving on to the stage that follows, so that a team will often go round in circles, unable to break out and move on to the next stage. This can be interpreted as inertia, resistance or even 'neurotic' homeostasis but it becomes a team norm. Although some teams will encounter these transition barriers at different stages for each project, most tend to find themselves getting stuck at the same barrier again and again, no matter what their task. For example, one team may keep its options open until the last possible moment and never move cleanly into the implementation stage or another may get caught up in details and never even get a clear opportunity to decide. A third team will even have trouble identifying the problem while a fourth tinkers endlessly with its strategy and never hands it over to the organization.

- *Transition barrier 1: Insight* This barrier prevents the team moving from recognition to understanding. The team knows the situation exists but cannot bring it into focus or clear resolution. Members are unable to see what is happening. They float ideas and even solutions but feel confused or at a loss. They may have conflicting opinions which polarize, one side being unable to explain itself to the other. The team never gets a clear run at the project or if it starts in one direction the effort is half-hearted and soon falters.

- *Transition barrier 2: Mobilization*   The team has done its research and has a clear understanding of the situation, yet somehow fails to make a final decision. There are still more factors to be weighed, more information to be absorbed. The team becomes bloated with information and ideas but has no sense of direction, no release, no commitment to a particular course of action.

- *Transition barrier 3: Commitment*   The team has taken a decision but for various reasons—lack of commitment or enthusiasm—doesn't follow through. It may not have the commitment, enthusiasm or strength of feeling to follow through. It may question the decision. It may be ambivalent or keep options open for something a little bit better. It may even be waiting for someone else to do it for them. It suddenly finds something more appealing and loses interest in the task. Members may not trust each other's commitment, particularly if there was disagreement during the decision stage.

- *Transition barrier 4: Integration*   The team has implemented its strategy but cannot make it work sufficiently well to hand it over and complete. It has not found an integrated strategy to bring the change into its daily applications. The plan is fine but no one is applying it. The training is great but no one is using it back in the work place. Alternatively, the customers for whom the product is intended want to apply it but the team will not let go. Either it does not feel ready or does not believe its customers are ready to use it. The team mulls over all possible variations, seeking some magic ingredient that will completely satisfy them. In fact, the team does not want to relinquish control.

- *Transition barrier 5: Withdrawal*   The team has completed the project but one of two things happens. Either it takes no time to savour the results, moving straight into the next task or it floats in an undifferentiated zone not knowing its purpose or what to do next. Without reflection, there is no learning. Rushing to the next project blocks any chance for release and rest—the team cannot reaffirm its identity. Eventually, waking up and finding itself somewhere in the next project, it is ill equipped to make decisions. On the other hand, when the team does not begin to chart a new course or direction, awareness of what is appropriate begins to falter and its actions no longer come from a place of strength. The transition barrier and the team task cycle are detailed in Table 3.1.

Table 3.1   The team task cycle

Stage of process	General features	Transition barrier

Stage 1:
Recognition
⇓
Transition barrier 1:
Insight
	Identify:
	  the situation
	  boundaries
	  input/output
	  ideal function
	  customer
		Not knowing what to do
		Not knowing how to
		  proceed
		Not knowing where to look
		Confusion
		Loss of identity

Stage 2:
Understanding
⇓
Transition barrier 2:
Mobilization
	Gathering information about
	  content, process, noise and
	  error states
	Mapping the system/ecology
	  of which the system is a part
	Generating ideas, new
	  processes and new solutions
	Identifying root cause
		Knowing what needs to be
		  done but not doing it
		Continuing to collect more
		  and more detail
		Afraid to proceed
		Afraid to actualize
		Caution

Stage 3: *Decision* ⇓ Transition barrier 3: *Commitment*	Establishing ways to eliminate the problem Planning changes Making robust Stabilizing process Improving process Re-engineering process Choosing design Deciding on strategy	Fear to commit No collective agreement Inaction

Stage 4:
Implementation
⇓
Transition barrier 4:
Integration
	Planning and implementation
	Replacing process
	Running experiment
	Refining product
	Training
	Consulting
	Producing
		Holding on to the project
		Not letting process move
		  forward
		Controlling
		Inability to integrate and
		  absorb the process into
		  the body of the
		  organization

Stage 5: *Completion* ⇓ Transition barrier 5: *Withdrawal*	Following up Refining Reviewing Improving Moving on Ensuring systems are in place	Caught between this and the next project Afraid to let go Stuckness

TRAVELLING THROUGH THE TEAM TASK CYCLE

Teams face other pitfalls as they travel through the team task cycle. They may not get stuck but may not perform a certain stage well enough—not knowing what needs to be done. Sometimes they omit an entire stage or give it only cursory attention. At other times they may have too many urgent projects, which create a drain on the team's energy as an over-stretched team may be unable to cope. Nevertheless, the team is unable to withdraw its attention or energy from any of them fully and this causes mental and emotional distraction from current concerns.

All teams are embedded in a customer–supplier chain of some kind. Customers, colleagues and other teams will be awaiting the completion of each project before being able to move on. Sometimes those directly affected will pursue complicated manoeuvring to circumvent the obstacles caused by tardiness of the 'delinquent' team.

Another problem emanates from team leaders who skimp on the implementation and completion stages, with the result that there is neither proper integration nor withdrawal. Loose ends or 'unfinished business' then distract team members from the new item of business.

Recognition of the team's effort and a decision to incorporate lessons learned into future performance also constitute a part of closure. Task closure is important for both the task and the people involved. Some direct benefits are:

- It allows customer feedback to be assessed.
- It supports self-assessment of the team's performance, providing a clear mechanism for feed forward to improve future performance.
- It ensures that procedures are in place to support the ongoing viability and usefulness of its solutions.
- Teams have time to recharge.
- Teams have time to acknowledge each other's efforts.
- Team members gain a sense of completion that enhances their job satisfaction.
- It clears the way for a 100 per cent focus on the next project. The team is not divided in its attention and no individuals are caught in 'the middle zone'.
- The team's view of its identity can be updated. This may result in some members moving on, others joining and a re-examination of current team norms.

The effective team is the one which:

- knows its own process
- knows how to observe its process
- knows its present stage in the task cycle
- knows the stage of its task cycle it should now have reached
- knows how to complete one stage and move on to the next
- knows when it is deviating from its process and structure..

In Part IV we look further at the cycle and see how it is followed by project teams.

PART II

Team Development

4

The team experience

INDIVIDUAL IDENTITY AND TEAM MEMBERSHIP

Many athletes claim that they are not team-oriented, that the reason they became golfers, swimmers or tennis players was primarily that they like to be judged entirely on their own performance and not to depend on anyone else. In sport, it is possible to maintain the image of oneself as a loner, although it can be argued that even an athlete like the golfer Nick Faldo has David Leadbetter (his coach) and Fanny Sorensen (his caddy) to consult and support him.

In business, this is more difficult. Despite the importance of personal performance, as underlined by the prevalence of annual assessment, the man or woman who does not clearly belong to some form of team is rare. Since a certain reluctance to depend on others is a common human attribute, life in a business setting can be uncomfortable and the tendency for certain team members to be present but to withold 100 per cent commitment is a situation experienced by many teams. When this is the case and the situation is not addressed or no answer is found, the team concerned never performs as well as it might.

The dilemma for the team member is how to become a part of the team without getting lost in the process. The twin fears of being isolated and being swallowed whole are first encountered in late childhood in the struggle for self-assertion within the family system. In families, as in sports and business teams, demands for total allegiance and conformity are not uncommon. 'Do this or your pocket money will be docked' is a precursor of 'Do this or you're out of a job'.

There is an old American college sports slogan that says 'There is no "I" in team'. Yet the question 'Am I an individual or am I a team member?'

that such pressure prompts only leads to confusion. Most people want to belong, have influence and express themselves in the team *and* want to be separate in the face of pressure to conform. In fact, staying present for others while maintaining a sense of self is a mark of maturity—the human condition includes relationship to others and being alone. Opting for isolation limits the incoming flow of information. Opting for immersion limits our ability to process information. Yet vacillation between the two can be paralysing.

The answer is to thoroughly explore both polarities, starting with a clearer understanding of ourselves. It is in itself something of a paradox that the more we know about ourselves, the less vulnerable we are to adverse manipulation by our team and the greater the contribution we can make to that team. Bill Luff, head of strategy and planning at BP Oil, once said: 'Good organizations are those where you can live your personal values in the workplace.' In fact, as we shall see in the next chapter, the process whereby individual members each learn more about themselves is an essential part of becoming a successful team.

WITHDRAWAL AND PRESENCE

In our society, strife and competition form a way of life. Yet in-depth profiles of 'captains of industry' sometimes hint that success is not all fight, effort and control. Jan Carlzon, the former president of Scandinavian Airlines Systems, admitted that 'to withdraw is one of the keys to going forward again'. Masanari Ikelani, chief executive of Tokyo Steel, is doing just this when he gets up at first light, not to steel a march on his competitors or colleagues but to tend his orchids.

Well-timed deliberate withdrawal from the team is actually a prerequisite for sustained effort in support of that team. Without an awareness of one's own needs and attention to one's own well-being, there is a real danger of burnout. Young team athletes often tire before a competition is over. Completely identified with the team and not knowing how to pace themselves, they compete flat out until first their attention wanders and then they make mistakes under pressure. In extreme cases they tire physically and may be injured as a result.

Steve Perryman, the captain of Tottenham Hotspur Football Club in the early and mid-1980s, played over 300 consecutive First Division League matches without injury. Working at the club at the time, we could not understand at first how he managed this. As captain he was tireless. He seemed to spend each day, both before and after training, in endless conversations with players, the coaching staff, the directors of the club, the people in the administration and ticket offices, the women in the laundry, the men who brought in the tea after training and, before a home match, he would stand outside the players' entrance signing dozens and dozens of programmes. We then noticed that when the match was over he would sit slumped on a bench in the dressing room long after the manager had had his say. Eventually he would take off his shirt—as Johnny Wallace the kit man chivvied him—then slowly made his way to the by then empty bath. By the time he was dressed and combing his hair in front of the mirror, only one or two apprentices were there, sweeping around his feet with their brooms.

Meantime most of the younger players had jumped in the bath as quickly as possible and were away before Steve began to move. By the time he climbed into the bath, they were up in the players' lounge with their friends and relatives. These, we discovered, were the players who were injured most frequently, whereas Steve had learned that taking things slowly after a match was what his body and mind most needed. Furthermore, such wisdom was not unrelated to his boundless ability to think and talk about the game.

When on tour, the youngest athletes in a team, and those who are travelling for the first time, often need to be told to arrange with their room-mate that they each spend some 15 minutes on their own each day. This allows their attention to switch inward not only to reflect on their performance or to do some mental rehearsal of technical skills but also to tune in to their physical and emotional needs. They soon find they know what these are better than anyone else and learn how and when to withdraw from the team. This is the point at which their true ability becomes apparent, for only then can they give of their best.

Sometimes, on the second or third day of a business team workshop, we will start with an experiment. We ask all the participants to be quiet for one minute, the only other instruction being to notice where their attention goes. At the end of a minute everyone makes a list of the things they became aware of in the silence. When that has been done, we ask them to note which of these things were outside themselves—people, objects, sounds or movement—and which were happening internally—thoughts, feelings or physical sensations.

Some people have difficulty switching their attention from outside to inside and back again, as if they were being asked to use a muscle they had not exercised before. Everyone makes such switches but, done unintentionally, they are often dubbed a loss of attention rather than a transfer of attention. Asked to report what they are feeling at any given moment, the first response of many people will be 'I don't know'. Yet this information can be as valuable to a business team member as it is to an athlete. Whatever the nature of our performance—a high board dive, negotiation with a tricky customer or leading an important meeting—our performance is affected by what we feel, whether or not we know what that is. Furthermore, unless we are aware of our feelings, we can do nothing about them.

RESPONSE AND DISCLOSURE

We always have some sort of response to what is happening in our immediate environment. If someone makes a point in too much detail, we may begin to fidget; if someone makes an unethical suggestion, we may get angry; if someone talks across us, we may feel hurt and not bother to try again. All this we may be vaguely aware of. On the other hand, we may feel tense without realizing that we distrust the person who is talking or have a headache without acknowledging our frustration at underlying issues being avoided.

One reason we often cannot discover what we feel—our response—is that it presents the dilemma 'should I or should I not disclose what I feel?' The chance of being ridiculed and thereby distanced from the rest of the team can seem too great—especially in a team that is new or poorly led. Since no one can ever know the inner state of someone else, we cannot be sure whether any other team members have the same response to a given situation as we do. This leads to another dilemma: 'If I do not disclose my true response because I fear being rejected—and then, as a result of being quiet or telling only part of the truth, I am accepted—the acceptance will mean little to me and I may even end up feeling scorn or frustration for the people whose acceptance I want'.

This paradox of team membership is one of many identified by Kenwyn Smith and David Berg (1987). They divide such paradoxes into three groups: belonging, engagement and speaking or action. The paradoxes of belonging centre on the question: 'Should I or should I not join this team?'

The paradoxes of engagement then occur: 'Should I or should I not take part?' (This group includes the paradox of disclosure noted above.) The paradoxes of speaking or acting arise from the necessity to stop doing something if one is to do something new. All these ostensibly revolve around the direct experience of the individual, but many paradoxes also apply at the level of the team and the organization.

TRYING TO CHANGE INHIBITS CHANGE

It is an axiom of our approach that trying to change inhibits change. At the personal level this means that if I try to be something that I want to be or feel I should be or that someone else wants me to be—if I focus on my ambition and my predetermined goals, blocking out the behaviour patterns of which I disapprove—I shall invariably be frustrated. While goals and objectives can be important as an orientation, the only way I can actually change is to pay attention to what I am doing and how I am feeling—the present patterns of my thought, reactions and behaviour. As Judith Brown once said:

If you tell me you want to be 'there', you have a problem. The first question to answer is: 'Where are you now?' You can't go 'there' until you experience yourself being 'here'. The problem is not 'I'm here and I want to be there'. The problem is 'I'm here and I don't even know where here is'.

This, as we shall see later (Chapter 7), is equally true at the level of the team or organization: the team can only change as each member becomes aware of how the team currently behaves. Any organization or team constitutes a system that, for good or ill, has great resilience—hence the observation 'the harder you push, the harder the system pushes back'. Efforts to change that begin with top management making some formal mission statement and end with their imposition of a new policy will not succeed. Nor will the most democratic of team leaders who organizes a retreat to decide on a team vision and then fixes that vision in stone. In the attempt to attain a set image of how the team should be, the fullness of what the team might become is denied. Reaching for perfection introduces limitation.

At their best, mission statements, organizational policies and team visions are up-to-date guides to current business decisions and contribute some temporary sense of identity to the organization and team concerned.

However, if a team is to reach its potential, the leader has to ensure that team members pay attention to what they actually do and how they relate to each other. They need support in increasing their awareness of the team's patterns of interaction and in reporting their perceptions, thoughts, feelings and fantasies, as they progress. As the team, and indeed the organization, learns more about itself it may also gain a glimmer of what it could become—and as this happens, vision, mission statements and policies will be refined and change.

The key step in this process is for team members to increase their awareness and appreciation of the masterful way (both intricate and invariably successful) in which they do those things of which they do not approve. We joined the new Ford Technical Education Programme management team in October 1995. Two months later, we noticed the team had acquired the habit of walking in and out of the room during our meetings. Knowing the way to change was to increase our awareness of what we were doing, we began to comment when it happened but then chorused, laughing: 'and we do this very, very well!' Members of a team have to become aware of the *advantages* of maintaining the status quo—what deeper needs they meet by such apparently aberrant behaviour. Until their awareness is heightened in this way and they can fully experience themselves as they are, nothing will happen. 'Change', said Fritz Perls,* 'is grounded in an acceptance of self that has been resisted.' Tom Peters is thinking along the same lines when he says: 'If we're resigned to being flawed (yet wish to succeed) we'll exploit to the hilt whatever we've got.' However, it was Alan Forrester, a founder of systems dynamics, who said this most cogently: 'Don't just do something: stand there!'

RELINQUISH CONTROL AND GAIN CONTROL

Leaders who strive for perfection usually experience a need for tight control, so that they may move the team in the right direction. Yet the way to win control can be to relinquish control. This is certainly true when the leader—or another influential team member—imposes rigid control to avoid an undesirable situation. We look at this further in Chapter 6: the

* Fritz Perls and his wife Laura were the prime developers of Gestalt therapy, upon which a Gestalt approach to team and organizational development is based.

topics and situations that are being avoided within the team—and also the wider organization—are often those that need to be embraced.

Sometimes, the leader's fear is not so much of the situation itself but of how he or she might respond, should the situation be allowed to occur. Both the leader and the team as a unit have traits that they do not like, do not trust and try to avoid. Both may fear that if they accept any such traits or behaviour patterns they will stay with them for ever. The reverse is true. By letting 'the worst' happen and by paying close attention to the way the team responds, a new ability to guide and a new mode of control emerges. As leaders trust enough to let go a little and move in this direction, they discover a related paradox: as they become more open to influence they become more influential.

HELP BY NOT HELPING

Another paradox the well-meaning team leader may encounter is that not helping often helps and that helping usually inspires resistance. If, as consultants, we offer a team detailed advice, we may be doing exactly what we are asked but we fall into the trap of taking responsibility for the outcome of any action. The team now knows that should things go wrong there is someone else to blame. It follows that, if our client is reluctant to move and we give *unsolicited* advice, it will be met with resistance, however sensible that advice may be. When the managing director champions a consultant's advice, the consultant has still taken responsibility for the outcome and resistance will come from further downstream. The consultant gives genuine help when offering objective information as to what the team is doing at the moment and what affect this seems to have on the rest of the organization. The same is true of the team leader talking to one of the team. This process is explored further in Chapter 7.

The detached but clear view of someone who is essentially an outsider can be of great value to the team leader. Even his or her presence can increase self-awareness and thereby cause change. If the team's consultant, whether internal or external to the company, can avoid the temptation to make suggestions, he or she is also free to explore the team's norms and identify those that are determining the way the situation or problem is currently viewed. In having its attention drawn to this framework, the team may become aware of other options, other norms, other ways of being and thereby other ways of viewing the environment with which it interacts.

YOUR PROBLEM IS YOUR SOLUTION

Some years ago, I was sitting in the office of the head of a leading design company when he leaned back in his chair and sighed. 'I've got a real problem with Joan, one of my co-directors,' he said. 'I just can't speak to her.' My immediate response was to ask him to rephrase his second sentence, using words 'I *won't* speak to her' and see how it felt to take more responsibility for his actions. This produced a startled return of energy and certain insights but nowadays I would probably take a different approach.

'What does your problem—not being able to speak to Joan—*do* for you?' I would ask. In other words, if two members of a team have a problem with each other, however frustrating the situation may be for each of them and however much their performance may be suffering, it is almost certain that each gains something from things being as they are. Another question to ask in such circumstances is: 'Can you imagine what life would be like if this problem between you disappeared?'

POLARITIES AND BEING STUCK

Within any team there are opposing opinions about how to act or react. Weeks of meetings may pass without arriving at consensus over a particularly important issue. This process may be a theme at all levels of the team's system—in the full team, in subgroups, in paired relationships and within individuals. For instance, whether or not they voice their thoughts, many team members will have similar dialogues going on inside their heads. Individuals can dither for days between two possible courses of action, wondering: 'Shall I speak out or shall I keep quiet?', 'Should I take a stand or should I give way?'

This state of being is called '*the middle zone*' and is extremely uncomfortable. 'Stuckness'—the experience of being in the middle zone—often results from a lack of clear experience of either polarity. In merely contemplating one possibility, the team or individual immediately shuttles back in the other direction.

This can easily become a team norm. The executive team leader of a national telecommunications company had had a heart bypass operation two years before we were invited to work with him. Speaking individually with each team member in turn, we found that he was very popular and everyone was deeply concerned but did not express these feelings openly.

Instead, the unspoken norm was never to challenge him at team meetings, to make few demands on him and to pour oil on troubled waters when arguments threatened in his presence.

Towards the end of one team development session, we finally asked the question no one had dared to ask: 'How are you?' Sensing the tension, he looked up surprised, saw their concern and was touched. He talked at length of his experience as a team leader, his health and his role within the organization, and finished by saying:

I've been much closer to death than most of you, so it should not be surprising that in some ways I value life more than you can know. Because of this I am more determined than ever to contribute my efforts in the community and world at large. Working in this organization is my way of doing that.

This deeply felt sense of purpose caused an abrupt change of norms. For the first time, the team had a heartfelt discussion about the direction of the company and its value in their society—what they believed they contributed through their work. They began to challenge their leader again, testing their briefs and ideas against him and each other. It was now possible to question, push and be pushed back. The log jam of polite middle-zone discussion was broken. Everyone named personal key values, agreed how these might be expressed within the organization and joined in formulating their mission.

Escape from the middle zone is not always so simple. In fact, the paradoxical way out is to stay in it as completely and as consciously as possible, to become fully aware of *how* one produces this 'stuckness' and to appreciate sincerely one's ingenuity in doing so. Part of this process may be to exaggerate one's behaviour in one direction or the other and see what happens. When working with a Ford Motor Company team that had ground to a halt over a specific issue, we asked team members to identify the two polarities of their dilemma and to describe what it would be like to take one of them to an extreme. Having some suggestions, we asked everyone to push their chairs aside and walk around the room making a case for such action to each person they met. The room was immediately filled with noise.

We then suggested that they act out the reverse polarity and, finally, to divide randomly into two groups, each group taking one extreme position. The two groups prepared their cases separately and reassembled for an evening session. They then conducted a full-scale parliamentary debate with someone to propose, second and oppose the motion, having appointed us as joint speakers. The arguments were wild and hilarious but also contained moments of illumination. The next morning a totally re-energized team quickly decided a course of action, with everyone contributing and all in agreement with the result.

We work with individuals stuck between two possible ways of behaving in much the same way. The client is seated and a second chair is placed facing him or her. The client is then asked to argue one side of the dilemma vigorously, as if talking to someone of opposite beliefs sitting in the other chair. The client is then asked to change seats and make a counter-argument with equal force. The somewhat surprising result is a detachment that allows an overall pattern to emerge and a decision to be made. Often the client gets a new insight that circumvents the dilemma completely.

When clients are unable to imagine either extreme position, we work at a different level of experience and ask how they feel physically as they think about their 'problem'. Whatever their response we could ask them to exaggerate that feeling—so, if they report feeling tense, we could ask where they experience that tension and to deliberately increase it. Doing this leads directly to the experience of the opposite polarity, a feeling of relaxation.

Such experiences allow the team or the individual to discover a way of being—a part of themselves that they had either forgotten or had never really known. The further one polarity is explored, the clearer the other also becomes and it, too, is joyfully played out. The word 'joyful' is apt because the experience evokes a great deal of energy and humour where very little existed before. At this point the team (or the individual) is able to assimilate or disidentify from both extremes and experience the relationship between them—the pattern into which they both fit. This allows freedom of choice, and action can be taken from a centred position.

There is a second less apparent form of 'stuckness' which is equally as unproductive and as frustrating as the first. This involves being stuck at one end of the continuum, identifying with one polarity at the expense of the other or simply being unaware of the paradoxical nature of a particular situation. A team stuck in this way might always be decisive and never free-wheeling or might always meet on Mondays at ten o'clock and never, in any circumstances whatsoever, consider the option of a different day or time. Or one team member can be so stuck on pointing out the drawbacks of every creative suggestion that his or her responses become predictable—

with the result that no one listens any longer and the occasional valuable observation is lost.

Again, nothing can change until the individuals concerned are aware of what they are doing and can appreciate how well they are doing it—despite the difficulties their behaviour may produce. Often they are unaware that there are other ways of behaving, let alone suspect that from someone else's viewpoint their behaviour may seem extreme. In such cases, an exercise that allows everyone to get some reflection of how they are *not* could, at the right moment, produce both laughter and insight. If each team member was paired with another and, alternately, one of the pair spoke while the other sat and moved in a manner that was as nearly as possible the *opposite* of the speaker—i.e. when the speaker smiled, the other frowned—they would both learn a lot about their partner *and* themselves.

Thereafter, one way out of this 'stuckness' is to do the opposite to whatever is the accepted 'correct' behaviour. For instance, when a team struggles unsuccessfully to clarify its mission, convinced that a mission is essential, it might explore the advantages of not having a mission at all— instead of moving forwards, what are the advantages of staying where they are? Exaggerating beliefs and behaviour that have been rejected or avoided usually lead to creative new perceptions. The motor restarts and, where there was listlessness or frustration and little contact, there is suddenly an abundance of energy, humour and contact.

As the decisive team acts out being totally casual or the creative team puts on a great show of precision, members are often surprised to find that, at some deeper level, they had always known what this unacknowledged polarity was like. In fact, the head of steam that had built up under its repression was probably leaking out in all directions without them ever noticing. The team that was so decisive may have been frequently frustrated by a casual attitude to putting decisions into action or the creative team members may have been keeping a jealous account of who used someone else's idea and when. The leader whose self-image is one of listening and quiet understanding might have a team of wary members who have been confused by unexpected flashes of sarcasm or harsh judgemental asides. When a group of leaders are asked in a workshop exercise to act as if they are the opposite of what they believe a good leader should be,* the

*An exercise called 'The Worst Possible Leader', designed by George and Judith Brown.

room is suddenly filled with noisy commands, interruptions, exaggerated gestures and gales of laughter. Everyone knows *exactly* what to do.

Such an exercise leads people to discover how the aspects of a situation or behaviour they have been avoiding—the opposite polarity to those they have pursued—are in fact complementary and can be integrated in a way that brings another dimension to their performance. In writing this book there have been long moments of 'stuckness' as we strive to be clear, logical and precise. An hour of intense effort can pass without anything acceptable appearing on the screen. One response to such intolerable 'stuckness' is to leave the word processor and take a long walk—to switch from complete involvement to complete withdrawal—and to find that a knowledge of what the next paragraph should say soon comes swooping into one's mind like a bird across the surface of an evening lake.

The other response is to write total nonsense, to be as illogical as possible and scribble whatever comes to mind for at least three minutes. The speed of writing is a release and out of the chaos there always emerges a pointer to what must come next on the actual page. Battling to discover an approach that is correct for the organization, a team finds that a period of irresponsible play or outrageous brainstorming can indirectly guide everyone to awareness of the next logical step.

SUMMARY

The experience of team membership is always a challenge. It involves a plethora of dilemmas and paradoxical situations—whether or not to join; whether and when to withdraw; whether or not to make oneself vulnerable; how to change and gain control by no longer trying; how to help by not helping; appreciating how problems serve us and consciously experiencing the nature of being stuck. Yet staying with the process always produces some surprising insights and allows the team to grow into an effective unit.

5

Team development

Industry desperately needs to foster teamwork. The only training or education on
teamwork our people receive in school is
on the athletic field. Teamwork in the
classroom is called cheating.

(Scherkenback 1982)

The silver-haired sales manager leaned forward, glaring down each side of
the table in turn. His right hand smacked the open file in front of him.
'We've *got* to trust each other,' he declared forcefully. 'It's the only way
forward.' Having spoken to several team members before arriving to
observe the meeting, we knew that the leader was highly respected and
had a good relationship with most of his staff. It did not surprise us to see
nods of agreement in response to his outburst. However, we also knew that
relationships between members of this senior group were poor and that
trust was indeed an issue.

Unfortunately, motivational speeches, however heart-felt, can only
reinforce the link between the speaker and his or her audience. Nothing
was going to change until the leader helped switch the attention of his team
members from himself to themselves and each other—a task many team
leaders ignore. Trust and team spirit are the product of awareness, not
motivation.

Team development* can be (somewhat artificially) described as a three-
part process. Firstly, team members increase their *awareness* of themselves, of
each other and of their differences—and come to appreciate those differ-

*This chapter presents a model for team development that is based on a concept
of George I. Brown. (See also Merry and Brown: 1987.)

ences. Secondly, members make *contact* and communicate with each other. Thirdly, there is a growth of respect, trust and *team spirit*. The description is artificial only insofar as the different steps of the first and second parts of the process can build back and forth—awareness of others, for instance, will also increase awareness of self and contact will immeasurably enhance awareness of others. However, the third part of the process is different. Respect, trust and team spirit that are *not* built on communication, contact and the proceding steps of the first part are an illusion.

The remainder of this chapter explores each part of the process in greater detail.

AWARENESS

Awareness of self

Ralph Waldo Emerson once wrote: 'What lies behind us and what lies before us are tiny matters compared to what lies within us.' In fact, good and bad memories of the past—and hopes, fears and intentions for the future—only exist in our minds, during the present moment. It is by increasing awareness of how we respond to the world around us and what we do—especially what we do habitually—that allows us to let go of past achievements and failures and to make it possible for the full range of our potential to emerge. The greater our awareness of ourselves, our current patterns of reaction and behaviour, the more we become aware of the options we have. Moshe Feldenkrais, the founder of a revolutionary form of movement re-education called 'Awareness Through Movement', said something about this in a class we attended a few years before his death. Slowly guiding his students through an unfamiliar sequence of movements he pointed out that 'when you know what you're doing, you can do what you want'. Although he did not say so, the reverse is also true: when you do not know what you are doing, you have no opportunity to change.

If a batter in baseball decides in advance where to hit the ball and keeps this shot in mind as the ball leaves the pitcher's hand, there is a high chance that he will not connect. The image of what 'should' happen obscures what does happen—how the ball actually approaches. It can also deflect the athlete's attention from his own response so that the same mistake can be made again and again.

One County cricket batsman with whom I worked some years ago frequently lost his wicket after playing himself in and complained that he had a problem with concentration. I pointed out that concentration is a mental skill (placing one's attention appropriately from moment to moment) that can be improved through mental training. Then I asked lots of questions. When did you last have difficulty concentrating? Where were you? What did you do? How did you do it? And so on. As the player replied, he became increasingly interested in the pattern of his thoughts and actions—of which he had not previously been aware. Gaps in his memory inspired an enthusiasm to return to the crease and discover what he did next time. He had adopted what is called a 'metaposition'*: he had become a rapt observer of his own 'process' and in doing so increased his self-awareness, his self-esteem and his ability to concentrate.

Interest is an important part of awareness. Walking down the street, our attention will go to post boxes if we have a letter to post, to food shops and restaurants if we are hungry, to our feet if somebody steps on us. However, although a child may wake from her daydreams or have her total absorption in her neighbour's antics broken when the school teacher calls 'Mary! Pay attention!', she is unlikely to become immediately aware of the point that the teacher is making. Her interest is aroused by the use of her name and the tone of the teacher's voice, not by the content of the lesson. It is possible to direct one's attention consciously but awareness cannot be forced: it is 'the merging of attention and situation that produces excitement' (Korb *et al.* 1989: 4).

Like the cricketer or baseball player, as I grow in self-awareness, I discover the excitement of new options. Such awareness may come from a video or audio recorder, from a mirror or from my passing reflection in a shop window but it is usually prompted by others—a team leader, coach or team colleague telling me what they notice me doing and how they feel when I do it. Although this information may be skewed by prejudice or judgement, true descriptive feedback does not give the option of change. Sometimes I may feel embarrassed or confused but, as Laura Perls was fond of saying,† embarrassment and confusion hold the seeds of creativity, a signal that I am on the edge of something new.

---

*See Judith R. Brown (1996: 11) 'It involves (i) a break from the on-going process [...], (ii) relinquishing the mental set of the interaction [...] and (iii) taking a metaview of ourselves [...].'

†Quoted by Claire Stratford of Cleveland Gestalt Institute.

It is the experience of having one's self-image challenged that normally gives rise to confusion. I may think of myself as kind and be told that I am experienced as being exacting or I may pride myself on being exacting and be told that I wear my heart on my sleeve. Ram Dass, the director of the Seva Project, a meditation teacher and formerly professor of psychology at Harvard University, was asked at a meditation retreat about the search for happiness and replied: 'Who you think you are may not be happy but who you are may be'—emphasizing that our self-image may be false, out-of-date or, at best, incomplete. The injunction 'Know thyself!' (suggesting we actually know very little about ourselves) and the idea that we are not our thoughts, our feelings, our physical body or even our actions are as old as philosophy itself. Ram Dass went on to tell a story: 'I was deep asleep one night, many years ago and was awakened by the phone. A woman was crying and screaming that she'd gone crazy. I said: "Would you please find the person who dialled my area code and number and let me speak to her? . . . because you're crazy!"'

The Johari window (Figure 5.1) is a matrix that shows the shifting relationship between self-awareness where others are also aware ('public'); self-awareness where others are unaware ('private'); lack of awareness where others are aware ('blind'); and lack of awareness where others are also unaware ('unknown').

When a team member begins to disclose more information about his or her response to things happening in the team, the public square expands and the private square contracts. When the team member receives and listens to feedback, the public square expands and the blind square contracts. And when the individual is prepared to both disclose *and* listen to feedback, the public square expands in both directions so that the unknown area is also reduced.

We may be exceptionally adept at our profession and yet this very success may blind us to our limitations. A maths teacher with a clear analytical mind may fail to make meaningful contact with a child whose thought

	Known to self	Unknown to self
Known to others	public	blind
Unknown to others	private	unknown

Figure 5.1 The Johari window.

processes are primarily associative and an art teacher may eventually ignore a child who demands reasons for everything. If the two teachers become friends and, in discussing the students, point out the limitations of each other's way of seeing them, the self/public awareness of each will expand and both will be able to improve their teaching. As we perceive our limitations and realize what we need, we gain the power to get what we need.

Increasing self-awareness is like waking from a dream that we were awake. All of us carry around parts of ourselves that have been asleep a very long time. Usually the sleep is protected by childhood rules about how we should be. 'Shoulds', especially childhood 'shoulds', invariably interrupt awareness of self. Joining a team that is committed to effective teamwork gives an unparalleled opportunity to 'wake up'. Self-awareness is heightened most easily by other team members giving dispassionate feedback and asking what? how? and where? questions, as opposed to why? questions which lead *away* from direct experience.

However, there are plenty of exercises you can undertake alone. For instance, given that one's earliest group experience was the family culture into which one was born, the question 'How did I behave in that situation then?' followed by 'In what way do I perform the same role and react in the same way in this work team now?' could lead to interesting insights. If you discover that you used to defend a sibling, ask 'Who do I defend now?' If you used to be the family member who challenged everything your father suggested, who do you challenge now? If you were a peacemaker between warring factions, in what way do you struggle to keep the peace now? Then experiment, be outrageous, try doing the *opposite* to what you did then. If you always spoke first, try speaking last. If you always withdrew your suggestions under pressure, try championing them to the last. Then reflect 'How did that feel? Was it scary or exciting? Did I feel powerless or powerful?' And if the experience was threatening in some way, what did you fantasize might happen? What, in short, did you discover about yourself?*

As we increase our self-awareness, we increase our responsibility for our own behaviour. We are better able to understand that we are not responsible for the world as it is, nor for the behaviour of others but realize that we *are* responsible for the way we interpret the world and for

*See Judith R. Brown (1996) and Syer and Connolly (1991) for a range of such exercises.

the meaning we give to our experiences. This becomes clear as we develop a metaposition, learning to observe ourselves. Siemens, in an article on work with a group of HIV-positive young men (Siemens 1993: 91–104), describes how psychologically strengthening it can be to take responsibility for our interpretations. 'We searched for self-support, to help members of the group restore it, so that they could again have contact with themselves and life.'

Victor Frankl, working with individual clients, also sought to increase their awareness of command and responsibility of self through what he termed 'sympton prescription'. An example of this would be to ask a client suffering from insomnia to make sure that he or she stayed awake. In following this kind of paradoxical 'prescription' clients become aware how they do what they do. Insomnia (or whatever) is no longer something that they experience as happening to them. They regain a sense of creating the 'reality of their existence'—and of being responsible for the interpretation they put on it. This renewed sense of being in control of one's own existence, brings a new lease on life.

Yet many people fight hard to protect a restricted image of themselves, usually through fear of the unknown consequences of viewing themselves differently. Even holding on to a restricted self-image is a 'symptom' that can be 'prescribed'. George Brown once said:

Whatever it is that you're doing, that's what you need to do. Don't judge yourself. Experience it as if it's the way you're going to be for the rest of your life—as if there is no hope of changing. Instead of trying the change it, do it with intention and enjoy it. Stay with the process. Nothing else. Only say, 'This is where I am and this is what I'm doing now.' Having to have a breakthrough is wrong.

Appreciation of self

If, having become aware of what we do, we judge ourselves adversely and leap straight into efforts to change, we shall have missed the point. Infuriating though it may be for the perfectionist in us, we cannot experience what we are doing until we have no negative judgements about it. Ted Turner, majority shareholder of CNN and owner of the Atlanta Braves, captured the essence of this cheerful approach when he said: 'If only I had a little humility, I would be perfect.'*

*Quoted in *International Herald Tribune*, 6 October 1993.

The way to change is in fact to stay with the experience, adopt the metaposition and notice the intricacies of the pattern. How subtly and faithfully we maintain it! In the previous chapter we discussed the paradox of change and made the point that one way to promote change is to exaggerate what we are already doing, to do it more, to delight in doing it, to share the process with others and laugh.

Believing that we have to be different or consistent in our behaviour inhibits acceptance of who we are. We learned to act as we do because it was the best way we could deal with the circumstances that originally faced us. Now is the time to appreciate how well we learned the lesson. Orson Welles once told critic Ken Tynan:

For 30 years people have been asking me how I reconcile X with Y! The truthful answer is that I don't. Everything about me is a contradiction and so is everything about everyone else. We are made out of oppositions, we live between two poles. There's a philistine and an aesthete in all of us and a murderer and a saint. You don't reconcile the poles. You just recognize them.*

Finally, for all the oddities and apparent defects of our behaviour, there are also times of well-being, an appreciation almost of oneself in relation to the world around us. I sit writing at this moment, by the open door of an old Spanish bar, somewhere on a remote unspoilt island. It is early morning and I have a café cortado beside me. Time goes by peaceably. People come in, stand at the bar, eat, drink, chat and leave and the next time I look up there are other people standing there. Local music tapes play, the sunlight slants heavily across the tiled floor and I'm aware of the clatter of washing up across the background of music. Words come easily. Sometimes people greet me. A fly lands on my arm and I shoo it away. I continue writing, experiencing a sense of rightness at being here and part of this right now.

Such moments of acceptance—the inextricable acceptance of self and of others—may be rare in the hurly burly of the daily routine. Yet accepting one's own behaviour is the starting point: at least it makes it easier to understand others who act in a similar way. Working on one's own performance—in this case increasing one's awareness of that performance—invariably contributes to the performance of the team.

*Kenneth Tynan: *The World of Orson Welles*, 1967 (quoted in Callow 1995).

Awareness of others

'We miss a lot of the good things in life by not seeing the fascinating things in other people,' says George Brown. Unfortunately there are many ways in which we can cloud our awareness of others. Acrimonious conflict can prevent us from seeing others or even ourselves as we get stuck in old patterns of defence and attack. What we imagine about people can be based on something in our past experience that has nothing to do with them. ('Who knows what part we play in other people's dramas', private eye Kinsey Milhone reflects uncomfortably.*) Hanging on to old ways of looking at other team members prevents us from seeing them as they are now. This is most likely to happen when some past exchange was unpleasant and in some way incomplete. Everything these members do subsequently is interpreted according to what happened then, which is stifling for those concerned who find themselves trapped in a negative thought form. Nothing they do can be right.

The manager of one well-known football team found it hard to forget the sharp altercation he had once had with a mid-field player, 'Dave Reid'. This led him to see Dave as an argumentative player. Shortly after the incident, the player had had a string of matches in which he incurred penalty points and the manager's opinion of the player crystallized. One day, two or three seasons later, we were sitting in his office, listening to him tell us that Dave was always getting penalized for arguing with the referee. On the wall behind him was a huge chart on which all the players were listed alphabetically with the number of penalty points they incurred written beside their names. It was April—near the end of the season—and we could see that Dave had only four points. This was fewer than almost anyone. When we pointed this out, the manager turned in surprise. 'Oh! it must have been last season,' he said. Dave had changed but the manager still carried his negative thought form around with him, ready to take the simplest question from the player as confirmation of his contentiousness.

Team leaders who talk a lot more than they listen may still believe they know and have a good relationship with each member of their team—and they may. However, they are probably not aware that each member responds differently to their every action and they will know next to

*See Sue Grafton (1993), p. 132.

nothing about how their members relate to each other. These responses and relationships are important, if only because they have a direct effect on the performance of the team members concerned.

When a leader fails to see a team member with full awareness, that member's contribution to the team is lessened. Any two members can inhibit their own joint contribution in the same way. When one person incorrectly assumes that another shows a particular quality strongly— either negative or positive—the relationship is never comfortable. If both make this mistake, especially when they unknowingly demonstrate in themselves the quality they think they see so strongly in the other, there is confusion as to what is going on in whom. As George Brown once said: 'When I confuse what I am doing with what you are doing and you do the same, it is easy to lose touch with who is actually present.' This is not unusual, especially when no attention is paid to team development. On the other hand, becoming aware that this is the game that we play, is enough for us to re-establish contact.

We can also avoid seeing people as they are by *wanting* them to be different. This also traps them in a thought form that is entirely our own. If we are in a position of power, it will slow their development and block them from making their most effective contribution to the team. In fact, if we were to see how a particular member of our team acts in a *different* team, we might be surprised. One of the difficulties with psychometric testing and with Meredith Belbin's attempt to categorize team members according to his set of roles, is the presupposition that people are consistent in their behaviour. They are not. We all show different, even contrary, aspects of ourselves according to circumstances, such as who the leader is, who else is in the team and external demands. Unless our awareness of others remains firmly based on what we see and what we hear, rather than fixed on assumptions about how they are expected to act, we are liable to lose touch with reality.

The head coach of one American team had been under pressure for some time. Many people in the organization claimed to support him and wished he knew that. However, since their impression was that he always walked around looking at the ground, they felt he did not notice them or did not want to hear from them. Some even wondered if he knew their names. When the coach asked what we had learned in wandering around the club, we told him and he laughed somewhat bitterly. 'You know, it's funny,' he said. 'I walk around and get the exact same feeling. I think all anyone sees is "the head coach". There are only one or two people in this whole organization who see me.'

To be fully aware of other members of our team we need to move into a place of 'creative indifference'. Judgement clouds our perceptions. We have to let go of what we imagine we see and look for those traits that would be obvious to an outsider. Patterns of behaviour—something that someone does several times within a limited period—then stand out and we begin to notice what happens in the team as a result. We need to take responsibility for the way we react, although this too could be important information for the team member concerned and is certainly a part of our relationship.

If our awareness sometimes seems based on intuition, as well as conscious observation, it may come from what Betsy Mintz calls 'subliminal clues—body language, tone of voice and so on' (Mintz 1987: 92). Hypotheses about what is going on in the person concerned emerge from a juxtaposition of our past experience and present observation. These elements of our response—often congealed into a belief system—need to be checked out, if we are not to risk acting inappropriately. In a feedback session after a British team pursuit cycling team training ride, Chris Boardman turned to a new member of the squad and said, 'I noticed that you went up early on your last couple of changes. When I do that it's because I'm struggling. What was happening for you then?' After listening to the reply, he asked the rider what he had noticed about the rest of them. In all this he was deliberately demonstrating the team's norm of making hypotheses explicit. It also resulted in the new rider contributing some valuable observations of his own.

Awareness of self leads to awareness of others but the opposite is also true: others provide awareness of ourselves. In his book on multicultural awareness, Paul Pedersen (1988: 44) writes:

As we increase our contact with other countries and other cultures, we can expect to learn a great deal about ourselves. We can expect to challenge more of our unexamined assumptions about ourselves and the world about us. We can expect to move beyond the parochial concerns of our culturally limited perspective. This is the experience of anyone joining a new team.

It is the leader's responsibility to help relationships within the team to develop and change. Relationships do change. The way we see our parents when we are the ages of 6, 16 and 36 is usually quite different. However, in order to see people in a new way, we must first let go of the way we used to see them. This is how we make it possible for our parents, our teachers and other people in authority to become our friends.

A group of individuals can only grasp the possibility of becoming a team as they become aware of each other. In a team development workshop we make sure, sometime during the first session, that each person talks in turn. Whichever exercise we choose, it takes the focus away from us as leaders and promotes their awareness of each other and their diversity.

Awareness of differences

Encounters with new and potentially very different people can be challenging. We often begin by trying to find ways in which we are similar. If I join a group and someone tells a story, I may respond with a story of my own that supports the point being made. Such initial conversation is chat—more happening at a non-verbal than verbal level of communication—but if the point is made seriously, I may find a way to agree, even if my own belief is different.

In some early research into communication patterns, three distinct phases in making contact were identified. The first is inconsequential chat, the second is meaningful discussion and the third includes shared 'in' references, mocking jokes and a deeper level of personal disclosure. If people new to the team miscalculate when they can move from one stage to another, progress is stalled. If they jump too quickly to the second stage, the team member to whom they are talking will probably clam up or move away. If they jump too soon to the third stage from the second, they will again be met with a cold look and find that their companion has retreated to stage one and is now talking about the weather.

This inhibits the development of a new relationship. Some people have the knack of racing through this process at full tilt, able to challenge or disagree with a view that contradicts their own early on, without coming to grief but most people err in the other direction. When we lead a course or a workshop we have several exercises to speed the process. One is called *pairs fantasy*. Participants divide into random pairs and take turns to state the things they do not know but guess about their partner. Each speaks for two minutes while the other listens in silence. When both have had a turn they check out the truth—and sometimes realize they were each describing *themselves*, not their partners.

In a second exercise with a new partner, the task is to find five ways in which each is similar and five ways in which each is different. Many pairs report it is more difficult to discover differences than to discover ways in which they are the same. Sometimes this is because the *speaker* has undeclared prejudices related to such differences and is afraid that his or her partner might guess. If this is the case it will involve such thinking as 'He is short and I am tall . . . and short people are . . .' or 'She is white and I am black . . . and white people are. . .' or 'He is a man and I am a woman . . . and men are . . .'.

A variation on this exercise can be done during the introductory phase of a course where participants have not met before. Each person comes to the Metaplan board, pins up two cards and makes a short statement about each. One card names a quality and the other a skill that the participant had but has since lost, has now or is in the process of developing. Meantime the remainder of the group watches and listens, writing down one way in which they feel drawn to the person and one way in which they feel distant, based as much on tone of voice and what they see as on what the person actually says. This helps them realize how often they are either drawn to someone and seek to make contact or feel distant and cancel them out.

First impressions can easily coalesce into inappropriate thought forms that are never checked out. Many leaders try to tone down differences, either through a doubt about their ability to manage conflict or to achieve some objective of their own. Yet no team can reach its potential in such circumstances. The more obvious the pressure to conform, the greater the hidden divergence. Effective leaders gradually coax team members with a strong preference for comfortable 'sameness' to become aware of differences. Each member will have a different experience of the team. If these differences of interpretation are not made explicit, confusion can surface at any time. Both apparent similarities and the obvious differences are valuable to the team.

Deepening such awareness is usually part of our consulting role, whether we are leading a workshop situation or facilitating a conversation between two team members in someone's office. When two people get caught in an argument or issue, they can lose touch with themselves, each other *and* the problem. We may then use a sentence completion exercise that was devised by Judith Brown to help re-establish contact. This slows communication

* Based on a Cleveland Gestalt Institute exercise.

down to the point where they can again become aware of each other, by (for instance) asking each of them to make a few statements, in turn, that begin alternately 'Now I . . .' and 'Now you . . .'. The job is made easier by the fact that, in most teams, individual members do have one clear similarity. This is the goal, mission or purpose that brought them together in the first place and serves as a focus throughout the team's life. (An alternative process is the Ury–Fisher negotiation model which clarifies conflicting positions before identifying the *interests* behind those positions. Shared objectives then form the basis for generating options to meet both sets of needs.)

A team cannot achieve its purpose without individual members contributing their differences. As Smith and Berg (1987: 65) point out: 'This means that differences must be brought into the group and then integrated in a way that provides unity while preserving difference. Difference alone is enough to provide a platform for conflict but the need to unify in the light of differences makes it almost inevitable that conflict will occur.' At a later stage of team development, when the team has a sense of its own identity, a conclusion is reached—after forceful expression of very different points of view—by taking a metaposition and tuning in together to the mission that unites them.

One learns about oneself from others, precisely because they are different. In fact, it is said that one learns more home truths from one's enemies than one does from one's friends. This can be hard to accept but one's reaction will depend on whether the feedback is judgemental or straight information (see Chapter 9). Whatever the case, there can be no clear *contact* between team members until they are aware of their differences. Contact occurs at the boundary between two people. When only similarities are seen, this boundary becomes blurred: 'Without distinction, there is only oneness and hence no opportunity to make contact, to vary, to assimilate otherness, to grow' (Korb *et al.* 1989: 39).

Appreciation of differences

Appreciation in this sense means being able to identify with the other person's position—seeing it is right for him or her without necessarily liking it. Appreciation is one possible response to the differences we see between ourselves and other team members. It is a way of 'framing' our experience. Paradoxically, the more we are able to appreciate ourselves, the more likely we are to respond to these differences with interest or even excitement, rather than feeling threatened and turning away.

It is possible to compete with someone and recongize the game behind it: most athletes compete without losing sight of the sporting context. Prosecution and defence can compete by all means fair and unfair and still be amicable colleagues afterwards. Keeping a functional paranoia without 'closing one's heart' is an art form taught by several martial arts. The creativity inherent in healthy competition arises from an intense awareness and appreciation of differences.

This is how Billy Wilder framed his response to the differences he saw between himself and Christopher Hampton, with whom he collaborated in writing the libretto for Andrew Lloyd Webber's *Sunset Boulevard*:

His world is a million miles from mine. His conversation is often sprinkled with intellectual references and his knowledge of literature and art is quite daunting. It comes as no surprise to hear him comment on Spinoza, Pushkin, 17th century composers or 19 century art. I, on the other hand, being an old stand-up comic, am more likely to quote Max Wall. And all I know about art is that it's short for Arthur ... [but a good collaboration is] work with someone you respect who thinks differently from you.*

The element of respect that lies in a true appreciation of differences includes a respect of personal boundaries. 'Being carefully attentive in one's approach to another person, respectful of differences, discriminating and able to treat coming close to another as though it is a significant event, is a great and civil virtue, the essence of community' (Miller 1993). One of the differences of which all team members need to be aware, while progressing from chat to talk to confidences, is the other person's pace. Members who jump fearlessly into debate are often critical of those who are reticent. Appreciating how another team member is different affirms that person's present existence by acceptance of his or her credibility. Many will fight for such acceptance. ('Violence', says Judith Brown, 'is the last step in an attempt to get one's existence affirmed'.) I want to be appreciated for who I am, not for who you imagine me to be or want me to be.

*Adelphi Theatre London programme notes, September 1993.

CONTACT AND COMMUNICATION

Making contact

In the words of William Wordsworth in *Intimations of Immortality*:

> The Rainbow comes and goes,
> And lovely is the Rose,
> The Moon doth with delight
> Look round her when the heavens are bare,
> Waters on a starry night
> Are beautiful and fair;
> The sunshine is a glorious birth;
> But yet I know, where'er I go,
> That there hath passed away a glory from this earth.

Contact, whether with nature or with another human being, is an experience of acute awareness that one can remember but not—as Wordsworth knew—easily recreate when it has gone. It is central to the team development process. Contact, in this specialized sense, is the crux of team development and central to quality teamwork. It is a concept that includes the lay definition—as in 'making contact', 'eye contact', 'physical contact'—with the specific overtone of mutual awareness. It is a concept to which we continually return throughout this book.

Some years ago I was invited to an American company to watch a communications team meeting. Three women were seated at the conference table opposite me. As the meeting came to an end, I realized that one of the three had not spoken. I was later able to tell her what I had noticed. She smiled and said, 'Oh! I haven't been invited to one of these meetings before'. Most of the team knew her but some only by name. The workshop we led a few days later allowed the other members to make contact with her and adjust to her joining the team but, without that, I wondered how long some measure of integration would have taken.

An invitation to say something allows the rest of the team to become aware of a new team member and a first appreciation of how he or she is different. However, something more needs to happen if there is to be any contact. Some team members may wait several days or longer before approaching. Others will walk up to the newcomer at the next coffee break. Contact requires this 'mobilization of energy' and is then energizing for both parties.

While contact is mutual recognition of how we stand, it is not necessarily getting what we each want. In Ed Nevis's words it is 'knowing what is possible' (Nevis 1987: 29). We make contact with other team members by making the effort to find out who they really are as opposed to staying in the fantasy of what we imagine. Contact brings a sense of the other person with all the impact of difference. It is the experience of being fully present for the other person, rather than standing with one hand on the telephone receiver or looking beyond that person at someone else talking on the other side of the room. This experience is mutual. Without it, the probability is that one or both individuals are stuck in a middle zone—neither making contact nor making a clear break. Fraught with uncertainty this is always uncomfortable (although the ability to stay with the discomfort can bring new insight).

Contact includes an awareness of the boundary that exists between us, as two team members. If one of us is not aware of his or her own boundaries, there can be no contact. The boundary between us, writes Harman (*The Gestalt Journal* 1982: 40), 'doesn't separate but defines and limits us, allows us to be in touch with what is not us'. Only at this boundary can we meet someone else. When our focus is on what we imagine rather than on what is, the boundary is unclear and we 'miss' each other. If one person avoids the other, deliberately or not—e.g. failing to respond to an overture or, in the business context, failing to give the advice or information the other needs— this is called a 'boundary issue' because there is a lack of clear contact and one or both is uncertain as to what is going on.

Boundaries are kept in place by the assumptions we make about each other and are there to be tested. This is the point at which teamwork can be improved. Giving clear information about what we think or feel— rather than sitting back, silently categorizing, imagining and judging things about the other person—may make better contact but it is risky! It is as difficult to admit 'I get bored when you talk at us for five minutes non-stop' as it is to say 'I get sad listening to that story and feel close to you'.

There is the risk of being rejected and there is the risk that by making contact we may somehow lose a sense of our own identity. 'Full contact', writes Miller (*The Gestalt Journal* 1992: 93), 'involves a certain degree of impact of the other person's differences.' This may mean being open to other opinions and behaviour so radically out of line with our normal way of doing things that for a while we feel lost. For many people, especially those in leadership positions, the risk may seem so high that they choose to avoid making contact at all.

The sudden insight that teamwork involves contact is enough to make some leaders and organizations back off. Having been invited to redesign a four-day problem-solving course to include team building, we sat in on the original version. At the morning break on the third day, most of the participants got coffee and returned to their desks to read their newspapers until the next session began. Still no one bothered to speak to anyone else. Clearly there was scope for change. A year later the new version was launched. The feedback was positive but within six months one of the company's continental divisions had gone back to the original version, cutting out the team-building component. Contact was either seen as unnecessary or as a distraction from the problem-solving methodology it had been designed to support.

A formal layout of a room, with people sitting in lines behind tables, the provision of plentiful notes, the semi-darkness required for projecting transparencies, the willingness of a presenter to take the focus of the proceedings throughout (except at the end when there *may* be some questions) provides a method by which contact between people sitting in the same room for the same purpose can be avoided. The leader who chooses this leadership style runs little risk of unscripted contact. The consultant who consults this way may sometimes be seen as contentious but rarely as threatening. The only problem is that the team concerned never discovers what it is capable of doing and in what way it is unique. Nothing ventured, nothing gained. For us this means a job half-done.

Fortunately there are many good leaders who have the skills, the courage and the will to lead their teams towards a full expression of latent ability. Instead of creating distance, they model 'contactful' behaviour, which is discussed in Part III of this book. As Charles Garfield (1992: 33) wrote:

Many of the peak performers of my research were managers whose team-building skills enabled them to reach levels of performance that they would not have reached on their own. Far from being radical individualists, they were collaborators who valued relationships and understood the importance of connection.

Recognizing the initial need for members to laugh off opportunities for increased awareness, these leaders will gradually establish a sense of safety that allows everyone to make contact with each other. This includes giving ample opportunity for individuals to check out what they imagine about other members, for without such checking there is no way of knowing who is there. Eventually, as contact increases, new ideas, new paths of action and new patterns of interaction emerge and the team's identity becomes clearer to all.

Interruptions of contact

There are a group of five personal behavioural patterns that interrupt contact. These are ways in which we block or inhibit our relationships with others, although there is a positive side to each. No change can occur in these relationships until we become aware of how we embody these patterns. They are (i) *projection*, (ii) *introjection*, (iii) *retroflection*, (iv) *confluence* and (v) *deflection*. (These interruptions of contact fit into the self unaware/public aware box of the Johari window.) All are linked and it is important to remember that each is a way of behaving rather than the description of a type of person. In different circumstances we all project, introject, retroflect, become confluent and deflect.

Each team member has a complexity of relationships within the team. Most of these are one-on-one relationships with other team members. However, the individual also has relationships with the team as a whole and with each subunit of the team, including each pair relationship of which he or she is *not* a part. In describing the five interruptions of contact, we focus primarily on the individual's relationships with one other team member, although it is interesting to shift one level in the system and see how a *team* may acquire a particular form of contact interruption as a norm.

Projection

Projection interrupts contact by overreacting to a quality in another team member, quite unaware that one shows it to a far greater degree oneself. It is a case of the pot calling the kettle black, when the kettle is still almost new. It is a way to disown a part of oneself. The person in a typical projecting mode is the sarcastic, angry or caring team member who is forever accusing others of being sarcastic, angry or 'too soft by half'. Having such qualities so prominently in their own make-up, they are hypersensitive to them in others, in whom the qualities are usually well-integrated. The person who says 'Don't you raise your tone to me, young man', in a tone that everyone else recognizes as being considerably more raised than that of the team member addressed, is a case in point.

Projection blocks contact, even in the most restrained of projectors, because there is always an element of judgement involved. One unconsciously projects onto others what one judges to be too good or too bad in oneself. You may like and admire me but if I disapprove of the image I hold of you, you cannot reach me. In the first place I am responding to the image I have created and in the second I have decided how you should be—a double barrier to contact.

Hypersensitivity to the quality one projects can lead to some unexpected results, other than attacking the quality in someone else. For instance, those who deny their own pain and suffering are those who surround themselves with people who suffer. Team members who cannot accept that they are cold towards others—this not tallying with their own self image—are nonetheless sensitive to the fact that there is 'coldness' somewhere, so imagine they are being rejected by the team. Communication with others becomes very unclear since the person who is projecting speaks to images of team members that are in his or her own head rather than to those who are present.

Projection can be mutual. Joseph Zinker (1978: 209) says that 'we often fall in love with someone who exhibits the polarities within ourselves that we do not see. . . . If a husband falls in love with his wife's softness, he should get in touch with the softness in himself'. This pattern is frequently complementary with the wife falling in love with the husband's practicality, for instance. In this way the couple get each other to do for them what they do not do for themselves, each projecting the quality they deny onto the other. As Zinker points out, when love fades and appreciation is no longer expressed, resentment comes to the fore. The husband's tone changes as he says 'Talk to her, she's the one who's sensitive' while the wife will say 'Talk to him about that, he's the practical one around here'. And 'after ten years of marriage, the attractive characteristic is no longer a nice thing'.

Many relationships in any team will have some elements of such collusion. It is not unusual for two people to co-operate in disliking each other in order to feel good about themselves. This may sound extreme but consider two supervisors we encountered some years ago, one who prided himself on being outspoken and the other who prided himself on being cautious. The first, unable to accept the doubting part of himself, labelled the second as evasive and slow; the second, unwilling to see the impetuous, forthright side of his nature, labelled the first as untrustworthy, brash and self-righteous. For everyone else in the team the relationship was to varying degrees a disruption and for the team manager it was a chronic source of frustration.

This evokes another way in which we differ philosophically from the popular concept of team roles. In our view, identifying team roles based on such qualities as 'confident', 'courageous', 'sober', 'mild', 'reliable', 'conscientious' and 'singleminded' (Belbin 1993: 23) reinforces the collusion of mutual projection. This builds a lack of awareness into the team framework—a hornets' nest of potential conflict and mistrust. The surface may be seamless, the tenor of meetings sternly efficient but, despite the comfort of one's self-deception being reinforced, there will be an all-pervading sense of something missing. These meetings will be a duty accompanied by very little pleasure. The absent component, of course, is the warmth of contact that provides an enduring sense of fulfilment for teams with quality teamwork.

The relationships between the various team members and the team leader can also contain elements of projection. A senior member of a research team we worked with acknowledged that he felt upset when a leader was appointed from outside the team. Unaware of this, the leader looked to him for support and, on occasion, a sharing of the leadership role. The senior member, however, secretly doubtful of his own ability (he had been rejected), projected his considerable leadership qualities onto the leader. He hung back and enjoyed the role of undermining authority— appearing to sympathize with the leader but invariably using his experience to point out drawbacks to the leader's suggestions. On the other hand, team members often project their leadership ability onto the leader in a positive way—by identifying personally with the leader's mode of leadership.

Negative projection creates considerable difficulties for both the individual and the team as a whole. The projector needs help to see what is valuable about the quality he or she resents so much in other people. When could it be useful? Looking again at the team member who seems so offensive, what are the positive results of behaving like that? What might the person projecting achieve by acting in a similar way?

Very often he or she has been brought up to believe that the quality is either wrong or a sign of weakness. One indirect approach to improve contact involves the whole team having a discussion of the quality during a team development session. This can help the person concerned to escape from long-held but unexamined prejudices, to be less harsh on himself or herself and to begin to use the quality positively. It is possible to achieve all this without pushing the person to take a central part (or sometimes any part) in the discussion. The result will still be increased self-awareness and the potential for re-owning the projection.

As team members glimpse elements in their own behaviour that they have so strongly disapproved of in others, they may feel confusion but also excitement. As they gradually learn to accept themselves, they become more accepting of others and re-open the possibility of contact with them. The chapter on speaking skills gives examples of how to take verbal responsibility for what one imagines about others, affording a way to check whether one's fantasy is true or false. Some formulae can seem tortuous to the outsider but to the recipient they do not. To take an example from Zinker (1978: 213), having become aware of one's own tendency to interrupt yet still feeling interrupted, one now has the option of saying: 'As an expert in interrupting, I feel you're interrupting me.'

This is already moving towards empathy, the positive use of projection. Clarkson *et al.* (1993: 74) give an example.

If I am in tune with my own shyness ..., I assume that the other person experiences similar emotions and I feel understanding. The projection or assumption is recognised as an assumption and I realise that I may well be mistaken.

Introjection

Introjection interrupts contact through a lack of discrimination, an unquestion- ing taking in and acceptance of information and ideas. Team members who have a strong tendency to introject may work closely with another whose superior experience they follow unquestioningly. They may feel unsure of themselves and lack drive when given a task to do alone. A leader who introjects may imitate the leadership style and words of his or her own superior and insist on the party line without thinking how it might be adapted to the needs of his or her own team. Introjection is expressed in Gestalt through the metaphor of eating: to introject is to swallow whole without chewing. What is taken in is then spewed out unchanged, instead of being digested.

The process of writing a good book on a given subject involves a long period of intake (listening, reading), chewing over (matching with own experience, discussing with others) and digesting (integrating and allowing new ideas to emerge). All of this needs to be done before a word is committed to paper—though the process continues during amendment and rewriting. As the first volleyball National Coach for Scotland in the mid-1960s, I travelled far and wide to learn what the top coaches in Europe were doing. I returned full of enthusiam, assembled the Scotland men's team and introduced a new tactical system of attack that I had learned in Czechoslovakia. The players responded with enthusiasm but played worse than they were playing before: this system was simply unfitted for the level of physical and technical skill possessed by my players at that time. I had introjected what I had seen in Prague, unquestioningly.*

Introjection is a normal part of learning. I did not have enough experience as a young national coach to assess what I was seeing and hearing in Prague that year. Later visits to Italy, Germany and Holland helped me to compare and experiment further. Although I had to reject much of the early information, I learned from the process. From then on I worked with the team to adapt new ideas to our own requirements. Eventually, too, we were able to re-incorporate some of the advanced Czechoslovakian tactics.

In some teams and organizations introjection is required. Many leaders who are unsure of themselves get angry when their point of view is questioned, despite the fact that until team members can find a clear answer to the questions 'Where am I in all this?' and 'What do I feel is the truth?', they will be unable to contribute fully. In the army, unquestioning obedience is the norm, on the basis that any emergency requires an instant co-ordinated response.

The best teams are those where individual needs, skills and potential abilities are allowed expression and where there is room for change when a new member joins. The team leader encourages members to challenge new ideas . . . and, where for one reason or another there is to be no choice, will give time for team members to voice their frustration.

*From a systems perspective, unless the input is transformed and integrated through the systems processes, it cannot be utilized properly. It remains a bolt-on skill or tool. Oxygen absorbed through the lungs is vital for life. Oxygen injected directly into the blood stream causes death.

Retroflection

Retroflection interrupts contact by doing to oneself what one would like to do to others or doing for oneself what one would like others to do for us. Feelings of guilt are a classic form of retroflection, in that I find it easier to chastise myself than to criticize someone else. The tight-lipped 'don't worry, it's my fault—how stupid of me' frequently hides the message 'how *could* you be so stupid?'. Behind guilt for something one has done to someone else, there usually lies at least an intense frustration with that person. On the other hand, I might sing my own praises to some quiet team member when I really want the leader to praise me. Either way, I am avoiding contact with the person in focus.

Retroflection is a superb form of defence. When I was coaching the Scottish team, one of the best players would always forestall any kind of feedback by saying 'Yeah, I know I'm a terrible player. I'm not sure if I should continue training'. He knew we depended on him for some of the complicated tactical ploys we had developed but, this way, I was unable to get across to him that he could be a lot better than he already was.

Team members with a strong tendency to retroflect know all about the withdrawal side of the withdrawal–contact polarity and can serve as a valuable model to the more raucous element of the team. However, they frequently withdraw at times when their presence—physical, emotional and mental—is needed. These are people who may well respond to someone talking across them by going quiet and eventually leaving before the meeting is finished—without ever saying how upset they are. This avoidance of contact creates a dead area in the team's web of relationships and leaves the team member concerned low in energy and depressed. 'The golden rule of Gestalt', say the Browns, 'is to do unto others as you do to yourself.'

The positive side of retroflection is that, in other circumstances, it brings self-reliance and confidence at being able to do for ourselves what we initially wanted to have done for us by others. It can also serve as a model for withdrawing to focus on a specific area of the team effort which needs personal attention.

Confluence

Confluence interrupts contact through a strong reluctance or inability to withdraw into oneself. Confluent behaviour is demonstrated by the 'team junkies', those team members who hang on to the bitter end of a social gathering, who feverishly exchange cards at the end of a course when it is near certain they will never meet other participants again and who rarely know how to pace themselves. Confluent behaviour does not draw distinctions or boundaries between one team member or one subgroup and another.

The 'pairs fantasy' exercise, described earlier, that asked participants to guess the lifestyle of their partners is a difficult task for those with a strong confluent streak: it pushes them to consider how different their partners are from themselves. To be confluent is to focus on similarity and sameness. Conflict is always toned down. Seeking approval at all costs, the confluent trait pushes us to hold back from saying anything controversial. 'A person who diminishes contact through confluence has difficulty speaking for themselves and experiences anxiety around those who do.' (Frew 1986: 60.)

Team leaders who themselves feel anxious that things might get out of control if real conflict emerged will value the 'dedication to the team' that they see exhibited by the confluent traits of certain team members. Their accent is on holding the status quo. Curiously, however, the team-orientation of such team members who hate to see things break up lacks the spark of energy that comes from an appreciation of differences. The trouble is that without differentiation and risk of conflict, there is no contact and little creativity.

The positive aspect of confluence is the sense of belonging that co-exists with respect for team members' individuality, within a healthy team. This was the experience evoked by Ray Clemence in the Wembley dressing room, half an hour before the 1982 Cup Final. For 20 minutes, clad only in his underpants, he ran on the spot repeating the words 'One for all and all for one'. This is the feeling shared by all members of a good team, just prior to a team meeting—'this is where I belong right now'.

Deflection

Deflection appears to be an instinctive avoidance of contact—either by sliding away from genuine interest that another team member shows in you or by interrupting another team member who is about to share his or her own experience. Common ways of deflecting interest in ourselves are changing the subject, generalizing rather than giving specific details, telling stories about the past instead of reporting what is happening now and intellectualizing our own emotional experience. As a result, we not only become isolated or at least distant from other team members but we lose touch with our own inner experience—and to that extent we are less self-aware. Ways to interrupt a team member who is about to make an uncomfortable observation or share his or her feelings include suggesting a coffee break, making some inconsequential remark, telling a story about someone not present and, most frequent of all, making a joke to relieve the 'awkwardness'—actually the awkwardness of up-front confrontation with a truth that the team needs to face.

A lot depends on the team leader in such situations. One member can sometimes steer a team into deflection being an accepted norm. If the leader gives support, those who object will eventually be seen as troublemakers or as displaying poor taste. The result is that team members again close down, trust diminishes, relationships, essential in a good team, are weakened and team development stalls.

Deflection is often used to avoid emotional contact. To this extent it could almost be called an English trait, with any show of emotion being frowned on as bad form. 'Keeping a stiff upper lip' is still the rule in many English business teams. In one exercise we led for a 24-man all-male manufacturing design team, where the floor was cleared and a few people took it in turn to arrange the rest in a way that reflected their experience of being a member, one person put everyone in positions facing away from him. He then said, by way of explanation 'I don't feel heard in this team'. 'So how do you feel when you have this experience of not being heard?', I asked. There was a pause, then 'Alone. Sad, really', came the reply. Before anyone else could give their response to this, the team leader laughed, said 'Hey! we're all facing the same way!' and began to sing: 'Row, row, row the boat, Row the boat ashore'. The deflection was the more striking in that it underlined the point that had bravely been made. Emotion is as threatening to some leaders as conflict is to others. However, emotion, whether expressed or hidden, conscious or unconscious, *always* affects our behaviour. Any top-class athlete knows this. The only way to ensure that feelings work to enhance teamwork is to express them appropriately, in the moment. As this is not always easy, we as consultants must sometimes model contactful behaviour. This involves showing our feelings when doing so can help reinforce a point.

The positive side of deflection involves timing. A team member who responds to every polite 'How are you?' with a catalogue of ills and distress, is soon avoided. To make a mild joke to distract the club bore from pinning a new member to the bar with an inquisition of personal questions is an act of common humanity. Similarly, if the leader of a new team were to press for personal confidences at the first meeting, anyone helping to diffuse and deflect with a lightness of tone would ensure that the team did not batten down before having a chance to take a first step forward.

Interruptions of contact: conclusion

Even while writing about each of these behavioural traits, there have been frequent reminders of my own behaviour. Perhaps as you read, you also thought of aspects of yourself and wondered about certain things you have seen in others. It is not a question of *whether* I have such patterns of behaviour but of discovering *when* I tend to display them, to what extent they are patterns that have served a purpose in the past but have little relevance to the present and how they affect—both positively and detrimentally—the functioning of the team or teams of which I am part.

Communication

As contact between members improves, the team reaches new levels of humour, excitement, directness, brainstorming and creative conflict. Engagement is total—as on occasion is deliberate withdrawal. The team adopts and refines productive norms of communication (described at length in Part III), allowing the free exchange of information and the discovery of new ideas.

TEAM SPIRIT

Respect

There are many documented cases of highly successful sports teams where members have not liked each other, but none that we know of where there has been a lack of respect and trust. Unless team members are fully aware of each other and are able to make contact, any respect is based on fantasy. The basic steps of team development must come first. Respect grows with awareness and is an immediate result of contact. A team member who withholds or avoids contact also withholds respect.

Trust

'I'm bitterly disappointed.' The paint shop manager looked around the circle of his all-male team in disbelief. In an exercise where each team member had written down one quality he saw in each of the others, and where no one was obliged to say what he had written, the word 'quiet' had appeared three times on one person's card. When the person concerned had asked 'Would those who wrote "quiet" like to say whether they think I am too quiet?', none of the three was prepared to be identified. 'I can understand', continued the manager, 'that where we've written negative words we might hesitate ... but "quiet"?!' He raised both hands and looked around again. 'Is there no trust here at all?'

To us this was less surprising. The team had been formed eight months previously. It was large, of several different grades and had never met before in its entirety. The manager spoke to individual members quite often but the main decisions were taken by himself and three direct reports who appeared still to have a certain caution with each other. It was not yet fertile ground for trust. Rightly or wrongly, several members of the team seemed to believe that speaking out might bring retribution—if not immediately, then at a later date. A careful reticence prevailed beneath the surface-level humour. The risk of giving each other feedback, let alone giving away technical information, was too high before knowing each other better. This would take time.

Most team leaders regard trust as a key element of a successful team performance but members will defend themselves and the information they hold unless they feel safe. Paradoxically trust needs to be demonstrated by team members before they are prepared to trust each other. Caught in this bind, many leaders resort to exasperated tub-thumping exhortations ('We've got to trust each other!') or the shrugged indifference of a past coach I knew who said: 'It's not my job to sort people out. You're adults. You do it. My job is to teach you to play volleyball.' Neither approach works.

We sometimes conduct exercises in which the team is divided into two groups, both groups voting—independently and yet at the same time—to choose one of two options. Initially it is assumed that the two groups are in competition with each other but sometimes, someone in one of the groups realizes that it is impossible to win by trying to beat the other team: the only way to win is to co-operate. Since the two teams are in different rooms and are only able to communicate with each other by voting, anyone who realizes the solution must first persuade the other members of his or her own team and then work with the team to get the message to the team next door. The only way to do this is to consistently vote in a way that would be illogical if the object of the game was for one team to win at the expense of the other. This is a daring path to follow, especially for those who remain unconvinced and are scared of being viewed as stupid.

At senior management level there is often little attempt to explore the team's potential. Meetings are short and largely a matter of putting out information for each team member to pass on to his or her own team. Any attempt by the team leader to form a team, to get members to commit to each other and to the team's performance is often sabotaged by silence, late arrivals and early departures. To admit to needing help or even to having an unusual idea is a risk that seems to promise meagre rewards. As Katzenbach and Smith (1993: 219) point out, 'by the time most executives get to the top, they find it hard to allow their performances to depend on people who are neither their boss nor their subordinates'. Given that the prevalent culture of job descriptions, career paths and evaluations all emphasize individual performance, team members are reluctant to take responsibility for results other than their own. In such teams, the team leader is usually left to take decisions and to take the blame personally should things go wrong.

In 1993, a BBC2 'Business Matters' programme on quality reported that managers were seen as the largest barrier to quality culture. People interviewed believed that managers were unwilling to trust their staff, fearing mistakes for which they would be held responsible. Yet without mutual dependence there can be no team. In a good team, individuals speak up when a discussion gets into an area of which they have personal experience or knowledge, even if the admission of such experience might make them vulnerable. In such a team, the team trusts the individual and the individual trusts both the team and him- or herself. How does this happen?

Some very practical answers have been suggested. When Honda bought Rover, trust was promoted by instituting common car parks, adopting similar routines, calling employees 'associates', giving the workforce the power to stop the production line and guaranteeing that if someone could see how to improve efficiency by eliminating their own job, they would be given a job of comparable status elsewhere. In short, responsibility for quality was passed to those doing the job. When personnel are given information and trusted to meet the needs of customers directly, customer service is seen to be a priority and individuals tend to support each other more.

All this is relevant but the smaller the organization or business or the smaller the unit within the organization, the more challenging is the issue of trust. Ultimately trust stems from team development as described in this chapter. If team members are aware of their own patterns of behaviour and the patterns of others; if they can appreciate and respect their differences and make genuine contact with each other, trust will follow. Appropriate self-disclosure becomes the norm and a sense of basic security prevails.

Team spirit

Before we work with a team in any depth, we always spend time with team members individually to learn about their different 'realities' or ways of experiencing the team. However, we often learn more later, when we quietly observe a team meeting. It is then that we see the team's outward pattern of interaction—who talks to whom, who interrupts whom, who looks at whom, who looks away, who sits forward and who sits back—and we get ideas that can be explored at a later stage.

Team spirit (see Syer 1986) is experienced by the successful team, sought avidly by the aspiring team and disavowed by the pseudo team. Defined as a combination of synergy and positive confluence (a sense of belonging experienced by team members) it can only be inferred by outsiders—but there are signals. These are primarily the patterns and norms of communication that we describe in later chapters on feedback, speaking, questioning and listening skills. There will also be conflict without judgement, contact without manipulation, humour without deflection and a fair measure of courage. Often team members will spend time together beyond the minimum that is programmed although, since successful teams can comprise people who do not particularly like each other, this may be purely in the interest of getting the job done.

Less easy to isolate is a willingness to experiment or take risks. This is related to the trust and security of mutual responsibility—a belief that if one fails, all fail—and is radically different to the experience of teams made up of cliques, each with its own agenda. Team spirit engenders the liberty to take initiative without constantly checking back for permission. Feeling part of something bigger than themselves, team members know they are empowered to make immediate decisions. In such a team there is strong support for members to explore their latent ability and constantly to improve their level of skill.

Team spirit is present when awareness of each other and of individual differences is so acute that (paradoxically) the direction and needs of the whole becomes clear. Such clarity is a source of motivation that has nothing to do with reward. It is a mutual appreciation—experienced by each member as an affirmative 'you belong and you are important here, miserable sod though you might be!'.

On the day of a World Championship or Olympic Games competition ride, the four members of the British team pursuit cycling team will do everything together. They agree on their movements down to the last minute at a meeting the night before. They are already paired to share rooms but on the day of the ride will get up, eat together and then ride to the track in a tight group. Once there, they will do their individual warm-up alone and eventually will be on the rollers, paired to face each other, doing their final warm-up in silence. Long before they sit ready at the trackside, as their bikes are placed in line by the officials, they are a team, each in touch with the additional power and resolve that they derive personally from themselves as a unit.

By contrast, I saw a junior British team—new to mental training and distracted as individuals—break all the agreements they had made with each other the night before. They arrived at the breakfast table at different times and rode to the track in two separate pairings. There was no surprise when gaps appeared between them early in this, their World Championship ride. Shortly afterwards, one rider touched the wheel of another and both collapsed in a tangled bleeding heap at the bottom of the track.

Synergy

Synergy is a term that describes the interaction of two chemical substances, each with its own attributes, that produces a new attribute, implicit in neither. Buckminster Fuller, the American architect, used the term to describe the quality of strength inherent in his geodesic dome—a structure made of comparatively fragile support struts, where the compression exerted by one strut on another is counteracted by the pull of a third. The term is now so commonly applied to the relationship that exists between all members of a strong team—the whole that is greater than the sum of its parts—that it can be seen at airports all over the world, advertising the Siemens Group.

Synergy is experienced by members of a synergistic team as a form of support or strength to which they both contribute and draw upon. 'Ian McGeecham, Scotland's rugby coach, observed that several members of his squad not only perform better as team members than as individuals but create a chemistry that allows the stars to shine more brightly'.* Most people are part of more than one team and, in the corporate world, it is not unusual to participate in the meetings or activities of three or four teams in a day. When each of these teams is synergistic, the participant will probably have the feeling of positive confluence each time: 'This is where I belong right now.'

There are poor teams that have no synergy or that are so blocked that they have negative synergy. In the latter the whole is *less* than the sum of its parts: the team has such problems that it is less than the sum of each individual's abilities. Individual members are each less effective as team members than they are on their own.

Katzenbach and Smith's concept of a 'working group'—the high-level team where members do not trust enough to share responsibility for producing something together—is an example of a team that has *no* synergy (as opposed to negative synergy). Here the team's efforts may be measured as only the sum of the individual efforts of team members and team goals can only be reached by everyone working independently.

There can be relatively *good* 'working groups', where members give and receive information, listen to each other's concerns, make suggestions and enjoy each other's company, but the focus is still on personal rather than team performance. What Katzenbach and Smith call 'real work' is done in the different teams at the next level down, not here. Not only has there been little or no attempt to increase awareness of self, each other and differences but no team goal has been identified that is different to the goal of the organization as a whole. These teams are often marked by such absence of synergy that members all feel like visitors, anxious to get home to their 'real' teams. The experience of being a member of this type of team is perfectly captured by Lily Tomlins's line: 'We are all in this alone!'

---

* *The Sunday Times*, 21 February 1993.

We have encountered such teams. Called in to one small manufacturing department within a multinational corporation, we were interviewed by the team leader plus three others and told they had a problem with their foremen who would not work together as a team. In the course of our initial research we discovered considerable cynicism throughout the department whenever teamwork was mentioned. Fingers were pointed at the top management group of 12 men. This was widely seen as fragmenting into a ruling 'Gang of Four' (who were mistrusted because no one ever heard what happened at their meetings) versus the rest, with loud arguments exploding in the corridors of the administration block, as a result.

Any system in which an inner team dominates creates so much internal 'noise' and so many error states that it can never be greater than the sum of its parts. In our experience there is always competition and a number of overlapping responsibilities between different teams within such an organization. Members of these teams are so caught up in their own experience and routines that they know little about contiguous teams. As a result, they build mythical pictures of how other teams operate and how they themselves are seen by other teams. Synergy can exist *within* teams at this level but the organization is blocked by the lack of synergy at the top.

Just as an individual is more than the various parts of his or her anatomy—more even than body plus mind plus emotions plus physical sensations—the team has an inherently different nature to the kaleidoscope of its membership. Once fleetingly experienced, synergy and the team's identity (see Chapter 7) become the holy grail of that team's life. The closer the team gets, the faster the team's purpose is accomplished.

6

Resistance

Shortly after the death of Jacqueline Kennedy Onassis from non-Hodgkin's lymphoma (cancer of the immune system) in May 1994, the *International Herald Tribune* carried an article noting a marked increase in the disease. One of several hypotheses for this connected the AIDS virus epidemic with the number of successful human organ implants. Since the body's natural response to the intrusion of a foreign organism activates the immune system, it has to be deliberately curbed to allow implantation. The significant increase in implants has lowered the mean level of resistance among the human race and, according to the hypothesis, this has allowed more virulent forms of AIDS and other diseases that attack the immune system to appear. In this context, resistance is an adjunct of good health.

Sigmund Freud, on the other hand, focusing on resistance at a deep-seated emotional level, viewed it negatively. He believed that his patients were each traumatized by a past sexual event that they were unable to remember consciously. He termed this form of amnesia 'resistance' and believed that the path to health lay in the resistance being overcome. Freud's intention of course (to provoke the patient towards conscious recall) was invasive. The patient's initial response to emotional invasion was in line with that of any physical organism: denial or 'resistance'.

Resistance is also experienced in the context of an organization or team, where it occurs at various levels. At the intrapersonal level, the level at which the immune system also operates, a team member may debate silently whether or not to act. The impulse to act is resisted by some conflicting element of caution. This experience can be highly stressful for the individual who may feel paralysed by indecision. However, the forms of resistance that occur *interpersonally* are more evident and impact the quality of teamwork directly.

CONFLICT

Resistance is normally experienced in a team or an organization by those who want to make some new intervention or change. An individual may resist the intervention of another team member, the team leader, his or her own subgroup, the team as a whole or the culture of the entire organization. A subgroup may resist another subgroup, the team leader, the whole team or the organization, while a team may resist interventions of other teams or the rest of the organization. At whatever level the resistance occurs, it too is an instinctive energetic response to intrusion—this time the intrusion of a new idea or of an expressed wish to do something differently. It is a refusal to introject (see p. 97). If the intruder persists, conflict is inevitable.

Some team leaders are unaware of having chosen a goal without consultation and are surprised by the resistance they meet. Others may arrive declaring an intention to create change, determined not to back down and refusing to allow discussion or feedback. Any resistance is framed as a struggle for control or as a problem that has to be eliminated and the battle lines are quickly drawn. When heads begin to fall, resistance goes underground and emerges in the guise of sabotage. The star quarterback gets transferred and no one argues openly any more but there is bad feeling in the locker room and less than 100 per cent effort in training. Further cuts are made.

When we are introduced as consultants, our presence immediately signals that someone within the organization—usually the person introducing us—wants change. However long we are allowed to watch quietly to see how things are done, we are rightly seen as change agents. As such we shall be welcomed by some and immediately mistrusted by others.

Invited to give a twenty minute introduction to mental training to the coaches of a professional sports team, towards the end of an initial five-day observation period, I began with a 'circle check'. The head coach had just given a fifty minute talk of his own and my idea was to allow a moment's respite, by asking people to check in to themselves before focusing on a second presentation. 'Let's go round the table', I said, 'and say one word that describes how you're feeling right now.' Of a group of 20 coaches, several said 'curious', others said 'interested', a couple said 'tired' but one folded his arms, looked straight at me and said 'bored!'. Since I had not even begun to speak, it was easy to assume that this person wanted me to know he thought I had been brought in to create change and that he did not trust me. In fact, any proposal for change could only be inferred since the head coach had kept a very low profile in the manner of my original introduction. Most people assumed that I was doing some form of academic research that would have no direct bearing on the club. This coach was not to be fooled.

Exploring conflict

In our work with sports teams, we sometimes differentiate between 'neurotic' and 'creative' competition. We define neurotic competition as competition where the intention of the participants is to prove they are what they believe they are, or what others believe they should be (usually the best). This is as much the experience of someone locked in a struggle with a rebellious subordinate as it is of the troubled teenage tennis player trying to live up to the ambitions of his or her parents. On the other hand, creative competition occurs when the participants use the contest to discover more about themselves and what they are capable of achieving. The youngster then dares to experiment and gains respect for strong opposition, while the executive learns to switch attention from the subordinate's behaviour to his or her own patterns of response and discovers the ability to improvise.

If conflict is an issue, we can help team members explore their attitude towards it during a team development workshop, by suggesting they write something or by introducing an interactive exercise. In the first case, we might ask the participants to complete some sentences. For instance:

'Conflict is . . .'
'When I see conflict coming, I . . .'
'The most productive use of conflict is . . .'

and then discuss what they have written. Similar sentences could be completed about change.

As an interactive exercise, especially if working with young athletes, we might divide them into pairs and ask them to try to push their partners off balance. Alternatively, we could give each pair a stick or a rolled-up newspaper and ask them both to hold it and pull their partner across the floor. When everyone is thoroughly energized, they can sit in their pairs (and later in fours) to discuss the experience. To prod the discussion further, additional questions could be floated, such as: 'If the object was to win, what constituted winning for you? Was it (i) keeping control, (ii) having most fun alone, or (iii) having most fun with your partner' or 'Did you give up? What was it like to give up? What was it like when your partner gave up?' Simple though these exercises are, they can lead to involved conversations that teach team members a lot about each other. In a team where change, conflict and resistance are current issues, counterproductive undercurrents will surface and be explored creatively.

Avoidance of conflict

Conflict is not so much something to be resolved as an experience to be explored. Conflicting views on direction and change within a team are never totally unrelated and have great value when considered as different parts of one story. Most exercises in conflict resolution aim at compromise, yet real difficulties arise if conflict cannot be expressed. Avoidance of conflict either drains interest, enthusiasm and eventually trust from the team experience or results in concealed tension, political infighting and the impaired performance of certain relationships within the team. Far from diminishing, resistance will then increase.

While some team leaders meet resistance head on, others do everything possible to avoid overt conflict. Those with most power can simply transfer the team member or members concerned. Those who are less decisive or less powerful, but still with an authoritarian style, may alternate threats and enticement. Others avoid the issue by holding meetings when 'difficult' members are absent. In each case, the underlying fear is that once conflict is expressed it could easily destroy team morale. Certain basic facilitation skills are required if the best is to be drawn from friction within the team and many leaders know they have yet to acquire them.

As consultants, we occasionally find that closer examination of an organizational structure results in our sponsor becoming less available to us. In such cases, having commissioned us to facilitate some form of change, he or she finds that the resistance we help make explicit is too daunting. We are then told that certain relationships or levels of the system 'are best not addressed at this stage' or certain members' reluctance to participate 'should be respected', or 'a way forward' is chosen that allows underlying issues to be ignored. All such responses can evoke sympathy and, while providing more data as to how the system actually works, they often indicate how other issues fit into the overall pattern. Yet they are nearly always based on the erroneous assumption that the resistance has to be suppressed and that the resulting battle will be catastrophic both personally and for the organization or team concerned.* In such cases, avoidance of conflict is itself a subtle form of resistance.

Not to respond to the team member resisting the proposed change is to become confluent with that person and thereby also avoid creative contact. If no differences are recognized, no appreciation of differences can occur. The same is true if they are recognized but not voiced. Here, the individual wishing to keep the peace is not putting his or her ability to think, react and challenge into the relationship. In the context of team development, this shows a lack of respect.

When the team leader heads us away from sensitive areas of the organization, the opportunity to discover new insights, to tap into the potential synergy of differing ideas—perhaps through creative argument—is temporarily lost. This delays change. The answer is not for us to say what should be done. Any consultant who makes suggestions rather than give descriptive feedback and model missing or polar opposite behaviour risks walking into trouble and hampering the team's development. However, when the team leader *does* have a consultant who makes suggestions and the leader resists some of them, the consultant will be forced to argue the case and this may prove to be more productive than the consultant's original advice.

Other leaders try to avoid conflict by using double messages. These only confuse people on the receiving end, who gradually realize they are trying to hit a moving target. One team leader made it clear that he wanted us to interview his staff and watch meetings but did not find time to make any introductions or inform his staff. We followed him into a meeting, as invited, but either his enthusiasm for change faltered or his attention was drawn to more familiar channels because we were still not introduced. Instead, his secretary had to introduce us at a later stage.

At the end of our first day, he wanted to know our suggestions for change. Since our brief had only been to observe, report and facilitate any subsequent discussion—a remit that exactly fit our approach—we were

---

* Systemic interventions might be made elsewhere in the organization and include (i) identifying interests behind positions, (ii) having a dialogue with perceived obstacles, (iii) identifying how homeostasis is maintained by procedures rather than individuals and (iv) force field analysis.

somewhat startled. We had some observations but no advice. He then suggested that he did not perceive 'just talking to people and watching' as work. This was frustrating until we realized that this was part of the picture we had been asked to observe. The leader's behaviour with us would reflect his behaviour within the organization and his team. Did this blunt form of challenge and changing of ground rules represent some form of test through which all his team members had to go (we learned later that it did) or did it just indicate ambivalence about our presence, now we had arrived? He did not answer when we asked but his manner changed and he arranged to meet us again the next day.

Another way to avoid conflict is to give a flat 'No' to a suggestion and turn away. Yet, as often as not, somewhere behind the 'No', there is curiosity and a willingness to consider saying 'Yes'. Rather than resistance to the idea itself, this type of response may be a reaction to pressure or a method of avoiding immediate agreement until the matter has been more carefully considered. In one workshop of ours Phil, a mild-mannered man, was hotly accused of negativity by one of his colleagues: 'You always say "no" when I make a suggestion!' 'That's because you always ask for an immediate answer,' replied Phil reasonably. 'Saying "no" is the only way I can gain the time I need to think. You're like my wife. She asks me the same thing: "Phil, why do you always have to say 'no' before you say 'yes'?" 'Sometimes,' he continued, 'I need a shower when I come home, before I'm ready for more decisions. Saying "no" rather than "maybe" seems to give me more space.'

Denial of conflict

Ed Nevis once said: 'If there's no resistance, look out! You'll be ambushed. It's always there somewhere.' All systems (except those specifically implemented to create change) resist change. When a team leader proposes change and everyone pretends to agree, the scale of resistance can be immense. This happens when the team has a strong norm that no dissension or negative views are expressed or where the core of resistance reflects a side of the team, or indeed of the team leader, that no one is prepared to discuss. The team may have adopted such slogans as 'We stick together, no matter what' or the leader may personally be in the habit of boasting that 'this team has flair and flexibility', so that no one wants to seem rigid. We would then have difficulty taking such statements at face value. Who is this 'we'?

Who is it that is so flexible? Which are the team members who are silent on these issues? In what circumstances would other people on the team question your loyalty? What are you not saying about the team or about yourself?

We were once in Germany with an extraordinary senior executive who relished his reputation as a tireless leader and charismatic spokesman for change, able to sweep all before him with a commanding tone and relentless argument. Just prior to our return to England we discovered that he had a severe migraine problem that he thought he was hiding from the rest of his hard-driven team. This man was hard on those who did not have a high level of stamina and was hypersensitive to any slackening of effort in others. Yet he was reluctant to recognize a part of *himself* that needed to slow down. Everyone knew he had previously had open-heart surgery and many of his loyal staff were very concerned.

On other occasions, denial of a particular quality may be cultural. Soccer, rugby and American football—at least as played by men—have a distinctly macho set of norms. Swearing, shouting, breaking wind loudly and an unending stream of sexual jokes and inneundo are commonplace. On a recent first visit to an American football club, all these elements were apparent, as I wandered around watching meetings and interviewing. Players received motivational speeches, were given briefs with little opportunity for discussion or for contribution of their own ideas and moved from lecture theatre to weight training to field practice on a rigid programme. Referring to this disciplined approach, one of the coaches said that his all-time hero was General Patten.

I then had a series of four one-on-one interviews in which each person in turn used the word 'mothering' in relation to their unofficial job function— the physiotherapist, the kit man, the head coach's secretary and the managing director's secretary. Used to this role, the coach's secretary even embodied it with an outsider like myself, making sure I had everything I needed and showing me a small room with two sofas that I could use if I felt tired when working late.

Superficially this system worked well. Players sat through the long lectures and motivational sessions without comment. If they were verbally abused in training they were schooled not to give excuses or complain. If they were exhausted by the physical demands of the training they said nothing—not until they were with the physiotherapist or the kit man. Meanwhile, upstairs, the coaches got in early to make final preparations, attended their staff meetings, spent the day with their players and stayed so late analysing videos of their next opponents or the day's practice that they occasionally did not bother to go home. Even the secretary stayed till nine or ten at night on certain evenings, exchanging humorous comments—a source of 'mothering' support—as she worked away in the midst of it all.

My interviews allowed me to learn a little more. In fact, by giving another opportunity for people to 'off-load', I was sometimes seen as an extra 'mother': I provided a place where responses and ideas could be expressed openly. I learned that, when the training sessions were cut from two each day to one, the players' spirits soared, now feeling able to last the pace until the end of the season but that 'they would never admit to such a response'. I learned that one member of staff was convinced that team performance was suffering through a specific piece of bad organization but that he would not voice his opinion because 'if you say anything, sooner or later it will come back and hit you on the head'. I learned that a key relationship did not work because one person refused to speak to another 'for days on end'.

None of the many perceived difficulties and frustrations was unusual but the denial of the need to express illogical feelings, the impossibility of even contributing one's own creative ideas in the macho training, briefing and competition context, where they were always evoked, meant that the team lost valuable information. This in turn meant that the head coach's immense efforts to improve the team's performance—and he was universally respected as working harder than anybody—never reaped its due reward. The existence of 'mothering' to compensate for the 'macho' prevented the system grinding to a halt but the lack of integration of the two polarities prevented anyone involved from reaching his or her potential. Any suggestion that this might be changed was bound to evoke resistance somewhere in the system—probably from among those acting out the polar extremes. The system was stuck in an uneasy homeostasis.

Anxiety

Avoidance and denial of conflict are rooted in anxiety. When a norm of behaviour is cultural, to consider behaving differently is to face the probability of isolation and ridicule. In the above example, macho behaviour and the projection of one's caring side on to people whose jobs are to tend to others' needs, may be a cultural norm. To help the players express their feelings in a team meeting and beyond that to express their own feelings of remorse, joy or frustration would have been a minor act of heroism for many of the coaches concerned.

However, none of the coaches was insensitive and all were presumably able to invite and express feelings in a different context—for instance, when they were at home. Also coaching, even professional coaching, is a branch of education. When done well, it involves both teacher and pupil in a caring relationship. It was precisely because these coaches were good that they did in fact know they could only evoke the best in their players by expressing the best of themselves—emotionally and spiritually as well as mentally and physically. However, cultural norms such as the ones in this club are so strong that change only comes with team development. When the norm itself is against taking time to develop the team, individuals who become more conscious of the value of change can feel uneasy and stuck and eventually feel like outsiders.

If some sports teams have a norm against the expression of feelings (discussed in Chapter 7) it is far more prevalent in a business team: at least an athlete is professionally in touch with his or her physical sensations. For many business people, feelings, whether physical or emotional, have little apparent relevance to their performance. Any suggestion that feelings always affect their performance, whether they are aware of them or not, can meet resistance and a break of contact through deflection—making a joke, intellectualizing or changing the subject.

The prospect of a team development workshop can cause considerable anxiety—usually built on false suppositions about the form or content of the programme—that cannot be easily expressed. Where a team has members of differing grades within the organizational structure, both senior and junior members can feel threatened. The junior members may fear that if they speak their minds they will be punished. The senior members fear that if they are open and honest they will be ridiculed. It is our job to provide support for all members to take small steps towards facing and exploring their anxieties and resistances, sometimes alone but often within the context of the team. In the same way, the team leader who genuinely wants to effect change has to guard against resisting resistance, otherwise his or her efforts will be sabotaged and everyone concerned will feel stuck. The way forward is to reframe such stubbornness as a healthy if inefficient defence of something valuable that exists in the system as it is.

In many situations, 'stuckness'—the unwillingness to change coupled with the inability to continue to act in the same way—is so frustrating that it can result in explosions of denial and resistance. An immense amount of effort is spent on 'not doing something, on avoiding change itself or on fearing a change' (Oakley 1993: 125). Whatever is actually said, much of the frustration comes from knowing that the battle is not with the intruder or 'change agent' but with oneself. It is difficult in such circumstances to maintain self-respect. Denial is the only defence.

'Stuckness' is usually compounded by a simple fear that the known way of doing things may come to an end. The person who said 'bored' when I was about to give my talk to the coaches may have feared his unofficial role as players' confidant would change. At a different club, we initially had the same uneasy relationship with the club chaplain. Change in the team system often threatens to reduce one's ability to meet one's needs—a loss of power. At a deeper level, a change of environment, role or relationships can threaten one's sense of personal identity.

RESISTANCE SEEN AS HEALTHY DEFENCE

Old-style management

The family member who does not conform to family norms and is described by the rest of the circle as 'being difficult' does not often see it this way. The same is true of the argumentative member of a basketball team or the head of department who avoids implementing change in the way his own team leader would like. A line worker may be seen as resistant but, as Ed Nevis (1987: 141) points out: 'Resistance is a label applied by managers or consultants to the perceived behaviour of others who seem unwilling to accept influence or help.' If the worker's fundamental need is for inclusion and appreciation for work done, the manager will not get much response to any proposed change until these needs are met. Even pay rises may not buy openness and full-fledged support. When managers speak of resistance—especially when the term is linked to discussions of how it may be 'overcome'—they usually experience it as a negative and frustrating phenomenon. They know that theoretically they are in charge—resistance rarely occurs between equals—and yet somehow these subordinates seem able to determine what does and does not happen.

The terms 'top dog' and 'under dog' are used to describe the thought processes that lead us to undermine our own best intentions. Writing this chapter in Italy, I wake each morning feeling somewhat full of food and deciding that 'tonight I won't have ice cream'. Come the evening, I eat my dinner, wash the dishes and go out for a walk. When I reach the ice cream shop I reason that all this walking down the winding steps and back up the steps to get home is going to burn up lots of calories. Without a second thought I'm inside. The woman behind the counter smiles. She is already holding an empty cone, reaching her scoop towards the lemon tub. 'Limone e cioccolata?' she asks, meaning 'the usual?' I nod, I smile and am having my first lick of the dark unctuous chocolate before I even get my change. In the morning I wake up feeling full of food and decide that 'I really will go without ice cream tonight'. The person who wakes in the morning is my 'top dog'; the person who drifts into the ice cream shop at night is my 'under dog'. Top dogs always appear masterful, making plans and telling the under dog how things are to be, but the under dog, appearing meek and acquiescent, is an expert at sabotage and nearly always wins.

A similar game is often played between manager and subordinate. One of our multinational clients appointed a long-term quality team with members from different parts of the organization and of different grades. This team was trained in part by us, in part by other consultants and in part by the internal directors of the venture. A senior member of the team in terms of grade soon became *de facto* leader, making demands and setting limits on behalf of the team as a whole. He used his rank to dominate the other team members—forcing through a decision on targets the team would and would not meet—and for a while they followed his lead.

But soon everyone in the team had had enough of being brow-beaten and one by one they disassociated themselves from their self-appointed leader. People found excuses for not working with him and spent more time with the directors of the programme. Some ignored their enforced team agreement by becoming involved in outlawed projects. Team meetings became infrequent and poorly attended and the 'leader' became increasingly isolated. Not surprisingly, the underdogs won the day without the 'leader' ever really understanding what had happened. The ability to undermine authority is also a form of control and one that is available to all subordinate parts of the system.

The more insistent a team leader becomes on a particular course of action, the more likely it is that someone, somewhere, will object. If the objections are not taken into account and are referred to as 'resistance', the more clearly will opposing battle lines be drawn. Not only do those with objections disengage from contact with the team leader, the team leader's own obstinacy will make contact increasingly difficult. His or her obstinacy is itself resistance—a refusal to hear the objections.

Different realities

The main challenge in leading a team is to allow the full complexity of individual peculiarities, talents, qualities and insights to emerge and be harnessed to the team's objective. It is far easier to set limits on expression and behaviour but the potential of the team's performance is then less. Since each individual sees the world and its events from the perspective of cultural and personal experience, any initiative for change will evoke a varied response. This can be subdued by heavy-handed leadership, but then attention span will be short, contribution minimal and interest low. Where everyone thinks alike, no one thinks much.

Ed Nevis—having described the Gestalt cycle of awareness that moves from awareness of a need (for instance, to post a letter), to mobilization of energy to satisfy that need (going out to look for a post-box), to making contact (finding a post-box), closure (posting the letter) and withdrawal (walking away), only to become aware of a new need (to satisfy pangs of hunger), and so on—points out (Nevis 1987: 35) that even within a family each member has his or her own cycle. These cycles will interact but there is no guarantee that all family members will be at the same point of the cycle at any given moment. Should all but the youngest brother coincide in awareness of a particular need, then at the moment he is about to satisfy a need of his own, this brother may be charged with not supporting 'the family', although in fact his needs are equally valid. Nevis calls this state of affairs an instance of 'multi-directional energy' and suggests that it is a phenomenon that accounts for much apparent resistance within the experience of any team.

Resistance then can be framed as a need 'in another direction'. It shows that someone else's view of reality is different and is only *experienced* as resistance if the person proposing the change claims that his or her way is the only way. The shift required of the leader or change agent is to become curious about the other party's reality and increase awareness of his or her own conceptual blocks.

The baby and the bath water

In every team there are those who want change and those who want things to stay the same and both positions have a certain insight to the true needs of the team. In order to ensure that neither insight is lost, we would help the team leader to establish (i) what is happening in the team right now, (ii) what is the force for change, and (iii) what counterbalancing forces seek to minimize change. In this way, both positions are respected and a creative dialogue can commence.

Those members who fight to resist change can be viewed as sturdy guardians of the team's traditional norms and beliefs. Klein* gives three reasons for their importance:

(i) They are sensitive to any indication that those seeking to produce change fail to understand or identify with the core values of the [team] they seek to influence; (ii) they see consequences of the change that are unanticipated by the initiators and that may threaten the well-being of the [team]; and (iii) they are especially apt to react to changes seen as reducing the integrity of the system, that is they are sensitive to the importance of maintaining self-esteem, competence and autonomy.

A few years ago, we agreed to lead a team development workshop at very short notice for a team of 26 male plant operators. The only occasion when everyone could attend was on the first few days of the year, when the plant was closed for annual maintenance. This period was sometimes used for meetings but many team members might have reasonably expected to get an extra day at home with the family. We met the team leader and his assistant in the middle of December. Although the team divided into five subgroups or shifts, the leader particularly wanted everyone to do the workshop at the same time. We pointed out that this offered the opportunity of learning more about the identity of the whole but, with such a large number, there could only be a limited amount of one-on-one contact. Each person would need to take more responsibility for his own involvement, everyone would have less air time in team discussions and we would not be able to give as much attention to small groups of two or three. Should anyone so choose, he could go for long periods without being directly involved.

*D. Kline: Some notes on the dynamics of resistance to change: The defender role. In Benne *et al.* (eds) *The Planning of Change* (3rd edn), 1976—quoted by Ed Nevis (1987: 112).

We only managed to interview a few team members before Christmas, with the result that the majority of the people were unknown to us when we met on the first morning of the two-day programme.

We soon realized that five team members were not taking part. As we began a warm-up process, these five ignored the invitation to change partners and did not follow the instructions. Our offers to clarify were brushed aside and their behaviour was soon noticed by other team members. When we changed gear to allow a facilitated discussion, it emerged that no reasons had been given for the workshop in advance and that when the leader had said at the start that it was to improve communication, these five members had assumed there was an unspoken subtext. Having voiced their scepticism and gained some reassurance from the leader, they agreed to take part. But, on the first one-day follow-up programme, held for two of the shifts six weeks later, the pattern continued.

This time the team leader was ill and his deputy was in charge. Two of the five 'recalcitrant' team members—'Alan' and 'Fred'—were present and, if anything, more resistant than before. It was easy to sympathize since it had been made clear that the method of choosing the two shifts that were to attend the session had been some measure of performance by which they had rated poorly. Alan and Fred sat side-by-side, arms folded, glaring at us right from the start.

Some 15 minutes into the programme, we asked each participant to sit on a chair we had placed between us and tell the rest of the circle something that had changed for them personally since the previous workshop. When Alan came to the chair, he looked straight at the deputy leader and said he did not want to be there and thought the session was a waste of time. Fred held the same opinions and the deputy, though invited, had no comment to make. Everyone looked at us, presumably to see what we would do. In the event our response was, first, to ask Alan and Fred if they would be prepared to stay, if necessary as silent observers and, secondly, to ask the remainder of the team if this was acceptable. Everyone agreed and we continued with the programme, Alan and Fred sitting together initially outside the group but sometimes later choosing to be in the circle.

Half-way through the afternoon the team were in a discussion that was becoming circular. Noticing that the two opt-outs appeared to have been attentive throughout, sometimes speaking to each other but apparently commenting on what was happening, one of us took a chance and asked Alan what he had noticed so far. 'You mean descriptive comments without opinions?' he asked, showing to everyone's surprise that he had not only heard a key point made at the first workshop but had understood and remembered it. He then commented on a pattern of interaction between the deputy and another member that he said he had often seen before with results that always made him feel frustrated. He asked if he could make a suggestion on the topic the team were discussing. Eagerly invited to do so by way of a lot of vigorous head-nodding, he took the discussion on to a new and more productive plane, by reminding people of factors and a decision made in the past that had an important bearing on what was happening now.

It is easy to be obsessed by a need to succeed. Since I tend to believe that having interviewed team members and having attended a few of their meetings, the programme we have designed is the one that will help them most achieve their objectives, I can confuse success with completing the programme. Double mistake! This is a certain way to set myself up for direct conflict with anyone who decides 'not to play'. Had I continued to focus on our programme (which we did have to adjust radically) rather than on Alan and Fred, I would have drawn the full force of their fire and would probably have alienated the rest of the team. Christopher would probably have been pulled down with me, Alan's contribution would never have been made and none of the team's objectives would have been met.

Resistance as a strength

Stubborn resistance is an affirmation of all that is valuable about the way things are now and actually contains pointers as to how to move forward. The 'that won't work because ...' statement is a valuable part of the change process. It insists on refinement of the original proposal—perhaps a step back to better take two steps forward. It also provides an in-built protection against the faddish change-for-the-sake-of-change scenario that is itself resistance to persevering in the face of difficulty. So rather than being something to overcome, resistance deserves respect for helping the team to discover *how* to change. Sullenness rather than stubborn opposition may characterize some who take on the role but resistance is never lethargic. It is characterized by a mobilization of energy, not by lack of it: 'It is just that their energies are pointed in different directions' (Nevis 1987: 143).

An inexperienced team leader is unlikely to face overt resistance with great delight. Yet, a team member's resistance, like that of the immune system, is a healthy creative force to meet the challenges of an often threatening environment. At least it ensures homeostasis and a consistent performance of the team system. Once curiosity is aroused (what is this person's reality?) appreciation and respect soon follow, allowing the discovery of a new way forward.

SUPPORTING RESISTANCE

The Gestalt approach

Whereas Freud believed his patient's resistance had to be overcome, and the approach of many old-style leaders is to force their way past objections, the Gestalt approach—whether followed by a team leader, an internal facilitator or a consultant—is to support both the need of team members to withdraw and their right to hold their opinions. Not everyone should be required to be the same or to move at the same pace.

One club with whom we worked had a norm that the coaching staff would speak patiently, both on the pitch and in the locker room, to any player who was slow to do what they wanted but, back in their own part of the building, would express all their frustration through a stream of sarcastic jokes and bitter comments. While they credited themselves with professional restraint for their 'public' behaviour face-to-face with the player, the constant whinging 'at home' clearly cost a lot of emotional energy and perpetuated their problem. The coaches were quite unable to make the shift from seeing the player as a trouble-maker to seeing his resistance in a positive way.

No doubt, as sports psychologists, we were better placed to help the player discover what he needed (while becoming more aware of his own behaviour and the response it evoked) but by working with the coaches as a group and leading a series of hour-long teamwork meetings with the manager and the players, the manager himself stopped labelling players as 'problems' and began to ask interested questions of his own. Describing behaviour instead of labelling it, questioning instead of interpreting and reframing obstacles as opportunities were some of the skills he acquired.

Exploring resistance

Resistance can be a bottomless pit down which all effort to create change gradually disappears. The greater the effort, the greater the resistance. Telling team members what they need to do differently almost always meets with resistance. The resistance may or may not be voiced but, if it is not, it is a near certainty that the lack of response will soon make it obvious.

The only hope is to stop pushing and see what can be discovered about the resistance—in effect, exploring the opposite polarity. In fact, since pushing for change ensures some measure of resistance, a time-honoured tactic is to suggest that things should stay as they are. Alternatively, exaggerate the need for change, as Laura Perls was known to do in her Gestalt groups, asking the team to make a case for disbanding all together. In our experience even the mildest suggestion along the lines of 'Okay, so perhaps we shouldn't bother after all' is enough for someone to accuse us angrily of picking up our ball and refusing to play. Play? Oh, so we *are* interacting! There *is* interest here! In that case, let's take a deeper look at what is going on. And as consultants our role is 'not to ensure that change takes place but to help the [team] to heighten its awareness of forces acting for and against its moving to a new place on a problem or issue . . . to help the [team] resolve the dilemmas that underlie that ambivalence' (Nevis 1987: 60).

This was the path taken by Dr Bernie Bulkin, Head of Oil Technology at British Petroleum, when he set up and led a team to find a better non-reward-based appraisal system. He suggested that they begin by taking a hard look at the system currently in place. How did it work? What did people like about it? What did they object to? Only later would they begin to consider possible changes.

Team development is a combination of one-to-one interviews, coaching sessions, observation and facilitation of all types of exchanges (including pairs, small group and team meetings). It can also include brief on-site and longer off-site workshop sessions. These sessions allow the implicit to be made explicit, as the unstated underlying factors, dilemmas, ambivalence and assumptions are expressed, checked out and resolved. Team members grow in awareness of themselves and each other, come to appreciate differences and make contact. As they become more open to change, the sessions become increasingly productive as a forum where new ideas can be modelled and discussed.

Although we will have asked similar questions in the one-to-one interviews, at a workshop the questions 'What are you doing now?', 'What is the force for change?' and 'What stands in the way of change?' can fuel the discussion. If the proposal for change has come primarily from outside the team, as in the case of an organizational quality initiative, the resistance to that proposal needs to be fully explored before considering what factors might give the proposal support. Even where the change proposed is for this team alone—perhaps a senior management team—the underlying unexpressed factors that constitute the core of any resistance have to be brought to light before any progress can be made. Such discussions could well start with a statement to the effect that 'there is no possibility of going forward without a temptation to stay where you are' (Smith and Berg 1987: 222).

Sometimes a more oblique approach brings higher dividends. When we have been with the team for a period of time and have come to know each of its members, we may ask more searching questions: 'What are you uncomfortable about in the context of this team?' And even, 'What is it that nobody likes to talk about here?'

This last question reminds me of a question I heard asked at the beginning of a personal performance workshop in Chicago, where the subject was also change but at the level of the individual rather than the team. All the participants were asked to stand up in turn, give their name and say one thing they wanted people to know about them and one thing they *didn't* want people to know. Such questions must be timed correctly and facilitated expertly but even then they produce surprise and much (often deflective) hilarity. Their value lies in raising self-awareness, even when the questions are not answered.

One of the prime paradoxes of the team experience is that trying to change inhibits change and that the path to change lies in paying careful attention to—even to accentuate—what we are doing *now*. In a team context this is done by giving descriptive feedback, which we shall discuss early in Part III.

7

Team identity

A team is a group of (often irrational) people with a complex set of relationships. As such, it does not feel, it does not think and it does not have goals or intentions of its own. The team's members have all of these— occasionally sharing similar feelings and usually having a common goal. The team does have systems of operation and norms of behaviour. Also, as a unique group of people, it has a history, a present existence and, most interestingly, a potential.

Our original concept of a team's identity was strongly allied to its potential. Just as an infant's genes hold the physiological characteristics of the potential adult, a group of people forming a team hold the potential identity of that team, an identity that is unique. However, many groups fail to discover the full richness of who or what they might become—either through a restricted life span, a lack of facilitation or an inappropriate style of leadership.

We now distinguish between a past, a present and a future team identity, while recognizing that in fact all three can only exist in the present moment. The past is a self-contradictory knot of personal memories of how things actually were; the present is a mixed bundle of current awareness of how things actually are; and the future is a dimly perceived maximally creative ideal interrelationship, open only to this group of people. By the nature of things, some team members will not want to see and will not be able to see this potential; others may be able to see it but not want to; others again may want to see it but be unable to; and still others may want to see it and be able to. The balance of these four categories may determine whether the team attains its potential identity. It does not change that identity's nature.

This chapter, which closes Part II, outlines some factors that affect a group's ability to attain its potential team identity.

DISCOVERY

Any leader without a deputy who can be trusted to give an unbiased second opinion runs the risk of confusing personal interests with those that are best for the team, although there are plenty of leaders who do not believe the distinction is important. When I was the Scottish men's team volleyball coach, I dropped a player because he always seemed to be arguing with me and I had difficulty communicating with him. I may have told myself that the player had a communication problem that was affecting the team. Without him, the team certainly seemed to be more in harmony but our play became more predictable and I noticed that, when I moved on, the new national coach immediately reinstated the player in the starting line-up. Many years later I did some work with another European national volleyball team where the coach was having a similar problem—but this time with four professional foreign-based players. The same scenario was re-enacted—the players were dropped, the team played less well, the coach left and the new coach brought the players straight back.

Each of us had focused on our own needs and our own preconceived structure for the team—backed though we may have been by other players in our teams. We each came close to restricting interaction between players, which would have ensured shallow, unproductive relationships. As long as we behaved this way, we were never going to guide our players to discovering either their potential as a team or their identity.

Discovery is now valued by educationalists as the way that people learn best. Learning by rote is outmoded. Teachers are asked to be imaginative in creating experiences for their students. Postgraduate courses in confluent education stress the importance of integrating the affective and cognitive. Where there are no surprises, where meaning is fixed, there are few opportunities.

As consultants we join a team with as few preconceptions as possible, holding hypotheses at bay for as long as we can. This allows us to become aware of a wider range of incidents, a more intricate pattern of behaviour and gives us a greater chance of discovering what is really going on. Joe Leaphorn, the Navajo Indian police detective in Tony Hillerman's books, (Hillerman 1993) was once asked what he was looking for as he circled the scrub around a newly discovered body. 'Nothing in particular,' he replied. 'You're not really looking for anything in particular. If you do that you don't see the things you're not looking for.'

Just as the human body constantly strives to return to health from a state of sickness, over-indulgence, injury or stress, so does a team appear to naturally gravitate towards discovering its potential when the forces against its doing so relent. Only when chronic misuse or abuse of human contact reinforces an altered level of homeostasis, do teams accept norms that restrain their performance.

As team members begin to glimpse the fact that their team is different to any other team of which they have been a part they gain a greater appreciation of their personal differences. This, in turn, further facilitates the expression of conflicting opinions, without which no team can ultimately survive. Abandoning both the 'stuckness' and the comfort of perpetual agreement, everyone realizes that each team member may see and respond to any idea or event differently, that within the team there are 'multiple realities' and that this opens the possibility of discovering and thereby achieving more than anyone had originally suspected.

Synergy

Such awareness both comes from and contributes to an increased willingness to listen and build on each other's ideas. The experience of new ideas flowing synergistically from this process brings the first intimation of the team's unique identity. This is true of teams of any size. Even a troubleshooting team of two, a tennis doubles team or for that matter a married couple can find themselves going in a direction that neither would have taken alone. Smith and Berg (1987: 111) are making a similar point when they write: 'While a group is not independent of its individual members, it does have a life beyond what any individual in the group is capable of understanding at any moment.'

A team functioning healthily will not only produce ideas that no team member could have thought of alone but will also be able to solve problems that even the technically most gifted was unable to solve. A Ford Motor Company TOPS 8D* engineering team is only *formed* when it has been established that no individual is able to solve the problem alone. Normally a team, like an individual, will always grow rapidly to become greater than

---

*TOPS 8D = Team Oriented Problems Solving (8 Disciplines). This title is soon to be changed to 'Global 80', as different versions are rationalized.

the sum of its parts. It is the dysfunctional team, the team riven with politics, power games, secrecy and fear—the team in which individuals accomplish *less* than they can when they are alone—that is psychologically out of balance. In systems language, this is a team that has acquired a homeostasis that is counterproductive and a large percentage of its energy has been side-tracked into error states.

Yet, at all levels of system, decisions are made to by-pass the team process. Tom Peters once wrote:

Pessimists about adaptivity support the models of 3M and Johnson & Johnson, which foster the creation of numerous independent divisions and eschew the allure of synergy. Optimists about change rely on co-ordinated strategic planning to guide the institution towards whatever ideal tomorrow it chooses.

(Independent on Sunday 13 June 1993)

Even at this level the choice is the same: to allow the open conflict that will always emerge from multiple responses to the same situation or to maintain a low profile, keep the peace and never discover the synergy inherent in one's team identity.

ATTUNEMENT

We have used the word 'attunement' in different contexts arising from our experience as athletes and the time we spent at the Findhorn Foundation.*
In sport, and indeed in business meetings, it defines the six-part process of warming-up. At 'Findhorn', 'attunement' had three connotations. The first was the short silence at the start of a meeting, which allowed attention to move from outside concerns to the purpose of the meeting; the second was a type of meeting—the weekly meeting held by each work department that was half maintenance and half task,† and the third was a silence observed in the middle of a meeting to allow a shift of perspective from personal needs and contradictory opinions to alignment to the needs of the community as a whole.

*The Trust, in Moray, Scotland. See Syer (1986) for further references.
†In this chapter, there are several references to 'task' and 'maintenance'. Task is the business part of a meeting. Maintenance is time spent attending to relationships and how people feel physically or emotionally. These parts of a meeting are the subject of Chapter 9.

It is this third type of attunement which allows the team to discover its identity. Paying attention to personal needs and opinions is essential groundwork, but opening oneself to the unexpected and continually affirming the team process is the way to clarity. The team's potential, like its identity, is unknown but exists in the present as a possibility. The shift of focus to the needs of the whole requires a belief that the team is always capable of improvement. When this is present, 'the synergy that accompanies alignment enables us to do seemingly impossible things' (Oakley and Krug 1993: 174).

As discussed in Part III, the last maintenance stage of warming up and the first of warming down—tuning in to the team—is a form of alignment with the team's identity. This might be pulling the chairs back into a circle, looking around and asking the question 'So how is everyone?' or it could be a more imaginative ritual. Many of the exercises in our team development workshops are designed to achieve the same objective. Guided visualization can also evoke a strong sense of team identity.

At the same time, while still in the task phase of warming down, a conscientious review of progress made towards the team's purpose—so that the next stage to be accomplished is clear—would be typically in line with any team determined to reach its potential. So, too, would a consideration of the consequences that any changes decided at the meeting might have on other parts of the organization.

Individuals and affiliation

The paradox of membership—how to become a part of the team without getting lost in the process—is most apparent when attuning to team identity. Many individuals only join teams that will allow them to retain a fair measure of autonomy, while teams usually prefer members who will put the team first. This accounts for the importance of the first part of team development and, on a much smaller scale, of warming up—when each individual voices his or her needs, concerns and opinions. This stage can neither be overlooked nor hurried. The team is defined by its membership and until members have tuned in to each other—heard and understood each other—there is no possibility of everyone tuning in to the team. It is this first part of the process that raises awareness and mobilizes the energy of everyone present, allowing everyone to 'turn to the same page'. Individuals become aware not just of others but also of themselves and their own patterns of action and reaction—and in doing so begin to appreciate alternatives.

Perhaps it is the length and intensity of this ongoing process and the investment of time and energy involved that produces the strong mix of feelings when the team's task is completed. Having overcome obstacles to consensus, having completed the task and withdrawn from the project, team members may experience both satisfaction and regret—the regret stemming from temporary loss of mutual awareness. In fact, if the team is defined by its membership, individuals will also define themselves by membership of the team. Even the fear of losing oneself in the team is only a Western cultural concept. In the East, particularly in China, the individual feels defined by the team and it is therefore in *leaving* the team that the individuals fears the loss of his or her identity.

Ritual and symbols

Agile and creative thinking is a prominent aspect of effective teamwork. Ask any strong team the question 'What song comes to mind that characterizes you as a team?' and a chorus of suggestions will come in response. One of these might make people laugh so much or create such instant and universal recognition that, for a while at least, it becomes a trigger to the shared sense of team identity—a form of instant attunement. In the East, it is perhaps a more solemn affair but organizational anthems played at the start of the day serve a similar function for many employees.

Any symbol arising out of the team's experience may also work. When Tottenham Hotspur won the FA Cup in 1981, the Cup itself became an instant touchstone to the team's identity when it was brought into the changing room before home Cup matches the following season. Katzenbach and Smith give the example of the team at Kodak, formed to heighten awareness of black and white film, that not only designed special black and white logos but gave themselves the name 'The Kodak Zebra Team' and wore black and white clothes to work, thereby affirming their identity. Badges, blazers and scarves presented only to outstanding athletes can have a similar effect—even on their team mates who have yet to make the grade.

VISION

The team's vision, once established, becomes closely allied to the team's identity. However, if the team's identity is 'who' or 'what' the team is capable of becoming, the team's vision is also 'where' and 'how' it wants to be. The vision also incorporates the team's purpose and objectives which are 'what' the team wants to achieve. This means of course that although a team is usually selected with a purpose in mind, it is conceivable that the same team might later work to achieve a different purpose and a different vision, while retaining the same identity. Most cross-functional commercial teams are disbanded after they have achieved their purpose. A football team winning the League is somewhat less likely to disband than the team that came last and the purpose simply shifts to winning again the next season (but perhaps winning the Cup for good measure as well).

In a sports team the vision might remain the same but, if the membership of the team changes, much effort has to be spent on discovering the new team identity before the team has any chance of realizing the same or a similar vision. However, the team's vision can still be an equal source of inspiration. Provided that team members have clarified their vision together or that members have joined because they were attracted by the team's vision, tuning in to it either separately or together can help the team to regroup in the face of apparent defeat. By refocusing on the desired future the unexpected present state of affairs is reframed into a new set of opportunities.

When George Bush, as President of the United States, spoke in his idiosyncratic way of 'the vision thing', his message was similar (if somewhat less direct) to that of Proverbs 29:18: 'Where there is no vision, the people perish.' This line is quoted by Oakley (Oakley and Krug 1993: 178) who himself points out that without a vision team members will tend to focus on what is going wrong rather than on what is going right—indeed, without a vision, the only distinction that can be made is between what is comfortable, at best enjoyable, and what is unpleasant.

Despite this, it can take a new member some time to realize that a team has no vision—especially if the team appears to have a function. In many large organizations the custom is for a company vision or mission statement to be defined by the top management team, all other teams being expected to accept it as their own. Such statements may have value, particularly to the prospective outside customer, but the job is not complete until each team has gone through some similar process of its own to affirm its role and team vision within the context of the whole.

If the newcomer asks the question 'Why are we doing this?', the answer may come easily enough: 'So that ... .' However, if that answer is met with another 'Why?' question and the next and the next also, a team objective may emerge but a lack of team vision will eventually produce the answer 'I don't know'. All members of a team on its way to discovering its identity are aware of the connection between what they are doing and the team vision. This is their source of commitment, rather than any company vision—at least in the West. In one of the unhappiest teams we've ever worked with, we discovered that not only was there no vision but no clear common objective, no formal meetings and no job descriptions. Everyone had a job title and the chief executive assumed that this meant members knew their roles. Instead there was endless confusion with—at any given time—three people taking care of one matter and no one taking care of many others.

Generating a vision does not ensure a strong business strategy, will not clarify roles and does not guarantee success. However, it does heighten awareness of the team's direction—providing an organizing principle—and, if pursued seriously, it does compel the team to question what it is doing, why it is doing it and how it is going about its business. A vision driven through to structure, function and objectives generates congruence and integration of personal and team will.

When we lead a team session on vision, we will sometimes supply crayons and ask everyone to draw. A vision can be described in words but it is primarily a product of right-brain associative thinking. A clear vision is a picture 'worth a thousand words', that evokes a personal, emotional response. We ask people to spread out around the room, each with crayons and three pieces of paper. We then lead a short visualization to evoke their memories of the team the day they joined—the atmosphere, how people communicated with one another and so on—and ask them to let an image come that captures this memory, open their eyes and draw. One member may show an apartment building with many people behind closed doors; another the wild confusion of a jungle; and a third a series of islands with a small tribe of natives on each. After a few minutes they write the word 'PAST' on one corner, put the paper aside and settle back for another visualization to evoke their present reality.

This one will reflect the current patterns of team behaviour. They visualize, draw, write the word 'PRESENT' on one corner and repeat the process with the future—how the team will be as it moves towards some form of fulfilment.

When the BBC did a 'Business Matters' television documentary comparing our work with athletes and with business people, the British cycling pursuit team all drew podiums and medals, while the 'Ford Motor Company 'KD' management team drew a variety of symbols all relating to success. On the back of the last picture we ask people to write a phrase that sums up their vision of the future. They ground this experience by taking their three drawings and talking about them for five or ten minutes with two other team members. Since each drawing describes a personal experience, all are valid and significant. The two others listen and question but do not judge. The process fosters creativity, awareness of multiple realities and an appreciation of diversity. It allows team members to escape the verbal clichés of ready-made mission statements and to contact a deep personal experience of the team.

Eventually, they come back to a circle and each person in turn pins up his or her future picture, describes it to the whole team and reads out the phrase on the back. We list the phrases on a flip chart. With these in view and all the 'future' drawings on the Metaplan board, the team begins to discuss what it has done. Although the drawings may seem poor or trite, most of them portray an intuitive feel for what the team might achieve. Such insights usually lead to full engagement as the team seeks to clarify its unifying vision. It takes time to reach consensus—a shared view of the big picture—and the process is rarely completed in a single session. However, the team is always able to agree on a few immediate action steps that will begin the move from where it is now to the general direction of where it wants to be. Realizing their similarity of intentions and their strength of will for the team's future increases their commitment and further clarifies their perception of their team identity.

Goals

Once the vision has been clarified, it gives life to the team's purpose and serves as a point of alignment for both long- and short-term goals. Considerable time is needed for the purpose to be affirmed and the subsequent goals to be agreed. Such a discussion will include a gear change—a moment to attune to the team's identity. If this process is rushed team members will leave the meeting with differing views of what was decided and communicate conflicting stories to people further down the organization. The goals have to be clear, testing but achievable and, above all, agreed. Teams lower in the organization and any subcommittees should have equal clarity, having subsequently undergone a similar process. However, the best team leaders remember that goals are also boundaries and, like the team's vision and purpose, need to be reviewed from time to time.

A team that establishes goals reflecting its shared vision, finds them easier to achieve than those that are imposed by some alien business plan because its process will have eliminated any conflicting objectives or confusion and surfaced any hidden agendas. It is also engaged in a self-regulating process, for goals that are in line with personal vision coincide with the goals of an effective system. By choosing the factors it considers primary and by organizing team structures to support the achievement of its target, it is merely 'co-operating with the process'.

NORMS

The newcomer's first hint of the team's identity—which his or her arrival is going to change—is on encountering current team norms. These accurately reflect how the team is now, but may also give some indication of what the team may become. Norms are unstated rules and patterns of behaviour that determine what is acceptable or unacceptable in almost every situation. The newcomer will immediately encounter the norms that this team holds in response to the arrival of a newcomer. Some teams appoint a person to introduce the newcomer to the other members of the team in turn; others wait until there is a full team meeting. Some will start the process of introductions but forget to finish it; others will assign someone who has also only recently arrived and cannot do the job properly. When I arrived at the Cleveland Browns, for my work with them during the 1994 season, special assignment coach Ernie Adams and Bill Belichick's secretary Linda Leone introduced me to each member of the coaching staff in turn. On my second visit, I found an office had been assigned to me with a stack of pads and pens and a note saying 'welcome' from the owner's secretary, Marilyn McGrath. More than a facet of American culture, this demonstrated a norm of a family owned club that prided itself on its old-fashioned human values.

Norms of unacceptable behaviour are often discovered by experience. At Tottenham, the first time the authors were invited to travel on the team bus, we each bought a new sweater to mark the occasion. As we stepped onto the bus, Keith Burkinshaw the manager, who was already sitting just inside, greeted us with a smile and the words 'John! Christopher! Good to see you! Now, how would you like to ride with a friend of mine today? He's got a Rolls Royce and travels just behind the bus. Come on, let me introduce you.' Mystified, we looked beyond the manager for a moment and then noticed that all the players were travelling in suits.

One European athlete we knew, fresh from a foreign club, challenged his new manager, mid-way through his first team meeting—unaware that no one ever did this publicly. He was instantly branded as a 'problem' before most of the team had had time to say 'Hello!'. No one knew that that was the way his previous manager had encouraged his team to behave. Assumptions underlie all norms. While the rest of the team assumed he was a trouble-maker, he assumed everyone else was either slow-witted or half asleep.

When we work in an ongoing consultancy role, we help make a team's norms and the assumptions that underlie them explicit. We do this in conversation, in one-to-one meetings with the team leader and in written reports—saying what we see and what we hear. We are careful to make neither assumptions nor interpretations although we may sometimes report how we respond personally to a given pattern of behaviour if we think an outsider's response could be useful. When we receive conflicting signals, we make this explicit. Watching a team meeting stuck in repetitive dialogue, we might voice confusion: 'As I sit listening to you, I realize that I'm not sure how you make decisions here.'

A team development workshop allows a team to re-evaluate its norms. To this end we might give each member some Metaplan cards and ask him or her to write down, on a separate card, at least three of their team's undeclared norms. Some norms will identify group behaviour—'we start meetings late', 'we sit at a long table' or 'we complain about decisions over which we have no control'—and others will identify functions of individuals in the team (for example, 'Elizabeth always asks for the bottom line' or 'Robert usually speaks first'). We stress that the norms described should be observable, although the assumptions made about the norms and the assumptions upon which the norm seems to be based can be discussed afterwards.

We then collect the cards and pin them on the Metaplan board. No one needs to admit to writing a specific card, although people usually do if asked. When no further norms are offered, we ask if any are unclear. (This is the opportunity to probe behind anything that appears to be an assumption, rather than an observation, and to get examples.) We then ask if there are any that anyone disagrees with. If even one person disagrees we mark the card concerned but leave it on the board. Finally, we ask the most significant question: 'Are there any that anyone would like to change?'

This is first discussed in smaller groups of three or four, taking whatever time is needed. The process of questioning these norms and considering whether they are still aligned to the team's purpose and vision allows the team to discover more about its identity. Whenever there has been a significant change in membership, this is a process to repeat. When a new team leader is appointed it is essential.

Change follows awareness. By making team norms explicit, awareness is heightened and members have a choice whether or not to continue acting out the same patterns of behaviour. There is now the possibility of making a shift from 'this is how things are' to 'what does each of us want to do in the future? let's discuss it'—a move that counteracts the assumption that the team has human attributes and an independent will. (It does not.) However, the team does have goal-seeking behaviours and it will strive to maintain homeostasis: it is through the will, individual or collective, of team members that the direction of a team changes. Self-regulation becomes possible for a team that has awareness and uses feedback to redirect itself purposefully.

The outsider and the newcomer may be biased by their own past experiences of other teams but still offer a fresh view of a team's norms. A team may be stuck, frustrated, trying to change and getting nowhere because it is locked into a paradigm that is no longer appropriate. For instance, a team that is trying to solve a problem may produce solution after solution to no avail, without ever thinking to examine the way they solve problems. A newcomer who is used to solving problems in a different way can tell the team what it is doing and, with that awareness, the team may change.

However, not all new members are as brave or bone-headed as the athlete who argued with his manager at his first meeting. There is not only a risk that the team will not listen—or at least that the individuals with the power will not listen—but also that the newcomer will suffer the athlete's fate and become a scapegoat.

Most newcomers who are rebuffed in this way take a back seat. Any member still feeling threatened will comment adversely on everything the newcomers do but eventually, if they persevere, support will come. From that point, if there is no open discussion, the battle for change may shift to a different field. Any team or organization behaves differently to its stated beliefs, rules, slogans and declared goals. It is an unfortunate fact that all human beings have standards they do not live up to. This discrepancy can be exploited to produce change.

The method is simple, effective—and infuriating to those in the team who are attached to the old way of existence. It is to act out rigorously the stated procedures and ignore the conflicting unstated norms. Where the stated procedure is half forgotten, question it until it is restated, then act on it accordingly. The whole moribund system begins to crumble and the entrenched implicit norms are forced to the surface, to be questioned and reassessed.

A new team has a different task. A long initial warm-up allows members to discuss their needs, wishes and expectations and the norms of behaviour they want to adopt. Everyone can write down a few things that they want to tell the rest of the team about themselves—their strengths, what aspects of themselves they want to develop, what support they would like and what they have to offer. They can start by discussing what they have written with a couple of other members or, if the team is not too large, go round the circle telling one or two of the things they have written. Eventually there needs to be a discussion of norms around meetings, attendance, roles, how decisions are to be taken, the importance given to time (strong teams value and protect the time they have together), the place of task, maintenance and process, how to give feedback and speaking, questioning and listening skills.

Image

Not inviting a newcomer or an outsider to report what they notice misses an opportunity to discover more about the team's identity and runs the risk of the team holding an entrenched unrealistic self-image that will hinder effective dealings with the world at large. Ignoring some of its own characteristics, it will be over-sensitive to a trace of them in other teams with which it has to deal. In fact, it will actively look for such characteristics and subconsciously its members may even create situations that are likely to provoke the other team to display them. This leads to misunderstandings at best and usually results in mutual distrust. Performance soon suffers.

Helping a team to face its pattern of denial needs sensitive facilitation. When people finally become aware of some unbalanced pattern of their behaviour, it can come as a shock. If we shift for a moment to the context of a two-person team and consider a married couple's relationship, we can give an example provided by George Brown. In a workshop where video equipment was used, couples were asked to take part in an exercise that simply involved pushing. The partners faced each other and put both hands against their partner's hands. The task was for one of them to push the other backwards until reaching the end of the room, then the other to push back until they reached the other end. This was to be repeated several times with each person's focus being on his or her own response to being pushed and to pushing. The video camera remained fixed throughout, focused on a line across the room, so that it recorded all the couples every time they moved past. After ten minutes, each couple found somewhere to sit together and discuss their experience with each other.

Eventually everyone came back to a circle and after some further discussion of the experience the video was shown. People were asked to watch themselves and their partner and to call out if they got any additional insight. A few people spoke before the group leader turned to a couple that had not said anything and asked what the experience had been like for each of them. 'Great fun!' they both agreed.

'Is there anything you notice about yourselves that is different to the other couples?' asked the leader. The woman frowned and said: 'I'm not sure. I did think there was something wrong'. She turned to her husband, then suddenly realized. The video showed that she was walking backwards, smiling and that her husband was pushing with lots of creative variation but every time they came into view she was walking *backwards*. They had never switched round: he had been pushing all the time! The woman became very upset—not just because she had been 'pushed around' but because she had not realized it. This was a significant awakening for her.

Such lack of awareness within the complexities of a team's relationships is not uncommon. While their attention is fixed on surface behaviour, members soon respond emotionally to the unspoken norm and the hidden message. Yet being unaware of these feelings does not reduce the effect they have on the relationship and on performance. Double binds—where someone says one thing and means another—undermine contact, respect and trust. The only way to increase awareness—changing the false images team members hold of their relationships and of themselves—is to seek descriptive feedback.

Tom Peters* suggests that teams should actively canvas for feedback on how they are seen from a range of customers—those lost as well as those gained—and from recent successful and unsuccessful interviewees. Whatever is mainly remembered about the team by these people, after some time, is a sure indication of how the team is widely seen. He calls this the 'big picture' or seeing 'naively' and believes there should be in-house sessions to discuss how team members see a variety of everyday service professions, so that they realize how the team's customers draw conclusions about them. By exchanging roles within the team, members would get further insight into their customers' experience but the main message on how to grasp the formation of the image that outsiders hold of the team is to 'try to stop immediately dissecting; stick with the big picture'.

We sometimes encourage teams to distinguish between (i) their self-image, (ii) the image they would like outsiders to have of them (which may or may not be the same) and (iii) the image they believe that outsiders actually have of them. We then ask them to clarify these images by sitting quietly for some 20 minutes, cutting out magazine pictures and making three collages. Only afterwards do we invite a verbal explanation and discussion of what they have done.

At some later date, we ask different teams within the same organization to check out their 'how we imagine we are seen' pictures with each other, before showing how they see themselves and how they would like to be seen. Eventually they may also choose to inform each other of any plans they have to change their outside image. Usually the result of such joint sessions is that both teams realize that the images they were holding—both of themselves and of the other team—were in many ways false. This allows an appreciation of real differences between them and contact that helps all future dealings.

LEADERSHIP

It has been said that leaders often know more about how to become leaders than they do about leadership, having focused much of their time and

*See *Independent on Sunday*, 1 August 1993.

energy on climbing their organization's pyramid. Outward bound course organizers have found that the person who eventually assumes the leadership role in extreme circumstances is often not the designated team leader. This may be because the leader already has nominal power and wants someone else to experience the role. Deliberately holding back would certainly create an uncomfortable vacuum with everyone experiencing an increasing sense of powerlessness until someone decides to take control. The ability to remain relaxed and sit out this discomfort, without rushing in to take charge, can itself be a leadership quality. However, leadership in such circumstances makes demands other than relaying information, considering strategy and keeping a meeting focused on its task. The additional ingredient required, which the designated leader may or may not possess, is the ability to make contact.

A British Institute of Management survey made in December 1991 found that although 86 per cent of the respondents believed teamwork was necessary, only 36 per cent rated the ability to contribute to teams as an important management quality. This would be understandable if the leader's only role was to lead meetings and that at those meetings there was always a good facilitator available to take care of maintenance and process. Meetings are more effective when the leadership and facilitation roles (described in Chapter 9) are split but both are part of the designated team leader's role when the meeting is over. It is an interesting fact that nearly all designated leaders will take the leadership rather than the more contactful facilitation role during a meeting. If the leader has the qualities required by the wider role, leading or facilitating a meeting should be equally simple and satisfying.

The human resources representative plays a related role and often attends the preliminary meeting we have with the leader of a team within a large organization. When the meeting finishes, we leave the leader and the 'HR rep' in the leader's office but meet the 'rep' again later to glean some additional information about the team.

Unfortunately, even when an 'HR rep' is available, the designated leader's role cannot be split successfully outside the meeting. The leader has to help clarify the team's purpose and guide the discussion that establishes specific team goals but afterwards, his or her role does not stop at focusing on the team's task. Nor is it just to relay information, consider new ideas or think about strategy, though it may include all of these things. The leader's prime role is to guide the team, with descriptive feedback, through each step back and forth on the path of its evolution until it eventually discovers its identity. At the same time, he or she is guardian of the team's vision, avoiding the mistake of trying to mould it to a preconceived form that may or may not satisfy some personal agenda.

Should the leader ignore this role, no HR rep can take.it over. Nor can any other team member without a formidable struggle that could only end in a change of behaviour on the part of the leader, a change of leadership or, more likely, the expulsion of the team member concerned.

Guarding the vision and continually tuning in to the team's identity, involves modelling the behaviour that is congruent to attaining both. The leader is supremely visible. For good or ill, his or her behaviour is more predictable and more discussed inside and outside the team than that of any other team member. Hence, the media creates and promotes a 'received' image of any coach or manager of a top sports team. The strength of the leader's commitment to and belief in the team carries great influence.

A leader of quality will create an atmosphere that supports and encourages the creativity of each team member. In a good team, all members continually learn about themselves and develop towards their own potential as the identity of the team gradually emerges. Throughout the day, when a leader interacts with any of the team members—be it formal in an office or informal over lunch—some part of the leader's role is a form of facilitation. In a context wider than the formal team meeting, this still means learning about each member's needs and the needs they have of each other, allowing people's feelings to be expressed, and occasionally checking their responses as a way of forming a clearer picture of what is going on. Leaders cannot afford to be too distant. While the ability to step into an observer's role is important, so is willingness to give an open and personal response. This does not mean giving endless opinions but saying what they feel. Unless leaders model such behaviour there will be little trust within their team that such behaviour should be the norm.

Good leaders continually look for new opportunities for the other team members to show their expertise, interceding where necessary on their behalf and not keeping all the best assignments for themselves. Giving power and responsibility to team members does not diminish the leader's power—in fact the leader's power increases. Oakley confirms this opinion when he writes: 'The empowered leader knows that giving away power, like lighting candles from a single one, does not subtract from their power but adds to it' (Oakley and Krug 1993: 227). Ricardo Semler, head of Semco, a

Brazilian manufacturer of industrial equipment, lets his staff decide work hours, work days, salary and dress code. He has chosen to be one of six people sharing the chief executive position, believing that if you treat people as responsible adults, they will act that way. All information is shared with the workforce and there is a profit-related pay which means that the company is not left with high salaries during difficult periods. In 1993, staff turnover was less than 1 per cent.*

Nothing is potentially more traumatic on the team's way towards discovering its identity than a change of leadership. Any change of membership results in a change of potential and team identity but a change of leadership will both alter the identity and enhance or inhibit the journey towards its discovery. British league soccer clubs and American NFL football clubs have the same custom whereby a change of manager or head coach automatically brings a wholesale change of coaching staff and often a considerable change of player personnel as well. Any inherent tendency a manager or head coach may have to mistrust the (admittedly often unsuccessful) existing format is exaggerated by an expectation that the stables will be swept clean. Inevitably the playing staff who stay behind are unsettled, guarded and often resentful. Since the manager or coach has total power, such feelings cannot be expressed, so that any desire to continue to discover the team's identity has to begin again. If the previous leadership was poor, many players may feel a renewed sense of hope and initial results might improve because of an improvement in their personal performance. Eventually, however, any lack of vision and absence of feel for the team's identity will result in renewed misunderstandings and mistrust.

In the context of business teams the formula is similar, but the option of continuity is taken a little more frequently. The new team leader is often appointed from within the team or, at worst, the team will meet with both the old and new team leaders to discuss vision, goals and norms, before the handover occurs.

Followership

One of Smith and Berg's organizational paradoxes states that until the new team leader makes a move, the other team members are unable to decide the extent of their support. Yet is is only when they give their support that

*See *Independent on Sunday*, 1 August 1993.

leadership happens. This interplay between leading and following means that team members actually help to determine the type of leadership they receive and need.

Katzenbach and Smith make the point that members of many top management teams prefer to allow the leader to take all the decisions and stick to the domain of their own teams. This way they do not have to subscribe to an 'only the team can fail' philosophy: no one can be held responsible for 'someone else's' mistake. Often this suits the leader as much as anyone else, unless it reaches the point where team members collude with failure by withholding information at critical junctures. The use of 'someone else' in this thinking betrays the fact that such people do not think of themselves as teams (which is why Katzenbach and Smith call them 'working groups'). This is the type of team that has no creative work to do together, no vision distinct from that of the organization and no concept of, let alone interest in, its team identity. It can work effectively, while giving the clear non-verbal message that teamwork is not important in this organization.

QUALITIES AND SKILLS

Both within the team and from outside, some reflections of the team's identity are seen in the norms, the leadership style, and the qualities and skills of team members. Each member brings a wide variety of skills and qualities to the team, some of which are shown and made available and some of which are hidden, or unrealized. In the usual pattern, members demonstrate those qualities that support the image they have or want to have of themselves within the context of the team. However, if there is a quality that describes me—kind, strong, expressive, dull—I also own the opposite quality. (We often develop relationships with people who display this polarity, so that we do not have to own it ourselves.) Each team member reacts to those qualities shown by each of the others and makes subtle adjustments of behaviour accordingly. As the team passes through different experiences new qualities are required, and are often discovered where least expected. A business trip to another country may not only reveal unsuspected language skills but a quirky humour in a member who had previously been seen as a recluse.

This evokes the third way (see pp. 85 and 96) in which we differ philosophically from the Belbin model, Myers–Briggs or indeed from most forms of character assessment or personality profiling. While understanding that many leaders feel more secure if they can be told how an individual will react to a given situation, we come from an educational orientation with the firm belief that everyone has the potential for demonstrating a wide range of qualities that reside in us all and can be developed by a good leader. Indeed, we see the enlightened leader as someone who makes this a central part of his or her role.

Nothing is more limiting and wasteful than to label someone as (for instance) cheerful and expect that person to be the life and soul of the party. There is a natural tendency for this to happen and we believe this is something that the leader should watch carefully and, where appropriate, deliberately counteract. When some personal problem besets the 'funny' team member, he or she rarely feels allowed to change role and show grief or anger. It can be as limiting to label someone with a 'positive' quality as it is to label him or her with a 'negative' one.

A similar tendency to label can be seen at all levels of the system, throughout the organization. A subgroup may find itself a doer, a thinker, a questioner and a carer. A full team can organize itself to have all these and more, while at the organizational level the Research and Development department may be called 'the creative guys around here', while Packaging and Marketing are deemed to be practical. Some executives have a 'fierce' personal assistant to guard their door. Those who are allowed in encounter a 'relaxed and affable' manager. This division of labour, conscious or unconscious, works well for both parties—the executive is protected and the PA has power. Yet the same result can be achieved with the roles reversed. One of our clients, who wanted to move freely from one work point to another, adopted the 'fierce' label and strode around glaring. Meantime his secretary was seen as the most sympathic person in the organization, with the result that almost anyone wanting to speak to her boss asked her to intercede for them.

It is always from the next level up that the link between the different parts becomes apparent. From the viewpoint of the manager's direct report team, the manager and the secretary are often thought about separately but they are frequently seen as a unit and as a unit they *together* possess the qualities of austerity and friendliness as part of their own team identity. In fact, not only does every member have a relationship with each two-person relationship within the team but every relationship within the team—having an identity to discover—is potentially full of surprises. If its members give any relationship a fixed label and meaning, other opportunities for that relationship may become hidden. This is equally true of the division of qualities within partnerships, subgroups and the full team.

If team members are locking each other into categories, the skilful leader will always encourage them to reframe their relationship in the context of the whole, seeing how, by aligning themselves again with the team identity, their various qualities are mutually owned. The team's identity is inherent in the relationships that exist between team members and, in an effective team, its various qualities and skills are aligned to its vision and declared purpose.

Modelling

Sometimes the adopted norms of the team omit the expression of some quality of behaviour that would appear—at least to an outsider or a newcomer—to be desperately needed. A new member would have to be brave and judicious to point this out but a consultant or a new leader is in a position to model the missing quality. Even for the consultant, this is not always easy. At the Cleveland Browns, where everyone nobly honoured what was referred to as 'our work ethic' but where some key people had had trouble pacing themselves, I noticed that I got sucked into a similar syndrome myself. I spoke and wrote about my perception of their need for more rest but was often there from 7.00 a.m. till midnight myself.

I had been more successful a year earlier as a member of a cross-cultural consultancy team. Working with a Glasgow hotel management team that appeared so stressed that none of them seemed to hear what the others were saying, we deliberately modelled a slower pace, checking that one of our own team had finished making a point before making another, looking at each other frequently, even sitting back in our chairs from time to time and proposing regular breaks throughout the day. When the time came to make explicit what we had been doing, we asked the client team what they had noticed. Their response was that we had been fair to each other and took each other seriously—which was an easy way into a discussion of their own self-image and how they wanted and would be able to change.

MEMBERSHIP

Any *ad hoc* group of people have a team identity they can seek to discover—the right way to be and work together. Anyone who played a minority team sport at college or university, where it was rarely a question of picking and choosing but rather of hoping enough people were available to form a team, will remember the experience of a motley crew of unlikely but dedicated candidates discovering how to act and play together—discovering in fact their team identity. The team may not have won too often but team members still found themselves capable of more than they ever thought possible. Amateur club sport has a lot to offer. Business and professional sports teams are a little different. Here the leader usually has the luxury of choice, with many candidates applying for each vacant place. The question then arises: 'What criteria should be used in selection?'

Although it would be silly to pretend that in selecting our own staff we pay no attention to references that attest loyalty, honesty and good humour, we believe that the criteria that really counts is the ability or potential ability to provide the level of technical skill required by the job. If we believe a candidate wants to join our team as opposed to any team, this would also make a difference when selecting a consultant. We would not, for instance, select someone who was wedded to the Belbin model or believed whole-heartedly in personality profiling.

This example is making me think more than usual as I write. We have long been aware that we are concerned to protect our image as humanistic consultants, trained in one of the humanistic psychologies. We believe whole-heartedly in this approach. It is the one that we like to project and it is also what makes us different. So, if we are not prepared to change the professional aspect of our image, to what extent are we attached to our team identity? How much danger is there that we shall fall into the trap we help others to avoid and only appoint people who will never challenge our norms, never question our ideas and will 'fit in perfectly'?

Very little, I believe. There is a lot more to team identity than one's professional image and approach. In fact, our current team continues to discuss and explore the finer points of our approach and we do reassess our norms, our purpose and our vision, although perhaps not as regularly as we should. Once, when two consultants joined us and two left within a six-month period, our team identity radically changed. This was painful. We 'mourned' the two members who left and, for some time afterwards, mourned the passing of the team identity we had been discovering together. This was not easy for the consultants who replaced them. They were good but they were quite different and were not unnaturally impatient for us to forget the past and see who we were now. Designing and writing a new brochure together was a major step towards discovering this new identity.

Football managers or head coaches have so much power that they often find themselves isolated from differences of view and opinion. This would be limiting when it came to selection were it not for the extensive scouting organizations that most clubs now operate. Business managers have their head-hunting agencies and personnel departments to perform a similar function but, in either case, it is possible for leaders to select teams that are built around their own image—an attempt to create a team identity rather than discover it. In such teams, members soon learn to withhold aspects of themselves, under threat of dismissal, and very little progress is made towards the group ever feeling or being a team. The team identity (which exists for any group of people) remains firmly 'on the etheric' with no likelihood of being found. The team may still be relatively successful if the members are highly skilled and the leader has a sophisticated tactical sense but will never be as good as it could be.

In summary, we believe in selecting according to skills or the ability to learn new skills quickly and, where possible, in selecting people who are not afraid to report what they notice and how they respond. Selecting people for their personalities, their apparent qualities, their compatibility or even to get the 'right mix' of interpersonal skills is limiting. A person may demonstrate one set of qualities in one context and another somewhere else, according to what is happening and the perceived need. A leader's job is to draw different qualities from team members as well as to develop technical ability. Leadership is an educational role and its use as such allows team members to find deep satisfaction in their work as a result of achieving their potential. Such achievement is synonymous with highly effective team performance.

Any problem-solving team is selected to solve a particular problem. As such, the team is composed of people who have the technical skills related to this problem. Members are also required to have a working knowledge of the problem-solving and decision-making process, and some rudimentary grounding in teamwork. The membership of the team often changes as the problem-solving process unfolds—once the root cause of the problem has been discovered one engineer's job might be done, whereas, in order to cost a chosen method of problem prevention, someone from the finance department might join. Any changeover of this sort needs to be done consciously with an extended period of maintenance to allow established members to adjust personally and as a team and to enable the new member to tune in to the purpose, vision and norms of the team. Everyone can then move forwards discovering the new team identity as they tackle the problem together. This is true of any team, yet is rarely accorded much attention.

After the original maintenance session is completed and the move towards a new team identity begins, there are still adjustments to be made. Over a period of time at the Findhorn Foundation one could see that new members invariably went through the same cycle of questioning, of encountering problems and finding solutions, of gloom and delighted discovery, in relation to the same recurring issues. The last part of this process is moving from being exasperated and wanting to help, to understanding that each person needs to make his or her own discoveries in order to fully arrive.

Size

On my first introduction to one problem-solving team at a large manufacturer of security products, ten members were in attendance. The team seemed large but potentially manageable. Then I realized that I could not identify the roles of the various members and asked for clarification. To my surprise, only three members had the relevant product knowledge and expertise. The others were there to represent their departments, to ensure that no blame was attributed to them for the cause of the problem and to ensure that no decisions were taken that might compromise their managers. Little wonder that after three months of debate they still had not found a likely root cause.

By contrast, a TOPS 8D team—formed to solve a problem that no one person can solve alone—consists of not less than four and not more than ten people, each of whom has some essential product knowledge. The principle that a team should be no larger than it need be is a good one. If one person's job becomes too much to handle alone, an additional member may be brought in, but the original job should then be divided in a way that the new person's role is clear. Finally, the more that each member knows about the roles of the others, the better.

Most teams larger than 12 subdivide into smaller groups. When we were with them, the BP Legal team had 29 members and both the Jaguar X100 and X200 design teams had 24. Each of these teams developed temporary or informal subgroups, reflecting functional, geographical or historical boundaries. Organizations do have a team identity, expressed though their specific culture, but it is most easily approached through the identities of long-standing top management and the various departmental teams.*

Each relationship within a team contributes towards that team's identity and a team can be said to be as strong as the weakest of those relationships. A relationship may be weak for a number of reasons. It will be weak when the two members spend little time together and know little about each other's role; it will be weak when they work together but instinctively avoid each other; and it can be weak because the two had a recent argument that leaves them still holding resentments.

A team of four has 6 relationships, a team of eight 28 and a team of twelve 66. The team leader, in guiding the team towards its identity, must tend each of these relationships—helping individuals to be more aware of each other as well as know more about each other's roles, ensuring that there is time to finish unfinished business and enabling individuals to appreciate each other more. From this a synergy of creativity and ideas will flow. However, the larger the team, the longer this takes.

Yet a team is more than the sum of its relationships. One-on-one encounters are not enough to promote team synergy. Head coaches who talk at their staff from the top of the table or who address their players from the foot of the auditorium may give clear information in an inspiring way but, unless they are fostering relationships elsewhere, they are not team building. A team discovers its identity by meeting regularly. If, when it meets, it is too large for everyone to have their say, this becomes a serious obstacle. It is better then to have a number of subgroups and a team of subgroup leaders. However, those large teams at BP and Jaguar had considerable energy and success and some idea of their team identity. In all three cases their interactive work was constant and intense. The potential of each team was probably much larger than they needed or had time to discover.

Our concept of team identity originally came from our experience of the Findhorn Foundation at a time when there were over 300 members. That

*Corporate culture and team identity were discussed in Chapter 1.

we were able to tune in to an identity of such complexity was probably due to the community norm of regularly switching focus between personal needs, departmental needs and the needs of the whole. We became good at it. Something similar can happen at the United Nations or even in the chamber of a national parliament, despite so much time being spent in scathing debate.

Absence

The team identity does not change when someone is absent for a short period, but there is a potential new identity standing in the wings. This accounts for the fact that a meeting without a certain member can feel and be very different from one at which he or she is present. Teams with a member who is frequently absent can be caught between the two identities—although a lot depends on the member's will to be present and the effort that member puts into renewing and maintaining contact between meetings.

We sometimes keep an empty chair in our circle for the absent member— at least during the warm-up and warm-down. (Having written that sentence, I phoned my office from Spain, aware that our Christmas party was in progress and was told that a champagne glass was there on the table for me.) We also make sure that messages from absent members are passed on at the start of the meeting—together with the reason—and we allow time to anyone who wants to give a response. At the Cleveland Gestalt Institute staff meetings—a team whose members live in different States of the USA—an absent member is sometimes included by someone saying 'What Ed would say now is ...' or 'What Claire would say is ...'. This affirms the team identity and vision.

BOUNDARIES

A team's boundary—the line that separates 'team' from 'not-team'—is defined most obviously by its membership and leader but also by its purpose, its vision, its norms and ultimately its identity. There are also boundaries within the team between each individual in a pair relationship, between each pair relationship within each subgroup and between each subgroup with the team unit. Such boundaries are the points at which contact is made between those involved. If there were no boundaries, there would be no distinction and therefore no contact, since contact can only occur between two distinct entities. However, contact between two entities—between two units within the team or between the team and an outside body—can be interrupted by the contact disturbances described in Chapter 5—projection, introjection, retroflection, confluence and deflection.

Boundaries not only enable the team and its internal subgroups to make an impact on entities outside themselves but also clarify the sort of action it is going to be. A football team is not on the pitch to play cricket and the strikers are not defined by their ability to defend goal.

Unclear boundaries

When the team's boundary is unclear, it becomes difficult for outside individuals and groups to make contact and for the team itself to make good contact. At the start of pre-season, an NFL American football team has some 70 or 80 players training together. No one at this stage is clear who will be part of the team and who will be discarded. The only identity that exists is for the entire squad. The team exists somewhere within the squad but at this stage it is unable to act and can be neither contacted nor described by coaches, administrators, fans or the media. When two companies merge and there is a duplication of many senior positions, contact with customers is crippled until the new company is reorganized. The reorganization destroys both identities, this being keenly experienced by those who stay through the initial clash of cultures. The path to discovery of the new organization's identity gives everyone a bumpy ride.

As consultants we often find that within a given organization there are teams whose roles, at least as understood by themselves, overlap. Sometimes virtually the same work is being done by three people in three different teams, with the result that the remainder of the organization or external customers are unsure how to make contact. The confusion is similar to that resulting from a misunderstanding between coach and players of a volleyball team. If the players are not clear on a new tactical combination, two players can collide in attempting to get the ball. In a business setting our role would be to heighten awareness of the situation, so that the organization is able to clarify its internal boundaries.

When such confusion emerges within a team we create the opportunity for the members concerned to talk to each other but also for others to voice how the confusion impacts their own performance and what they need for good contact. This is another situation where our role is to highlight the missing entity within the team, as opposed to (or as well as) what we see happening. Internal confusion will also impact on suppliers. When a team or organization is able to exchange similar descriptive feedback (discussed in Chapter 10) up and down the supplier chain, it is received with interest.

Permeable boundaries

The boundaries of most teams are permeable. A problem-solving team frequently co-opts people from within the organization to give information and advice on the problem the team has been formed to solve. A good problem-solving team leader will ensure these people are included if they are to be in the team for a period of time—clarifying the team's wider purpose and introducing the individual to both the task methodology and the team's maintenance and process norms. Sometimes permeability is used to expel or marginalize members who are saying things the rest of the team does not want to hear.

A team we worked with in the early 1980s saw itself in the image of its leader as charismatic and creative. One meticulous member, initially a subgroup leader, became increasingly uncomfortable with what he termed a lack of conscientious commitment and began to voice his concerns. The team did not want to hear them as they threatened its self-image, so instead of expanding its vision to include a degree of meticulousness, it became a norm to make jokes about the 'fuddy-duddy' who always had his nose down in his papers. This person never left the team but attended fewer meetings, was divested of his subgroup and eventually was given a desk on the outer edge of the team's office space. Scapegoating a team member is always an attempt to create rather than discover the team's identity. A key quality is being 'split off'. The team still has the quality as part of its actual identity but the quality is disowned. This allows the team to maintain its lopsided performance and feel good about it.

Too much permeability is demonstrated by a team that rarely holds meetings and, when it does, has the norms that (i) virtually anyone in the vicinity may attend and (ii) once there, anyone can be called away to the phone or back to their workplace, at any time. The result here is that team members eventually feel isolated, as they completely fail to make contact with their team identity.

Teams of any size can demonstrate all degrees of closedness and permeability. A subgroup of two can be so involved with each other that their individual response and input are not available to the team or can each be so available to everyone else that their joint responsibility is poorly fulfilled.

It is a commonly observed phenomenon that when a team has an adversary or is focusing on a competitor, 'team spirit' seems to be more intense. The boundary between inside and outside is strengthened. On the other hand, when there are no clear adversaries, competitors or immediate challengers, insiders who are in some way seen as different or strange become marginalized again.

Potentially, the hardest assignments I have had as a sports psychologist have been with national volleyball teams—particularly the Scottish men's national team, having once been a coach. The danger was that I would stray too far inside the team's boundary to see clearly what was going on and, perhaps, to be taken seriously in my new role. Being too friendly, too at ease, I might have been too confluent with the team. The 'prophet in his own country' often has such a problem. In fact, I was able to maintain my boundaries—partly because I had been away for so long that many of the players had not heard of me and partly because the coach who called me in was a friend who by then identified me with my new role and did not invite me to give technical input. Working with the Netherlands men's team was a little more difficult because the coach knew of me as a coach but knew little about sports psychology.

On the other hand, being with the British cycling team when I was quite ignorant of the sport was relatively easy—and I worked with the Cleveland Browns during the 1994 season, precisely because the head coach wanted someone who not only knew nothing about the game but, not being American, was unlikely even to pretend to. Actually, the danger here was the opposite—that I would be seen as unlikely to say anything of relevance and therefore not heard. Struggling with the fact that sports psychologists are often marginalized, the British Olympic Association has even advised newcomers engaged by Olympic teams to spend time being friendly to athletes in the cafeteria queues. In our experience, there are no such problems if boundaries and responsibilities are agreed between sports psychologist and head coach and announced to staff coaches and athletes before work begins.

Yet the thinking is right. A consultant will not get far unless he or she is able to make contact with all parts of the client system. Learning when and how to give personal response, when to give feedback, how to listen and which questions to ask takes time. As in any profession, mistakes are valuable points of learning. Eventually one learns how to be oneself and to *present* oneself in a way that achieves the right level of contact, without imposing personal opinions or articifial changes on the system. At this point, according to Ed Nevis, one is both different and interesting.

Being outside

In Part III we state that facilitators need courage because their role is to interrupt: to ask the team what it is doing or how individuals feel in response to what is happening is to cut across the topic of discussion. If the facilitator has been designated from within the team, he or she is stepping outside a specific boundary while fulfilling the role. This is not the boundary formed by team norms, vision, identity or overall purpose (the individual is still a team member and continues to play a role in pursuing the team's objective) but one that defines the task of this particular meeting. The facilitator focuses on maintenance and process and is no more concerned with the task of this meeting than is a team member who is absent. This temporary boundary excludes the facilitator and allows him or her to make contact with the team rather than be part of the team. This is underlined by the formula a facilitator often uses to preface his or her comments or questions: 'Do you mind if I *come in* here?'—which asks permission to cross the boundary. Although this may occasionally be to offer an insight on the topic being discussed, it is usually to invite the remainder of the team to step back over the boundary together and notice how they are feeling and how they are conducting their discussion.

When the different roles are practised during the four-day TOPS 8D course, it is the facilitator role that is least popular. This is partly because the role is the most demanding and difficult to learn—but only partly. When the session is completed and the team does a review, the facilitator's most frequent answer to the second question—'How did you feel?'—is 'isolated'. In this role the participant misses being part of the team, even though he or she may only have met the other participants a few days earlier.

Internal boundaries can seem permanent or they can last for just a moment. The boundary between designated leader and the other team members is ongoing but if another team member takes the leadership role during a particular meeting, he or she crosses that boundary for the interim. In the same way, when one member turns to another and uses that person's name—as in 'Jane, I'd like to know what you think of that'—that member is drawing a boundary fleetingly around the two of them that exludes the other members of the team. Were this to develop into a relationship, to the point where they operated as a duo, the remainder of the team would relate to them as a subteam with its own norms, relationships and identity.

Boundaries redrawn

Finally, *absence* was mentioned above in relation to membership but has an equally significant relationship to boundaries. By putting an empty chair in the circle during warming up and warming down—especially at the moment of tuning in to the team—or saying 'What Ed would say now is . . .', the absent member is still included within the boundary. On the other hand, when someone leaves a meeting early or fails to arrive, the decision to take the empty chair *out* of the circle is a way of redrawing the boundary to exclude that member for the duration of the meeting. This can significantly help the people left behind when there is regret at the person's absence. The gesture allows them to tune in to their *own* identity—that of the team that is still present—and put aside any distracting sense of loss.

Over a longer time frame the glaring absence of someone important to the team—due perhaps to illness or, as is common in professional sport, to injury—means that the member becomes marginalized. The team adapts, closes ranks and the boundary is redrawn. The same thing happens when a team member is known to have a significant contribution to make to a meeting but for one reason or another declines to speak. Initially, that member's silence is figural and considerable energy and attention will be spent on either trying to persuade the member to say something or wondering nervously why he or she is silent. During that phase of the meeting, the member's power increases but, after a while, interest wanes, the boundary is redrawn to exclude him or her and the power returns to the reconstituted team.

Such experiences were epitomized by a programme I attended where a prominent member of staff left before the end of the first session and—despite sending messages of regret and support to subsequent sessions—never reappeared. As so often happens in such systems, what had happened at staff level recurred at participant level, as various people dropped out, arrived late or left early. Speaking of this at the final meeting of the programme, some 18 months after the start, a member of the staff who had kept to his original commitment said: 'First Fred and Astrid disappeared, then Alex and Jean left early, at the next session someone arrived late and yesterday it was Mark and Laura who weren't here. I get depressed, saddened ... And then *I assign them to the margin* and my energy becomes more available'.

A final example here is of a small organization we consulted that had successfully completed a major management project eight months prior to approaching us. At preliminary interviews, we discovered that the leader was considered brilliant and that he still felt exhausted from his efforts. It then emerged that for the preceding seven months he had threatened to leave, to take a year's sabbatical but, at the last moment, had always decided to stay. When questioned, he admitted to his dilemma; he was too tired to stay but he could not trust the rest of the team enough to leave. The resulting confusion had reached a point where two others were now ready to go. The distress of being unable to either maintain or redraw the team's boundary had become too great.

RESISTANCE

When we began our five-year involvement at Tottenham Hotspur Football Club in 1980, Keith Burkinshaw asked how he should introduce us to the players. We said that we were sports psychologists. 'Oh no,' he replied, 'I can't say you're psychologists—they'll all imagine you've come to analyse them.' So when we went into the meeting room with him, he said 'This is John and Chris and they're going to be with us for a while.'

Inviting an outsider into the team to help with some aspect of their process can evoke one of two responses—confidence and commitment to doing everything possible to achieve their potential or uncertainty and resentment at the fact that they appear to have given some of their power away. The first response carries optimism that this is an opportunity to learn more about their individual and team identity, the second carries a fear of losing the image they have of that identity at the moment. A consultant will encounter both types of response, sometimes from the same individual on different days. The second response always entails some measure of resistance.

Our experience at Tottenham helped us to clarify that we were not there to diagnose and treat problems but to facilitate our clients' discovery of their own skills. If a player said, 'I've got a problem with motivation,' we would reframe his statement and say 'Okay, motivation is a mental skill. Let's see what you might do to improve it.' We refused to be placed in a medical model and asserted our place as educationalists on the coaching staff. Mental training complements physical and technical training and has its own set of exercises and training routines. We still make clear that this is our approach and the way we want to be seen, when working in the corporate sector. Resistance is reduced when we are heard and understood but we are and in fact need to be outsiders.

PROJECTION

A team that cannot accept what it considers to be negative aspects of itself will unconsciously deny these aspects and project them on to another team. By steadfastly maintaining that 'the enemy is out there', the team avoids confronting its own 'shadow'—its unintegrated qualities. Such blindness to its own behaviour will inevitably inhibit its performance and block it from discovering its identity. The only way forward is for the team to become aware of what it is doing and re-own the characteristics concerned.

THE TEAM SYSTEM

The team, with its inner boundaries, is a system with different levels of operation. As such, anything that happens at one level affects or reflects what happens at another. As sports psychologists we began our careers working with a number of golf professionals who wanted mental training exercises to improve their personal performance. It was not surprising, therefore, that when we were first invited to work with team sports, the coaches of those teams called upon us to 'deal with' individual athletes whom they thought had a problem.

While it is quite possible to work with a team athlete to improve individual performance—in a business context this is called 'coaching' or 'mentoring'—it is impossible to ignore that the support, stresses and strains that impact on the individual's performance are in large measure a function of the team system. So if we are called in to work with a team member because the leader sees this person as 'having a problem', we have to assume that the problem is a function of the team. In such situations there is always a choice. Either we work with the individual to improve whatever skills he or she wants to improve in order to deal with the challenges of his or her situation, or we focus on the situation (the team system as a whole) to help the team discover what there is about its norms, roles and structure that may be blocking its ability to reach its potential. Looked at one way, the problem belongs to the team and the team leader, not specifically to the team member.

There are no rules that dictate where a team problem will become most evident. It could be at any level of system—individuals, pairs, small groups or the whole team. It can also be worked with at any level, provided the client understands that any work at one level will affect the other levels. This was the case with the manufacturing organization mentioned earlier— where an inner 'Gang of Four' of an unhappy 12-man management group was concerned about the lack of teamwork between foremen on the shop floor. After our initial audit, we started with the management team, instead of the foremen. Our job was to help them to understand how their 360 member organization worked as a system. Eventually the managers focused on improving their own team, realizing that *their* performance could influence how the rest of the organization performed.

A good team leader helps each pair relationship, particularly those whose performance is high profile, to seek actively for their own pair identity. However, what happens at the pair level also impacts the whole—as was clearly the case in the cycling team pursuit team, where anything affecting one of the six relationships affected the whole team the next day at training.

Which level I worked at—with the pair concerned alone or with the 4-man team plus coach Peter Keen—was immaterial, although I usually felt in the later stages of our preparation for the Olympics that there was more to be gained more rapidly by working with the team together. If for some reason I had not been able to work at the level of my choice—if the pair had wanted the others present when I preferred to work with them alone or one of the rest of the team had been away when I had thought it best to work with everyone present—the effect of me working at the other level would eventually have been the same.

As the leader helps the team to discover its identity, boundaries within the system are certain to change. Contact improves. Each time someone does something different the whole system changes, often in unpredictable ways. Teams are like families and when one brother expresses previously withheld affection or resentment to another, it is a fair bet that other family members will respond so that lines are drawn differently.

A facilitator from outside the team or an internal or external consultant will not change the team identity, although he or she will change some of the boundaries between team members, just by being there. In some teams, contact and appreciation has been so rare that the interviews and further interventions of a consultant are events of major proportions. Sometimes, modelling ways of relating that are new to the team or to units within the team is enough for substantial change to occur. Lasting change, however, will only happen when the team reaches a new common understanding of itself as a system.

PART III

Team Meetings

8

Warming up

A team leader who jumps straight into the agenda as soon as members arrive for a meeting and closes without any kind of review slows team development and limits performance. Members will often be distracted, are likely to misunderstand each other and will probably discuss each other afterwards with people who have nothing to do with the team. In many such teams, some members arrive late, others leave early.

Part of the team development process is a growing attentiveness to the start and the end of each meeting. Sports teams, acting and circus troupes, dance companies and orchestras all warm-up and warm-down as a matter of course. Business teams do not—not as a matter of course—and if challenged would probably say that, since their activity involves little physical movement, there is no need. Yet any top athlete or dancer knows that the physical warming and stretching of muscle groups is only part of the process. Warming up and warming down always include emotional preparation and review together with an important element of mental activity.

Warming up and warming down—sometimes called 'attunement' and 'closure'—help the performance of team members at any type of discussion meeting, for two or more members of the team. Both are part 'maintenance' and part 'task'.* The time required for these phases of a meeting is in direct proportion to the meeting's length. A 90-minute meeting might have a warm-up and warm-down of five minutes each whereas, on a two-day workshop, the team can usefully invest in an hour-long warm-up on the first

---

*Maintenance is attending to how members feel, task is the business of the meeting—see Chapter 9.

day and the same length of time for warming down on the second. Meetings that institute some major change—the appointment of a new leader or a change of team objective—should be longer than the normal meeting and include a correspondingly expanded warm-up and warm-down programme.

From a system's perspective, warming up is a ritual that allows a number of disparate individuals to reclaim their identities as team members and acknowledge a clear boundary differentiating team from not-team. In doing so, they identify with the roles, functions, tasks and team norms which characterize the system of which they are now a part. They all begin to act and speak as they do in this team, letting go of the way they were acting and speaking in other teams a short time ago. Here one person may be a member, having just come from the team where he or she is leader; others arrive back at home base from a different role in a cross-functional engineering team or a line management team. Warming down marks a reverse transition and allows members to ease out of the team system and revert to the identity each assumed elsewhere.

Although there are distinct stages of warming up that form a useful structure, each team has to discover its own routine. This is difficult because teams are heavily influenced by their culture. At Findhorn, all teams began (and in fact ended) their meetings with a minute of silence. This was ostensibly to allow members to tune in to themselves, each other, the group and the reason for meeting—virtually the entire warm-up process. Many business teams start by serving each other with coffee and then address the first item of business. Tony Lewis's Education and Training presentation team at Ford Motor Company used to meet at the hotel the night before, explore the room assigned to the event, then gather for a Tony Lewis pep talk.

Professional soccer and cricket teams in England have a lot in common. We have seen players at White Hart Lane and the Oval, Anfield and Lords, lounge in interchangeable dressing rooms, playing strip hung on hooks above the benches, a table or massage table in the centre of the room and an elderly white-coated attendant serving hot sweet tea, milk and sugar all mixed in, from a huge aluminium tea pot. That said, football teams are probably more focused, a policeman outside the door barring the way to anyone not part of the manager's immediate circle, as the players gradually work themselves and each other into a state of intensity. Cricketers remain relatively relaxed and disconnected from each other, rarely all in the room

together. Any attempt at motivational speech is made (often half-heart-
edly) by the captain. The captain is a player and if he or she happens to be
an opener, as was Hugh Morris of Glamorgan when we were there, speech
making can conflict with personal mental preparation. On the other hand,
cricketers tend to warm up on the pitch together, whereas footballers
straggle out in their own time.

The underlying structure to warming up has close parallels with the team
development process described in Part II. It is accomplished by paying
attention to several background factors, all of which have some impact on
the quality of the meeting or event. These factors are: (i) the *place* where the
meeting is conducted, (ii) *oneself*, (iii) each of the *other people* attending, (iv)
the *team* as a whole, (v) the *purpose* of the meeting and (vi) the *agenda* or the
way in which this purpose is to be achieved. The first four phases are
'maintenance', the last two are 'task'. In warming down, the process is
reversed.

THE PLACE

The business team on site needs to pay as much attention to the meeting
room as a sports team does to an away venue. In each case, ignoring the
environment can result in poor quality performance. (Tom Peters once
quoted architect Christopher Day on the surprising lack of attention paid to
business surroundings: 'Day-to-day corporate existence is flattened by
sterile work environments. I shake my head in wonder—and sometimes
am moved to rage or tears or both—by most facilities I enter.') Yet here, the
main difference between the two is that business teams can take full control
of their meeting venue—organizing the room to suit the purpose of their
meeting—whereas sports teams have only marginal control.* In fact,
having taken note of any distracting factors that cannot be changed,
members can still adjust their response to these factors.

Most business meetings, even those between two team members, take
place in a room with the door closed. This makes it easier to concentrate
than meeting out of doors in bright sunlight or indoors pressed against the

*This is not always so when the team has home advantage. In the semi-finals of
the 1995 Davis Cup, the Russian team put so much water on their clay court that
the visiting Germans, Michael Stich and Boris Becker, were quite unable to play
their own powerful game, losing well against the odds.

wall of a busy corridor. Yet many leaders, with a choice of rooms available, let someone else decide the venue without checking the room beforehand. They then end up in a space that is too small, too dark or too noisy for their purpose and have to tolerate conditions that limit their team's performance.

Furniture can and should be moved to match the type of meeting and style of communication required. This can be done as the meeting starts by the people participating—and can indeed become a team ritual for larger and longer meetings. One-to-one meetings between the manager and a junior team member or between the manager and two senior direct-reports may usually be held in the manager's office but even there it is better to be conscious of the effect produced by the various possible arrangements of desks, chairs and tables than to assume that one formula is always right. Focusing on the environment of the meeting is not just a ritual, it should be part of the overall strategy.

Task teams can enhance their performance by occasionally meeting in non-habitual environments. Creative teams have met in art galleries and zoos to spark unexpected associations. Problem-solving teams can discover new information by visiting their suppliers of components or systems. The executive team that is occasionally hosted by different members is both managing by wandering around and increasing awareness of each other. On the other hand, Bob Dover's X100 'war-room' at Jaguar Cars, with its charts and simulated pictures of the final product, target dates, newspaper clippings, messages and jokes provides instant access to the team system and instant reconnection with the team identity for any members entering the room after a few days away with their functional team.

Most designated leaders and most team members are unaware that the way the room is arranged affects them—they do not pay attention to their *response* as they walk in and as they sit there. Intently focused on the task, they rarely notice that the windows are closed (although a lack of oxygen has slowed their creativity) or that because one half of the team is unable to see the other the interactive flow of ideas is reduced.

The traditional boardroom with the long boardroom table ensures that attention is focused on the person who sits at one end. It is ideal for a leader who wants tight control. The norm and the phrase 'speaking through the chair' is directly related to such a format. Discussion is replaced by a series of dialogues between the leader and individual team members. Direct contact between members is almost impossible, especially between those sitting on the same side of the table. There is usually an 'above the salt below the salt' split, with the more important team members sitting each side of the team leader. Those at the far end of the table are excluded from swapped asides by the top members and have to make a greater effort to voice their questions and views. If they speak quietly to the members near them, they have no impact on the outcome and, if noticed by people at the leaders's end of the table, they may be assumed to be making negative comments.

A small meeting of four or five people around one end of the conference table allows less contact than sitting around a small table (and much less than sitting in a circle without a table). However, everything depends on the situation: the point is that the choice should be deliberate. In November 1994, the weekly meeting of the new three-man management team at the Cleveland Browns took place in the rarely used conference room because the members knew it would impart a message of seriousness to the rest of the organization, at a time when such a message was needed.

It is unusual for such decisions to be taken so consciously. Teams become locked into their old norms: a new team leader, with a much less authoritarian philosophy, may find him or herself seated at the end of the conference table puzzled by the fact that making contact with the rest of the team, especially those guys down the far end, seems so difficult.

A strong team always adapts its surroundings to meet its own needs. When travelling, this includes creating a sense of 'home'. When Tony Lewis arrived at a hotel with his Ford Education and Training presentation team, the large seminar hall was changed into a theatre for the next day's seminar but some small break out room became the team's 'home' base. Similarly, a volleyball team competing in a top European club tournament may find itself in a large hall with many courts, limited locker room space and no meeting rooms. In such circumstances, as coach, I would search the premises until I could find a 'home base'. Failing all else, we would appropriate a corner of the hall and mark out an area with our bags, where we would sit or lie on the floor until it was time for our physical warm-up. Provided we had someone to keep an eye on our belongings, we would return to this space whenever we had time between matches.

Companies with a *kaizen* approach to quality, have found that suggestion boxes fill up with practical ideas. These are contributed by employees who have information about specific aspects of the job they are doing that few managers upstairs would have been able to guess. Some factor like the height of a working surface or the distance between two instruments can have a significant effect on output. Any informed suggestion for change is an attempt to make the workplace more practical, but also more like a home base. The same purpose is achieved by emptying ashtrays, clearing away coffee cups, tearing off old flip sheets, moving aside tables and making a circle of chairs at the start of a team meeting.

Circles are an ancient way to evoke a team's sense of security and home. The world's first dances were circle dances which represented an inner circle of light beyond which lay outer chaos, danger and darkness. Centuries later, in similar vein, explorers in the wild west would rest around a camp fire. The obvious effect of changing a meeting room arrangement from a boardroom table or a line of benches (in the case of Tottenham football team) to a circle of chairs is that everyone can see and talk directly to everyone else. Anyone involved in such a change will also notice some personal inner response.

This experience can best be expressed as making contact with each other and the team identity. Not everyone finds it agreeable. Anyone who feels alienated or prefers to be separate can be threatened by such an arrangement. Yet it seems significant that the upper echelons of many leading organizations now hold meetings at round tables. In November 1993, President Clinton, holding an APEC summit meeting in a log cabin on Blake Island off Seattle, went one better: the picture of that meeting published the next day in the *Financial Times* showed delegates dressed casually, sitting in a circle with no tables in sight. Some business meetings require participants to refer regularly to sheaves of papers, which is difficult to do without a table to lay them on. Inevitably, a choice has to be made between reduced personal space and reduced contact. This choice should be deliberate, according to the occasion.

ONESELF

Without a warming-up routine, any team falters under the pressure of a big occasion. When we went to Wembley Stadium with Tottenham for the 1982 FA Cup Final, the warm-up was precisely the same as prior to a mid-season league match. The same bus driver drove us in the same bus. Before going into the dressing room, everyone walked through the tunnel and on to the pitch to 'get a feel' of the atmosphere and a look at the pitch. The pitch and the atmosphere were very different to a normal match, as was the dressing room (the dressing rooms at Wembley were surprisingly small). However, each player had a well-established personal routine, within the framework of the team routine and, on returning from the pitch, each spent time following this. Some silently rehearsed some element of their game, others stretched, had a massage or tapped a ball around in a corner. One player locked himself in the lavatory and read the programme several times over; while Ray Clemence did his 'One for all and all for one' routine, mentioned earlier. These were personal routines with which everyone was familiar. Although each person was focusing on himself, there was an intensity about it all that unified the team—everyone knew that the warm-up process was under way.

At this stage, such mutual respect is rarely so evident in the average business team because very little attention is paid to preparation. Yet effective business teams do have a short parallel process that is equally important. We suggested earlier that members must pay attention to themselves and their own needs in order to contribute fully to the team's goal and this should be done before the business of a meeting commences. Ideally, each member prepares physically, emotionally and mentally for any team meeting or event, checking personal needs exactly as the athlete does. This includes stretching, visiting the rest room and getting a drink (all physical); releasing frustration or excitement generated by the last meeting and evoking the feeling he or she wants to have in view of his or her current role (emotional preparation); and getting a clear image of his or her reason for attending (mental preparation). Tuning in to oneself before the business of a meeting begins allows one to be fully attentive from the start.

The team leader needs to ensure that everyone has had time to do this. Most people occasionally arrive distracted and unknowingly tense and can easily misunderstand (or not hear) what is said. Arriving at a meeting physically is not the same as arriving mentally. Business people have either left their place of work or another meeting and often arrive with their heads full of concerns and ideas related to what they were doing previously. Other members of the team may have problems that they have been considering all day and cannot deal with until later. Still others may arrive with preconceptions about the meeting—perhaps based on past meetings—that can prevent them from noticing what is actually happening.

Findhorn's minute of silence can be mildly uncomfortable for the unversed newcomer but it only differs from the silent element of an athlete's preparation* in that the whole group are doing the same thing. In either case, it allows mind and body to slow down and is an option we have seen some business teams adopt.

Many people know intellectually but few are physically aware of how much tension they accumulate during the day. Creating the opportunity to notice it is usually enough to let it go but taking a deep breath and exhaling slowly will always work. In very unusual circumstances, tuning in to oneself might lead to the realization that one is not in a fit state to attend the meeting at all. Foster Dulles used to say that if he had known how jet-lagged he was in his meeting with President Nasser, he would not have made the mistakes that led to the 1956 Suez Canal conflict.

The team leader can ensure that no one skips this part of warming up by asking everyone to make a note of the main thing they received from the interaction or meeting they have just attended or to write down a list of things they have to do when the current meeting ends. Writing gives the additional benefit that the members are silent and are reflecting inwardly while they write. The quieter the room, the more easily most members can settle. A question that directs everyone's attention towards their own needs can be particularly effective at this stage. For instance, 'What do I want from this meeting and what can I contribute?' will lead people away from prior experiences and increase their commitment to the present. As consultants, we have to be grounded in our own needs if we are to be successful at looking after those of our clients. In the same way, team members who are not clear about their personal needs, objectives and potential contribution at the start of the meeting will be less than fully present.

OTHERS

This phase of warming up (and the next) improves as the team develops. Its objective is to enable members to make *contact* with each other. Many sports

* See Syer and Connolly (1984: 14).

teams fail on the day of an important competition because the coach, despite having built up some sort of relationship with each of the athletes, has done little to develop relationships *between* the athletes. Motivational speech does not do this. Once the event begins, the relationship of the coach to each athlete is of minor importance.

Although we found different atmospheres and local differences of procedure between various soccer clubs, the cultural similarities were stronger. One of these was that the substitutes, nearly always much younger than the regular first team players roomed together, ate together and changed together before the match. When the established players started to put on their strip, they began to remind each other of their roles, walking around the dressing room to do so. This was their way of tuning in to each other—at least to people they combined with tactically. Yet at none of the clubs did any of them talk to the substitutes, even though everyone knew the position each substitute was covering. As the substitutes were generally younger and respectful, they did not approach the starting players. Only at the end, immediately prior to going on to the pitch, did everyone join in the ritual of shaking hands with everyone else and wishing them good luck. Consequently, when the manager made a substitution, the player coming on the field was rarely tuned in to the rest of the team, which led to an immediate misunderstanding, if not an opposition goal.

Lack of contact between key players prior to a business meeting does not often have such dramatic results but there are similarities, especially if the meeting is held at a boardroom table where the physical distance between people can be great and where most people can only see two-thirds of the rest of the team. As on the football pitch, misunderstandings then occur. The football players talk about tactics but the key factor is increased awareness of each other through eye contact and sometimes physical contact as well. This evokes the positive elements of their relationship— what they have achieved together before. When a subgroup of business team members is combining to present an idea to the rest of the team, their performance depends on their preparation—not just in the days prior to the meeting but in the moments immediately beforehand. Contact evokes awareness of the effort they have each contributed over the preceding week. The more relationships within the subteam that can connect at this stage, the better. This applies to preparation for *any* form of team effort.

Occasionally the first three stages of warming up are completed before the team sits down but the longer the occasion, the more important it is to include warming up as a part of the programme. Tuning in to others may be left to encounters over coffee before a short Monday morning meeting but, if team development has been neglected, members will chat with the same group of friends, little being done to affirm the other relationships.

This can change if the norm is made explicit by putting warming up as a topic on the agenda of some future team development session. It can then be pointed out how many one-on-one relationships there are in the team: 15 in a team of six, 28 in a team of eight, 45 in a team of ten and so on. Each member also has a relationship to each paired relationship and at some point in the session everyone should consider those relationships that are already strong and those that need some attention. Any team is only as strong as the weakest of its relationships.

In a longer meeting that allows for a programmed warm-up, the leader or facilitator can move to the third stage by asking members to find a partner and discuss something they have each written down. In a work-shop, we include two or three different pairs exercises, emphasizing the number of relationships there are in the team and asking members to pair up with someone they know less well. Even though certain members may never normally interact, everyone has come to this meeting for a shared purpose and, by implication, has something to contribute. How well the team performs in this situation depends largely on the contact that members make with each other. If I can find some point of contact with Fred Bloggs who always sent me to sleep at previous meetings, I shall probably hear him better this time.

A team member who arrives late, sits down noisily, greets everyone and objects to the first proposal someone makes, is usually unaware of the resentment he or she can evoke. Having missed the team warm-up, the easiest way to tune in to the meeting is to hold a personal warm-up. This would parallel that done by the team—noticing the room arrangement and finding the right place to sit, taking the time to let go of the speediness inherent in any late arrival, looking around and silently greeting those who are looking at him or her and then tuning in to the team as a whole. Behaviour on late arrival (and early departure) is a topic for team discussion when it becomes a pattern.

When the meeting itself is between just two people, nothing much changes. This third phase of warming up is maintenance,* not task, so any exchange that allows them to connect with each other on a wider front would help. This can include discovering the right place to talk or arranging for coffee, reflecting before speaking, sharing some personal concern of the moment and referring to some successful past collaboration between them. All shared experience of past team development—awareness of others, awareness and appreciation of differences—now comes into play.

THE TEAM

A two person subteam does have an identity but a one-to-one conversation, however formal, is not the same class of experience as a full team meeting of three, six or 18 people: the fourth state of warming up is different to the third. In a team of more than two people, the identity of the whole is radically different to the identity of the components—even of the component relationships.

I saw this clearly when helping the Cleveland Browns' management team to form, during their penultimate season. Previously most organizational decisions had been made by one of three individuals. Usually the person concerned first consulted the other two but this was always done separately—the three did not meet together formally. I pointed out that the proposed team would not only consist of three people but also of three existing relationships. To emphasize this I conducted three separate pairs sessions, asking each pair to talk about their relationship—what they considered its strengths and weaknesses to be, how as two individuals they were similar and how they were different, what they wanted to achieve and how they imagined the third person in the new team saw them as a unit.

The next step was to get the three of them back together, each pair to report their experience of their session and then to check out with the third person how he *actually* saw them as a two-person unit. This process marked the point at which the new three-man team was created, the richness of differences and potential represented by the three component relationships clearly adding to the talent and expertise each man brought to the team as an individual. However, they then scheduled an urgent meeting for the next afternoon, despite the fact that one of them—the head coach—would only be able to attend briefly.

The difference between the two meetings was immediately apparent. Not only was the atmosphere more casual but the coach's absence quite changed the experience. This was indeed the old pattern, the one that

*Taking care of relationships and how people feel—see Chapter 9.

they were committed to leaving. More importantly they realized that, in the absence of one team member, two-thirds of their contributing paired relationships were absent, even though two-thirds of their membership was there.

The final maintenance phase of warming up is precisely this process of focusing on and affirming the identity of the whole team, be it the 25 + membership of a Jaguar design team or a doubles team before a tennis match. Team spirit is experienced by the individual as a feeling of contributing towards and being supported by some entity that is greater than the sum of its parts—a combination of positive confluence and synergy. All pre-competition motivational speeches aim to evoke such a feeling and occur at this point of the warm-up, although they count for little if the team has not already developed to a point of contact, respect and trust. The team has not completed this stage of the warm-up until every team member has the feeling 'this is where I belong right now'. A sports team achieves this through their chosen rituals and through the sound of the head coach's or manager's voice during the pre-competition team talk. It is the process of evoking its team identity. Any team improves its ability to do this, as it works together to discover 'who it is' and what it is capable of doing. This takes time and, in particular, the complete dedication of the designated team leader.

PURPOSE

Whereas the first four stages of warming up were maintenance elements of the meeting, the last two are task. Having paid attention to where we are, what I need, who I am with and who we are as a unit, it is now time to address the question 'Why are we here?' Any team that does not have a strong response to this has little idea of its team identity and can soon drift apart again. However, most business teams jump straight to this warm-up phase and deal with it well. Team members usually arrive knowing the purpose of the meeting in advance. Everyone present has made the meeting a priority. For most people its purpose is the prime motivating factor for their attendance. Restatement of this purpose ensures that everyone has interpreted the message they received in the same way and mobilizes the team's energy towards achievement.

The purpose of a particular meeting normally has connections within the wider context of the team's long-term vision. This acts as a form of self-regulation, not only guiding the purpose of each meeting but helping the team adapt to meet many challenges. The vision is the organizing principle that attracts or guides the team to seek out those elements—skills, processes and resources—that will help it to grow to its potential. Many teams inherit an organizational vision and mission statement that they then discuss, formulating their own complementary vision in response. This process usually includes all team members clarifying their personal roles in helping the team fulfil its objective. From then on, all business meetings are steps taken towards the team's goal. A business meeting between two team members usually relates to the work being done by their subgroup or directly to the work of the team as a whole. Each subgroup has an agreed remit set by the team as a whole and the team itself has a role within the organization.

At this fifth stage of warming up, the team leader helps team members reconnect with the team by clarifying the link between the team's formulated vision and the meeting's purpose. In fact, the best teams continue to refer to and re-evaluate their vision, in the light of the ongoing stream of information that they receive and generate. Such periodic discussion allows the implications of their vision to be further clarified for each team member.

This is a step that is easily forgotten. At Tottenham one home match day, after Keith Burkinshaw had given his talk outlining the afternoon's tactics, Ricky Villa, one of the team's two Argentinean players, was sitting beside me. 'What was that all about?' I asked, somewhat ingenuously. 'Oh, he was just telling us what to do', said Ricky. 'Like what?' 'Win! We got to win,' he laughed. 'So how are you meant to win?' I said. 'Oh', replied Ricky, 'Keith says we must close them down for the first twenty minutes and earn the right to play'. 'And what does that mean you're going to do?' I asked. 'Who me?' 'Yes. I mean "close them down" and all that is general, for the team isn't it? What does that mean for you playing in the mid-field?' 'I don't know, I suppose it means I'm going to have to tackle back more than usual.' 'So how many times is that? What would be more than usual during that twenty minutes?' Ricky looked at me in surprise. 'I don't know may be twelve, maybe fifteen?' 'Shall I count and tell you later?' I asked. 'Look Johnnie! You see! For you I do fifteen!'

Few employees have a say in determining the vision and policies of a large organization. Usually these are well publicized but organizations vary in the amount of care taken to ensure that subsidiaries know how their role fits within global policy. When little is done and a team has a leader who consults no one when establishing the team objectives and vision, team members rarely get excited about their work. Commitment stems from involvement. A team may have no say in global policy but if it is helped to understand its role and is left to work out how to perform that role, commitment will depend on its own leadership norms. A meeting's purpose can be agreed in broad outline at the end of a previous meeting or be presented by the team leader. Provided there is an explanation of the relationship between a particular task, the team's role and the overall policy, consensus on the meeting's purpose is not too difficult to achieve.

AGENDA

International athletes of the calibre of Ricky Villa have little trouble translating an objective into specific action. In the story quoted above, Keith Burkinshaw had already given both purpose (to win) and team tactics (to defend aggressively for 20 minutes before looking to attack). For the athlete it is vital to translate purpose into a clear image of specific action that will make that purpose a reality. In the same way, an organizational vision needs to be translated into specific action steps and a team's purpose in holding a meeting needs to be translated into an agenda, by which that purpose will be achieved. This sixth and final stage of warming up is totally focused on task—as indeed was the previous stage, attuning to purpose. Sometimes, without discussion, the leader will decide both purpose and agenda but ideally this is the exception rather than the rule. All team members can be invited to make suggestions in advance. If the team is large enough to appoint a facilitator and a time manager, the leader has a priority to discuss with them the proposed agenda as well as other aspects of the meeting. This allows the leader to build the support of a team within the team, to guide the meeting. It also helps to ensure a realistic time frame for each item and allows contingency plans to be made for the case where an item proves to need more time. (Every design has its unintended consequences.)

A full team meeting requires an agenda as its essential structure, to which all processes, methodologies and discussions are attached appropriately. The structure is agreed by the team during this final stage of warming up and affirmed by the leader or anyone taking the leadership role, at different times during the meeting. Making an agenda for meetings of small subgroups of two or three members is usually a more casual process. Once some attention has been paid to the maintenance aspects of warming up and the purpose of the meeting has been clarified, the question 'Okay, so how shall we go about this?' is often enough to produce a clear plan.

9

Task, maintenance and process

Team development can only occur when team members meet. Whether it then does or does not depends on the way the meeting is conducted. Any form of team interaction constitutes a meeting. It may be between two members, a small subgroup or the whole team and it can be either formal or informal, productive or unproductive. Whatever its nature, it will have throughout three possible points of focus: task, maintenance and process. The balance of focus between the three depends on the norms of the team concerned, the type of meeting and interpretation of the leadership and facilitation roles within the team but this balance determines the meeting's level of success.

TASK

Team members focus on task when they attend to their meeting's purpose and follow or readjust its agenda. This may include collecting, organizing, presenting and discussing information, solving problems and taking decisions. A chance meeting in the corridor between two team members may quickly develop a purpose of its own related to the team's defining objective. However, if the two later decide to leave the building and talk about politics, this meeting may constitute valuable team development but no longer has the task focus. On the other hand, although team development normally has a maintenance focus, it may sometimes be the specific purpose of a meeting—as it is in any team workshop we lead. Task is defined as the business of the meeting.

We offer three ways to categorize the business of a meeting: the Past–Present–Future approach, the Plan–Do–Study–Act (PDSA) cycle and the team task cycle.

The Past–Present–Future approach

This approach has evolved from our work with Ford Motor Company, who in turn learned the basics from the Kepner Tregoe organization in the early 1980s. After our initial work with Ford of Europe, we found it simpler to move away from an analytical approach to the more flexible 'where-to' approach presented here. This allows a team to decide which methodology to use for any particular task. There are four stages. The first is *analysis*, which identifies whether the situation being addressed by the meeting is focused on the past, the present or the future. The team then follows one or more of the other three stages: *problem solving* (if the focus is the past), *decision making* (if the focus is the present) and *planning* (if the focus is the future). Although this approach was formulated for a manufacturing organization, it can be used by a service industry equally well. Each stage of the approach incorporates different methodologies.

Analysis

The first stage, *analysis*, includes studying the history of the problem, challenge or point of interest; obtaining, sharing, questioning and giving feedback on information; doing a concerns analysis; and using other basic quality tools. When a team focuses efficiently on some business item pertinent to its objective, the meeting often takes the following format. Someone is invited to give background information, that is amplified through questioning. The team then discusses the information and, if it is a complex item demanding action, does some form of 'concerns analysis'.

A concerns analysis is a method of identifying and prioritizing the various aspects of the situation that appear to need attention. Some aspects will be obvious while others may need to be discovered. After a Sunday game, the coaching staff of the Cleveland Browns used to spend Monday afternoon and evening and the whole of Tuesday watching, minutely analysing and discussing the film of the most recent performances of their next opponents. On Wednesday they presented this information in a coherent form to their players. Similarly, our office administrator Debbie Shepherd and her assistant may spend the first part of Monday morning listing and prioritizing the items of business they know they will have to deal with during the week.

A full concerns analysis consists of (i) identifying the issue, (ii) deciding whether it concerns the past, the present or the future, (iii) breaking any complexity down into manageable subdivisions and (iv) prioritizing in terms of seriousness, urgency and growth (whether the impact of the situation is growing, stable or decreasing). It then moves from focusing on the current situation towards the different forms of resolution: problem solving, decision making and planning.

Problem solving

Problem solving is past-oriented. It is a systematic way of dealing with the basic cause of the current situation. Here it can include such additional tools as *force field analysis* and *cause and effect diagrams* as effective alternatives to problem analysis but the formal eight-step model, team-oriented problem-solving TOPS 8D is the system preferred by Ford—at least when confronting manufacturing problems.

The original TOPS programme was designed by Ford Motor Company in the United States. Towards the end of 1988 we were invited by Tony Lewis, then head of Education and Training (Manufacturing) at Ford of Europe, to help design a new programme by incorporating a strong team-building element. This initial team-oriented approach to problem solving subsequently came under the much wider umbrella of a Ford of Europe total approach to engineering excellence, called Engineering Quality Improvement Programme or 'EQUIP'. Now this in turn is being replaced by the Ford Technical and Educational Programme (FTEP)—a 'global approach' to training—and is to be called 'Global 8D'.

The TOPS problem-solving method is best suited to problems where no one in the team knows the basic cause, where this cause has to be discovered, where the problem is some variation from normal functioning and where no one person can solve the problem alone. It is a method that can deal with complex data in a new way and shows the team where it must call upon outside specialist help. Great attention is paid to gaining an accurate description of the problem through meticulous questioning, relying primarily on the questions 'what?', 'where?', 'when?' and 'how big?'.

This leads to a brainstorm on possible causes, in which the team focuses on changes that have taken place in the system that might have produced the problem. The process establishes the root cause of the problem and the final steps involve deciding how to deal with the established cause of the problem, putting this plan into effect and ensuring that the problem will nor recur—that is, decision making and planning.

Decision making

Decision making is present-oriented. Formal *decision making* in a complex business-oriented context is the orderly process of making an informed choice from a number of plausible alternatives. The more an informed decision requires that the team obtain some multi-functional input, the greater the need for a visible systematic decision-making process. There are many methodologies to choose from, the most commonly used involving prioritization. These include decision analysis, SWOT analysis, risk priority numbers used in failure modes and effect analysis, Pugh concept selection techniques and Moody preference charts. The three main criteria for choosing are:

1 Horses for courses. Many techniques are designed for a particular arena, for instance, Pugh concept selection is used to choose between different designs, whereas risk priority numbers identify which potential failure modes in a design should receive the most resources to avoid their effects.
2 The amount of systems analysis input should depend on the complexity within which the methodology is operating. The more complex and variable the system, the more systems analysis input is required when prioritizing.
3 The team has to be comfortable with the methodology and trust it.

Prioritization is one of five forms of decision making, each of which is more difficult than the last. These are: unilateral decisions, polling, prioritization, compromise and consensus.

Planning

The nature and scope of the task also determines which of a wide range of planning tools should be used. Critical path analysis, Gantt charts, interrelationship diagrams, PERT charts, a 'to do' list, a detailed action plan or a project management schedule are all valuable when used appropriately.

The focus of the tools forms a basis for looking into the future, considering what might go wrong (based on past experience) and making a secure plan that will avoid such an occurrence. In this context, one's view of the future is determined by decisions that have already been made. Each step of the proposed course of action is examined for possible mishaps, asking the questions: What could go wrong here? How could that be prevented? What if it still happens? Who is responsible to take action? and What precisely is the signal for action to be taken? Not surprisingly, once this process has been completed, some changes are often made to the original plan.

Figure 9.1 gives a fuller picture of this approach.

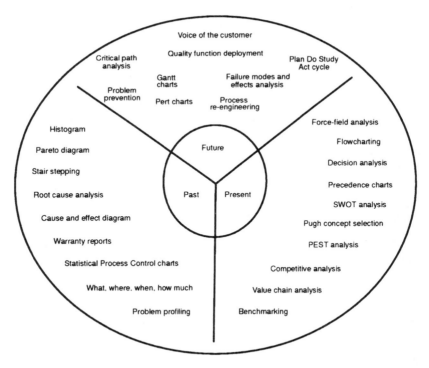

Figure 9.1   The team's task: past, present and future.

The Plan–Do–Study–Act cycle

The PDSA cycle—also called the Deming cycle or the Shewart cycle—is another highly analytical system for monitoring task progress (Figure 9.2). It is frequently used to describe the sequence of activities involved in planning, running, analysing and reacting to the results of an experiment.

The 'plan' part of the cycle includes a procedure for carrying out the experiment and gathering data. It provides some first ideas as to how the data should be analysed and a provisional list of the actions that might follow (a comprehensive list would be impossible). The 'do' part of the cycle consists of running an experiment or pilot project and collecting the data it generates. The 'study' part of the cycle consists of analysing the results. The 'act' part is to refine the first pilot and either run it again to confirm the results or start the full project. In the context of research, this knowledge is the result of sharing and co-operation between subgroups within the team and becomes part of the team's expanding fund of knowledge.

The most interesting aspect of the PDSA cycle is that it is repeated until the team is satisfied with the outcome—an element neglected by more linear models which do not explicitly account for feedback into their process.

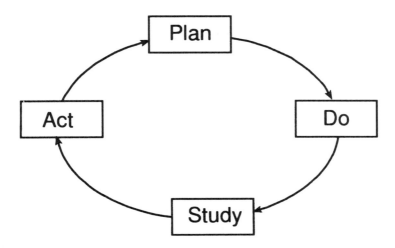

Figure 9.2   The Plan–Do–Study–Act (PDSA) cycle.

This is a task approach used primarily to conduct experiments. It assumes that the purpose of the task has already been identified and that the team is planning how to generate data. Much of the initial analysis of the situation and the identification and planning of a course of action are subsumed within the primary 'plan' stage of the cycle. It is therefore limited as a model for situations in which teams know neither the problem nor the criteria for success—and cannot begin planning their strategy for some time.

The team task cycle

This is the approach described in Part I. Its advantages are:

1 As it mirrors many typical organic and creative processes, it is easily understood.
2 It is cyclical, allowing teams to build in feedback and feed forward from one stage to another. It can be followed through several iterations.
3 It allows teams to 'plug in' different methodologies at each stage of the cycle.
4 Its internal constancy allows the team to apply it to almost any task.
5 It is easily supported by a systems approach.
6 Simplicity: it only has five stages.

Optimizing team task effectiveness

The Past–Present–Future and the PDSA approaches to task are highly analytical. They involve reports, briefings, recording ideas and prioritizing decisions, using Metaplan boards, flip charts and overhead projectors. Participants may be referring to books and other written material and between paying attention to these, to the boards and to the charts (which they are probably all facing) they may not look at each other for long periods of time. This format reduces their awareness, their contact and their ability to maximize the potential of team performance. Most of the work is conducted in an analytical mode, with no recourse to associative, intuitive or visual thinking. Without any variation, members will lose interest, especially those who feel neither heard nor seen.

The team task cycle allows creativity and innovation to impact task performance. These are qualities more readily associated with right hemisphere than left hemisphere thinking. Any use of brainstorming, slides, slides with music, visualization, collage or drawing would not only bring analytical thinking into balance, making the task more enjoyable and satisfying but could also improve the quality of the results. New ideas, new ways of viewing old situations and the stimulation of dormant creativity would be accompanied by increased awareness of individual team members and of the team's identity as a unit. Humour would be another by-product. Where interaction is intense, humour becomes a *positive* form of deflection, helping to give some needed distance.

Finally, a group of people who have no clear function and no task to fulfil are not a team. As stated earlier, for Katzenbach and Smith, they are only a 'working group'. According to them a real team 'must be linked to a specific purpose . . . and then pay relentless attention to progress' (1993: 250). They 'roll up sleeves and do real work together such as interviewing customers, digging into analyses [and] experimenting with new approaches' (1993: 221). Even an upper management team that meets to report on work done by their subordinates and leaves most decisions to the team leader is only termed a working group. Although we would call any group of people that meets for a purpose 'a team', we would agree that a team that does not do 'real work' together is one that has still to discover its identity and potential.

MAINTENANCE

Breaking down

A meeting is in a maintenance phase whenever attention is paid to (i) how team members are feeling physically and emotionally, (ii) the relationships that exist between them and (iii) the immediate environment. Maintenance ensures a continual focus on team development. If a car is not serviced, it will eventually break down. If the task is the business of driving towards the team objective, maintenance is looking after the engine and bodywork. If no attention is paid to how team members are feeling, many will eventually lose interest and either slow down or leave. Others may work even harder in a desperate effort to be noticed and, unsupported, will eventually burn out.

Task inevitably fosters conflict, polarizing members according to their personal beliefs. When the conflict is around power and direction, the connection and underlying unity of the two opposite sides can be forgotten.

As an increasing number of members are drawn into taking sides, the sense of team identity is easily lost. People lose touch with themselves and with each other. Friendship is forgotten, open contribution to the team becomes restricted and contact is lost. Where teams are cross-functional, multi-graded and perhaps multinational, when many members may share their allegiance with another team and the team itself has a limited life span, polarization can easily result in members being seen only in terms of their position.

Periods of maintenance guard against this and ensure that conflict remains creative. Katzenbach and Smith (1993: 230) may be right to suggest that good 'personal chemistry' is not important but, unless someone in the team knows how to ensure that dissonant chemistry is productive, it can bring progress on the task to a virtual standstill. No one is going to experience conflict as being creative until periods of maintenance are included.

Unresolved conflict between team members inhibits their performance as much as a car's performance is affected by dirt in its carburettor. Crosby, having plainly defined 'hassle' as 'the unnecessary difficulties or harassment placed in the path of someone trying to do a reasonable thing', makes the equally plain statement that 'Hassle means ... the people inside the company spend more time working on each other than they do making something happen' (Crosby 1984: 178). This happened at a multicultural course that I once attended. Despite the focus being on organizational development, little time was scheduled for exploration of relationships within the large team of participants nor in the smaller groups. Eventually the programme had to be changed, as participants—experiencing high tension—insisted on a long maintenance session. Inter-personal dilemmas had become so figural that cognitive learning ground to a halt.

Acknowledgement

Awareness of others and of differences integrates an awareness of how others feel, how they respond and what they need. Contact enables communication *and* healthy negotiation. Differences become a spur to new solutions, in the context of common goals, interests and aspirations. When individuals feel positive, relate well to each other and can appreciate the range of skills and qualities each member brings to the team, there is full involvement and quality work.

Sometimes we visit an organization to meet team members on a one-to-one basis before making a specific proposal, only to find that people have never had an opportunity to give their views of what happens around them. The response can be overwhelming. Sixty years ago, a team of efficiency experts went to assess the effect of improved lighting at the Hawthorne, Illinois plant of the Western Electric Company. In the subsequent experiment, the group working under better lighting did indeed improve output but so did the control group. Further research showed that the increase in productivity was due to the increase of attention that was paid to all the workers by management during the experiment.

Many people working in large organizations still receive so little attention and such a meagre amount of feedback that they feel no sense of affiliation and may even wonder if they are visible. 'You can give people raises and incentives', says George Brown, 'but in the long run, if they are not "seen"—if you do not bother to make proper contact with them—you might as well not bother'. From our earliest childhood, one of the things we need most is to be acknowledged. At some level, as we say in the context of listening and being heard, this need is always there—a need to be acknowledged for who we are, not just for what we do.

Two-thirds of the way through the 1994/5 American Football season, when it became clear that the team would make the play-offs, head coach Bill Belichick sent a letter and a 'game ball' to each of the 80-strong Cleveland Brown's administration staff, expressing appreciation for the support he had received during the difficult early years of his tenure. This caused a sensation within the club because Bill had been closeted on his side of the building and had not seemed very approachable. What hit home, however, was a perceived change in his behaviour. People who had been unsure if he knew of their existence were proud of their game ball but said they found renewed commitment to their work at the Club, the day Bill stopped to say hello.

When and how

Passing encounters in the corridors and unscheduled meetings at the coffee machine between different team members are a form of maintenance in the larger scheme of things but, within team meetings, the focus can be on maintenance at the start, in the middle or at the end. Warming up and warming down at the beginning and end of a meeting are mostly maintenance. Maintenance in the middle of a meeting is usually part scheduled and part governed by the ongoing situation.

Times for coffee, lunch, tea and checking out of the hotel at an off-site workshop—all maintenance breaks—are usually built into the programme. However, maintenance also includes making sure that team members can still all see each other whenever the format of the meeting changes, opening a window when the room gets too warm, telling a joke when things get too solemn and, in teams that are quite at ease with each other, taking a moment to stretch.

Personal response

Any member who checks how individuals are responding physically or emotionally to the intensity of a long task discussion is also shifting the focus to maintenance. This can bring a sudden awareness of how the internal environment of the team system is affecting its performance. Sometimes, the sense that it is important to ask such a question comes from the people who have just been speaking, suddenly aware that they have not been sensitive to anything other than their own words. More often it comes from someone in 'the audience'—someone who has been quiet and less involved and has been alternately watching any visible reactions of other team members and checking in to his or her own response.

However, the questions 'How are you feeling?' and 'Are you okay?' are unlikely to produce anything much more than the answers 'Fine' and 'Yes'. Such responses may be cultural and automatic or they may be the result of habitual reticence. On the other hand, by declaring what prompted the question—'I notice you haven't spoken for ten minutes' or 'I notice you don't look at Tom when he speaks and I imagine you are feeling frustrated about something'—the likelihood of an informative response is greatly increased.

Although feelings always affect performance (as thoughts affect feelings and physical performance) it usually takes courage to disclose them. When the questioner gives some personal information, thus modelling disclosure, it becomes easier. Each person who does this makes it easier for the next, until declaring one's response to what happens in the team has, at least in certain circumstances, become an acceptable norm. It is usual, in any workshop exercise where each person does something in turn, for a self-confident team member to go first. Yet often this person will be less outspoken than more reserved members who wait to take their turns later. Personal response usually clarifies the team process and always increases contact. This is exciting and draws commitment from all concerned.

We sometimes suggest a (maintenance) circle check where each person finds a word to describe how he or she feels and says that word in rotation. This is an easier option for those who would normally avoid taking any sort of risk. A few people will find it hard to find a word but not usually those who have been quiet. Often these members have been sitting on some feeling evoked by something that happened half an hour earlier. If so, they will hardly have followed let alone contributed towards any of the subsequent discussion. The circle check allows them to express themselves and returns their attention to the present.

This maintenance check can also produce surprising information. People who most team members had assumed to be disinterested and aloof may declare themselves committed or involved and someone who was considered to be patient and supportive may admit to being restless and ready to move on.

Disclosure of feelings

A new team leader, a consultant and an internal facilitator have a lot in common. They all need to spend quite a lot of time observing current team norms before modelling other possibilities—however inhibited and detrimental to performance the existing norms may be. Both the form and timing of any intervention must be right. Coming from the rapid fire of competitive sport, the openness of Findhorn and the directness of Gestalt, it took me time to readjust my pace to the corporate world; I gained some unexpected insights along the way.

Norms around disclosure of emotion can be particularly rigid and comments on contrary norms may be harsh. Those who insist on expression will call those who are more cautious 'rigid', while those who are cautious will sneer at those who speak clearly for 'letting it all hang out'. In either case a new team member may consider caution to be the better part of valour and take a low profile, while gauging how best to behave in the future. Ostensibly, facilitators and consultants are in a very different position, since their role is simply to serve the team. Judgement as to when they should express their feelings has to depend on when they feel it will help the team's process. However, people who keep quiet at a meeting, for whatever reason, need to be aware of their emotional response to the discussion, otherwise they may say something inappropriate when they finally speak.

Difficulty with feelings

Some people block out their feelings and deflect any attempt to help them say what they are experiencing. They may contribute ideas and information and be highly respected yet they are difficult to contact and are often emotionally isolated within the team. 'Good' or 'fine' or 'I feel great' is the most they will say, perhaps unaware that these words describe nothing. These are evaluative statements that serve to conceal their feelings, as much from themselves as from everyone else. If time spent on maintenance is threatening they will dismiss it as a waste of time. When other team members are committed to team development this lack of contact creates uneasiness.

Feelings are not logical and therefore cannot be wrong. In a moment, the only possible genuine response to the expression of feeling is a feeling response. When someone in the team trusts enough to speak of his or her anxiety, grief or anger, those listening may feel empathy and for some this can be frightening. For some, the admission of sadness is particularly hard, for all other emotions will have been restricted by its denial. To experience sadness could be to lose control. (The emotional response of survivors to downsizing is rarely expressed but can have a deep influence on future motivation and team performance). A joke or a change of subject is a way out. That said, they can also be a viable way back for the speaker who suddenly feels too vulnerable or for the team leader who is aware of the importance of returning to the agenda.

The importance of skilled leadership and skilled facilitation working hand in hand cannot be overrated. The team must walk a delicate balance between disclosing personal feelings and respecting the boundaries of the individual.

Physical clues

Physical and emotional feelings are closely linked and both can relate to what is happening in the team context. If I feel sleepy during a team meeting, it may be partly because I stayed up late the previous night. Yet the moments when I feel sleepy, as opposed to those when I feel alert, are as often as not when that Joe is yabbering on again. If you do not know what you are feeling, consult your body. Are you cold? hungry? stiff and cranky? Do you have a headache? And how could this relate to what's going on? What do you need right now? The answers may tell you as much about the pattern of your team's behaviour as it does about yourself.

Taking time out to consult one's physical body—in effect attending to one's own maintenance needs—is ultimately a health issue. Not to do so from time to time is to invite burnout or, in the case of a physical occupation, injury. However, balancing effort and rest—and, in the context of the whole team, task and maintenance—also offers positive rewards. Rollo May once wrote of the artistic process, 'Insight comes at a moment of transition between work and relaxation' (May 1969: 66). This is my experience when, tired of writing (literally dozing over my lap-top so that I wake to find five lines of the letter 'k' recording my sleep on the screen) I get up, change and go for a jog on Hampstead Heath.

Invariably, this half hour of 'maintenance' brings me a couple of insights into what I was writing, so that I go back to drip sweat all over the keys as I record them—before taking my bath. 'The conscious work has been more fruitful because it has been interrupted and the rest has given back to the mind its force and freshness. This is not just a break from fatigue—the rest has been filled with unconscious work' (May 1969: 69). And Rollo adds: 'the receptivity of the artist must never be confused with passivity'.

Integrating feelings

Communication without a clear mental structure is difficult to understand but the artist also knows that communication without any emotional engagement will make little contact and will probably be forgotten. Without integrating feelings and thought, it is often difficult for the speaker to know *what* he or she wants to say, let alone communicate it— which is another reason why team members out of touch with their feelings often say nothing during periods of maintenance. A simple exercise to help people think about what they feel and to increase the vocabulary of their emotions—their 'affective' vocabulary—is to list as many emotions as possible in the space of five minutes. Having done this, go down the list and score out of 5 the degree to which you have ever experienced each of these emotions.

There are far fewer differences between business and sports teams than most people imagine but probably the most notable is that athletes are usually more in touch with their feelings. Many people in business organizations like to maintain that a team member's feelings are private and do not belong in the workplace. Yet resentment, for instance, will always escape in unpredictable ways and will affect the performance not only of the person but of all the relationships and teams of which that person is part. It can also lead the person to feel increasingly isolated, even destructive. On the other hand, when team norms and good facilitation allow the anger that is so often dammed up behind resentment to be expressed in a way that respects others and is contactful, it is always productive. Whereas unexpressed emotions inhibit performance, emotions that are acknowledged and transformed through a period of well facilitated maintenance allow the team to return to its task with renewed commitment.

The Tottenham discussion on 'loss of confidence', described more fully in the next chapter, allowed players to disclose feelings and assumptions that were inhibiting their performance. Although it turned out that one or two players had not felt any loss of confidence and 'the team' as such certainly did not feel anything, it was still true to say that lack of confidence and unease was, to use Smith and Berg's term, a 'group-based feeling'. Some players were no longer confident in their own performance, others were no longer confident in the performance of other team members (whose support they needed) and others were continuing to play, without taking any of this into account. The result was an incoherent losing team performance that needed discussion. At Queen's Park Rangers, when I was there, a similar issue centring around 'trust' became figural and a concern about 'honesty' has emerged in many settings, business as well as sport.

On such occasions something has to be done because, when the task or business of the team has become tangibly affected, every team member is affected directly or indirectly. Concern eventually reaches a level of negative synergy where it is considerably worse than the sum of individual concerns. At this point, from being a simple need for maintenance within a meeting, a special meeting or residential workshop needs to be arranged, the purpose or task of which will be to facilitate the expression of team members' concerns and to address them properly. This allows the suppressed energy bound up in the issue to be freed to work constructively. The sense of relief is usually so great that worry changes to excitement, to renewed interaction between team members and to effective action. Timely well-facilitated periods of maintenance lead to a clearer sense of team identity and that, in turn, promotes an increased synergy in addressing the task.

PROCESS

If task is the business part of the meeting and maintenance is the part devoted to relationships, process occurs in those moments where attention is paid to how the meeting is conducted: the dynamic of the meeting. Process is stepping back for a moment and taking the metaposition—the position of the observer. At its simplest level, if someone in the team is timekeeper, any comment made in this role is a process intervention. A facilitator will shift the focus from task into either maintenance *or* process.

Good meetings start (and end) with maintenance, whereas process always occurs after something has happened. Maintenance is always a break from task, whereas process can be a break from either task or maintenance and focuses on whatever was happening at the time. In either case, process is normally introduced by the words 'Okay, so what's happening here?' (or something similar), whereas the focus of the meeting shifts to maintenance when someone suggests taking a break or doing something different for a while. The person who asks 'So what's happening here?' is inviting descriptive feedback—'What is it that you notice?' Anyone who gives descriptive feedback ('I notice that you've said nothing, John, since Paul contradicted you' for instance) has also taken a metaposition and is making a process observation.

The need for process may only occur once or twice in a well-run meeting but there are times when everyone except the person or people speaking is aware of the need. When the shuffling of feet, the tapping of pens and major chair-bound calisthenics occur after 90 minutes of clarity and pace, they normally signal a need for shifting to maintenance—probably a five-minute breather. However, when the same restlessness occurs earlier, during an involved discussion between two team members that ignores the presence of everyone else, it is a sign that someone should comment on what is happening.

If the meeting is a long one and especially if there is no designated facilitator, the team leader would do well to shift from task to process at least once, even if he or she does not experience the need personally. Since leaders tend to do most of the talking, they are least likely to realize the need for change. Good teams normally have an understanding that any team member can ask for a shift to process. Processing is required when the meeting has somehow become derailed: when it has stuck in a circular argument or dialogue, when it has lost touch with most of the participants or when it has broken into separate discussions.

Process interventions

In the broader context, any discussion of team norms constitutes focusing on process. If some people are continually late for meetings, if certain people always hold up the agenda, if decisions are either rarely taken or never recorded nor acted upon, someone will eventually demand a break from either task or maintenance and initiate a serious discussion about the process that keeps the team stuck in such unproductive patterns. It may be a case of asking for agreements that have never previously been made or it may be that the team has drifted away from agreed procedures, with the gradual change of personnel. Either way a new agreement can then be made.

A process intervention during a meeting results in a decision—a decision to move on, to refer an issue to a subcommittee, to get more information, to get back to the agenda or perhaps to shift to maintenance and break for coffee. Process at the end of a meeting, addressing the question: 'So, what's been happening here?', is covered in Chapter 14, 'Warming down'.

We have described circle checks—each person in turn responding briefly to the same question, with no responses until the circle is completed—as a way to gain a quick picture of the full range of reactions, experienced in the moment by various members of the team. If task checks ask the question 'What's your opinion on this?' and maintenance checks asks for 'one word that describes how you feel right now', a process check asks 'What is it that you actually notice (an observation not an opinion) as we talk like this?' And, as before, it is often the quieter members of the team who have the most acute observations to offer. This illustrates one good reason for respecting the silence of those who prefer to be quiet most of the time. Being quiet allows them to take a metaposition and get a perspective on how the team functions much better than those who are naturally in the thick of things.

A shift from task to process can produce surprising insights. A team that is stuck in problem solving without reaching any solutions may find, by shifting to process, that it is the way they are trying to solve the problem that is keeping them stuck. On one occasion when we were called in to meet with representatives of a high-level research team, with a view to our working together, we found ourselves increasingly confused as the meeting went on. What did they want us to do? Why had they invited us there? Whenever we asked the question, someone would tell us that they wanted team building but although there were connections between the 80 people in the department, they could not decide if they were actually a team. After a whole morning of meeting them together, then meeting them separately and finally meeting them together again, each of us felt at a loss. When it was time to go the senior manager walked with us to our taxi. Suddenly, one of us thought to comment on our experience from a metaposition.

'I'm totally confused', I began. 'How did you do that? How did you confuse me?' The leader smiled apologetically, 'Yes,' he said. 'I'm afraid we do that to each other all the time.' 'So could it be that this is your problem and that what you would like us to do is to work with you on communication? Wouldn't that avoid the question as to whether or not you are one big team?' And it did. By letting go of the preordained solution—team building—the problem was solved but it was only by stepping back from the task that we were able to guess that the solution was in fact the problem.

In our view the consultant's job is to draw the clients' attention continually to what they are doing, how they do it and what happens as a result. They may wish to change and they may even need to change in order to survive and prosper. Yet no change is possible until they are fully conscious of what it is that they actually do. The more they know about the way they function and how they attempt to solve their problems, the better they are able to find out what they need to do. Discovering this themselves is always of greater value than receiving a proposal from someone else. However, by modelling the act of taking a metaposition and focusing on process occasionally, rather than being 100 per cent caught up in the task, the consultant offers a tool they can learn to use. This is a process they can then sustain.

One last refinement of process is to take the meta-metaposition and process one's processing. This is not as complicated as it might sound.

Normally done at a workshop where the concept and practice of processing is being introduced, it involves taking a final few minutes at the end of the review of a discussion or exercise to answer the question: 'And what did you notice about the way you did this review?' When we lead the workshop, we will sometimes suggest this position be taken in the *middle* of the ten-minute review, by asking: 'Are you aware of each other? What are you seeing, imagining and feeling as you do this review?'

THE RELATIONSHIP BETWEEN TASK, MAINTENANCE AND PROCESS

Task, maintenance and process are all essential to a successful team meeting. Appropriate timing and the precise balance of the three will vary according to the type of meeting. A meeting between two team members during a coffee break may be 100 per cent maintenance; and short talks or presentations, one person standing and the rest of the team sitting, can succeed with a minimum of maintenance and no process at all, provided there is an opportunity to have a proper meeting on a regular basis at another time. On the other hand, any *discussion* meeting that does not spend approximately 10 per cent of the time on maintenance and 5 per cent on process is unlikely to achieve much.

Unfortunately, many business managers (and coaches) have a leadership style that allows little time for discussion. They mistake question and answer sessions for discussion and even those who include discussion rarely allow time for any maintenance or process. Meetings that have no maintenance or process are exhausting, unsatisfying and devoid of humour. Unexpressed resentments smoulder and there are splits and cliques not far beneath the surface. These meetings constitute talk without contact, in which everyone is in the 'middle zone'. Decisions are then ill-advised or have no one's commitment. Teams that make decisions that work make them from a point of contact—contact with personal inner reality and contact with each other.

Yet meetings that have too much maintenance and process—where an overzealous facilitator interrupts an agenda item every few minutes or fails to interrupt when members have lapsed into swapping jokes—will ramble on aimlessly and be equally unproductive. In either case, the team performs poorly and eventually experiences a crisis. Team spirit is a product of working together consciously towards a clear common purpose.

All teams require meetings that include maintenance and process on a regular basis. At the Findhorn Foundation, each department would have an 'attunement' once a week. This began over coffee, everyone reporting on their personal experience of the week, with a clear shift to 'task'—discussing departmental and community business—about half way through. The three-man Cleveland Browns management team, mentioned earlier, agreed that during the hectic 16-game playing season their meetings would be restricted to 30 minutes. They also agreed that, if there was no business to discuss on a particular week, they would still meet and share their feelings and experience for at least 15 minutes.

TEAM MEETING ROLES

A creative and productive balance between task, maintenance and process ultimately depends on the ability of team members to assume the roles of leader, facilitator, time manager and scribe. Over time, a good team becomes so skilled in the use of these roles that different team members adopt them at different times, depending on the topic of discussion. Initially, it is important to identify at least one person who is capable of performing the function of each of the roles and assigning the roles accordingly.

Team leader

Most teams have a designated team leader, giving the parent organization easy access to the team. Part of the team leader's role is to report the team's progress or concerns to the next level of the organization and to bring back to the team information about the organization.

Leadership styles will affect the way the person concerned conducts a team meeting. An old-style authoritarian or autocratic leader normally discounts maintenance and process. If he or she allows any discussion at all, it will be entirely related to business. This is acceptable, provided that there is also a facilitator and that the leader and the facilitator work in tandem, respecting each other's roles. If there is no facilitator or if the facilitator is ignored by the leader, teamwork suffers.

A designated leader makes sure that the team has a clear purpose, that meetings are held to facilitate that objective, that the right people are present and that there is an agenda for each meeting. This includes monitoring one-to-one meetings and the meetings of subgroups that he or she will probably not attend. During a meeting the leader forms a team with any designated facilitator, scribe and time manager. Where these roles are not assigned, the leader becomes responsible for ensuring that they are carried out informally by the team as a whole.

The leader's own role is to state the meeting's purpose, establish an agenda, provide criteria for success and direct all matters related to the business of the meeting. This means making sure that people with relevant information give that information, that the information is discussed, that decisions are made and recorded and that any specific problem-solving or brainstorming methodology is followed correctly. It also means leading people back to the agenda or the point at issue when the discussion becomes too discursive. The leader has to be aware that when he or she is making proposals and agreeing or disagreeing with the proposals of others, this is not leading but taking the role of a team member. Ideally, except when there is no time for a discussion, the leader should focus on eliciting information and ideas and only add his or her own when everyone else has had a chance to speak.

Facilitator

Facilitation has such an important part to play in quality teamwork that we have already made many references to it in this and previous chapters. Adopting the role means fixing one's attention firmly on the form of the meeting rather than the content. This means that a team member who has an important contribution to make to a particular phase of the discussion, cannot also be the facilitator. It is impossible to have one's attention on two things at once. When the designated facilitator joins in the discussion, it is a sure sign that no one is facilitating. It probably means that no one has been facilitating for a while.

The first challenge encountered by the facilitator is to avoid getting caught up in the story—the content of discussion. If I allow myself to get caught, I am no longer aware of the obvious. Similarly, if I get stuck reflecting on something that happened a few moments ago, I miss what is happening now. As facilitator, my job is to look and to listen, without either waiting expectantly or digging for something to happen. When I get frustrated, I get a chance to be aware of my expectations for the team—which, again, are preventing me from seeing what is. Even the principles I hold as to how a good team conducts a meeting will get in the way of what actually happens.

Secondly, the facilitator has to be prepared to interrupt whenever something is hampering people's attention and ability to contribute. This requires a degree of courage, since interruption is often considered ill mannered, if not hostile. The leader can help the facilitator by occasionally asking if there is something the team should be noticing. The facilitator can help the leader by asking if the meeting is still on target, addressing the issues it was agreed to address.

The leader counts on the facilitator to monitor teamwork by ensuring that there are periods of maintenance and process. Although a good leader remains in contact with other team members, the facilitator watches the people who are not speaking as well as those who are and only looks at papers, flip charts or Metaplan boards when asked to step out of the role and give an opinion.

Learning to facilitate is easiest sitting beside any visual aid rather than facing it and practising the role by taking notes of what one notices. This develops the ability to watch and listen—listen to the tone of voice and the structure of the language—without getting caught up in the content.

A question like 'What do you think, Jane?' or 'Are you happy with that, Reg?' is a question relating to task and therefore a question asked by the leader, not the facilitator but, if the facilitator sees something that appears to be a reaction by one team member to a statement of another, he or she might ask 'Do you know how you respond—what you experience—when someone does something like that?' or 'What do you notice happening right now, Keith?'—Keith having been quiet throughout a heated episode. In other words, while it is the leader's job to ask for opinions, it is the facilitator's job to direct attention to the way the discussion is being conducted (process) and to how team members are feeling in response (maintenance).

Facilitators can do this either by asking for descriptive feedback or giving descriptive feedback (see p. 206). In the first case, the facilitator might address someone who has been talking for a while (on the hypothesis that he or she has not been paying attention to anyone else) or someone who has not spoken but may have tried, only to be talked over by someone else. In the latter case, the invitation to comment needs to be done without pressure on the assumption that if the individual had had no reservations about speaking (or at least being heard), he or she would have done so.

Although it is more time-consuming and cannot be used too often, an easier and more effective way to get descriptive feedback is the circle check described previously. Whereas the leader will call for a task circle check (asking 'What's your opinion on this?' to each person in turn), the facilitator will call for a maintenance circle check ('Can you find one word which describes how you are feeling right now?'—not 'How are you feeling?' which will produce a bland 'Okay' and certainly not 'What do you feel?' which will produce an opinion) or a process circle check ('What is one thing that you notice happening right now?'). Sometimes the facilitator will call both kinds of circle check but should call for the process check first as this allows people to first report an event, then say how they respond to it. The picture of the team process that emerges is like a snapshot taken by flashlight and can produce an immediate change of behaviour.

Sometimes a theme will emerge that can be tentatively labelled by the facilitator, who might say 'Am I right in sensing relief that we've given ourselves time to do this?' or 'It seems that the main concern here is honesty' or, after a circle check at the end of a meeting, 'It seems that one of the underlying themes for us today was commitment'. Such statements give an analytical equivalent to 'the big picture': they are another way to capture a broader focus.

Facilitators model descriptive feedback and ensure that all interpersonal feedback is descriptive, not evaluative. This means helping everyone to pay particular attention to speaking, questioning and listening skills. Since descriptive feedback raises awareness of such patterns, it makes change possible and is the facilitator's prime tool.

Good facilitators, like consultants, use themselves as instruments for the team by shuttling their attention from what is happening 'outside' themselves—in the meeting room—to what is happening 'inside themselves'—their personal response. This evokes hypotheses as to what other people are experiencing and that can be checked out by describing their own experience: this is what I see and this is how I respond (what I imagine and what I feel). The finer points of facilitation, including knowing when to interrupt with such information, can only be learned through demonstration, supervision and experience. Happily, the response to a correctly timed intervention is unmistakable and immediate, whereas a wrong hypothesis offered tentatively is barely noticed by the other members of the team. In fact, there is no such thing as a wrong intervention, as long as one is aware of what happens as a result. Reviewing one's performance and experience after the meeting, perhaps with the leader, the timekeeper and the scribe, can be invaluable—not just in terms of the timing and content of one's interventions but also as to one's style. Feedback gives a metaposition on one's own performance. Eventually one even becomes aware of the use of one's own voice.

The designated facilitator pays attention to the room environment as well as to the people in the team. This means checking the room from time to time, in terms of the temperature, the quality of the air, the seating arrangement, the number of empty cups and glasses—for 'clarity' and tidiness. The facilitator plans warming up and warming down with the leader before the meeting.

Time manager

A designated time manager supports the team leader by insisting on a clear time allocation for the agreed agenda. He or she then monitors the progress of the meeting against the agenda, warning the team of approaching deadlines and reminding them of the items still to be addressed. When a discussion of any item exceeds its allocated time, the time manager suggests a reallocation of the time remaining. Since time is such a precious resource, this is a key role. As the leader gains confidence in the time manager and the facilitator, a team within a team begins to form that allows the leader to focus better on his or her own performance.

Scribe

The scribe, the fourth member of this inner team, has the job of recording any decision-making process, usually on a flip chart. A good scribe helps the leader to maintain the flow of information and to organize it in a way that makes key issues clear. The leader checks views of the team and then tells the scribe what to write. The scribe only takes part in the discussion when invited to do so by the leader. The phrase 'power of the pen' refers to the abuse of this role that occurs when the scribe filters or interprets the leader's instruction or simply writes down his or her own opinion.

Recorder

The recorder's role is to take notes and to publish and distribute the minutes before the next meeting.

Combining roles

The easiest roles to combine are those of facilitator and timekeeper. The most difficult to combine, especially when the team is following some complicated problem-solving or decision-making methodology, are those of leader and facilitator. The most sophisticated way to handle the roles is to have them change according to the topic and stage of the meeting but changes of leadership and facilitation, particularly, require a great deal of experience.

These two roles complement each other and are by far the most complex. Although it is possible to shuttle one's attention rapidly from content to form and back, one is always likely to miss some important piece of information while doing so. However, an effective team leader would be at ease in either role: if the leader is unable to appreciate the role of the facilitator, the team's meeting will not be productive.

Whenever we totally identify with our role within the team or the organization, we limit our own awareness and tend to box others into their roles too. If I am always focused on being a consultant, my clients can only act the role of being clients. When you are identified with being a leader, your team members become boxed in to the role of following. Our objective must be to fulfil roles without identifying with them. It therefore becomes important to find times during the meeting and during the day to appreciate one's essential difference from one's role. Ram Dass tells a story of his first interview with the Indian Minister of Health, when setting up his Seva Foundation for the blind. He had expected a businesslike, time-driven official but was surprised when he walked into the man's office. 'He wasn't busy being the Minister of Health,' relates Ram Dass. 'He was just sitting there wearing his Minister of Healthness'.

10

Feedback on performance

All systems employ feedback as a self-regulating mechanism. The furnace has its thermostat, the human body will sweat or shiver, the bat sends ultrasonic calls into the darkness. They all have internal processes, structures, goals and mechanisms for gathering information. Most feedback mechanisms are used unconsciously but individuals within teams receive both unconscious and deliberate feedback on their performance. Their team colleagues will smile or frown, lean forward or hang back, often unaware of the messages they give, but each individual may also have formal performance appraisals or sales targets.

Teams, like any functional system, are dependent on continuous feedback to regulate the process whereby they achieve their goals. Sports teams use video replay but, somewhat surprisingly, business teams have few disciplined mechanisms for generating such feedback on their performance. They receive feedback on their product but little on their process—their ongoing performance. Even where they do have access to such feedback, it can be extremely difficult to use because it contains two flaws. Firstly, the relationship between the feedback they receive and the internal processes in which they engage is unclear or non-existent.* Secondly, since the feedback is often inadequate or distorted, it is useless or actually damaging to use it as a basis for modifying team performance. This chapter shows how to rectify such flaws.

When we comment on what someone is doing, we are giving that person feedback. This is how the first step of team development—awareness of

---

*See Part I for use of feedback in a team's self regulation.

self—is usually reached. However, feedback may be either *evaluative* or *descriptive* and the impact of each is quite different.

EVALUATIVE FEEDBACK

Evaluative feedback is very familiar. From an early age most of us have been told that we are right or we are wrong, that we are good or we are bad. Evaluative feedback is either positive or negative and always expresses someone's subjective opinion: it is not a precise report of what we actually did. In fact, if we can agree or disagree with the feedback we receive, it is by definition evaluative. All forms of grading or assessment of performance, unless they are objectively measurable and mutually agreed before the performance, fall into this category. Evaluative feedback tells us how we 'should be'.

In business teams, most evaluative feedback is negative and is given to subordinates by their manager or team leader with the explicit or implicit message that they should change. This often creates problems. On the one hand, the team members who receive it might disagree, might consider it unfair or might have a string of excuses for their performance. All such responses, whether or not they are actually expressed, block spontaneous change.

On the other hand, if the 'shoulds' of evaluative feedback ('You should be more assertive', 'You should plan better') are accepted, the individual's awareness of self is diminished. 'As soon as I buy what anyone tells me', says Judith Brown, 'I am lost'. The 'shoulds' become introjects—accepted but not digested. In any case, the person doing the telling automatically takes on the role of 'top dog' (see p. 119) to the individual's 'underdog' and ultimately never wins. There is no difference between 'I should be more assertive' and 'I shouldn't have ice cream tonight'.

DESCRIPTIVE FEEDBACK

Change, if that is the purpose of feedback, is more likely to occur when the feedback is as impartial as that given by a mirror, a tape recorder or a video camera. We may not like what we see and hear but, as long as we can take it at face value, the feedback turns our attention inwards, rather than inspiring gratitude or defensiveness towards the person who offers it. Any resistance we may have to the information will tend to be intrapersonal rather than interpersonal. We notice how we feel after our actions and from this perspective, we also become more aware of the impact our behaviour has on the team.

As evaluation decreases, so too does our resistance. Instead of being faced with truculence or deflection, the person giving feedback may find us asking for more information. Have you seen me or heard me do this before? Is there a pattern to this? And we may ask how this person *responds* to our behaviour. What do you feel when I do this? Are you withholding some form of judgement about what you describe me as doing? And if so what is it you are not saying? Many of us are so used to being judged that when we receive some clear, descriptive feedback we assume that there has to be something more that the speaker is reluctant to express.

When we give descriptive feedback, it is an account of what we see, hear, touch or smell. It can also include how we respond but if the response is to be non-evaluative it is limited to a description of how we feel physically or emotionally and does not include what we think—no judgements, no interpretations and no advice. Becoming aware of our response means slowing the flicker of our attention from leaping into the future or plunging back into the past and getting in touch with what we are experiencing and what we may need right now. Our ability to increase the awareness of others is related to the level of our own awareness.

Descriptive feedback brings awareness to others—a gift like any other in that it may be discarded, put aside for a while or used immediately—but a gift nonetheless because it creates an opportunity for change. Moshe Feldenkrais's maxim 'when you know what you are doing you can do what you want' holds true for every member of the team.

Stating the obvious

Descriptive feedback will either describe what happens *outside* you—what other team members are doing—or it will describe what is happening *inside* you—your own feelings. Giving 'outside' feedback is sometimes called 'stating the obvious'. 'What I'm most aware of right now,' said Chris Boardman, half-way through an evening pre-competition meeting of the team pursuit cycling team at the Barcelona Olympics, 'is that Bryan hasn't spoken yet.' Bryan Steel looked up. 'You're dead right,' he said, correctly tuning in to a message beyond the straight feedback. 'I don't agree with any of this.' And the meeting then moved into a new productive phase as Bryan's objections to an organizational suggestion were aired and discussed.

This team had long been using descriptive feedback, primarily after each practice ride of their training sessions. Simplifying a routine we designed for the European version of the Ford TOPS course (and later included in EQUIP and FTEP (see p. 182), where each syndicate group reviews each of their meetings, the cyclists would get off the track, park their bikes, sit down facing each other on the waiting circle of chairs, rummage in their bags for their plastic water bottles and answer three questions: 'What precisely did you notice?', 'What did you feel?' and 'What, if anything, do you want to change?' Responding to the first of these questions is 'stating the obvious'.

Since each member of the team would have a slightly different perspective on the ride, a variety of factors affecting their performance could be mentioned: the wind coming up the back straight, an acceleration of pace by the rider in front of them, the gap that appeared between them as a result, a comment on another rider's position on his bike, something about who went where as they broke line for the finish or a reference to their lap times were all possible observations. How they each responded physically and emotionally to these events is added to each observation, in response to the question 'How did you feel?'

Team meetings in a business setting become more focused and creative as team members learn to use descriptive feedback. This is the prime skill of a good facilitator (see p. 200).

Focusing on speech

Taking a moment to notice how other team members are speaking rather than what they are saying can raise awareness of the different characteristics and effects that these speech patterns produce.* Most of us can differentiate between, if not describe, quite subtle changes in voice quality which suggest shades of meaning that are not contained in the words alone. After just a few days, members of a new large team find they can recognize who is speaking without having to look. Unless we are trained phoneticians, the only way to give descriptive feedback on such intricate patterns is either to mimic or to switch on some form of voice recorder, which can sometimes

*For more on speech and body language, see p. 273 (listening at all levels).

be valid since voice quality forms part of the speaker's overall message. As we shall see below, any part of the speaker's 'performance' can be the basis for assumptions and positive or negative evaluation.

Even a comment on a speaker's 'grammatical construction' can bring surprises. A simple statement like 'Now you are asking another question' can shift the speaker's awareness to a different perspective and prompt a significant change.

Focusing on physical presence

Easier to describe is the speaker's posture and movement, of which he or she may be completely unaware. We tend to associate certain messages with the visual experience of watching another team member speak. Since the association is subjective, any feedback of the 'Your-arms-are-crossed—you-are-obviously-resistant-to-what-I-say' kind is evaluative. However, sometimes the message received by our eyes seems to contradict what the speaker is saying, in which case we shall trust the unconscious visual message more. If we see Max's colour change, his fists clench and hear his voice tighten as he says 'I don't care *what* you do', we may feel uncomfortable. Descriptive feedback can help: 'Max, your face is red. It's easy for me to imagine there is more to it than that. What's going on?'

A good facilitator, like a good therapist, has a child's ability to see clearly and state the obvious: 'Look at the king! Look at the king! Look at the king! The king is in his all-together . . .' cries the boy in the old Danny Kaye film version of Hans Christian Andersen's 'The King's New Clothes'. The adult villagers meantime were bowing and scraping and throwing their hats in the air as the king drove by, not only ignoring the obvious but, through force of habit, quite blind to it. The boy's cries raised everyone's awareness, including the king's and there was a dramatic change. The haughty tailors were thrown in the dungeons and the relationship between the vain king and his obsequious subjects began to improve.

However, children are frequently scolded for stating the obvious—be it that Granny has got a big nose, Uncle John has drunk a whole bottle of wine or that Daddy and Auntie Sue are whispering together again—when the rest of the family pretends not to notice. In the same way we find that members of a newly formed team with only one woman or only one black person may not mention the fact for months, even when diversity is a cultural issue.

Mirroring

A child who tries to mimic or 'mirror' an adult is in particular danger of being sent to bed early. Yet, go to the sloping cobbled square in front of the Centre Georges Pompidou in Paris or to the open space in front of the railway station in Amsterdam or to almost any festival town on a warm summer's day and you may see a mime artist walk behind oblivious passers-by imitating every gesture. Those who are watching laugh nervously, fascinated yet appalled that they might be the next victim. In our culture, to mime or mirror someone's unconscious movement or posture is to show that you notice what we are bred to ignore. It is the same culture that allows me to wander around all day with egg on my chin, unless I meet a close friend.

Yet 'mirroring' is a highly effective way of stating the obvious and raising awareness to allow change. As consultants, our very presence tends to make people more aware of what they are doing and when we state the obvious we are not necessarily aware of the significance our client may attach to the particular pattern of behaviour we describe. When we mirror what they do we intend to be supportive—perhaps talking their language or idiom rather than our own, to confirm that we have been listening and are interested. At other times we may reinforce a 'negative' norm by mirroring it unconsciously and without anyone noticing. We are then 'confluent with' the system we are meant to observe.

This happened to us once in Sweden: we accepted a team leader's plea that there was no time for us to interview his team before our workshop, only to discover that a lack of consultation before important team events was a key issue with the team. We had unwittingly colluded with this behavioural pattern.

Modelling

Sometimes it is the *absence* of some practice, norm or quality that strikes us. Then we might model what is missing rather than just comment on it. The cross-cultural consultancy team mentioned earlier used this as a prime intervention.

On one occasion we were counselling an overworked voluntary organization. Our own team was made up of three men and three women—all of
different nationalities. Sitting opposite us were our clients—also three men
and three women. The symmetry was so striking that after allowing some
time for introductions and for our clients to explain what they needed, we
split up into six pairs, male–female, consultant–client, to gather more
personal input. That evening our consultant team met to share and discuss
our impressions before having a second meeting with the clients the next
day. What emerged as we talked was the image of our clients being so
stretched and worried that they never looked up to support or make contact
with each other.

As a team of consultants we had our own sense of pressure and
uncertainty. In our initial session together, before meeting the clients, we
had each shared a lack of certainty in what we were meant to be doing and
confessed that, though we all had our own way of working, we had little
experience of improvising a team with other consultants from different
cultures, with different training and different personal styles. As a result, in
this first session with our clients we had each hesitated before speaking and
spent a lot of time looking at and checking with each other. Noting this
essential difference between ourselves and our clients we decided to
consciously emphasize the process during our next session and model the
contact that we felt their 'system' lacked. We decided to stop periodically
and ask our clients if we might discuss our impressions among ourselves
while they watched and listened.

When we did this our clients seemed transfixed. Towards the end of the
session we asked them each to say what they had noticed happening in the
room during the afternoon and, without exception, they mentioned the
contact that we made with each other. When we asked what they would
like to do with the time remaining they looked around as if seeing each
other for the first time, checked and then said they wanted to spend the next
20 minutes talking to each other while we watched and gave feedback.
Three months later, we heard that our clients were still under pressure but
felt closer to each other and better able to cope.

Sudden awareness of one's own behavioural patterns can give the shock
of a cold shower but it also brings a renewed sense of excitement. Another
client team whose members also discovered their lack of contact agreed to
what is called a 'paradoxical intervention'. In addition to having team
feedback meetings, they decided that every Tuesday they would deliber-

ately not look at each other from 3 p.m. to 4 p.m. By doing deliberately what previously they were doing unconsciously they further increased their awareness and ability to change a debilitating pattern.

Awareness and contact

Stating the obvious brings choice because, for some time afterwards, the behaviour described can only be continued with awareness. Judith Brown once visited a colleague with a small, very active child who was running from one side of the room to another. The mother repeatedly told the child to sit down but the child took no notice. After 15 minutes of this, Judith turned to the child and said with a smile 'Cindy, I notice you're running around and around and around today'. The child looked at her for a moment, then sat down and began to play with her toys.

Although stating the obvious results in awareness of self it can also bring contact with the person giving the feedback. Another of Judith's stories is of a married couple who had come to her for a counselling session. The wife had been to her doctor earlier in the day because she had long had something wrong with one of her tear ducts. In the middle of the session, the couple were speaking angrily to each other and the husband turned to Judith for support. 'I see I've done something wrong again', he said. 'Okay', said Judith, 'now look at your wife. What do you actually see?' The man turned and looked for a while and said 'I don't know ... it's hard to say ...' and then suddenly he turned to Judith and said 'She's crying!'. So Judith said: 'Don't tell me, tell her.' The man turned back to his wife and said 'I see that you're crying!'. This time the woman turned to Judith and said: 'I don't know what happened then but I feel better.' For the first time in weeks the man had noticed his wife. He noticed her tears, let his wife know and made contact.

Personal response

Personal response is information given by one team member to another or to others. It allows those being addressed to know how one other person reacts to what they are doing. The second of the three questions that the team pursuit cycling team riders answer is 'What did you feel?'. The question is not 'What do you feel *about* ...?' but 'What did you feel physically and/or emotionally, when someone did some specific thing or a particular thing happened?'.

On one occasion during a week's pre-Olympic training in Belgium, Glen Sword evoked strong reactions by pulling out of a full-speed practice ride but continuing to circle the bottom of the track. The first feedback question 'What precisely did you notice?' had evoked responses ranging from the unrelated 'I noticed that a gap appeared between us at the start of your last turn' (Simon Lilliston to Chris Boardman) through 'I noticed that you shouted at Glen' (Paul Jennings to Bryan Steel) to 'I noticed that you stayed on the track after pulling out and that I nearly ran into you' (Bryan Steel to Glen Sword). The second question 'What did you feel?' then produced 'I felt surprised' (from Simon), 'I felt strong' (from Chris), 'I felt angry' (from Bryan), 'I felt my bum muscle go' (from Glen) and 'I felt scared and furious' (from Peter Keen, the coach, who had been showing the lap times at the side of the track). Despite the emotion evoked—especially in Bryan and Peter but with a resulting effect on the others—the feedback contained no judgements, no accusations and no advice. The third question, 'What, if anything do you want to change?', allowed them to build on their descriptive feedback and express their needs—in this case a repeated demand that no rider stay low on the track after pulling out.

The full sequence of questions and descriptive responses allowed the team to move unscathed through a minefield of recriminations that would have blown a great hole in the agendas of many a business team meeting. The information given in response to the question 'What did you feel?' was, as always, of particular importance. By allowing them to learn more about the effect they had on each other and by reminding them how differently they could respond to the same event, their answers actually contributed further to their team-building process. It is a short step from team members appreciating their differences to feeling the strength they possess as a unit. However, personal response, by definition, means personal disclosure and, as noted earlier, although disclosure increases trust and team spirit, most people need to trust the team before making any significant disclosure.

We work with this paradox by insisting that (i) feedback is non-evaluative, (ii) no one gives advice or 'interprets' another team member, (iii) everyone takes responsibility for his or her own response and (iv) the differing levels of comfort in disclosure within the team are respected. If we ask for feedback on some deep exchange by two members or on some personal disclosure by another team member, we ask that any response be either a report on how people felt as they listened or some related personal disclosure. These boundaries protect everyone from attack and judgement. They support the integrity of the individual and make it easier for members to take the leap into personal response. When they are sustained over time, trust emerges as a team norm.

At the end of my first involvement with one sports team, I made a short presentation to the staff. It was the only time I had had to outline our concept of teamwork and I would have liked some feedback. One or two people said a few words before leaving but the head coach disappeared. I did not see him again that day nor the following morning, when I was due to fly back to London. I made a last search of the building and found him exercising alone in a corner of the vast gymnasium. 'Good-bye,' I said. 'I'm on my way.' He looked up. 'Bye. Send me that report' and he continued his sit-ups. In that moment I felt a confusion of shock, disappointment and anger (our original agreement had not included a report—one that I would be pushed to find time to write). Yet as I drove out to the airport, I found this all turning to acute interest. This was all part of a pattern; I realized that I had never heard him thank anyone for anything all the time I had been there. It was possible that my own 'personal response' was but an echo of the feelings of his staff who worked 16 hours a day throughout the season. I wrote my response into the report, suggesting that the lack of appreciation and support that he modelled could contribute to the lack of consistency on the field—his prime concern at that time.

Although voicing such hypotheses goes beyond descriptive feedback, it is valid as long as the hypotheses are firmly rooted in our observation both of what is happening in the team system 'out there' and what our personal response is 'in here'. It is valid when accompanied by the assertion: 'This is my observation. It isn't how you are.'

Writing about the consultant's role, Ed Nevis calls this skill 'the use of self' and points out that it includes 'the articulation of awareness of all kinds, such as feelings and sensations, thoughts, images and fantasies' (Nevis 1987: 125). However, this is not just a skill to be developed by the consultant or the facilitator. In highly effective teams all team members hone and practise such skill, thereby maintaining awareness of each other at the highest level. They may not particularly like each other but they report their experience and requirements without any fuss.

FEELINGS

Feelings are the substance of personal response and facilitate contact and team spirit. However, it can take time to know what our feelings are. Family norms may have reinforced a broader cultural norm that inhibits the experience and expression of feelings. Many of us, especially men, consider that feelings are a sign of weakness and should rarely be shown. This allows us to be indifferent and indifference is not just safe, it is also a source of power. Even team members who are open with their feelings at home are usually more guarded at work and when the team leader is uncomfortable in the presence of emotion, the team acquires its own norm against the expression of personal response.

Constant denial of our feelings can put them almost out of reach so that everyone else in the team may have deduced what we feel long before we know ourselves. This means that we are often unaware of our response to what is happening around us—either we are distracted or we retreat into analysing the situation or we do not give our response any value. We can lose touch with it by judging ourselves, well in advance of giving anyone else a chance to judge us. As a team member watching or listening to other team members, our response can be something as simple as 'I feel disappointed', 'I feel pleased', 'I feel disconcerted'. Yet some people nearly always hold back what could be valuable information, deciding it does not make sense.

As a cultural group, athletes—especially young athletes—are often more in touch with their feelings than many engrossed members of business teams but cultural norms still affect *when* they express them. A few years ago, I was asked to lead a morning session at a British Olympic Association camp for a group of promising junior cyclists, who had not done any mental training before. At the end of the first session, I brought them back to a circle and (as with the coaches referred to earlier) asked them to say in turn one word that described how they felt. The first one said 'Okay'. The next said 'Okay'. The third said 'Normal' and the round continued—'Okay', 'Normal', 'Normal', 'Yes', 'Okay', the next one just nodded, 'Okay', 'Normal'. So I then asked, 'When you are in an important race, coming to the top of a long steep hill and someone comes up and starts to overtake you, what do you feel?' Immediately there was a chorus of words—'Determined!', 'Stronger!', 'Frustrated!', 'Powerful!', 'Angry!', 'Tired', 'Hopeless', 'Tense!'. 'So,' I said. 'We've just spent ninety minutes doing all these strange exercises. We're going to take a break. What do you feel now?' There was a brief pause as they all looked at me in surprise. Then one of them laughed and said, 'John!' Do you *really* want to know?'

There are a few other points we should realize about feelings:

1 Feelings and thoughts are easily confused. 'I feel trapped' or 'I feel confused' are usually ways of labelling thoughts, not feelings. They can easily imply blame—'you are trapping me' or 'you are confusing me'— which would be evaluative statements and lead to dissent. On the other hand, they may be a sign of retroflection and invite the response: 'so how do you trap (or confuse) yourself?'

2 The words 'I feel that . . .' presage an opinion not a report on how the speaker feels. Even an admission like 'I feel that I'm on the spot' reports an assumption not a feeling, so that one could then ask: 'And what do you feel when you're on the spot?' Differentiation requires a practised ear, since it is possible to leave out the 'that' and still express an opinion rather than a feeling. 'I feel we should go to lunch' can be challenged, whereas 'I'm hungry' cannot.

3 'Pseudo' feelings are commonplace in a repressed team. They reflect how team members believe they should respond. Most members only discover and express what they feel as the team begins to move through the team development process.

4 Feelings are usually thought of as strong emotions but they are more often a subtle response to other members of the team.

5 Feelings are our response to what we imagine is happening or what we imagine another team member is thinking or doing, rather than to what might actually be the case. We say more about this below.

6 Feelings do not have to be logical and cannot be wrong—no one can disagree with what I feel. Personal response—giving feedback on how we feel—is by definition genuine. It is what we experience, whether or not we choose to report it to others.

7 When we do express our feelings we often relieve our embarrassment by explaining them away. Explanation and analysis always lead us away from our feeling experience, making their message less accessible.

8 Feelings are my own responsibility. I cannot change and am not responsible for what other team members choose to do, even when they are reacting to an action or words of mine but I am responsible for my own feelings—the way I respond to others. This is because I have a choice and can learn to expand my awareness of the different options available.

Frustration and discomfort, for instance, come from the way we 'frame' or interpret what happens, not from the situation itself. You may think you know how to make me angry and, indeed, I may respond to your taunts in the same way each time but, in fact, each time I have the option of responding differently. It sometimes helps to remember that feelings are something I *have*: I am not my feelings, I am the person with choice.

9 Feelings contribute. Even so-called 'negative' feelings are a contribution to the team's evolution, provided they are owned and expressed directly. Statements like 'I'm angry' or 'I'm bored' not only allow the rest of the team to know how I respond to what is happening but open the way for others to speak. Sometimes one admission of 'I'm bored' is enough for everyone to realize that the two people talking were the only ones still paying attention to the topic under discussion. Problems only arise when, being angry or bored or frustrated, I let the feeling 'leak out' without admitting it, I admit it and blame someone else for my experience or I consistently time my outbursts uniquely for my own benefit.

10 Feelings are personal: the team does not feel anything. Although it is theoretically possible that every team member responds in exactly the same way to a given event, it is highly unlikely—and, even then, they would be making a number of personal responses. When we were at Tottenham, Ossie Ardiles (then still a player) once said after a run of poor results: 'The trouble is that we're not confident.' When we asked him 'Ossie, who's not confident? Are you confident?' his reply was: 'Oh, *I'm* confident but many of the others are not.' A quick check established that in fact several players, like Ossie, still had confidence in their own play. However, confidence was an issue worth discussing. Some players were unsure what they felt and were worried about what the *others* might be feeling. Others, like Ossie, were less than fully confident in the performance of others. Having made this explicit it was possible to ask for more detail: 'So who are you not confident in? When are you not confident in him? What could he do differently that would allow you to be more confident?'

11 Physical and emotional feelings may be connected. Body, mind and emotions do not function separately. Physical and emotional warmth and coldness, tension or lassitude are often experienced simultaneously, so that if we are unsure how we respond emotionally to some pattern of the team's behaviour, it is sometimes possible to discover the answer by focusing on physical sensation.

12 Feelings are inside but may connect with what is happening outside. Paying attention to oneself can provide information about what others are doing. 'Be in touch with what's going on in yourself,' says George Brown: 'Personal response is legitimate. There's something going on in you when you see, hear or smell someone else. It's mostly stuff we don't pay attention to.' If you went to bed late, you may well feel tired during the following day. However, the precise times at which you feel sleepy during a meeting will still be linked with what is happening around you and a bold declaration like 'I don't know about anyone else but I'm feeling sleepy' may well result in a change of topic or a coffee break.

This is another example of the 'use of self' (see p. 214) but here one switches attention from what is happening outside to one's physical feelings, in order to discover something that would be helpful to the team's process. For example, becoming aware that I am tapping a pencil on my writing pad, I may realize (a) that something is bothering me, (b) what that is and (c) if I dared to declare what I notice and how I respond, the team might benefit from our intervention. In the same way, if I suddenly notice that I am biting my lip, the sharp kinaesthetic experience can make me aware that I am embarrassed, that I am tense or that I want to get away. Perhaps I have a strong feeling that the person talking is not telling the truth. Very often such keen feelings and the intuitions that they prompt go unexpressed because we are afraid of being wrong. Even realizing that two team members have been discussing the same issue for a good ten minutes creates a challenge: do I let this continue or do I tell them that I have lost interest, that I'm drifting away—and see if I'm the only one?

13 Feelings *always* affect our performance, even when we are not aware of what our feelings are. This is connected to the two preceding points. All athletes know that physical performance can alter from day to day and from moment to moment, depending on what they feel (and think), just as what they feel will be affected by their performance. Resentment can make us tense, induce a headache or cause a serious accident on the shop floor. Taking a walk or going to the rest room can clear our mind and allow an important new idea to emerge or can allow us to calm down after making a stupid mistake. Mind, body and emotions are inextricably linked (which is the genesis of our company name, Sporting Bodymind Ltd).

PAST, PRESENT AND FUTURE

Two of the three process questions used at the end of a meeting (What did you notice? What did you feel? and What if anything do you want to change?) are in the past tense. For this reason, it can be important to finish with the question 'And now? What do you feel now?'

A negative experience between two members that is not resolved is likely to resurface as 'unfinished business' that affects their performance at some future date.*

'Unfinished business' can be carried around indefinitely and dull our awareness of the present. Jessica Mason, an internal consultant we were training some years ago, had an older brother with red hair who used to taunt her mercilessly when they were children. Years later, when leading a course, Jessica found she had ambivalent feelings she was unable to explain about one of the participants. As we did our review at the end of the first day's session she suddenly made the connection: this participant had red hair and reminded her of her brother. It was one of her first conscious experiences of a 'fixed Gestalt', later defined by Ed Nevis (1987: 12) as 'figures developed out of past experience that become adhered to rigidly in the present situation'.

In effect, during that first day, Jessica was neither dealing with the past—her unfinished business with her brother—nor paying attention to her present relationship with the red-haired participant. In the meantime, having been unable to accept and make contact with the participant, she had been in the process of creating a new lot of unfinished business with him. By sharing her insight on the second morning, she was able to clear the new relationship and, by talking over past times with her brother on her return home that summer, she was finally able to close the issue for good.

We can inadvertently pour so much energy into powerful memories of the past or into vivid fears and fantasies of the future that we are left with very little for the present moment. We then only see the present through our highly coloured lenses of past and future. Ram Dass,† who wrote the 1960s classic *Be Here Now*, said recently that he still gets caught himself:

*See Chapter 14 for more on closure and unfinished business.

†Much of his current work is with the dying. He once said that 'it is the holding on to the old—how things used to be—that creates suffering'.

I travel giving workshops for nine months of the year. A month ago I was sitting alone in a run-down, very plastic, American hotel room and found myself thinking of my base and calculating how soon I would get home. So I walked out and closed the door. Then I turned around, went in again and called 'I'm ho-ome!'.

A facilitator has to be capable of letting go of what has just happened in order to tune in to what is happening now. For members, another way to *interrupt* or lose touch with our response is to rehearse—another route back to the future. If the meeting consists of several presentations and I am making one of them, it is easy for me to completely miss the presentation before mine, even if it has an important impact on my team role. We know that when we ask for a circle check during one of our workshops, there will always be some people who will not hear what the member before them said: they become anxious and rehearse their own contribution. In both of these cases, personal response has been interrupted.

My most powerful experience of 'returning to the present' from a fantasy trip into the future came some years after surviving a non-fatal air crash one summer in the late 1950s. I had managed to avoid flying throughout my volleyball career and, indeed intended never to fly again. Eventually, however, I had to travel to America and had neither the time nor the money to go by ship. When the time came, I somehow talked myself into leaving the asphalt and walking up the steps into the plane but I was sure that that was the last moment I would be on the ground alive. The plane took off and I sat there shaking.

After a while, I became aware of a small Scottish voice beside me saying: 'Excuse me but are you all right?' I turned and saw a well-dressed elderly woman, looking at me with concern. 'Actually, no,' I said. 'I'm busy falling apart.' 'Are you frightened?' she asked. 'Yes, very,' I replied tersely. 'So *where* are you frightened?' 'Pardon?' I stared at her. What on earth (*on earth?!*) was the old biddy wittering about? 'Where in your body do you feel frightened?' she pursued gently. 'What's happening to you physically? What do you notice?'

'Oh. You mean like, like I'm sweating?' 'Yes. What else?' 'My fists are clenched?' 'Yes. And what else?' I was becoming interested. 'Oh, my chest is tight and my arms ... and my *thighs* too ... and my *feet* are cold,' I said in surprise. 'Good. Good. And are you breathing?' Pause. *Wow!* I'd stopped breathing. 'No!' I gasped. 'So breathe. ... Breathe in to the count of four. ... Hold it for the count of four. ... Now let it out very very slowly, maybe to the count of eight.'

To begin with it was difficult. I could manage to gasp some breath in but the muscles in my chest did not seem to want to let it out. Yet as the woman watched and began to count softly for me, I gradually got the hang of it and, miracle of miracles, I was beginning to relax. Much later, of course, as we talked (and I learned she was Dr Winifred Rushforth, an 85-year-old Jungian analyst living and still practising in Edinburgh at that time), I realized that she was pulling me away from my traumatic memories of the past and my hideous fears of the immediate future, to being fully aware of the present—first of my own body and then of the seat beneath me, then of the different sounds of the plane and eventually of the taste of the food they brought us to eat. I survived—survived to fly many, many times again.

This experience helped me first as an athlete and later as a sports psychologist, to work with anxiety before and during high-level competition. (Fritz Perls called anxiety the gap between the present and the future.) The key realization is that there *is* only the present—a concept that manages to be both obvious and obscure. The past only exists as a collection of imperfect and highly personalized memories that we hold at this present moment. In the same way, the future is only a current collection of suppositions, hopes, fears and fantasies that exist in our minds now. Our attention can be on them, as it can on our night-time dreams and nightmares or it can be on the physical sensation of the book you hold in your hands, the smell of the paper or on the keyboard beneath my fingertips. When we focus on our past experience of other team members or on the things we imagine about them that we have never checked, we are unable to see them as they are now and cannot make contact. We are also incapable of giving meaningful feedback.

Expectations and interpretations that you have in my regard may drive me crazy but meetings at which members constantly refer to the past are interminable and can have that effect on everyone. When you get caught up in what happened, you not only do not see what is happening you get hopelessly stuck. Even when a team member is genuinely concerned to put things right, the question 'What did I do that made you so upset?' can easily lead into justification, defence and arguments. It is far better to ask: 'What can I do when we work together that will make you happy?' It can be argued that problems that are not here now are not real problems.

ATTITUDES

Most attitudes are a useful pattern of beliefs and assumptions about the present that are based on our past experience and help us prepare for the future. They are one form of inner response to what we see happening 'outside' us and, in the context of a team, this is usually a response to what another team member is doing. However, they are sometimes outdated and lead to evaluative rather than descriptive feedback, which then prevents clear contact between the two people concerned—the image that one holds of the other masks the way that person really is.

Who's there?

Jonathan Males, now a member of our consultancy team, joined the Australian national canoe squad while still living in his native Tasmania. He discovered that the core of the squad came from Victoria, where most of the training was held, and they believed that no one from out of State ever contributed. They had seen many out-of-State members come and go. Tasmanians particularly were assumed to be amateurish, for no better reason than that people from Victoria went to Tasmania on holiday. Jonathan, seen through the veil of this negative thought form, was warned several times not to go partying at night although he had never considered doing so. It took him two years to establish real contact with the Victorians and change their attitude.

Attitudes are always out-dated when they are carried forward from one relationship to another. The story of the trainee consultant above was one such example but the situation is considerably worse when the confusion is mutual. If your voice reminds me strongly of Dennis (who was so boring at university) and my clothes remind you of Peter (who gave your sister such a difficult time a few years ago) there is a real chance that we shall be wary of each other, without realizing why. In the beginning, any conversation will be between 'Peter' and you or 'Dennis' and me but never between you and me. When the first real challenge hits us and our unwarranted mutual dislike surfaces, the result could unsettle the entire team. It would be equally uncomfortable for you if I confused you with someone I liked. Eventually you would feel trapped—expected to behave in a certain way and to express certain characteristics but not others. You would never feel appreciated for being yourself.

The heart of any team development process is an increasing awareness of who is 'really there'. The potential for confusion in a repressed, rigidly controlled team is immense. Since there is no place for any of the suppositions to be checked, interpersonal relationships depend on what members *suppose* about each other. There is very little contact.

Trapped and de-energized

Members of such teams are often unhappy in their work despite not knowing why. Since people's imagination of their character is never expressed, it cannot be confirmed or refuted. Expressed or not, attitudes are acquired the moment a new team member attends his or her first meeting. A healthy, creative and vigorous team will insist that these attitudes be made explicit and checked.

Inappropriate and out-of-date attitudes can also drain energy and the ability to achieve. Gifted young tennis players find it difficult to beat a top seed, not only because they think the top seed has more experience but also because they rarely believe themselves to be as good. When they learn that a player of even lower rank than they has beaten that top seed, the youngsters acquire a new attitude and will play a much closer match against the same player next time. Success breeds success precisely because successful individuals or successful teams have a clear image of their strength.

The way out

What we see and hear can be the basis for assumptions and hypotheses but, in many cases, these need to be voiced and verified before taking any definitive action. I once watched George Brown working with a member of a group who had been smiling while talking about something quite serious. Taking a facilitator's role, George interrupted her for a moment to check: 'You're smiling now. . . . Is something funny? Are you happy? Do you have a secret?'—making explicit both the dissonance between the story and the person's facial expression and a number of possible conclusions he might draw.

We sometimes use a Gestalt exercise called 'See . . . Imagine . . . Feel . . .' to underline the speed at which people normally jump to and act upon, conclusions. It is one we first saw used by the late Janet Zuckerman at the

Esalen Institute, during the 1970s. In three parts, the first consists of the team walking around making statements about each other that begin with the words 'I see you ...'—for instance, 'I see you have your hands in your pockets'. The second section, the hypothesis stage, involves adding an 'I imagine ...' statement—for instance, 'I see you have your hands in your pockets and I imagine you are relaxed'. The final stage returns to descriptive feedback and reports a physical or emotional response. 'I see you have your hands in your pockets, I imagine you're relaxed and I feel surprised.' There is no fourth part to the exercise but, in fact, what we *do* subsequently is based on or at least affected by what we feel.

It is the second stage of this process that is often the least conscious. Yet as long as we are not conscious of our assumptions, we are never going to check them and any contact we may feel with the rest of the team will be largely unreal. This brings us back to the paradox there is around trust. In order to make contact we must already find the courage to check some of our assumptions about the basic intention or motivation behind what the other team member is doing.

If you said 'I see you looking at the floor every time I speak to you, George. If I was doing that I would be showing that I was angry or not wanting to be there. Could I ask what's going on with you right now?', one of three things could then happen. You may get confirmation, in which case you have made contact and can explore your relationship further; you may get a surprised response, such as 'I was just thinking about what you were saying'; or you may get an apparently angry denial, still without the person looking at you, in which case you have to continue stating the obvious and making your assumptions overt. At least you will be modelling clear behaviour to the rest of the team and the likelihood is that someone else will eventually join you in your efforts, with more success.

INTERPRETATIONS

When we first introduce the meeting review questions—What precisely did you notice? What did you feel? What if anything do you want to change?—to a Ford engineering team the second question is always misunderstood. Someone will jump straight in with an opinion: 'Well, I felt that we did pretty well' or 'I felt that the leadership was quite strong'. We point out that these are opinions, not feelings, and although the expression of opinions is the only way to solve the problem, in the context of feedback on the way they performed their task, the most effective route is descriptive feedback. Anything else can lead to a long discussion. ('I felt the leadership was strong' might produce 'I'm not so sure', 'I think it was', 'No it wasn't' and 'What do you mean by "strong"?' just for a start).

However, even in this context, an opinion can be a valuable clue to what happened. Hang on to it and see if you can remember an example— something that you actually saw or heard on which your opinion is at least partially based—and you will be back into descriptive feedback. (This can produce 'I thought the leader was strong when he banged his hand on the table and said "Just a minute, I would like us to get back to the point here".' The facilitator can then extricate the descriptive feedback: 'Okay, so what you noticed was that the leader banged his hand on the table and said "Just a minute, I would like us to get back to the point here".' For the time being opinions are left out. They can be addressed in answer to the last question: 'What if anything do you want to change?')

Opinions and interpretations of other team members' performances constitute a major cause of meetings running over time unless they are expressed under the 'See .... Imagine .... Feel ....' format. Usually offered as a criticism and an implied desire for change, the interpretation is then disputed and thereby actually hinders change. Interpretations also have a more subtle drawback even if they turn out to be correct, which is that they deprive the recipient from discovering his or her own patterns of behaviour. This may not seem to matter much but it reflects a significant philosophical difference between the Gestalt approach and psychoanalysis.

In psychoanalysis, the objective is to understand something first and experience it afterwards. In Gestalt, we experience first and come to understand afterwards. Where the psychoanalysts get their patients to interpret their experience by asking the question 'Why?', Gestalt therapists help their clients to go deeper into their experience by asking the questions 'What?' and 'How?' and by using the present tense: 'What are you doing?' and 'How are you doing that?'. 'The problem with psychoanalysis is that the history you get is the history in that person's eyes,' says Judith Brown. 'I get history from the way they act, not from what they say.'

Family therapist Virginia Satir once said: 'whenever I find myself making an interpretation, I look for another one.' We believe that interpretations of another team member's experience are always question-able and can be harmful. When they are voiced, the recipient can either agree or disagree—both options causing potential problems. If the person agrees he or she is probably introjecting—accepting someone else's idea of how he or she should be. Should the person disagree, endless justification and counter-justification can follow. A good team leader pushes members to question assumptions they make about themselves or each other. 'One explanation is as good as another,' said George Brown, feigning indifference to a client's self interpretations.

Team respect includes not laying interpretations on each other and appreciating that there are as many realities as there are team members. George tells a story of a wise Middle Eastern khalif, the local judge, who lived in his one-room dwelling with his wife. One day two men came to ask him to settle their dispute about the ownership of a donkey. He asked the first man to tell his story and sat listening quietly. When the man had made his case, he nodded slowly and said: 'You're right. You're right. You're absolutely right.' Then he turned to the other man and asked him to give his account and as the man spoke he listened carefully. When the second man had finished, he nodded slowly and said: 'You're right. You're right. You're absolutely right.' His wife who had been listening in the corner snorted crossly and, despite herself, turned and said to the khalif: 'You stupid old man! They told two completely different stories! How can they both be right?' And the khalif nodded slowly and said: 'You're right. You're right. You're absolutely right.'

Logical analytical thinking and the ability to interpret data is an important part of the creative process. Yet analysing other team members and telling them how they 'really are' blocks contact. Someone in the team—preferably all team members at different times—has to take a more passive facilitative role. Communication and contact are improved by allowing a hypothesis to form based on observable fact and offering both the hypothesis and the fact for consideration, with complete readiness to discard the hypothesis if it is not accepted. Something else can then emerge.

'Give me the data; don't give me judgement!' The senior American member of a European Division finance team appeared to be cross, as he halted the colleague who was busy pontificating, in mid-flow. We pontificate almost by definition when we forget the existence of multiple realities and judge only on the basis of our own. There are many ways to perceive the team and all are equally valid. Eventually, however, one specific view may be imposed, crystallize and become the team's self-image. Someone new who openly questions or disregards this view and the related team norms evokes hostility.

ADVICE

Bias or an established viewpoint always leads to evaluative feedback and a certainty as to what people should do. This blocks understanding and contact and wastes a great deal of time. Few things are more fruitless than discussions in which team members give each other advice and refute such advice. Anyone who tells people what to do can be blamed when things go wrong. Giving advice to someone means taking responsibility for that person's actions and the result. The facilitator should never get drawn into this role and nor should consultants, who nonetheless are often asked to give advice. In accepting the responsibility they get caught in the system and can no longer maintain a metaperspective. Providing a context for decision making—perhaps by helping the client to redefine the problem—ensures that it remains the client's responsibility to respond. This is what Fritz Perls (1971: 125) meant by helping his clients move 'from environmental support to self-support'.

What the client or the team leader sees as the problem and wants help to remove is always a symptom of some deeper pattern. As long as this pattern is denied, it will soon reassert itself after the symptom has been removed. Our job is to help him or her to stay with the problem and explore it, not to make it temporarily disappear. The athlete who came from a club where open discussion was valued and stumbled against his new team's norm of denial—denial of conflict, dissatisfaction and freedom to question—was soon depended on by others in the team to make disagreement overt. Before his arrival, any disagreement had been expressed covertly in cliques away from the team forum, resulting in a lack of trust and respect.

The pattern was the same in a team that had a charismatic leader and one carefully pragmatic questioning plodder who became the butt of jokes but in fact provided the missing element in the team structure. In both cases we were invited to 'deal with the problem character' and in both cases we focused instead on making the team's system and patterns of behaviour more explicit. Both the managers concerned supported this switch, with far-reaching positive results. Not all managers have the confidence and courage to 'stay with the process', however. The prospect of examining the issue in the context of the team as a whole, rather than working with the designated person in isolation, can be daunting. In the next three chapters we suggest some ways in which the task may be made easier.

11

Speaking skills

INTERACTION AND CONTACT

Although team members may 'communicate' without making contact, there is no contact without communication and no chance of good team-work. Communication fails or results in confusion when the speaker's intended or overt message is different to the one received. The gap between the two is created by the way the message is conveyed, the way it is received or (often) a combination of the two.

In the best teams, verbal communication between members includes certain norms of speaking, questioning and listening, which we explore in the next three chapters. These norms all bring clarity, increase contact and thereby ensure the development of effective teamwork. They reduce time spent arguing or talking at cross-purposes and both shorten and enliven team meetings. They are all skills that can be learned through informed facilitation. Below are a number of interactive speaking skills, listed in no particular order.

Talk, not chat

When team members talk clearly about their experience in relation to a topic being discussed, they are contributing to the team and making contact with other team members. 'Chat,' on the other hand, is a form of speech that gives little or no information about the speaker's experience, relating instead stories about someone else doing something else somewhere else.

Lacking the power to make contact, chat either sends people to sleep or, conversely, makes them restless. As often as not people who chat are unaware of this and assume that whatever they say is of interest to everyone else. They are often accused of 'loving the sound of their own voices' or of 'suffering from an acute case of verbal diarrhoea'. In fact, they tend to be so insensitive that if they were told this to their faces their response would be to laugh and reply at some length. Chat is what Joseph Zinker would call 'confluent conversation' (Zinker 1978: 68). People who chat in meetings rarely have any sense of boundaries. They are so unaware of the differences between themselves and the other team members that they have no idea when to stop. These people, especially if they hold a senior rank, take up a high proportion of available air time and unless they are checked they can drain all enjoyment from the team experience.

Of course, they are not entirely to blame and, from a systems perspective, we would wonder what function they were serving for the rest of the team. What do they imagine might happen if the chatting stopped? Similar inane conversation is common in many families where it is preferred to silence and awareness of the weighty issues that are *not* being discussed. Airspace is filled with chat in order to avoid contact.

When team members decide they want to change the subject, various means are available. The simplest is to interrupt giving some descriptive feedback, along the lines of 'I notice that for the past three minutes you have been telling a story that you've told us before and that doesn't involve anyone present. My attention is beginning to drift and I'd like to move on. Could I check how others are feeling right now?' Other options are more brutal: turning chairs away from the table, getting up and walking in and out of the room and, if all else fails, pulling faces. Once the speaker has finally got the message, there needs to be a discussion of this particular norm. This will involve 'the chat merchant' and the rest of the team in making some new agreements.

'Language may distort, delete or generalise ... experience' (Korb 1989: 101). Chat is not always confluent. It can also be used as deflection by the team member who still finds contact with others too threatening. Deflection, as we pointed out earlier,* is either a way to avoid an uncomfortable truth or a sliding away from emotion. An example of the latter is Zinker's story (1978: 154) of a group member arriving very late for a meeting and announcing that he had just smashed his car. Before anyone could express

---

*Confluence, deflection and the other interruptions of contact were described in Chapter 5.

concern and check how the man was feeling, someone jumped in with the question. 'Oh! What sort of car was it?'

Fritz Perls would sometimes consciously use language to shock his group participants if he thought that, by doing so, he could shake them out of their deflections and into direct human contact with others. He called heavy intellectualization 'elephant shit', explanations 'bull shit' and chat 'chicken shit'. Perls did not mince words and could be brutal when faced with those who did. Yet, when group members struggled to stay with their confusion and discomfort and *not* slide away into triteness, he would show an extraordinary gentleness. It is a lesson would-be facilitators need to learn—when and how to challenge the 'chicken shit', when it can help to interrupt with the words 'That doesn't mean anything to me. How would you say that directly?' or 'What exactly is your experience right now?'.

Look at the person you're talking to

Books on body language suggesting that a certain posture indicates a specific non-verbal message ignore the fact that any message depends as much on the person receiving it as it does on the person sending. The social scientist Edmund Sapir told the story of an American diplomat on his first posting abroad, finding himself in the office of a senior Arab official somewhere in North Africa. Neither he nor his host was aware of the cultural difference between Americans and Arabs that exists in the norms of physical proximity. Arabs prefer to stand closer to each other than do Americans. The result was that when the Arab greeted and started talking to the American, the American felt uncomfortable and stepped back. And when the American stepped back, the Arab felt uneasy and took a step forward. For the next few minutes, an observer would have seen the Arab apparently chasing the American around his office. The Arab felt the American was stand-offish, the American felt the Arab was pushy. Neither was right. Each was giving a message to the other quite different to the one intended, while each was quite fruitlessly attempting to make contact. Body language is cultural and the same posture or movement may indicate completely different things to different people in different parts of the same country. In fact, there are as many completely idiosyncratic variances of movement and posture as there are variations of voice quality. We can recognize a particular team member's way of walking from a great distance as easily as we can recognize his or her voice with our eyes closed.

Looking out of the window while talking to other team members may not indicate a lack of interest in either them or the message but it is normally interpreted as such in our society. Despite the fact that I sometimes find it difficult to express a complicated train of thought while looking directly at the person to whom I am talking, it is hard to make contact with that person and get my message across unless I do. When I talk while looking at the ceiling. I am in an abstract world and not fully available to the team. Even when lecturing, I lose contact but in a normal team discussion it becomes intolerable. Eventually I trap everyone in a 'middle zone'. I once heard the member of one team explode with frustration: 'Mark! For God's sake *look* at us when you talk! You sound as if you are reading from some impossible book!'. Many teams make things worse by allowing a meeting room to be arranged so that no member can see more than half of the team. In these circumstances, any discussion produces less creative ideas than it would do otherwise. This is the problem with most boardroom tables and has been discussed in Chapter 8.

A team that has adopted descriptive feedback and has done the 'see ... imagine ... feel ...' exercise mentioned in Chapter 10 has the tools to check with team members who decline to look at the person to whom they are speaking: 'John, I notice you're looking out of the window as you talk to me. I'm finding it difficult to concentrate on what you're saying. Do you need more time to think this out?'. Statements and a question of this kind quickly re-establish contact.

Who looks at whom during a meeting (and therefore who appears to speak and listen to whom) is of considerable interest to a facilitator or a consultant. In fact, *scan the whole circle when addressing the team* is another speaking skill and the leader or member who addresses one person while speaking should check the message that he or she is understood to give. Even the most diligent 'scanners' in the team may forget to look at the two people sitting on either side of them—which is why, in most teams, a chair beside the team leader can be the best place for someone who does not want to be noticed.

Speak up

The two of us have an ongoing argument. He says I mumble, I say he is deaf. Unfortunately, I have to admit in support of his contention that certain other members of my family *do* mumble (such habits are often cultural) and that I do sometimes speak before I am sure of what I want to say. When I do this I probably am mumbling to myself as I think things out. This would be all right if I was alone in the fields but does not work so well in conversation or in a team meeting.

Many established relationships within the team will have set norms of their own. I have seen Judith Brown lead a pairs session where one partner had a habit of speaking while the other was still talking, with the result that his words were often not heard. Judith helped the man become aware of what he was doing by asking him to exaggerate his behaviour by speaking to his partner with a cushion held over *his* face. One senior executive committee we worked with had eight men and one woman and it was the woman who held everyone's attention, simply by speaking so low that everyone was hunched over the table, straining to hear. She appeared to offer contact but ultimately always withheld it. Whether done consciously or not, such behaviour can drive everyone crazy.

Occasionally use the person's name

I recently watched a team of 28 people sitting in a circle, lethargically discussing some internal concern. The meeting had been going on for some time when one team member, who had himself been fairly quiet, suddenly turned to another and said: 'Luke, I'd like to hear your views on that.' Despite the fact that my name is John, the tone of voice and the use of Luke's name made my attention snap back. Everyone turned to look expectantly at Luke. Contact had been re-established.

If an unknown voice calls your name in the street, you will probably look around to check if the person is shouting at you. In a team sport, the use of names is the single most effective way to transmit a message. Sitting in the Tottenham dug-out with Keith Burkinshaw, the manager, was an electrifying experience. He would shout so long and loud that he was barely able to speak when he returned to the locker room and usually left the half-time talk to his assistant, Peter Shreeve. During the match Keith would vent his exasperation and shout complex instructions, throwing up his arms in despair when any of his players did anything wrong. His instructions were always lost in waves of noise from the crowd but occasionally a player would hear his name and show some form of reaction.

(This used to remind me of a Gary Larsen two-picture cartoon of a woman talking to her dog. The first picture was entitled 'What Rover's

mistress said' and showed the woman, her finger raised, giving a complicated message along the lines of 'Now, Rover, you be a good dog. You
guard the house. If anyone comes to the door, you bark. Do you hear me?'
The second picture was entitled 'What Rover heard' and had one small
balloon saying 'Rover!'.)

On joining a team, a member's first step to make contact is to give his or
her name. In sports teams particularly, this is sometimes replaced by a
nickname. This is acquired through some mutual team experience and can
be a trigger that evokes identification with the team, both for the team
member concerned and any team member who uses it.

Speak to people present, not about them

It is possible for two team members to be so angry (or embarrassed or
confused or frightened) in the presence of each other, that they refuse to
address each other directly, even during a team meeting. If they do have
anything to say, it is conveyed through a third party, usually the leader,
without looking at the person concerned. A good facilitator makes this
avoidance of contact explicit but without forcing the issue.

Often, however, the 'talking about' is unintentional. When I am asked
'How do you feel when Ann leaves the meeting early?' I could easily say,
'Angry. She's always doing it,' while Ann is sitting across the table from me.
It is the point at which I use the word 'she' that I have gone off course.
'Angry' is information about myself, given in response to the third person's
question. 'She's always doing it' is a statement about Ann and could be
made directly to her. If someone taking a facilitator's role draws my
attention to this by saying 'Tell her!', I will probably back-track, turn to
Ann and say: 'Ann, you always seem to be leaving the meeting early and I
get angry when you do that.' Speaking directly to other team members
rather than about them to a third party ensures contact.

When team members are unable to see each other during a meeting, they
are more likely to talk about than to each other but the likelihood is further
increased when the team leader sits at the head of a boardroom table, opens
the proceedings and 'controls' the meeting. Some team leaders still believe
that addressing all remarks 'through the chair' is the only way to keep a
meeting on target. This reduces discussion to a series of dialogues between
different team members and the leader, with the result that team members
inevitably talk about, rather than to, each other.

When direct contact between team members is minimized or blocked, there is little opportunity for the growth of either respect or trust. Some team members will lean forwards or backwards so that they may at least see the person who is speaking but a keen observer of such teams will probably surmise that just as many people are deliberately keeping out of view. Such teams are often plagued with hidden agendas and undeclared political alliances.

Another distinguishing quality of these teams is that team members disperse into small cliques and talk about those who are not there. Irrespective of whether this is gossip relating to what the person is reputed to have done or a report of something the person did when the speaker was there, it is a drain on team spirit. Even where appreciation is being expressed, the potential for team development is lost if the same things are not said directly to the person concerned.

In an off-site workshop, where we have already worked with the team for a period of time or in a facilitators' training programme group, we might help people to talk to rather than about another member, even when that member is absent. Sometimes an issue concerns an absent member but appears to have more to do with the attitudes of the people who are there than with the person who is absent. Occasionally, the person concerned has left the team altogether but some unfinished issues remain.

In such cases, the speaker is clearly projecting and the facilitator's role is to make this explicit so that the projection can be re-owned. The quickest, least demanding way to do this is to ask the speaker to repeat his or her gripe or appreciation and then imagine and say what the person concerned would say in reply. The advanced version of this, which we might use where the issue is central to the team's experience, is the Gestalt dialogue exercise* described on page 74. Here the speaker talks to his or her projection, as if that person was sitting in the chair opposite. The speaker then switches chairs, carrying out an imagined dialogue with the absent member. One of the big advantages of this format is that the person volunteering to do the exercise discovers his or her own solutions to the unfinished business with the absent team member, without explanation or advice from anyone else.

*This exercise is described in full in Syer and Connolly (1984: 113)

Say 'I', rather than 'we', 'you', 'people', 'one', 'the team', etc.

When expressing an opinion or reporting how I feel, my words will have a far greater impact if I begin my sentence with 'I' rather than these other pronouns and collective nouns. Each of them has the effect of placing a veil between my meaning and you, the person I am addressing. If I have made contact with you directly in the past, you will feel the difference and wonder what is the matter. Loss of contact with a team member who has suddenly retreated behind 'we', 'you' or 'one' has its parallels with Wordsworth's experience *vis-à-vis* nature, (see p. 91).

In using these locutions, you may retain my interest and attention—and as a *facilitator* I would myself be interrupting contact if I always insisted that someone relating something difficult and personal switch from 'you' (as in 'you know, you feel quite sad when that sort of thing happens to you') to 'I'. However, often I shall not be quite sure that I understand you. *Who* is this 'we', this 'you', this 'one'? How do you know what 'the team' is feeling? Does 'the team' feel anything?

In nearly all cases, people using such idioms as 'we', 'you' or 'the team' are in some way talking about themselves. Normally, if asked 'And you? Where are you in all this?', they are quick to correct themselves. These forms of speech can be so habitual that such a question comes as a surprise. The team member who begins 'People aren't sure whether ...' and is interrupted by the question 'And you? are *you* sure?', usually laughs in surprise. 'Oh! ... No. That's right. *I'm* not sure. ...'

When Ossie Ardiles said 'The trouble is that we're not confident' (see p. 217), he was talking about his own experience not the team's—even though he was personally a touchstone for confidence within the team. When pushed, he admitted that he was not always confident in the support of certain other players in the team. His *own* performance was suffering through this lack of confidence because he thought he had less viable options when he had the ball. To that extent, it made no difference whether the lack of confidence was in himself or in other players. Having established this the remainder of the linguistic confusion could be untangled. 'From whom specifically would you like more support?' we asked. And 'If [player X] was to play "confidently", in a way that would support you, what would he be doing? Tell him now.' Then we asked this player to respond—a response that included telling Ossie what he needed from Ossie, to make the identified situation work.

Ossie Ardiles was trained as a lawyer before becoming a professional footballer. Lawyers, like business people, are taught to be sharply rational and perhaps sometimes also learn to block the connection to their experience of contact—at least in certain circumstances within a work setting. Contact carries excitement as an in-built component and the experience of excitement—as of all feelings—can have unpredictable results. To open oneself to the unpredictable is to allow the possibility of losing control and for many of us this constitutes a major threat. (Or to be congruent, I should write 'I feel vulnerable when I lose control—and I imagine many other people do as well.') Using such words as 'we', 'you' or 'one' inhibits real contact and thereby lessens the possibility of overwhelming excitement. The trouble is that the rest of the team may lose interest or get confused and may confuse me with my role.

Interrupting excitement or creating distance from our own experience, by using the words 'we', 'you' or 'people' instead of 'I', is one form of projection. A statement that begins with 'people' get upset when you ...' usually means 'I get upset when you ...' but saying 'people' allows me to avoid responsibility for my feelings or at least suggest that I'm no different from anyone else. Similarly, when your partner shouts 'Now look at what you've made me do!', that person is obviously hiding responsibility for his or her actions and putting it on you. A clearer message would be 'Now I'm so angry that I've dropped the plates!'

Say 'I' instead of 'it'

Using the word 'it' can also be a way of separating myself from and not taking responsibility for my experience. The absence of any up-front proper subject to the statement not only withholds clear contact with the person to whom I am speaking but also avoids contact with myself.

For instance, saying 'It's lucky we didn't follow your suggestion' avoids making explicit the real message, which is 'I'm glad we didn't follow your suggestion'. Or 'It makes me uncomfortable when Sheila tells those stories' suggests that some vague unknown force, if not Sheila herself, is responsible for my feelings, whereas, in fact, irrespective of what Sheila does, I am always responsible for my response. In such a case, a good facilitator will ask 'Have you any idea what the "it" might be?' so that the speaker may get in touch with any deeper feelings, beneath the polite protest, that are blocking the relationship. This could provoke something as dramatic as 'I detest you Sheila' (which may well astonish the speaker as much as Sheila) but by taking responsibility in this way, the speaker discovers a wide-shifting range of personal responses and is able to begin building an honest relationship.

The word 'it' can also cause confusion in other contexts. 'We've learned to live with it,' one supervisor explained wearily when talking about the difficulties of working with a particular colleague. 'Tell me more about this "it",' I asked. 'Can you get a metaphor or a picture that captures the experience?'

An even more subtle form of distancing myself from involvement and contact is to drop the word 'I' in such statements as 'See what happens'. These belong to a category George and Judith Brown call 'magic talk'—'it' does not happen. The responsible statement is 'See what I do'.

Say 'I would like you to . . .' rather than 'you should . . .' or 'we should . . .'

'You should . . .' is invariably followed by an opinion, which can lead to a long debilitating discussion, outright argument or silent rebuttal. 'I would like . . .', on the other hand, is followed by a statement that makes my needs (or at least what I want) explicit. Being a clear descriptive statement, 'I would like . . .' makes contact and, when substituted for a 'You should . . .' statement, will shorten meeting time considerably.

The opinion that follows the words 'you should' comes in the form of advice, which is implicitly offered 'for your own good'. However, my hidden message is nearly always that I am not happy and I want you to change. Provided that I give this message up front, you can choose whether or not to comply.

Make a statement before asking a question

Behind every question is a statement. When I make this statement before asking my question, you will find it much easier to answer: the statement clarifies the question. I will also have shown something of myself in the process, which probably makes you more inclined to reveal your own position.

This is why, at the courses and workshops we lead, we often draw people back into a circle after a pairs, threes or small group exercise and ask 'any statements? any discoveries? any excitements?' rather than 'any questions?'. We expect questions and are happy to answer them but the issue becomes more interesting when you make clear your response to the exercise first. Often you will have decided what you believe, but instead of this being clear we go round in tiresome circles of vague question and unsatisfactory response. When this happens or when we are unclear as to the questioner's message or concern, we ask: 'What's the statement behind your question?' Steve Marcus, one of the staff on the Confluent Education programme at UCSB, used to warn his students, 'If you ask a question, be sure it's one you're prepared to answer', which takes the principle still further.

'But' negates

'I think you've met nearly all your targets this year but . . .' Any team leader beginning an assessment session this way provokes elation, deflation and frustration in the span of a single sentence. Listen carefully to any typical team discussion and you will notice that the same sentence construction is used repeatedly. If challenged, the speaker would probably defend the sentence as a polite formula but it always deflates the person on the receiving end. The formula restrains team development, showing careless-ness at best and usually a lack of respect. This is another example of one team member 'cancelling out' another.

In a book addressed to the aspiring manager, Crosby (1984: 156) shows how the same formula can be used to kill an idea or an initiative. It is a familiar example: 'Quality is important but don't forget we still have to sell things.' As he then points out, '[just] one phrase [will] turn the successful process back into the same old thing'. The word 'but' negates all that goes before it. One's attention immediately shifts to the real message, which is contained in the second half of the sentence. At best, this formula shows indecisiveness or lack of conviction, neither of which is easy for a sub-ordinate to handle.

In a team meeting with a designated facilitator or where it has become a norm for listening members to pick up this role, as and when required, someone can volunteer to help the speaker to work with the underlying dilemma. This might involve exaggerating first one position and then the other, keeping the word 'but' but reversing the two halves of the statement or even staying with the dilemma and restating the double-barrelled sentence with the word 'and' replacing 'but'. Any of these interventions will help the speaker to re-establish contact.

Make responsible 'I' statements

Even the pronoun 'I' can be used in a way that avoids responsibility. The apologetic statement, 'I'm afraid I can't attend the next team meeting as I have to go to see the people in Brussels that day', avoids responsibility on two counts. The responsible statement would be 'I'm not coming to the next team meeting as I want to see the people in Brussels that day'. This might be considered rude or provocative but in fact is the truth. Many teams prefer to avoid challenges of this sort but they are not teams that have any deep level of trust and are not, therefore, teams in which people choose to stay very long.

'I'm guilty for not returning your call' is another example, given by Korb (1989: 42), of an 'I' statement that ducks responsibility, this one being tied in to retroflection. (I punish myself before you get a chance to do so, thereby depriving you of expressing disappointment or irritation in a contactful way.) Fake humility is tricky to pin down and it takes a good ear to pick up the deliberate block to contact presented by this sort of 'confession'. Retroflection *is* tricky. In this case a good facilitator might suggest: 'How about trying, "I decided not to return your call"?'

Even some of the examples of personal response that we gave earlier can be made more responsibly. For instance, loudly exclaiming 'I'm bored', when Joan takes a deep breath between two parts of a long rambling proposal, is less responsible (and more disruptive) than something like 'I'm not paying any attention any longer, Joan. I would like you to stop there for a while. Could I check how the rest of us feel?'

Say 'I won't ...' rather than 'I can't ...'

This is a special case of the previous speaking skill. We know from our workshop experience that it is a suggestion that is often resisted, probably because it requires the speaker to take responsibility for his or her own experience. However, when a team member confides 'My problem is that I can't speak to Sid', the underlying statement is, for whatever reason, 'I *won't* speak to Sid'—the speaker is making a choice. A facilitator's response might be 'And if you *were* to speak to him ...?'. Or, responding to the statement being presented as a problem, the question might be 'And how does it serve you not to talk to Sid?', on the principle that problems are often attempted solutions to other problems.

Untie reification

'Reification' is the act of using language to turn a process into a thing. An example of this would be 'our relationship is never going to work properly'. This statement suggests that what each of us does in relation to the other is actually a thing with a life and intention of its own. Fritz Perls encouraged his clients to experiment with the use of language and experience the change in their feelings when changing reified nouns into pronouns.

Don't try

When I visited the Esalen Institute early in 1979 most of the staff I had known previously were no longer there. Fritz Perls had died nine years previously, Will Shulz had moved up the coast and Ida Rolf was no longer around. However, I attended workshops led by Dick Price, Ken Dychtwald and George Leonard, all early leaders in the human potential movement. Gregory Bateson was still in residence and lent me his van to drive to San Francisco one weekend and I attended in-house evening sessions with a quartet of formidable trainers—Betty Fuller, Janet Zuckerman, Betty Dingwall and Janet Lederman. It was one of these four women who gave the icy response 'trying sucks!' when I promised to try to do something.

It took me a while to digest this experience but the principle is simple: either I do something or I do not. To say 'I'm going to try to do ...' it is actually more insulting than the rejoinder 'trying sucks!'. When I said 'I'm going to try ...' there was so little energy in my choice of words that it was clear to everyone but me that I had no intention of doing it at all. The insult was in the off-handedness of my lie.

Say 'when ...' not 'if ...'

The promise that I shall do something for the team if something or other happens also avoids commitment. 'I'll read your report, if I get time' will produce little confidence in my intention. This statement contains a double avoidance of responsibility: that implied by the 'if' and that implied by the 'get'. The more affirmative sentence would be: 'I will read your report, when I make time.' Even this is not perfect but now that the speaker has taken responsibility for action, the team member being addressed can at least push for greater precision so that the 'when I make time' is eventually changed to a definite date.

Reconsider 'either–or' statements

At best, either–or thinking and speech patterns are limiting. The statements 'either we finish this project tonight or we forget it' and 'either he leaves or I leave' suggest a low tolerance of ambiguity, where such tolerance can be a valuable source of creativity.

Yet, while certain 'either–or' statements carry an implication of power-lessness and frustration, behind them is often a misuse of power and the desire to create division. Responsibility for the Trojan War can be traced back to Discord, the Fury who threw a golden apple with the inscription 'FOR THE MOST BEAUTIFUL' into the midst of the Greek goddesses, Aphrodite, Hera and Athena.* The 'either–or' statement creates the same unnecessary polarization, causing team members to take sides against each other, where no conflict existed before. The situation is best defused by focusing on the saboteur's motive.

Avoid generalizations

A child's common whining refrain begins 'Why do we always have to . . .?' or 'Why can't we ever . . .?'. The generalizations 'always', 'ever', 'never', 'anyone', 'no one' and 'everyone' often occur in adult speech too. 'You always say that', 'Stuart never says anything in one word if six will do', 'Everyone accuses me of that' are commonly heard in everyday conversation in the office and carry the same whining qualities as the child's complaints. Such speech patterns become highly irritating to other team members, who are constantly obliged to contest the generalization and do not feel seen or heard. Speaking this way blocks contact.

*Paris, prince of Troy, was asked to settle their argument. When he chose Aphrodite, she gave him Helen as a reward—the most beautiful woman in the world and wife of Greek prince Menelaus.

A further problem with generalization (as well as abstractions) is that, although two team members may be quite honest with each other, they may each hold quite different pictures of the situation they are discussing and of any decision they may eventually reach. In such cases, a facilitator needs to be particularly clear. If a previously silent team member is pushed to speak and suddenly bursts out 'I find it difficult to say anything!', the generalization needs to be checked—if not, each member projects his or her own interpretation on the speaker. 'Paul,' the facilitator might say, 'I don't know if you mean "I find it difficult to say anything and I'd like to try" or "I find it difficult to say anything and I don't want to". Would you like to say more?'

Reframe problems

Working with Andy Bern, Ted Fairbrace and Mike Holman of the Ford Motor Company, we finished designing the European TOPS (Team Oriented Problem Solving) programme in 1989. When we ran the first course, we encountered an unexpected up-front objection from the engineers participating: they had been told not to use the word 'problem' and did not like the course title. It appeared that a few years earlier an edict had been handed down that the word 'concern' had to be used instead.

We had some sympathy with their objections, primarily from a speaking skills viewpoint. Changing the word 'problem' to 'concern' had been an attempt to reframe or change the way employees thought about situations they encountered. We ourselves had designed an exercise that involved changing the word 'difficulty' into 'challenge' and reframing many problems as skills. When athletes come to us saying they have a problem with concentration or a problem with motivation we ask them to consider concentration and motivation as mental skills, comparable to the technical skills of their sport. This 'reframe' provides a basis for a mental training work programme.

Leave out the 'really'

'Believe me, I really tried!' is one degree less contactful than 'Believe me, I tried', which itself has no chance of making any impact. George Brown says simply: 'I don't believe any statement with "really" in it.' If you find that hard, you may discover you do not trust some of your own assertions—a sure sign that not many other team members do either.

Maintain metaphors

When one team member uses a metaphor to explain something to the rest of the team, others will sometimes build on it. When they do, the original speaker always feels heard, it allows them to empathize with his or her thinking and it brings new associative insights to the team's awareness.

TALKS, PRESENTATIONS AND CONTENT

The way we frame information provides guidelines to its content. Well framed, it allows the listener to respond clearly and constructively and to organize it into an overall picture. There are five such frames: headlines, signposts, boundaries, key points and links.

Headlines

A headline ensures that the relevant information is communicated clearly and concisely at the start of the story. Neither buried in the middle nor saved till the end, it is an 'up-front' statement that makes the subject clear. For example:

- 'The variation in sales last month reflects the introduction of a customer contact procedure, introduced three years ago.'
- 'The root cause of the problem is seasonal labour on the assembly line.'

Signposts

Signposts may also come at the beginning of the communication but indicate structure and direction, rather than subject matter. Sometimes they are used to open a new chapter of information or to indicate the story's change of direction. The headline says, 'this is what I want to talk about'; the signpost says, 'This is how I propose to go about it.' For instance:

- 'Problem solving. First I will describe our methodology, then the need for a company wide standard and finally the reporting format.'

Boundaries

Boundaries are statements which mark the beginning and end of a subtopic. They help the listener to stay in touch with the conversation, compartmentalize information and store it in discrete sections—just as we use discrete files on a computer disk to organize data. For example:

- 'That ends my thoughts on listening. Now let's consider formulating effective questions.'

Key points

Key points are phrases which highlight the main ideas of an explanation or account by using bullet points (or numbering) or they remain within the text, flagged by strong openings. For example:

- 'So the main point is . . .'
- 'Now—and this is important . . .'

Links

These are words or phrases connecting one part of an account to another. They help the listener to understand the relationship between different parts of the communication or the place the communication has in the big picture. For example:

- 'When building a powerful team, it is important to establish consistency and then move on to optimizing performance.'

CONCLUSION

The way we use language determines not just how other team members perceive and interpret us but also how we see others and the world at large. When we speak, we show how we position ourselves in relation to (i) the content of our speech and (ii) those to whom we are speaking. When our context is congruent with that of our listeners, our message is received in the way it was intended. Assumptions we make about the nature of our relationship with others influence the meaning of the message and the degree of contact between us. Roles, social distinctions, race, gender and company grading all affect the way we are perceived by others and are worth considering as we frame our message. They create the context that gives our message meaning.

The bulk of this chapter has described ways in which language can either enhance or interrupt contact between team members. Because making contact demands courage and self-confidence, we sometimes avoid taking responsibility for our own feelings and the messages we want to give. It is then that we use clichés, abstractions and impersonal forms of speech to make insinuations that allow us to keep our distance.

Effective teamwork involves a constant willingness to push at these self-imposed boundaries. Teams achieve this by developing a set of team norms that challenge any lack of clarity. Even the response, 'I feel uncomfortable saying this or doing this', is enough to enhance each team member's experience. The use of descriptive feedback leads the way to effective speaking skills. As each team member takes an increasing degree of responsibility for his or her own statements and response to others, clarity and contact rapidly improve.

12

Questioning skills

Questioning may either enhance or hinder teamwork—both in the context of team development and in the pursuit of a specific team goal. Any team has questioning norms, just as it has norms of speaking and listening. These are the patterns formed by how questions are used, when they are asked, who asks them and to whom they are addressed. Such norms are not usually adopted consciously (although they could and probably should be) but are the result of organizational culture and leadership style. As members become aware of these norms, they gain the opportunity to re-examine them and modify those that do not support their performance.

In this chapter we look at a range of supportive and unsupportive questions in both areas of the team experience—that of the team's patterns of behaviour, response and relationships and that of the team's task. We start with the unsupportive questions.

UNSUPPORTIVE QUESTIONING

Team development questions

Questions with a hidden subtext

These questions inhibit contact because the person addressed knows that some response other than a direct answer is required yet cannot be sure what sort of response that might be. The questions may focus on the individual's emotional experience and relationships or on task performance. In either case they mask a message and are not therefore genuine questions. 'What's wrong now?' carries the underlying accusation 'You're always complaining'. 'Haven't you finished yet?'—a question relating to task rather than emotional experience—carries the message that you should have finished.

Questions with a subtext are never entirely clear to the person to whom they are addressed because they hide more than they reveal. Although one is fully entitled to respond to a question like 'Why are you so upset?' with 'What gives you that impression?'—asking for descriptive feedback—it is easy to get caught up in an interminable 'I'm-not—Yes-you-are—No-I'm-not' type of exchange, without the questioner owning the frustration and petulance that prompted the question in the first place. Such questions are usually put out as bait to provoke an emotional response.

Similarly, the question 'Are you sure?' frequently carries the hidden message '*I'm* not sure' that needs to be challenged. Sometimes it is something in the tone of the speaker's voice that makes one uneasy and leads to the suspicion that the question has a hidden subtext—that there is something relevant, perhaps a strong opinion, that is not being stated. Strictly speaking any question is 'manipulative' in the sense that it is designed to get information without giving any. That is why, in Chapter 11, we suggested that behind every question lies a statement and that communication is usually clearer and more contactful when the statement is made first. What is the questioner's *own* view or experience?

An invitation to offer evaluative feedback—for instance, 'What do you think of her performance?' or 'What do you think of his idea?'—usually masks an opinion that the questioner already holds. Such a question is often asked with genuine interest and when the question is from the team leader or a senior team member to a new or junior member, it can help this person to learn and allow the team to receive a sometimes interesting alternative view that would not otherwise have been expressed. Yet there are other leaders who allow questions after giving instructions but no other response. In this case, team members may ask heavily loaded questions—for instance, 'Don't you think that might be a little complicated?' or 'Do you really think that the London office will accept that idea?'—in the hope that the leader will finally ask for an opinion.

Asking for advice

In the brochure we say we differ from most other consultants: we help to improve teamwork and both personal and team performance but we do not give advice. When it was first printed and we showed it to a friend, the head of human resources in a large insurance company, he had doubts. 'I understand your philosophy,' he said, 'but most managers will come to you looking for advice.' He was right—in the first instance they often do. However, asking for advice (asking for information or feedback is different) is a way to get someone else to do what one can do for oneself *and* take responsibility for the result. Such questions do not support *oneself*. Most of the time, the people concerned have the answers to their own problems and their real need is for some careful questioning that will lead them to discover what these answers are. They then gain confidence and the energy to act. When consultants lose their metaperspective, get caught in their client's story and fall into the trap of giving advice, they are no longer very useful. All they can expect are long explanations of why they are wrong or blind acceptance with little integration with existing team norms.

A prime role for coaches, managers and facilitators is helping team members to take responsibility for their own experience. When they ask for permission to do something or ask what they should do, they abrogate this responsibility. When the manager gives permission or gives advice and things do not work out, the manager will be blamed: it is his or her fault, not theirs.

Asked for advice during a one-to-one conversation with a client, we would normally begin by posing questions designed to help the client review the circumstances and bring them into clearer focus. We might then ask what solutions have been tried already and whether these solutions could be the cause or contribute to the cause of the current dilemma. Sometimes we are invited to accompany the client through his or her working day which allows us to give descriptive feedback and ask further questions (which we call shadowing) or at a team meeting. Should the client still be seeking advice, we could then suggest putting us on the empty chair in the exercise described earlier (see pp. 74 and 234) and giving him- or herself some sensible advice. Our objective throughout is to help untangle unconscious manipulation and help the client to discover his or her own way forward.

Deflective questions

Questions can be used to deflect another team member away from the expression of feeling and the experience of contact. The person who asked

'What sort of car was it?' (p. 230) was clearly unsupportive and was probably reacting to his or her own sense of discomfort. Similarly, the question 'What do you think?' can be used to deflect someone from reporting what he or she feels. When this is done frequently and no one objects, team development becomes a slow process.

'Why?' questions

The question 'why?' is useful in the context of fulfilling a task, particularly in convergent problem solving but in the context of maintenance, it almost always hinders team development. Psychiatrists believe change will come by giving their patients the 'correct interpretation' of their experience, so that they are able to understand it. Their frequent use of the question 'why?' is designed to elicit explanations and thereby understanding. On the other hand, humanistic psychologists believe that an experience can only be properly understood by experiencing or re-experiencing it. They believe that understanding and change only come with awareness. Asking why someone in the team does something or feels something leads straight out of the emotional and kinaesthetic experience and into rationalization. The colloquial expressions 'She's in her head' or 'He's not got his feet on the ground' echo the humanist's view: to rationalizing emotional experience often means losing touch with reality.

Although team development cultivates openness and clarity, all team members have some undeclared needs and agendas even—if not especially—with the people to whom they are closest. In the context of team relationships, 'why?' questions always hide a statement beginning with 'I', that is often a thinly veiled accusation ('Why haven't you finished this on time?', 'Why are you still here?'). This usually evokes appeasement or prevarication from the member being questioned, sometimes defiance but rarely the truth.

At best, this kind of 'why' question produces rationalization after the fact. We learn very early in life that explanations are a marvellous way to avoid experience. Words maintain a distance so there is a gap between the team member's response to the question 'Why?' and his or her actual experience. Explanations do nothing to evoke genuine insight into what one has done and how one did it. They therefore do nothing to facilitate change.

No questions

Many team leaders, focused on achieving their goals, find it difficult to
formulate questions which explore emotional response, relationships or
even patterns of behaviour. My time as a national athlete was under a
gifted coach whose response to being told that there was trouble in the team
was: 'This is none of my business. I expect grown men to sort out their
problems on their own.' His focus was entirely on technique, tactics and
results and he did not seem to realize that his efforts were frequently
sabotaged by other factors. Nevertheless, he was more in touch with his
team than some other leaders we have met. He held team meetings that
were not just lectures; he offered the players an opportunity to make
suggestions and respond to his.

In professional sport and in industry it is not unknown for managers to
ask no questions at all, other than those designed to make sure that the rest
of the team has understood what it has been told. Questioning in the
educational mode of 'leading out'—helping team members to discover and
express their experience—is not part of their repertoire. Even in the context
of tactics they assume they know best and see little point in consulting their
staff—especially those at the lower end of the scale, whom they take to have
a very limited view and understanding of the game or the business. Even
from the team performance angle, this is a mistake. The eyes of the
inexperienced notice more, precisely because of their inability to discriminate and in a business setting the junior employees are often closest to the
customer.

Task development questions

Biased questions

Whereas questions with a subtext, whether focusing on an individual's
task performance or probing his or her relationships within the team,
usually carry an emotional charge, biased questions tend to come from
unquestioned or even unconscious attitudes. Even facilitators or consultants, focusing on the team's interaction, will have a view that is affected
by their own past experience and present concerns. Their choice of
questions and their other interventions will inevitably reflect this bias,
raising team members' awareness in some areas but leaving it dormant in
those areas in which the facilitators or consultants are themselves uncom-

fortable—those areas to which they give little importance and those to which they are blind.

Where the purpose of questioning is to obtain task-related information, the questioner's own beliefs can determine the way the question is asked and thereby bias the response. Valuable information can be discounted because of the questioner's unconscious assumptions and the implicit suggestions that are contained in the question. The way in which the question is couched determines the response that it evokes. This can depend on (i) the vocabulary, (ii) what might be called the 'expression' and (iii) the grammatical structure of the question.

Vocabulary

The way a question is worded may determine or at least affect the response. If I ask my secretary the question 'So how early did Peter leave *today*?', I clearly imply that Peter always leaves early. The chief executive who opens a meeting with the words 'So what's gone wrong in the design department this week?', limits the scope of any response.

This phenomenon is well known and has been the subject of research. In one such project, two groups were shown the same picture of a person standing. The first group was asked the question 'How tall do you think this person is?', while the second group was asked 'How short do you think this person is?'. The first group consistently estimated a greater height than the second, with a difference of 10 inches between the highest estimate of the first group and the lowest estimate of the second. This was consistent with the experiment where two groups viewed the same film and the group that was asked 'How long was that film?' estimated up to 30 minutes longer than the group that was asked 'How short was that film?'.

In a different project, three different groups were shown a film of a motor accident, each group being asked a different question: 'How fast was the first car travelling when it (i) contacted, (ii) hit and (iii) smashed into the other car?'. Estimates of the first group averaged 31 mph, of the second group 34 mph and of the third group 41 mph. And in one other experiment participants were shown a video of a car travelling through the countryside and were then asked 'What colour was the barn?' Despite there being no barn in the video, a number of people said they couldn't remember what colour it was, while a few actually named a specific colour.

Expression

In the context of questioning, 'expression' means the flow (rate, frequency and sequencing) of the questions, the emotional tone and the questioner's underlying attitude—specifically the presence or absence of judgement. Piling one question on another can confuse and upset the person being questioned. It is a way of asserting authority, occasionally used by the maladjusted teacher or a good inquisitor. The questioner maintains control and pushes for a predetermined response, rather than for the relevant knowledge that the person being interrogated may actually possess.

When questions have an emotional bias, the person addressed tends to respond to the underlying emotional message rather than to the overt verbal one. Apparent anger, frustration or disappointment frequently produces an awkward or defensive reply. Questions asked humorously may get a casual response.

Other questions that give a double message are those that imply what the speaker feels you should or should not have done. 'Haven't you finished yet?' contains the question 'Have you finished?' and the statement 'You should have finished'. Such questions can lead to explosive results if used in crisis situations. A senior plant manager questioning a process engineer in this way, when the engineer has just stopped the production line at some personal risk, may get a variety of responses. These could range from outright defiance (a forceful account of all the things that management should have attended to long ago) to cowed incoherence (a mish-mash of pseudo facts that the speaker believes is what the questioner wants to hear). What the questioner will *not* get is a clear comprehensive account of what happened.

Structure

The grammatical structure of a question also helps to determine the message that the questioner will receive. It is in this sense that the structure also biases the question, although as often as not this bias is used to help the member being questioned. We look at this later under 'effective questioning'; here we are concerned with the way question structure can *impede* contact.

Questions are either *open* or *closed* and it is closed questions that—for good or ill—limit the team member's response. They always focus on eliciting specific information. Quite often they determine the concepts and vocabulary that are contained in the answer and they rarely if ever give any opportunity for the person addressed to offer an opinion. The questioner manages this by giving only a restricted option of possible answers.

There are three types of closed question: *yes/no* questions; questions that provide two alternatives (*dichotomous* questions); and *multiple-choice* questions.

YES/NO QUESTIONS

These are the most limiting. When a team leader wants the team to suffer and does this by haranguing one member publicly in front of everyone else, he or she assumes the role of barrack-room lawyer. The victim is backed into a corner by a barrage of yes/no questions that give no chance of explanation or excuse.

'Did you take it?'
'Yes, but ...'
'Did you take it knowingly?'
'Yes, but ...'
'Did you know the rules?'
'Yes, but ...'

The leader has made sure that the victim's answers are entirely framed by the structure of the questions. The 'buts' can never be expressed.

We know of coaches and team leaders who deliberately act this way in certain circumstances but we know others who inhibit team members with their yes/no questions unknowingly and are mystified by the result. The simplest player or staff interview seems to turn into an interrogation. 'I have no trouble talking to the team as a whole,' one well-respected soccer manager confided as we drove to the training ground one morning, 'but I just can't seem to get through to them one-on-one.' Business managers can be exactly the same:

'Did you do all right then?'
'Yes, thanks.'
'Was the plane on time?'
'Yes, it was this week.'
'Did John meet you at the airport?'
'Yes.'

'You don't like him much, do you?'

'No, I don't actually.'

'But you got on all right though did you? No upsets?'

'No. Everything was okay.'

'Well that's the main thing isn't it?'

'Yes, I suppose so.'

(Manager looks at watch)

'Well, if that's all then? Okay? Nothing else right now?'

'No, not really.'

'Right oh. Will you ask Muriel to come in as you pass her desk?'

(Young team member leaves the room. Pause. Muriel comes in)

'That Joe!' exclaims the manager. 'Not a word to say for himself. I can't understand what people see in him.'

DICHOTOMOUS QUESTIONS

These demand an either–or response and have a similar effect to yes/no questions. At Tottenham, the day before a home match, we would all be asked our food preference for the following morning's 11 a.m. meal: 'What do you want to eat tomorrow? Chicken or sole?' Eventually that particular question became multiple choice—'Do you want chicken, sole or omelette?'—but no one ever mentioned vegetables, even though the player who had pushed so hard for the third option had given as his prime argument that he was a vegetarian.

Sometimes the either–or questions are presented as counter-arguments with an appeal to a third party. 'Jeff says we should sell today, Danielle says we should sit it out. Which of them is right?' Whether or not the third party feels able to side-step the issue with the response 'Neither, actually' will depend on his or her status in relation to the other people concerned.

Research appears to suggest that where two options are given, more people will choose the first. One project discovered that when one group of people were asked 'Is the United States running out of oil or does it have plenty?' and another we asked 'Does the United States have plenty of oil or is it running out?', a majority of people in both groups chose the first option.

Alternative questions often fall into the trap of over-simplification, even when the questioner's intentions are the best. They can also give the illusion that clear answers always contain relevant information. If I consult the most experienced people on my team but fail to offer an alternative that corresponds to their position, I will not receive any significant help.

MULTIPLE-CHOICE QUESTIONS

These offer more than two alternatives but still limit the team member's ability to express an opinion. Questionnaires often do give at least three choices rather than two. However, a significant number of people will then choose the middle option—'all right' from 'excellent'/'all right'/'poor' or 'average' from 'very good'/'good'/'average'/'below average'/'bad'—as the safe reply. This is why many closed questions deliberately restrict the choice to two alternatives.

SUMMARY

In summary, closed questions, while having *benefits* that we look at later, are not appropriate when new information is needed nor for discovering the opinions of different team members. They limit the quality of information that is received and often miss important details. Sometimes they even falsify results. One survey that asked parents the question 'What do you think is the most important thing for children to learn to prepare them for life?', found that 60 per cent replied 'To think for themselves' when this appeared as an option on a multiple-choice questionnaire. However, it was later discovered that only 20 per cent of parents put 'To think for themselves' when given an open question without specific options. The same study found that 20 per cent replied 'Obedience' when it was listed in the multiple-choice survey but only 2 per cent gave this reply when asked the open question.

SUPPORTIVE QUESTIONING

Supportive questioning is an integral part of effective teamwork. It is used to enhance performance in two ways. On the one hand, it is the point of entry for anybody—team leader, consultant, facilitator or fellow team member—who wants to increase contact, respect and trust within the team. Used appropriately, it can help team members to focus their attention and heighten their awareness of self and others. This gives them a wider perspective of the team—its identity, its patterns of behaviour and the ways in which it functions. On the other hand, supportive questioning can help team members to frame information and formulate observations and opinions that contribute towards the team's efforts to achieve its goal.

Both forms of supportive questioning are used by the most successful teams because they complement each other. Questions designed to enhance contact are not enough to ensure that the team reaches its objective; questions designed to help the team fulfil its task will not succeed unless the team operates in a contactful way.

In any successful team, team members will give each other descriptive feedback. When the team has someone in the facilitator's role, this person will not only *give* descriptive feedback but will also ask questions to evoke such feedback from the rest of the team. Our three review questions, 'What precisely did you notice?', 'What did you feel?' and 'What, if anything, do you want to change?'—are all designed to improve team development through the use of descriptive feedback. However, in doing so, they also have an immediate impact on task performance.

Team development questions

The first set of supportive questions develop self-awareness, relationships and team identity and are asked by someone who is taking the facilitator's role. This may be the team leader but, unless a discrete section of the meeting is being devoted to team development, it is more likely to be another team member or someone invited from outside the team. In an effective team, this type of questioning reflects an orientation. When the team is together, it allows members to help each other explore and express how they respond to any team situation.

'What?' questions

'What?' questions can serve to heighten awareness of the situation of an individual, of a particular relationship or of the team as a whole. When we are called in to help specifically with team development, we usually find that our clients are answering the question 'What is your problem?' before we have thought of asking it. After some time the torrent of words subsides and we can then ask 'So, what do you want from us?'. As they become more aware of the situation they describe, further 'What?' questions, together with a few 'How?' questions, help the client to think about the problem in new ways. Claire Stratford of the Gestalt Institute of Cleveland once said:

The good consultant is a travel agent: he or she doesn't have the power to determine a destination for the system or the client, nor the power to determine the speed ... it is only possible to show the route.

Any team member feeling out of contact with another has a variety of 'What?' questions available to help re-establish contact. These same questions also serve to help someone who is worrying about some past or future event, by bringing that person back to awareness of the present and of his or her own behaviour. A team member taking the facilitator role might break into a discussion being dominated by the talkative member of the team with the words 'What are you doing now?' and may get the surprised response 'I'm telling a story that I've told before'. (If not, the facilitator might give this information as descriptive feedback.)

Gestalt questions

Common Gestalt questions are 'What are you experiencing now?' or 'Where do you feel that?' (the questions Winifred Rushforth asked on the transatlantic plane, to dispel my fear of flying) or 'What's happening with you?' or 'What's going on with you, right now?'. Fritz Perls would maintain that, in helping an individual to become more present, the three main questions to ask are: 'What are you doing?', 'What are you feeling?' and 'What do you want?'. These allow the individual to stay in touch with what is happening in his or her experience, from moment to moment. In this context, it is worth pointing out that the question 'What should happen?' or 'What should I do?' limits our awareness of both what is happening and what I am doing.

'What?' questions asked in the context of team relationships help the person being questioned to clarify personal perceptions—to explore further without ever feeling manipulated. 'I feel women are my sisters,' said a nurse in a medical team. 'And what are the rules for sisters?' came the interested response. The result, in answering, was not just that the nurse discovered more about herself but also that the rest of the team felt closer to her, many members choosing to say so later.

An off-site session is ideal for furthering the team development process. This is best done by a skilled external facilitator who can make timely interventions and model close attention without any personal agenda. No one exhibits this ability to increase self-awareness through questioning better than George and Judith Brown. The questions come gently but are full of surprises.

R   'I'd really like to go away . . .' (long pause).
JB 'Because if you go away . . .?'

D   'I'm not sure if he means that.'
GB 'Do you have a history of not being sure that people mean what they say?'

N   'I'm really angry . . .'
JB 'How do you know when you're angry?'
N   'My stomach muscles are tight . . .'
JB 'I tighten my stomach muscles.'
N   'I tighten my stomach muscles.'
JB 'I tighten my stomach muscles so that . . .?

P   'I want you to *see* me, George . . .'
GB 'And if I should see you . . . then?'

GB to client sitting beside him, who appeared to be stuck: 'If you had a T-shirt with one thing on the front and another thing on the back, what would the messages be?'

One team of paint shop managers we were observing had been arguing loudly and repetitively for a good half an hour. An older man, of a relatively junior grade, had been sitting stiffly silent, arms tightly crossed, mouth pursed, throughout. Someone in the team noticed and turned to him saying: 'Rod. I know you prefer to keep out of this emotional stuff but you've been quiet for a long time and this matters to me. What *would* you say, if you were to say what you feel?' 'I can't stand it much longer,' came the instant reply; 'I'm getting very angry', and the meeting shifted focus abruptly, as the squabbling was dropped and the deeper issue addressed.

'How?' and 'Where' questions

These carry a similar quality of non-invasiveness while retaining the power to prompt unexpected insights. 'How do you do that?' is a question we ask any athlete who is struggling to improve some technical skill but it is a question that can just as easily help people to become more aware of their mental and emotional patterns and of the way they relate to others in the team.

'*Where* do you feel scared?' Winifred Rushforth's odd question transferred my attention from fear of what might happen in the future (the plane could crash) to interest in what was happening at that particular moment (I was tense, sweating and did not seem to be breathing). 'What?', 'How?' and 'Where?' questions evoke a descriptive response. 'Why?' questions lead to opinions and evaluation.

Task development questions

Our collaboration with Ford Motor Company on the 40-day quality training programme for all Ford engineers in Europe—the Engineering Quality Improvement Programme (EQUIP) and the new 'global' version (FTEP: Ford Technical Education Programme) has produced a library of course material. The *People Skills Manual* that we wrote is a complete book, the skills we describe having been integrated within each 'module' with the technical skills.

Re-reading what we wrote about questioning, it is striking how task-oriented the material is, despite focusing on human interaction. Whereas the first set of supportive questions seeks to develop teamwork *per se*, this set—*task* development questions—is designed to achieve a team objective. The first kind gives attention to the individual's relationship with self, others and the team; the second extracts information for the team from the individual being questioned.

'*What?*', '*Where?*' and '*How?*'

There are many 'What?', 'Where?' and 'How?' questions that fall into this task-oriented category, including such well-known formulae as Lewin's force-field analysis questions 'What is your objective?', 'What helps you achieve it', 'What blocks you from achieving it?', 'How can you reinforce what helps?' and 'How can you reduce the restraining forces?'. These form a subcategory that are overtly goal-oriented and usually addressed at a team brainstorming session. Another variation focuses on successful procedures, asking 'What is going right?', 'How does it go right?', 'Where are we going?', 'What do we achieve by going there?' and 'What is the next step towards this goal?'. All such questions are task-effective because they encourage a variety of answers.

Task-oriented questioning is also the basis for engineering problem-solving methodologies (see p. 182) which use the questions 'What?', 'Where?', 'When?', 'How?' and even 'Why?'. A clear 'problem profile' is established by asking questions like 'What is wrong with what?', 'Where do you see the defect on the object?', 'Where else on the object could you have seen the defect but did not?' and moves on with such precision that if the process is followed correctly, the 'root cause' of the problem is invariably found.

Closed questions

Earlier, under 'unsupportive questioning' (p. 251) we said the vocabulary, 'expression' and structure of questioning could determine the answers received. Specifically, under 'structure', (p. 252) we showed how closed questions with yes/no, alternatives or a multiple choice could bias the response. When used in a task context, this bias has the positive effect of reducing ambiguity and clarifying information. Yes/no questions can narrow the details, once sufficient information has been generated and help discriminate between the significant core and the surrounding dross. A succession of alternative closed questions—'Did the problem begin before or after 21 June?', 'Is it appearing on Line One, Line Two or both?', 'Is it occurring at regular or irregular intervals?'—can clarify by helping a team member give a cogent account of an otherwise complex situation. Although closed questions restrict the amount of information received, even this factor is valuable when the information needs to be categorized and converted into statistically significant data. This is the case when taking a census or when aiming at specific groups of people for marketing initiatives. Closed questions can be used to highlight significant information.

Open questions

Open questions allow people to tell their story in their own way and can result in a far richer haul. There are two types of open question—'narrative' and 'directive': narrative questions allow people to organize their own thought processes, whereas directive questions focus on a particular part of the story. Narrative questioning produces more 'dross' but also allows those questioned to access information that could be bypassed by more direct questioning. This was demonstrated when a group of students were tested after reading a passage about South America. The students were first asked narrative questions (e.g. 'What do you remember about South America?'), then directive questions (e.g. 'What does Peru export?'). It was found that the students had made three times more mistakes under directive questioning than narrative. Some students even gave the wrong answer to a directive question when they had already given the right information in response to a narrative question.

Open questioning may take longer and large parts of the response may be of little interest to the questioner but since the response includes direct experience, accumulated knowledge and personal opinions, it can provide a more detailed and accurate account. These are the questions beloved of the apparently vague and disorganized detective. Their use reflects the belief that we all see the world through different eyes and that subjective opinions are also important. In these circumstances, it is also possible that the people responding will give information that was not specified, that to them is not important or that they would otherwise have hesitated to mention—but which is of considerable importance to the questioner.

When we interview members of a team prior to a team development workshop, we ask open questions. On those occasions our goal is to gather as much information about the team from as many different sources as possible, so that we may subsequently design an appropriate programme. We may arrive with a mixed list of narrative and directive questions but neither of us is attached to getting them all answered. Sooner or later there will be a narrative question—often something of the order of 'So, what is it like for you to be in this team?'—that hits some spot. From there on we just listen, watch and take notes. On the other hand, there are usually a couple of directive questions that we like to get answered by each team member, including 'What is it that you would like to get from this workshop?'. This means that the interview starts with one or two directive questions to set the scene (for instance 'When did you join the team?'), continues with narrative questions until one of them gets things going and finishes with a couple more directive ones.

Where a cross-functional project team calls in experts from different parts of the company, a similar procedure is often followed, although the respondent is faced by a team of questioners, some of whom will ask highly directive questions that relate to their function within the team. Since the visitors have been briefed on what the team needs, they usually arrive with papers and overheads at the ready. A simple narrative question from the team leader is usually all that is required to get the ball rolling.

Questioning for clarification

The cultural and environmental context in which a team operates and its impact on understanding and learning determines both the way people understand questions and the way the questioner interprets their answers. The beliefs, attitudes, attributions and experiences of people being questioned give meaning to what they hear and to what they say. The implication of the answers becomes clearer as the questioner tunes in to the personal context of the response.

This rarely happens overnight but communication eventually improves as team members become more aware of (i) how they obscure the task information they are attempting to convey and (ii) the questioning style they can use to help each other to communicate more clearly.

The most obvious way information gets blurred is through inappropriate use of language. There are countless examples of this but, for the sake of convenience, we group them under three headings: *deletion, generalization* and *distortion*.

Deletion

Team members who are in the habit of deleting are usually trying to simplify their message. Someone may once have told them that they were long-winded or they may assume that the rest of the team is hyper-intelligent and telepathic. Deletion simplifies and codes a message but the message is often incomprehensible without some details of underlying personal experience. The context is all important. Although several people might respond in the same way to an opening question, each is responding in the context of his or her own personal experience. Since meaning is embedded in this context, the response may not be understood without it.

A *comparative* deletion is one where a standard of evaluation is missing, as in 'He's a better salesman' or 'It's best not to force the issue'. This has to prompt the questions 'Better than whom?' or 'Best as compared to what?'.

An *unspecified noun* deletion is one where the subject or object is unstated, as in 'They haven't returned my phone calls' or 'Meetings can be exciting'.

The questions to be asked here are 'Who, specifically?' and 'Which meetings?'.

An *unspecified verb* deletion is one where the lack of any adverbial clause leaves too many possible interpretations, as in 'Jane rejects me'. This prompts the questions 'How?', 'When?' and 'Where?'.

Generalization

Team members who generalize also leave out information but in their case they offer just one experience to represent an entire category. Rather than trace the generalization back to its source, the best line of questioning is to ask for exceptions: 'When doesn't it happen?', 'How can it be avoided?'. Asking for the exceptions will help both the person questioning and the person supplying the information.

Universal generalizations were mentioned in the last chapter. They are signalled by such words as 'all', 'never', 'always' and 'every', as in 'Betty never listens to me' or 'No one tells me the truth'. The response would then be 'What, *never*? Has there ever been a time when she listened?' or 'What would happen if I told you the truth?'.

Imperative generalizations identify a limitation, imply there is no choice or require a particular action as in 'I have to attend every team meeting' or 'You can't run over time when you make presentations'. This time the effective questions would be 'What would happen if you didn't?' and 'What stops you?'.

Distortion

Team members distort the information they are attempting to offer when they include inaccurate opinions, logical processes or conclusions within the framework of their statement. In doing so, they make an unconscious shift in their experience of sensory data. Avoidance of a direct challenge and the use of effective questioning allow those offering information to re-examine and re-evaluate the line of logic and the set of beliefs upon which their conclusions are based. The process allows the questioner to understand the context of the statement better and to decide how best to assess and use the information provided.

Normalization renders an ongoing process static. Actions are obscured by verbs being used as nouns, as in 'I want recognition' or 'Our relationship is improving'. The questions to ask here are 'How do you want to be recognized?' and 'How is your relationship improving?'.

Cause and effect distortions embody the belief that some specific and possibly unrelated stimulus causes a specific experience, as in 'This lecture makes me bored' or 'His voice irritates me'. The effective questions would be 'How do you bore yourself during this lecture?' and 'How does his voice irritate you?'.

Mind reading distortions are assumptions made by the speaker that he or she knows what another person thinks (or feels) without any direct communication, as in 'You never consider my feelings' or 'He should know I really care'. The questions to ask would be 'How do you know?' and 'How should he know?'.

Value judgement distortions are opinions about the order of things that fail to acknowledge that someone else's 'order of things' could be different and equally valid. Such distortions are often signalled by the use of words like 'good', 'bad', 'right' and 'false', as in 'Waterstone's is the only good book shop in town' or 'This is the right way', to which the responses can be 'What makes you say that?' or 'According to whom?'.

... AND ANSWERING

We have already quoted Dr Steve Marcus who once warned his students at the start of a new semester: 'If you ask a question, be sure it's one you are prepared to answer.' He was asking them to become aware of the difference between unsupportive and biased questions on the one hand and effective questions (of both types) on the other. The distinction is crucial. Members of an effective team learn not to suppress contact or skew information by unsupportive questioning and to challenge anyone who forgets. Members who answer a question like 'Why do you always bite my head off every time I speak?' with 'I'm sorry, I didn't mean to' or answer 'What's wrong now?' with 'Nothing' are no help to themselves, the team or the person asking the question. As members work to establish a norm of challenging such questions, the team moves further towards the embodiment of quality.

There is a difference too between an answer and a response. Both can offer information but my response comes from some deeper level within myself and is of corresponding value to the team. In fact, I could choose not to answer you but still communicate my response. Naranjo (1980: 37) gives two such examples: 'I am excited by your question and afraid of answering' and 'I admire your perceptiveness and would like to discuss this with you later'.

CONCLUSION

Team development questioning and task questioning have different objectives. The first is designed to improve contact by helping the respondent to become more self-aware, more aware of others and of relationships within the team and more aware of the identity of the team as a whole. The second is focused on content and helps team members gain clear information from each other, so that the team's objective may be achieved more efficiently. The link between the two is that supportive questioning between team members heightens commitment and appreciation—both to and for each other and for the team's existential mission.

13

Listening skills

A team's communication skills—speaking, questioning, listening and giving feedback—are intricate patterns of behaviour, unique to that team's membership. Who speaks first, who rarely speaks at all, who speaks loudest, who looks out of the window when certain others are speaking, who leans forward, who looks at whom, who is never and who is always interrupted, who is most likely to interrupt, who checks to make sure they have understood before commenting on an idea—are all details of a complex picture. Such patterns have a significant effect on the team's performance and, to a practised observer, suggest where the team is and how it might progress in relation to its potential. However, since the attention of team members is nearly always on the content of communication rather than its form, much of this goes unnoticed.

In point of fact, whereas speaking skills can be recorded, listening skills can only be inferred. Team members cannot know whether the others are listening. If they know each other well, the 'body language' of those listening may give a clue but only their verbal response gives a relatively clear indication. The mother–child argument that goes 'Michael, you're not listening!', 'Yes, I am', 'No you're not' is not resolved until it reaches the stage at which the mother says: 'So, all right, what did I say?' In teams, as in families, members can mistakenly assume that someone never listens or someone else always does—and can react to this with sustained resentment or goodwill—without ever checking out their assumptions. This detracts from both the quality of interpersonal contact and the quality of information exchanged.

Equally, one team member can listen intently to what another is saying, but not hear. Just as some subtleties of intention can be lost in translation from one language to another, so can they be lost as they are transferred from the thought forms and processes of one team member to those of another. The intentions behind our messages are often very different from how these messages are understood. This gap between intention and reception is the source of much misunderstanding and confusion but it does not inhibit action. It is in this sense that the receiver is as important as the sender in deciding what the message means.

Good communication occurs when the speaker and the listener are able to tune in to each other and make contact. In the previous two chapters we have suggested ways in which the speaker may avoid erecting barriers to understanding and how, in what is already an interaction between the two participants, the listener may use questioning to help the speaker to be clear. In this chapter we focus on the mechanics of listening, first on poor practice and then on ways in which listening becomes creative.

POOR LISTENING

Inattention

Poor listening can be temporary or habitual. If I am worried about an ongoing situation at home or am incredibly thirsty, my attention to what you are saying will diminish until I have made a phone call or have quenched my thirst. On the other hand, there are often one or two team members who never seem to listen well.

Speaking and listening are so closely bound together that it is a viable generalization to say that team members who habitually fail to listen are in the same category as those who do not make contact when they speak. The worst cases seem to be shut off in a world of their own. They may smile and nod while you speak but eventually you realize that they must be thinking of something else or are at least deciding or rehearsing what they want to say. When you stop talking they jump in with a complete *non sequitor*, appearing to talk at you or the team and sometimes almost to themselves. The team eventually accuses these characters of being full of hot air, of loving the sound of their own voices and of preaching. Many members feel resentful but the person concerned is rarely aware of these reactions.

Many such characters are isolated by what Smith and Berg (1987: 125) have defined as 'the paradox of intimacy'. For whatever reason, they find it daunting to learn about themselves and this makes it almost impossible for them to make good contact with others. 'Preaching' and 'refusal to listen' are two different ways to maintain distance and avoid feedback from others. Whereas direct speech is a way to connect with oneself and others and listening is a way to understand oneself and others, these team members have difficulty doing either. Their membership of the team indicates that either (a) there is some strong constricting factor that prevents them leaving or being thrown out or, more often, (b) that they are a valuable source of information to the team and can function more normally on a one-to-one basis.

Selective attention

If such characters are rare, there are others who only listen for the remark that gives the opportunity to say what they want to say. They too, while looking for a way in, make no attempt at contact and hear nothing. Still others may be more bluntly uncaring of appearances, show their impatience and pitch in with their own ideas the moment the person speaking takes a breath. The only difference between them and the 'preachers' is that they are still addressing the same topic.

It only takes a few team members to behave like this, for the problem to escalate. An impression grows that one has to fight for air time. Voices become louder as more people talk at once and many interesting ideas are lost. Meetings become ragged, never staying long on the key point of discussion, jumping from proposal to proposal as one idea is shouted over another and drifting from topic to topic. Eventually these meetings lose all dynamism and creativity as those who get interrupted stop trying. Goodwill is eroded and dedicated team members stop competing, go silent and become increasingly disillusioned.

Many team leaders contribute to this, perhaps by over-identifying with their responsibility for the team's final decision, product or service. Whatever the reason, they are less likely to support and develop ideas suggested by their staff. This has been the pattern with nearly all the football coaches with whom we have worked. However thoughtful and attentive they are, they still do 80 per cent of the talking at team meetings and only 20 per cent of the listening.

All the different characters in the scenario—non-listeners, aggrieved team members and the team leader or coach—are equally responsible. Through their lack of awareness, they all suffer the results of poor contact, negative synergy and an insufficient exchange of information. In fact, each of them has the power to create change; but they cannot see this because their focus remains on the content rather than the form of their discussion or, if they are aware of the form, they abide by the norm that no one ever mentions it. So the team-oriented members, apparent victims of those who do not listen, compound the situation, choosing to 'interrupt' themselves rather than interrupt the crescendo of competing voices. Pushing to be heard on the topic under discussion or fighting for air time on the topic, is getting them nowhere whereas some blunt descriptive feedback—an announcement that they have been interrupted three times in the past half hour and are becoming angry—would have a dramatically different effect. Such words are close to the surface but they choose not to speak them, still preferring to conform to the norms of a team for which they are losing respect.

Deflection

Talking so loud that everyone else gives up or thinking about something else while you nod sympathetically are not the only ways to not listen. Another is deflection. When someone in the team starts to share a confidence, shows emotion or is asking for help, this 'non-listener' avoids contact by turning to talk to someone else, changing the subject or making a joke. At other times, the 'non-listener' gives a glib answer to an embarrassed questioner or a deliberate deflection of information that someone is trying to impart. Deflection is often a team norm supported by the other forms of not listening. The team member who deflects can hear but refuses to listen. Young children are past masters at this. On the other hand, parents can be so quick to fit what their children say into some pet category of their own, that they also avoid listening.

Not hearing

Few non-fiction books have one word titles and most that do have prominent subtitles. A book entitled *Teamwork*—at least without a sub-title—would soon gather dust on the shelf because almost every manager knows what teamwork is, 'even if we haven't quite got there yet'. The concept is so widespread and the term so hackneyed that few people imagine there could be disagreement over its meaning. Why buy a book that tells you what you already know?

In the same way, the labels and language team members use can prevent the rest of the team from hearing what they have to say. It is particularly difficult to make contact with those who think they know it all already. Preaching to the converted is known to be a waste of time. The converted 'do not need' the information because the meaning they ascribe to the words that are spoken prevents them from hearing the message. Philip Crosby (1984: 58) ends a story on a quality initiative with the words:

No-one is against quality and yet very few have it . . . Nothing worked dramatically because everyone thought they understood it all. It is difficult to reach the mind of someone who is enthusiastically agreeing with you.

This is like Judith Brown's story of the small child frightened by a dream: 'Tell me about it,' says the mother comfortingly. 'I don't need to,' replies the child in surprise. 'You were in it.' We assume that our own reality is shared by everyone else.

Any unfounded assumptions or prejudices we hold *vis-à-vis* the team member who is speaking prevent us from hearing well. At a three-day conference I attended recently, one delegate left the small group he had originally chosen to join, just before they had to prepare a presentation and formed a new group with another delegate who had done the same. When they were invited to make a presentation of their own, I felt such sympathy for the two groups that had been abandoned that I did not hear anything the new group had to say. Ideally, I would have 'bracketed' my reaction but I allowed myself to stay stuck in the prejudice I have around 'team loyalty'.

In the same way, one team member can spend so much time complaining that when he or she does eventually offer a compliment to someone, it is either interpreted negatively or not heard at all. The child who cried 'Wolf!' too often was not heard the day the wolf came. Thousands of people will refuse to hear a politician speak on television—however heart-felt the message—because they belong to the opposite party or because they are tired of politicians. And a true heckler, almost by definition, will *never* hear what the speaker has to say.

In some way or another most of us are stuck in the past. Resisting change, we are locked into a certain way of viewing the world and do not realize that we have become 'nothing but a set of obsolete responses'. Friends, relations and even opponents can predict our reaction to certain events, behaviours and suggestions. Such unquestioning beliefs, what we have called 'fixed gestalts,' act as a filter that determines what we hear and what we see.

A man who struggled unsuccessfully in childhood to gain the attention and approval of an emotionally detached father, may still carry his struggle with him in new situations—hypersensitive to the hint of cool behaviour in a superior and responding with an intense and inappropriate wish to please. Fritz Schumacher, the economist, was once in a restaurant at breakfast time, when a waitress came to the next table where a young family was sitting. 'What would you like today?' she asked. The father looked at his wife and said 'Bacon and eggs dear?'. His wife nodded. 'Three bacon and eggs, please,' he said to the waitress. His young son turned to him and said, 'Daddy! I want an omelette!'. 'Two bacon and eggs and one omelette,' said the waitress and walked away. The little boy opened his eyes wide and turned to his father. 'Daddy!,' he said, 'she thinks I exist!' To some extent, all employees in any organizational structure continue to carry this child in them so that the most important factor in making people feel they belong and are really a part of their team or organization is showing that they are heard. This is a fundamental human need.

A senior manager of one small company said of the chief executive: 'He is tough on his staff and it doesn't always have a positive effect. You have to be secure in your own feelings and thoughts not to be intimidated. Maybe that's his intention. He's a perfectionist and works very hard. He doesn't realize how people respond. Those that it bothers the most are the ones that work really hard. They want appreciation.' The chief executive himself recognized his tendency to be a workaholic and be very demanding. However, like the head coach mentioned earlier, he also felt that many of this staff allowed themselves to be blocked by his title—*Chief Executive*—and did not feel seen or completely heard either.

Finally, it is possible to listen so intently to the story someone is telling that we miss the 'big picture' or the subtext. You have to pay attention to the whole person to know if the story is the message or if it is just words. This is similar to the question that hides a statement. A good listener can often hear the statement behind a tentative question without inviting the speaker to make it.

Being out of touch

A senior coach or manager will not receive information from the lower reaches of the organization unless he or she actively seeks it. 'My door is always open' is an assertion we have often heard made by people in such positions who cannot understand why they often appear to be the last to know what is going on around them. Some executives are so isolated at the top of their particular tree that they do not even suspect how far they are out of touch with their own domain.

Reality can be increased by creating new channels of information. If the head coach wants to discover what issues really concern the team, he must go down to talk to the players. It will take time but eventually the players will respond. In most clubs, the easiest step to take is to visit the kit manager whose office is adjacent to the locker room. The players treat this staff member as an equal and talk in front of him without restraint. No one is better placed to gauge the team's morale and know the current issues. Similarly, the senior executive can visit the shop floor. The line operators will be wary for a while but the supervisors will have something to say.

Different strategies can be devised that are appropriate to the organization concerned. The current trend towards a flatter organizational structure, with management having 12 good people reporting directly rather than six or seven, is a step in this direction. Information cannot travel from the bottom of an organization to the top without something happening to that information. Sitting behind his or her mahogany desk, the chief executive who has asked for a summary on a single sheet of paper will never really know the truth. It is not possible to summarize information without interpretation.

GOOD LISTENING

Making contact

When one team member listens attentively to another they make contact. They enhance their quality of understanding of each other, of themselves and of the unit or team that they constitute within the larger whole. Listening is more than being quiet while the other person speaks, it is actively moving into an attentive space where one is poised to hear.

Listening is not passive. It involves an active interchange between the person who is sending the message and the person who receives it. A sympathetic listener is not one who necessarily agrees with what the speaker is saying or even passively condones the opinions expressed. Good listeners are able to detach momentarily from their own opinions but are not afraid to shuttle attention from what the speaker is saying to awareness of the impact that the message has on themselves. It is in this sense that good listening is the process of understanding or making contact with oneself as well as with the speaker.

This can only be done by leaving aside the assumptions and preconceptions that one may have had, based on one's own past experiences and paying full attention to the speaker's voice in this shared moment. Ram Dass once said: 'If I empty myself and listen, complete strangers tell me intimate things and then thank me for a good discussion.' The good listener is present for the speaker. In the words of the old Gestalt saying: 'When you hear, you're here.'

Listening to the sound of the voice

Someone taking the role of facilitator during a discussion or a team member exploring his or her relationship within the team, needs to switch attention from what is being said to *how* it is being said. This includes noticing the verbal structure (whether sentences are involved or simple), listening to linguistic structure (distinguishing between questioning, making judgements, telling stories, agreeing or disagreeing, complaining, appreciating and so forth) and listening to the voice quality (lilting, monotone, soft, sharp, commanding, etc.).

Practice reveals that we have unexpected sensitivity to what the speaker is doing. Listen to the sound of the voice. Would you call it whining? Pleading? Laughing? Notice how you *respond*. Do you feel alive? Sleepy? Cautious? It may be illogical but this sort of listening is an intuitive, not an analytical process. For instance, what is the effect of the voice that can hardly be heard? Judith Brown suggests that a soft voice reveals cruelty and that 'soft-voiced women have a core of steel'.

Watching

The role of facilitator also includes 'listening' to body language, although such messages can be particularly difficult to interpret. This involves being in a receptive mode that allows hypotheses and intuitions about secondary level messages to emerge. Each team member has a pattern of non-verbal language which is partially overlaid by team and organizational norms.

The trick at these moments is not to become absorbed in the story being told or the point being made—listening 'with compassion but without attachment' and occasionally becoming aware of one's own response. Fritz Perls, in the context of therapy where an individual is talking about his or her own experience, once said that 'verbal communication is usually a lie. The real communication is beyond words.' Clarkson, who quotes Perls (Clarkson and Mackewn 1993: 111), suggests that he 'exaggerated his case ... to ... shake his trainees out of their complacency', getting them to 'shuttle their attention backwards and forwards between words, gestures and facial expression'.

Movement, posture and facial expression send messages that sometimes seem incongruent with the content of speech. A male executive leaning forward with his hand on the phone, asking 'Now, are you sure there's nothing else you want to say?' appears to be giving a double message, one conscious ('I'm concerned and want to help you') and another of which he is probably unaware ('I haven't got time to listen so don't say "yes"'). The non-verbal message is far more powerful for the person to whom he is speaking, so that some variation of 'No there's nothing that won't wait' is the likely response.

Noticing a double message requires a degree of detachment. One of the reasons that we usually share leadership of a workshop is that, while we are all good at watching the team and picking up likely subtexts when others are speaking, we also give some explanations and theory. It is then more difficult to watch the participants and almost impossible to pick up any double messages that we might ourselves be giving. Sometimes I get attached to the scheduled programme and behave like the executive with one hand on the phone. 'Well, it's coffee time now,' I say. 'Does anyone have anything to say that won't wait until afterwards?' It is then my colleague has to slow me down, giving some descriptive feedback that makes everyone laugh.

Watching and listening at different levels and knowing how to time one's interventions requires training and considerable practice. Since facilitation is a skill that develops teamwork and is a role that can usefully be practised at different times by different team members, we often include some simple training exercises in our workshops. The simplest of these involves dividing the team into pairs and asking one person to talk about anything while the other pays attention not to the content but to the verbal structure or to the tone of voice or to any physical posture, movement or facial expression.

When working with posture, movement and expression, they are asked to pay total attention to what they see—not what they would like to see, not what they expect to see but just what is there. This involves scanning the whole body, not just fixing on their partner's eyes.

At the same time they give descriptive feedback, sometimes in words— 'Now you are telling a story ... now you are explaining ... I notice that your voice has become scratchy ... I see that you are smiling ...'—and sometimes by miming their partner's movements or mimicking his or her voice. Attention is shuttled from watching and listening to noticing how they respond.

The impact of first impressions on the observer is important, if it can be held without analysis and interpretation. Eventually, a 'big picture' will emerge, one that captures the essence of the situation. This is a skill that can be learned. Watching two team members explore their mistrust of each other in one training exercise, someone said suddenly 'You're like two snakes circling each other in the stillness of a cold cave'—an image they both liked and that led them to talk about the potential strength of their relationship. When such an image arises from unforced attention, it is often on target and heightens awareness of repeated patterns of behaviour.

SYNERGISTIC LISTENING

Up to this point we have focused on various personal patterns of listening and on listening in the context of the team system. The quality of listening also has a more direct impact on the team's performance. Any team attempting to solve a problem, think of a new design or discover how the enterprise might best be reorganized will have long discussions at which a variety of proposals are made and considered. Task-focused listening is a process that few teams get completely right.

At its best, task-focused listening produces ideas and action plans that are better than anything that any one member of the team could have produced alone: it assures a synergy of ideas. It is not uncommon, however, for a comparable discussion to end up with an action plan that is *worse* than what many team members could have produced alone. This negative synergy results from the overtalking, lack of attunement and attention and the inability to listen or to hear that we have already identified in the context of team development. Synergistic listening is a process that begins with one team member making a proposal, continues with someone restating that proposal, then with the appreciation of some aspect of that proposal, followed by the expression of a concern and a period of mutual building. Many years ago, we designed an exercise to introduce this process; we called it 'the listening circle'.

The listening circle

The team divides into groups of three, consisting of a proposer, a listener and an observer. At each stage of the exercise each participant takes each of these roles in turn. There are four stages. In the first stage, A makes a proposal, B restates the proposal and C observes and gives feedback. In the second stage, A makes a proposal, B restates the proposal and says three things he or she likes about the proposal and C again observes and gives feedback. In the third stage, A makes a proposal, B restates the proposal, gives three 'likes' and voices one 'wish' or concern, while C continues to observe and give feedback. In the final stage, A makes a proposal, B restates the proposal and expresses three 'likes' and one 'wish', A restates the wish and adapts the original proposal to include it. C observes and gives feedback to both A and B.

As workshop leaders we usually give everyday topics that have no connection with the team's current concerns; this enables them to concentrate fully on the process. Thus, for the final stage of the exercise the topic might be 'How to reduce international terrorism' and one of the groups of three—Dawn, Ian and Meg—might suggest the following sequence:

A   Ian. I would reduce international terrorism by insisting that everyone got their luggage to the airport one day before departure.

B   Dawn. You would reduce international terrorism by insisting that everyone takes their luggage to the airport one day before departure. Is that right?

A   I did'nt say they had to *take* their luggage to the airport.

B   Oh okay! You said you would reduce international terrorism by making sure that everyone gets their luggage to the airport one day before travelling. Right?

A   Yes.

B   Okay. What I like about that idea is that it would mean that I wouldn't have my usual last minute panic on the day of departure. I like it because I wouldn't have to stand in line so long for check in; and I like it because I imagine it would give the airport authorities time to make a more thorough check of everyone's baggage. What I *wish* is that I could take one piece of hand luggage with me otherwise I'm going to need to buy a second wash kit and not have the book I'm reading with me the night before I travel.

A   So, Ian ... What you wish is that you could take one piece of hand luggage with you. Okay, so I propose that we reduce international terrorism by insisting that everyone gets their heavy luggage to the airport a day before departure.

C   I noticed that Ian made one mistake in restating the original proposal but that Meg, you helped him get it right. I noticed that you used each other's names and faced each other as you were speaking. And I noticed that neither of you clarified how the luggage would reach the airport!

The complete exercise—each participant having a turn at each stage followed by a period of discussion—takes about an hour. On another occasion or later in the same workshop, we might invite the team to go through the same process with some of their own current issues. However, between times, we observe and give feedback on one of their team meetings, making specific reference to overtalking versus restatement and rubbishing suggestions rather than expressing likes before wishes.

There are a number of points to be made about each stage of the exercise.

The proposal

The proposal is a message for which both speaker and listener are responsible. Either can contribute to its clarity or confusion—the speaker in the way that the message is conveyed and the listener in the way it is received and interpreted. One's ability to hear well is partly determined by how clearly the speaker makes his or her proposal. If the speaker headlines the message and then enlarges on it logically point by point it will be relatively easy to hear. This may require the speaker to determine the details in advance. Although whimsical meandering spur-of-the-moment insights may sometimes break a log jam of grimly traded analysis, the clear succinct statement is usually an easier way to get things rolling. Few teams show any patience with a long-winded, muddled idea that is full of contradictions. Time is too short, air space too contested.

Restatement

As in the example above, an attempted restatement is repeated until the speaker is sure that the listener has understood. The speaker may often confirm part of the restatement but realize that the remainder of the message needs to be rephrased. In this way, restatement helps the speaker to headline and clarify his or her message, often making the long-winded train of thought more concise. Restatement also gives the speaker a sense of being valued, making clear that he or she has someone's undivided attention (Figure 13.1). From this point on, these team members are fully engaged in the interaction. By slowing the process down the listener has eliminated any possibility of glib assumptions being made.

By adopting this format, the listener is obliged to respond with words like 'I think what you're saying is . . .' or 'Hang on a moment. Let me see if I've got this right . . .' or again 'What I hear you say is . . .'. This can be surprisingly difficult if the people listening are genuinely interested in the topic and have firmly held views of their own. It is then that the listener's interruptions usually come or the impatient hovering until it is his or her turn to speak. Only those team members who are able to clear their minds

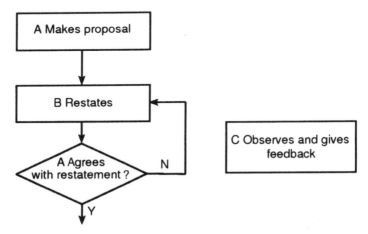

Figure 13.1   Listening: first phase.

of their own ideas and reactions are able to hear the speaker properly. The exercise often surprises people into realizing how fast their minds jump ahead to rehearsing their response and how little they actually hear beyond the opening words. Good listening demands that you relinquish your own position for a moment, trusting that the speaker will at least inspire some new creative idea.

Contrary to many in the field, we believe the consultant's prime task is to 'listen' and 'restate': listening includes both watching and listening to *how* the client speaks and restating is synonymous with giving descriptive feedback. While others might feel obliged to jump in with suggestions as soon as there is a pause, we do our utmost to slow the process down and disidentify from any such impulse. When Bill Belichick, head coach of the Cleveland Browns, invited me to work with the team and the organization as a whole, for what proved to be his penultimate if most successful season, he made two things clear: he was inviting me precisely because I was a foreigner, with no preconceptions as to what the club should do and, at least on my first two visits, he wanted me to do nothing more than observe and give feedback. In a team discussion, where a team member has a definite opinion as to how a matter should be addressed, it is much more difficult for him or her to slow down sufficiently to absorb and restate.

Likes

As co-authors, we are a two-man team with the objective of producing a well-constructed readable book. As a team we are capable of pushing each other to insights and ideas that neither of us would have had writing alone. We are also capable of not paying attention to each other, arguing bitterly and compromising with a second-rate half-baked construction that neither of us really like. This is the fourth book we've written together and the excitement of positive synergy and the despair of the reverse are still both part of our experience. However, we have learned to interrupt ourselves and recover from a negative non-listening spiral and one way we do this is to abide by the 'likes before wishes' rule.* '*Jo-ohn!*' Christopher will chant, stopping me as I launch into a careful but nonetheless rubbishing dismissal of his latest hair-brained idea. 'What do you *like* about it?' And when I slow

* The terms 'Likes' and 'Wishes' derive from early work of the Synectics organization.

down enough to find something I like—three things I like when I disagree strongly—we make contact again and as often as not my wish then leads to some new insight that excites us both.

By interrupting each other and slowing the pace in this way, we actually save time. A team discussion may speed ahead without interruption for hours but very little is ever achieved unless members build on each other's ideas. The 'likes before wishes' rule becomes a trigger, as we have made it in our writing relationship, to interrupt a negative communication pattern. Following restatement in the exercise, it puts a further restraint on the listener's impulse to jump in with his or her own views.

When our attention is entirely locked into our own needs, idea or point of view, we do not listen very well to others and, indeed, can only perceive them through the veil of our own preconceptions. If you were someone I liked and respected, I would probably wait until you had finished talking before I broadcast my own cherished idea but if I had a long-held image that you were stupid or pigheaded I would not give you a chance. I would pay no attention at all to what you might be saying, missing the fact that you were in fact particularly well qualified to speak on this issue. I would probably start talking loudly long before you had finished. However, if I were to adopt the format of the listening circle and not only pause to restate what you have just said but also find three things I like about it, I might see you clearly for the first time in years. Perhaps among all the apparently endless nonsense I think you habitually pour out there is something of genuine value.

Even in the best teams, some team members do not like each other. However, in such teams, appreciation, respect and trust are universal. A formula or team norm that ensures restatement of a proposal, followed by 'likes', demonstrates genuine appreciation through attention and begins to build respect between the team members concerned. From this point on, *your* idea begins to become *ours*. The previously closed doors between us and between your idea and me have been opened to new input. We break our pattern of unthinkingly rubbishing the other person's ideas and begin to build something new.

A wish

A wish in this context creatively reframes what would precisely have been expressed as an instant objection. It is more even than a carefully expressed

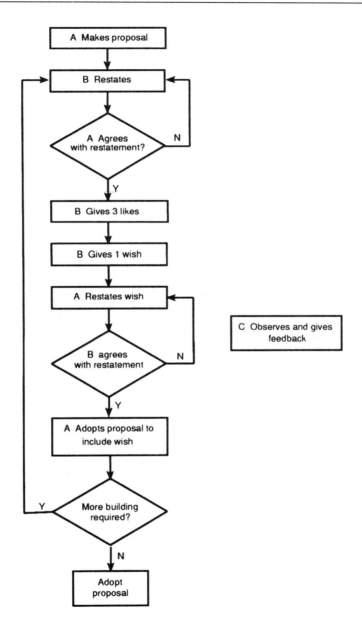

Figure 13.2 Listening: complete progression.

concern and is certainly not a linguistic device to avoid saying 'but . . .'. The wish can, however, arise from a reconsideration of one's own idea: 'If I take in this suggestion and hold it beside mine, what new insight does it provoke?' Precisely because you come from a different position you have something more to offer. Where does this lead? In what way could the original proposal be bettered? In this way a 'wish' becomes a suggestion for improvement.

Your 'wish' invites the speaker to leave his or her original position and to move forward into a productive dialogue. It also, in fact, contains the germ of an idea as to how the 'grey' area of the original proposal might be clarified. Together, your 'likes' and 'wish' push the speaker to take the proposal further.

Restatement and adaptation

If I am the original speaker, the first part of the final step requires that, having listened to the wish, I restate that wish. Sometimes I may want to respond to the wish more fully, following my restatement, with my own likes and wish. You can then restate my wish and adapt your own to include it or make a new enhanced proposal. Eventually, though, we can adapt my original proposal, taking into account this additional development.

When this happens, listening has become proactive. Although my new proposal may in turn be further explored through restatement, likes and wishes, the process of exploring and building on the idea now accelerates, with each new circuit further clarifying the suggestion and building common ownership until its full potential has emerged.

As said earlier, effective listening is not passive. It is a circular process which not only takes in the original information but can also add to it constructively so that the quality of mutual understanding is enhanced. The result is a process in which everyone is involved and a final proposal to which everyone is fully committed (Figure 13.2).

14

Warming down

An underdeveloped team tends to have a warm-down at the end of its meetings that is even more perfunctory than its warm-up. Even if no one leaves early, there are usually one or two members who begin to fidget towards the end. Members who avoid closure are either distracted or distressed and are barely conscious of the effect their actions have on the rest of the team. Usually, this has something to do with the team leader's style, of which he or she is quite unaware. I once wrote something like the following for one team leader who had asked specifically for personal feedback.

I've seen hastier warm-downs than yours. Nobody left any meeting I attended before it was declared closed. You always asked if there were any questions after your information sessions, even if you didn't always leave time for them. Occasionally at the staff meetings you asked if anyone had anything else to say. However, in some way people may not feel truly invited to speak. It may be that, having listened to a concise, carefully reasoned speech by you, they don't want to follow it too fast. Or perhaps you are leaning forward as if about to get up or don't make a point of pausing long enough to catch each person's eye—whatever it is, at least three people expressed frustration to me about the way meetings end (for instance: 'I wish we could leave meetings with everyone agreed' and 'Some guys come out of a meeting furious').

Clearly there was something missing.

Taking time to check what has been accomplished at the end of a meeting renews commitment to the team's vision. Taking time to check how team members feel at this point shows the respect for each other that is inherent in effective teamwork. Warming down is a form of closure and retraces the attunement steps of warming up, in reverse order. Like warming up, it marks a transition, allowing members to ease out of the

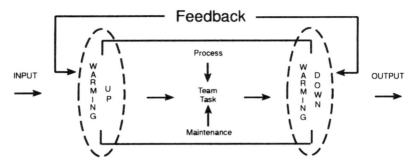

Figure 14.1 Warming down after task completion.

team system and back into the identities they each assume when they are not a part of this team (Figure 14.1).

Warming down differs from warming up in that it includes some periods of process, as well as the task aspects of tuning in to the agenda and purpose and the maintenance aspects of tuning in to the team, others, oneself and the place. From a systems perspective, the 'task' part of warming down includes releasing specific roles, particularly in project teams where members may go straight back to a different 'home' team and re-adopt a different role. The 'maintenance' part of warming down includes recognition that feelings inspired by the developing system of relationships that constitute the team need to be contained within that system and that what cannot be completed before the meeting finishes should be bracketed until the team meets again.

AGENDA

Warming down starts by checking the agenda: Is it completed? Is there some item to be postponed until the next meeting? Is there any other business that needs to be discussed before the meeting ends? These questions are all discussed in relation to the time remaining. If there is no more time, it may be possible to hold a subgroup meeting to consider the issue and report back to the next full meeting. Most teams use the agenda as a feed forward mechanism to help formulate the agenda of the next team meeting. However, warming down, like warming up, should be a scheduled item on any meeting agenda, the team learning through experience how much time to allow for this first stage.

PURPOSE

Since agenda and purpose are the task aspects of warming up and warming down, it is usually the leader who asks the questions: 'Did we achieve what we wanted to achieve?' and 'Where does this leave us in the pursuit of our overall objective?'

The last time the cross-cultural consultancy team (p. 147) met, our clients were a high profile controversial German organization. This was a small team of administrators who had exhausted themselves conducting a major international symposium the previous year. Since then, they had run into a number of relationship, planning and budgeting difficulties. We soon learned that they had been so burned out by the end of the symposium— having spent three years preparing it—that they had never met subsequently to review their experience. They had reconvened a few months later and found so many practical issues to deal with that their entire focus was on new problems that had emerged. This two-day meeting with our team was the first time in almost two years that they had agreed not only to spend time on maintenance (paying attention to each other's concerns, resentments and appreciations) but also to recognize what they had achieved together, how they each had responded to this achievement and what they each saw as still needing to be done.

Towards the end of the two-day consultancy period, we modelled precisely what they now felt to have been missing from their own past experience. With our clients watching us, we moved into a circle and checked that we had covered each of the items on our original agenda. We then revisited the purpose we had set ourselves before leaving—which included learning more about cross-cultural consultancy—and moved on to our experience as a consulting team, our feelings about each other and how far we had met our personal needs. Although we were to do this in greater depth the next day, alone, we were also doing it for real. When we had finished we invited and listened to the feedback our clients wanted to give us (they said the experience had made a deep impression, that it was something they had wanted without recognizing it). We then asked them to go through the same process while we watched and this led to some more discussion before we warmed down as one group, at what was the end of our client/consultant experience.

When a team has clarified its purpose at the start of the meeting, the warm-down question 'What do we take away from this experience?' has particular significance. How does what we take away relate to our stated objective? As consultants, it is a question that we usually ask our clients at the end of each meeting we have together: 'What do you take away from this?' It is also a question that we ask ourselves about our own experience, as we return to our Hampstead offices. In an ongoing relationship with a client, the question becomes 'What did we accomplish and what still needs to be done?'.

Looking back at the original objective, it is perhaps rare for a team to feel that there is no unfinished business. However, the objective was set as a pointer. Usually something has not only become clearer and has indeed been achieved as a result of the meeting but it is possible to view what happened as a completed task—what Ed Nevis would call a 'unit of work'. Taking time with our clients to view the meeting in this way helps them to clarify their next step and allows them to leave with a sense of achievement. In fact, a lot of work is done in the space of short encounters.

THE TEAM

Reviewing the agenda and comparing results with the original purpose can lead to the wider question 'What have we learned about ourselves as a team?'. If the task of the meeting was such that everyone had to split up into small groups or turn to face a screen (or Metaplan board or flip chart) or if people had to consult files and a spread of papers, the team should now move back to a position where everyone can see everyone else. At the end of a day-long meeting, it is best to close any files and put them and even the tables aside. Talking about 'what we learned from this' and sitting in a circle, the warm-up experience of 'this is who we are . . . this is a place where I belong' re-emerges for a moment. Many sports teams do something similar.

This constitutes the maintenance aspect of tuning in to the team—the third part of warming down—but tuning in to the team also has a process component. Even at the end of a relatively short business meeting, a few minutes spent answering our three basic review questions (p. 208) ensures continued team development from one meeting to the next. The first and the third questions—'What precisely did you notice (about the way we talked to each other)?' and 'What, if anything, do you want to change (about the way we talked to each other)?'—lead to a consideration of the team's patterns of behaviour, a prominent aspect of the team's identity. The second question—'What did you feel?' (physically or emotionally—this does *not* give opinions about the meeting)—is a maintenance question but is linked to the other two.

As an exercise, ask everyone to write down their answers as this makes it easier for them to reflect on the questions (it is quiet) and reach a broader range of information. Answers to the first and second questions can refer to the same moment during the meeting—what happened and one's response. Everyone in turn then calls out one thing they noted down in reply to the first question and any linked one-word reply to the second. This continues until no one has anything new to say. Suggestions for change prompted by the third question are then given on a final circle check. In a very large team, when time is short, members can discuss their answers in pairs or threes before coming back to consider as a team what they want to change. If the responses to the third question are captured by someone on a flip chart, a quick check can be made to see which suggestions have everyone's support. These can then be reiterated at the start of the next meeting and supported by someone taking the facilitation role. For instance, a decision may be made that any proposal be restated and appreciated, before a new proposal is made.

The final three parts of warming down focus on other team members, on oneself and on the place or meeting room. Most of the remainder of this chapter relates to the fourth stage of warming down—'other team members'—while covering some broader aspects of team relationships. Under this heading we have included closure, saying good-bye and unfinished (relationship) business.

OTHER TEAM MEMBERS

Closure

Closure is the experience of completion that allows attention to move to other unfinished issues. It builds trust through contact. Each time closure is waived, trust is diminished. In the context of relationships, closure happens when differences and misapprehensions have been clarified, contact has finally been made and the individuals concerned begin to move on.

It is not uncommon for two team members to clash repeatedly over a wide variety of issues throughout a meeting in a way that makes the rest of the team sigh in frustration (or boredom) and conclude that there has to be 'some deep personality conflict'. The end of a meeting can offer opportunities for closure or at least movement towards closure, that go beyond the settling of disagreements over specific business items. Romantic film script writers with their black-and-white steam-filled rail station dialogues have always known what the therapist knows: pay attention to the last moments of the session, for that is when the truth will out.

It is axiomatic that there is no closure without disclosure. As Judith Brown once said: 'If it's all inside, nothing's going to happen.' Deeper issues need time or at least facilitation and there may not be much opportunity for that until some form of team development workshop is held. Yet if the development of awareness, appreciation and contact is seen as an ongoing process, then warming down at the end of a meeting does present the opportunity to take one step in the right direction—to complete one small 'unit of work'. Even an agreement between two people that the issue between them is not finished—in some instances an agreement to disagree—is a form of closure. The occasion often allows nothing else. Closure does also mean acknowledging what is unfinished and there is an integrity in voicing this before the meeting ends, rather than keeping the unfinished issue hidden until the meeting is over and then speaking of it to people outside.

We have worked with a team in which two members finally decided to leave the team entirely. No one liked this—closure here equalled fracture—but closure is not always resolution. It is ultimately an awareness of what the ending is, a shared perception. In the same way, a marriage counsellor's job is not to make the two partners stay together but to ensure that, if separation occurs, it is done with integrity and awareness. Unfinished business can be left with awareness or without. The difference is learning: if we are not aware, we cannot learn. Most organizations by ignoring all but the first phase of warming down, do not allow even the acknowledgement that certain relationship issues may be unfinished—with the result that nothing is learned and the team gets stuck in unproductive patterns of behaviour.

Despite moments of closure, completion and withdrawal, any two-person relationship within a team can develop further; the process is never finished. However, an honest effort to expand awareness and challenge assumptions does ensure change over time and is also an integral part of the development of the team to which the two people belong.

Saying good-bye

Being able to say good-bye is a prerequisite to the ability to change, yet for many of us good-byes are not easy. Fritz Perls called the inability to say good-bye or achieve closure a 'hanging-on bite'. It is immaterial if a man feels he was in some way abandoned in his early childhood; what is significant is that he knows what he does now as a team member—be that invariably supporting any move for afterwork social events, feeling let down easily, being inordinately loyal or believing that a particular programme would lose its integrity if it was ever changed.

Organizational consultant Jonno Hanafin has pointed out that it is in our culture to avoid good-byes—to promise at the end of a week-long course that one will write (one never does), to observe the ritual nineteenth hole at golf or to know that when the stage darkens at the end of a concert the group will return after the statutory three minutes of applause. These are all ways of saying that the end is not really the end. Yet not to say good-bye is a way to avoid contact and closure. It devalues the time spent together. Sadness is a feeling and is therefore neither wrong nor logical—it does not have to be justified. To say 'I don't expect to see you again and I'm sad about that' takes courage because it is direct and reaches out to make contact. If I feel this way and leave without saying good-bye, my growth from the experience of being with you will be less. It is a matter of integrity and integrity builds trust.

Sometimes it is comforting to remind ourselves that although we might rehearse our good-bye scenes, what actually happens is quite unpredictable. One of the most powerful closure meetings I have attended was at the end of the 1992 Olympic Games in Barcelona. I had been working with the British pursuit cycling team for several years. One member of the team had won a gold medal and the team itself had surpassed expectations in finishing fifth. Now it was over and the team would split up. I had had all sorts of thoughts as to the format for this exercise but in the end the riders took charge. They decided to do a simple 'pass-the-pen' circle check in which each person in turn said what our time together had meant to him and what he was taking away from the experience. As one of them said much later—it was 'awesome'.

Ritual celebration often supports the process of closure. This has always been a part of my sporting life (and—remembering the ride back from Wembley in the Tottenham bus with the FA Cup in May 1982—part of my sports psychologist's life too) but it is something we find many companies are also very good at, especially in the United States. There is clearly a parallel here between closure and the Irish wake or the funeral rendering of the traditional jazz song 'When the Saints Go Marchin In'—the last of all good-byes.

Unfinished business

Research has shown that people remember those things they did not complete much better than those that they did. We seem to gravitate towards situations and experiences that are unfinished, without ever achieving closure, returning to them again and again. Such a pattern is unhealthy in that it drains us of energy that might otherwise be devoted to something new or might even allow us to notice something new. For example, the manager who mistakenly imagined his player was frequently penalized for arguing with the referee (see p. 84) was holding on to his own resentment for arguments the player had had with him, early in their relationship.

There are various ways in which we manage to avoid finishing unfinished business. One is to hang on to the past, as the manager did in this instance, rather than see the present as it is. Another is to not to forgive people. A third, stemming from a fear of change, is to hold to the belief that the devil you know (the image you hold of reality) is better than the one you do not.

Some of the saddest organizational examples of unfinished business are members of teams that have been reduced in size and in importance and are no longer sure of their role or identity. Here members cling to their past, missing both their departed colleagues and their lost sense of mission. This experience scars the survivors and drains them of committed energy.

Resentments

Resentment is such a strong word that we replaced it in one of our manuals with 'gripe'. Yet, in any dynamic team, most members will at some stage do something that another team member does not like. If such a reaction is not expressed or transformed it is easily reinforced later and can grow into resentment. Since a business meeting is a complex interaction of ideas and feelings and, since each team member is only aware of a part of this

complexity, an effective warm-down includes the opportunity for individuals to tell each other of any ill feelings that have been evoked.

When we lead a residential team development workshop for a particular
team, we usually include an exercise in the warm-down that gives every
team member the opportunity to meet every other team member, so that
each can make two statements to the other: 'One thing I would like you to
do *or* to do more *or* to do less *or* to stop doing is . . .' and 'One thing I
appreciate about you is . . .'. This not only allows any minor irritations to be
expressed but also, when two members have been sniping at each other for a
period of time, it allows all the other team members to give them feedback
as to how this relationship is affecting them. It is surprising how often
people come away from the exercise with a consistent set of messages. Of
course it also gives the chance to voice appreciations (see below). The
formula asks that no one tells anyone what he or she should or should not do
and that no one gives advice. It is a personal response information-giving
session: when you do that, this is what I feel—and this is what I want. There
is nothing that the person listening has to do or say in response.

Resentments are unfinished business and, as with all unfinished business,
the person holding the resentments will return to them again and again—
sometimes long after their object has left the team or even after the team has
disbanded. George Brown's paradoxical advice in such cases is to *appreciate*
these resentments—to appreciate them and discover what personal need
they satisfy. 'What do these resentments *do* for you?' he asks.

The resentments one team member holds for another call out for closure.
They need to be dealt with either in the main body of a team development
session or in a separate meeting for the people concerned. They also usually
require some facilitation.

Some leaders are not comfortable with the expression of feeling, especially 'negative' feeling. Some members do not dare to speak out and,
instead, complain later to someone outside the team. (Complaints usually
betray what it is that we have somehow learned *not* to get.) When no
opportunity is given during warming down for members to express any
frustration caused by something said or done in the meeting, this frustration
turns to resentment.

Eventually the resentment turns to guilt, the individual being unable
either to let the issue go or to express the frustration. It requires less courage
and energy to keep quiet and blame oneself for having such 'unfair' feelings
than to tell the member concerned. Guilt is a dead end. Increasingly

preoccupied, it becomes harder for the individual to contribute to the team, so the team also suffers. And, if blocking resentments is a team norm, there will be a complexity of such situations, each reinforcing the others.

A facilitator can help the members concerned to express their feelings, so that guilt can be switched back to resentment. There are two principles governing this form of exchange:

1 Feelings do not have to make sense and are not fair, logical or justified (for instance, someone might say 'I can't stand the way you are always so positive!' but is not invited to give an explanation).
2 Such a statement is a *report* of what the person concerned is experiencing. The person being addressed is not required to do anything in response.

The facilitator listens carefully, keeping them on track. If the speaker says 'I hate you criticizing me', the facilitator can suggest: 'Try saying "I resent you criticizing me"'. Remember that it doesn't have to make sense.' As the speaker stops trying to be logical, energy returns and the person being addressed usually finds it easier to relax as there is no need to do anything. Expressing what has been held in does not mean that it is forgotten but a block has been diffused and the speaker now has freedom to move on and contribute fully again.

Demands

Each resentment has an implicit demand or expectation. In fact it is the reluctance to make demands that leads to resentment—one actually can resent people for not doing something one wants them to do but has not had the courage to ask of them. When the demand is expressed, the other person can respond and, whatever that response, closure is now possible. When a demand is met by a refusal, each can now recognize his or her differences.

Thus, in the pairs meeting, after all resentments have been expressed, the facilitator will ask for demands. Again, the demands do not have to be logical but should be made energetically. They can be outrageous—for instance, 'I want you to pay attention to me throughout the meeting!'. It sometimes helps if the person making the demands stands over the other team member and waves a forefinger in mock command. Again, too, all the demands need to be expressed but they do *not* have to be met. This is made clear from the start, so the person listening does not put up a defence and stop listening in the process. The only thing asked of the listener is to hear the demands and appreciate the other person's experience.

Appreciations

Very often, closely following a demand, comes an initially grudging appreciation and respect for the person who was previously resented. This does not mean that the speaker would not still like him or her to act differently but it is a recognition that what this person does can be legitimate, credible and appropriate. This appreciation is in much the same vein as that of a woman who can appreciate that her husband works long hours, though she may not like it. The response is the opposite of telling her husband what he should do. When one team member can appreciate the irritating actions of another, he or she has decided to accept the situation as being correct in the context of that person's existence and will no longer agitate to get that person to change. This appreciation is of the other *and* of self and is in fact an appreciation of differences.

Judith Brown, especially known for her work with couples, sometimes uses Victor Frankl's concept of 'symptom prescription' (see p. 82). In this sort of situation she might give the two participants 'homework', asking them to give each other five resentments and five appreciations—making sure that they do this without explanation. Alternatively, she will focus on a recurring theme of the session and again give 'homework' that is purely designed to help the dyad to play the game they have long been playing with each other—but consciously.

So this might be to have a piece of paper on the wall to keep the score of not giving in, to see who cannot give in the most often! Or alternatively, if the pattern is for each to reject the other's attempts to make peace, Judith will say 'I want one of you to make a bridge-building statement at least once a day and the other to knock it down. Take turns.' This is all done on the now familiar principle that where there is awareness, there is choice and where there is choice, change again becomes possible.

Any warm-down exercise that asks everyone to give an appreciation to another team member produces some insight that improves the team's performance. Years ago, at the end of a pairs session I led for Mark Falco and Clive Allen at White Hart Lane, I asked each of them to say one thing they wanted from the other and one thing they appreciated about the other on the field of play, they responded easily. However both looked surprised at what the other had said. 'You know,' said Mark, referring to the appreciation Clive had just made, 'I always wondered if I should be steaming in in that situation. I always felt selfish and slightly guilty. I'd meant to check it out with you but never did. It's *great* to know you really like it when I do!'

More on others

A maintenance review with other individuals in the team is often more simple than any of the above. On a two-day workshop we use the exercise described earlier, where we ensure that each member has two or three minutes with every other member in turn. It takes half an hour with a team of 12 for each to complete two statements, one expressing something they want and the other an appreciation. In a normal meeting this is reduced to two or three haphazard pairings, each person giving the other his or her experience of the meeting. Sometimes this will also be formalized, everyone telling their partners their answers to a specific question, displayed on a flip chart. Sometimes we ask everyone to write their answers, stand behind their chair when they have finished and pair off with someone else already standing. The point is to ensure that at least some inhabitual pairings are made.

At short meetings a task and maintenance circle check combined often replaces this process, although, in fact, each person speaking in turn is tuning in to the team again, rather than to 'others'—the component two-person teams that contribute to the complete unit. The two statements we suggest for the circle checks are to give an opinion of the meeting that begins with the words 'I feel that . . .' and immediately afterwards to tune in to self and report what he or she feels, either physically or emotionally, with a sentence beginning with the words 'I feel . . .'—only three-word statements being allowed.

ONESELF

Focusing again on oneself at the end of the meeting, as part of a warming down, usually involves reflecting on the objectives one set for oneself at the start. The day Ricky Villa spoke to me (see p. 177), he set himself the objective of tackling back 15 times in the first 20 minutes to support the team's purpose. At the end of the match, he reviewed his performance in the light of this objective. Before pushing back their chairs to leave, business team members can draw a line under their notes, reflect for a moment, write the word 'review' and jot down one immediate observation on their performance. This might include an insight into what they take from the experience that was unexpected. Further reflection might be done later on their way home.

The important thing is not to race into another meeting without returning to 'home base'. Those teams with a norm of starting the meeting with a 15-second silence will also end with one. The 'black box' visualization we use with both sports and business teams at the self stage of warming up (Syer and Connolly, 1984: 14) only 'works' next time if the person using it goes back to the visualization very briefly before leaving and retrieves the piece of paper from the box.

THE PLACE

The last stage of warming down is to reorganize the room so that it is ready for another team's use. It includes returning the furniture to its original layout, tearing off used flip sheets, cleaning any white boards, throwing empty plastic cups in the bin and opening the windows if the room lacks fresh air. This serves to affirm and reconnect with the greater organization of which the team is a part.

PART IV

Team Task

15

Recognition

We may derive the three purposes of human work as follows:

First, to provide necessary and useful goods and services. Second, to enable every one of us to use and thereby perfect our gifts like good stewards. Third, to do so in service to and in co-operation with, others, so as to liberate ourselves from our inborn egocentricity.

(Schumacher 1979: 4)

THE PROJECT TEAM

Teams vary in size, function and life span. They now play a central role in most organizations and a strong case could be made for most teams being reoriented to a project focus. Such teams reassess their structure, membership and norms at the end of each project, thereby ensuring that they constantly adapt to a more appropriate form for their current objectives.

Team members also have an increasingly varied existence. A team's size may be determined but its membership may change constantly. Its life span may be that of a project, which could be weeks, months or years. A reporting format is central to its direction and focus and it may be responsible to a project manager or a champion or it may even be self-governing. Members are assigned to the project team but many members may be involved with more than one project, either independently or as members of other teams. This state of flux creates a dynamic context for a team's life and is reflected in its process—the prime focus of this book.

The following chapters apply the five-stage team task cycle to the project team system. This underlying structure allows the team to adapt continually to its ever-changing context.

Typical project teams

The structure, processes and identity of project teams vary widely, according to their task (Figure 15.1). Here are some typical examples.

Functional teams

Functional teams have long held a prominent place in most organizations, where they concentrate knowledge within a geographical and hierarchical focus. This expertise is either used for their assigned task or is offered as a specialist service to other departments within the organization. Finance, marketing, human resources, planning, accounts and legal services are typical functional teams. Others specialize in particular subsystems or products. A telecommunication company will have functional teams running call return, conference calls, telemarketing, business services and long-distance calls. These teams may have little opportunity for cross-functional teamwork, being confined to discrete elements of a product or service and rarely communicating. They often become protective of their territory and erect rigid boundaries. This restricts the quantity and quality of feedback they receive and makes it difficult for them to modify their processes.

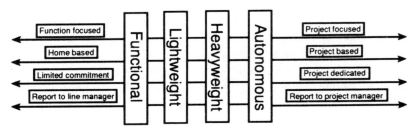

Figure 15.1   The spectrum of team responsibility.

Lightweight teams

Members are assigned to these teams on a part-time, advisory basis. Their main focus and physical location is at their home site and they act as representatives for the project to which they have been assigned. The project manager is not usually their direct superior but acts as a co-ordinator between the project's different support functions. While these teams may be run without demanding extra resources, they often struggle to succeed. Conflicting obligations, insufficient resources, time conflicts and members being called back to their home base all undermine their potential for success. The resources necessary to support the effort are still controlled by the functional areas rather than the team itself. Lightweight team project leaders are often tolerated rather than supported and are sometimes ignored or obstructed for political reasons. The flexibility and maximization of resources claimed by the advocates of such teams are rarely in evidence.

Heavyweight teams

The members of heavyweight project teams have these teams as their prime assignment. The team leader has direct control and responsibility for the work of each member. While members still liaise with their functional home base, they are responsible to the project and report primarily to the project leader, who usually has a senior grade. The team relies on its members to mobilize resources from their home bases and the leader is able to back them when necessary.

The case for design and manufacturing engineers to work together in a single process is overwhelming. For example, in 'over the wall' engineering, when a problem with the product arises ... the amount of effort expended by each side (design and manufacturing) to show they were not to blame for the problem ... equals or exceeds that spent in solving the problem. The separation into design and manufacturing is of course an artificial one since the design of a product will affect its manufacture in the same way that the limitation of a manufacturing process [can] ... affect product design. ... The path from product concept to product production is continuous, with numerous iterations and constant feedback loops.

(Coombes *et al.* 1995)

Heavyweight teams are very effective for specific longer term projects. However, they can put great strain on those members who must repeatedly justify the team's demands on their local resources, despite the leader's support.

Autonomous teams

Members of autonomous teams are seconded to the project team and are fully responsible for its outcomes. The team members report only to the project leader and the team has all the resources it requires. Such teams establish their own structures, norms, membership and functions and create their own processes. They can often define the product as they see fit and generate bright ideas. They can also go wildly off track, exceeding their remit or wasting their energy on side issues. They may even create products or concepts that require major redesign, have unconsidered consequences for certain areas of the company or fail to give due return on investment.

Some other teams

Three other teams that should be mentioned are the executive team, the small operations team and the 'skunk works'.

Executive teams

The executive team is central to the functioning of any organization and yet can struggle more than any other team to discover its identity. Members often view the team meetings as a reporting forum rather than an opportunity to work. Team members tend to maintain a primary allegiance to their home team (which they lead) and fight battles for that team rather than develop and align themselves with an executive team vision.

Small operations teams

This is the archetypal team, best represented by a sports team or the management team of a small business. When a small business is built around a product or concept, its entire workforce may be involved in design, development, production and sales. Team members represent all the functions of the company, taking all major decisions including many of the implementation and production responsibilities. The small size of such teams, their diversity and flexibility promotes adaptability and flair. They usually have a clear identity but suffer from the paradox of team identity: the more the members identify with the team the more likely they are to lose touch with their own identity and needs. Since little movement is possible within the company, members' ability to function effectively over time depends on their ability to withdraw from the fray at appropriate moments.

Skunk works

These teams were identified and described by Peters and Waterman (1982). They embody all that is quirky, non-conformist, anti-authoritarian, non-structured and anti-organizational in the creative process. Such after-hours teams steal resources from the central design office, get together over beer and pizza in someone's garage, play with outrageous ideas until morning and are the prima donnas of the design world. By nature they are disinclined to follow a strict design process or structure and they include most of the team elements outlined below—but spun together in a pattern of their own. If creative ideas are a major source of a company's market value, these teams have to be given licence. Their output is unpredictable but can bring enormous success.

FORMING A TEAM SYSTEM

Beginnings are important. The way a new team approaches a task or an established team approaches a new task, is the basis of all subsequent team action and directly influences its chance of success. The team must establish its process and structure. These go hand in hand, the process focusing how the team operates and the structure providing support. At first more attention is paid to maintenance and the general guidelines of how the team will operate. Once the team has identified its task, it chooses specific methodologies, continuing to do so throughout its task cycle.

Team development (described in Part II) comes into focus at the recognition stage of the task cycle, even with a team that has worked on other projects. The principle would be the same for a process re-engineering team, as for a team formed by the quality department and seeking areas for process improvement. Whatever the case, the team has to be a small group of dedicated people who have the knowledge, time, authority and technical disciplines required to take decisions and implement change. A new team has team development as its first task; a successful ongoing team reaffirms its commitment to maintaining a balance between task, maintenance and process. The transformation of a group of individuals into an effective team is a continuous process, not just a first step in the task cycle. Awareness of self, others and differences (a prerequisite of good relationship) is a framework within which problems are solved, decisions are made and the team achieves its objective.*

Structure

Membership, expertise, identity, meeting skills and roles are central to this initial stage.

Size Different tasks require different sized teams but most effective teams have between four and ten members. It is easier, though not necessarily more satisfying, to discover the identity of a small team. A motor vehicle development or launch team will have between 20 and 30 members, which will include project planners, finance personnel, marketing personnel and representatives of all the various elements of the vehicle. Cross-functional teams also need members from an appropriate organizational level.

Roles Teams function poorly if the roles of leader, facilitator, time manager and scribe are not adequately filled. Often a champion and a minute taker are also required. Leadership and facilitation are essential and may be adopted by any team member but not combined. Although elements of each role may be assumed by different members at different times, a young team probably needs a skilled practitioner assigned to each.

Formalization The larger the team, the more it needs a formalized structure. A large team is often broken down into a steering committee and a number of subcommittees which re-assemble to make reports. Roles are unambiguous, agendas precise and the team leader has clear authority to direct the team, otherwise such teams find it difficult to manage their process and tend to divide into cliques. Whereas subteams that are built into the team facilitate performance, unstructured cliques that emerge in conflict around unresolved issues do the reverse.

*Team membership should be reviewed periodically. Some members' contribution may be complete midway through the project and other people with other skills may have to be added to the team. Membership, expertise, identity, meeting skills and roles are central to this initial stage.

Knowledge This is a prerequisite for team membership. Increasing competency, expanding horizons and empowering members to conduct their own research evokes support, enthusiasm and creative, networked outputs.

Boundaries Boundaries often come from preconceptions of what the team should be or how it should behave. If they are not identified, exceptional opportunities will be missed. Time limits, budget or resource constraints and collaboration with other teams are *valid* boundaries that, once identified, can be stretched, moved, modified or even crossed, if not eliminated. Boundaries should be used to get the best leverage on a situation, not as a restraint.

Process

Contact The ability to convey and process information, ideas and personal feelings increases as the team develops. Members learn to express their ideas about the task, their observations about the process and their response to each other. Descriptive feedback skills fosters this capacity for contact.

Identity As a team's identity begins to emerge, members experience the entity that is greater than the sum of its parts. Norms and rituals which evoke the experience take root. Set exercises can speed team development, allowing the identity to be discovered. Team development, an ongoing process, begins with heightening awareness and appreciation of the present. Effective communication then builds understanding, respect and trust.

Networks Subteams that are formed through necessity bring life to the best teams. One of the four key elements of a CORE team is the capacity to support a wide network of informal contacts among the team members. These show how the team needs to grow as the project unfolds. Rigid structures may minimize conflict in undeveloped teams but may also impose mechanical patterns of response. Such teams do not have the inherent equipotentiality of flexible, human systems: they cannot adapt, learn and grow.

Communication Team members develop the ability to conduct and participate in meetings that share information, provide feedback, plan, develop recommendations, solve problems and make decisions. In an effective meeting all participants speak, question, listen actively and provide appropriate feedback. These skills can always be enhanced. The meeting is enhanced and contextualized by warming up and warming down.

Leadership   Poor and dispersed leadership are common and although the team leader may not always lead, at any given moment someone is adopting the role. Commitment and the ability to articulate, to inspire, to make decisions, to resolve conflict and to recognize and reward successful performance are all associated with competent embodiment of the role. While these tasks are usually assigned to the designated leader, they may be performed by any team member.

INPUTS TO THE TEAM SYSTEM

The type of information and the best way to receive it—its quality, its interpretation, etc.—are matters that the team needs to clarify.

Background information

Situations range from the very specific to the general and require quite different approaches. In a project team, the leader or the champion normally presents the issue. Whether it is a formal presentation or an informal explanation, this first input sets the tone. An offhand, casual or incoherent introduction hampers both understanding and attention.

Context   Many preconceptions, experiences and conceptual models are brought to a new situation. Most operate unnoticed, even when they have a significant impact on thinking. A relatively straightforward and familiar story will not require detailed background analysis. However, if the project involves, for example, the launch of a new product design or the implementation of some long-awaited plan, the context will need much more consideration.

Dominant idea   The idea currently organizing the team's approach to the situation must be made explicit. When a situation is inherited from another team, that team's reason for pursuing it may also be inherited. This rationale needs to be questioned before a search for solutions begins. Once grasped, the dominant idea may be pursued as defined, modified or re-examined. Either way, the act of making what is implicit explicit is of assistance.

Assumptions Assumptions can bind the team to a particular approach or restrict effort to a specific arena. Some assumptions will be correct but many will no longer be appropriate. Ideas, solutions and information should not be categorized too soon and team members, other teams, other departments, other divisions and 'the organization' should not be categorized at all.

Resources

Access A team within a matrix organization or performing a cross-functional or project role within the organization, needs access to key personnel and activities in order to carry out a proper needs analysis and assessment of the situation. When a team is part of a larger project or has process lines of authority to other teams, it needs to identify its customers, suppliers, line managers and functional authorities.

Meeting a clearly perceived need The team is asked to deal with the situation in a way that will bring quantifiable benefits to the company.

A clearly defined target area The team needs the point of intervention to have clear boundaries to enable it to receive the resources and authority necessary to implement recommendations.

OUTPUTS FROM THE SYSTEM

Restating the objective in its own language allows the team to comprehend a situation. Listening skills—restating, expressing likes before wishes and building on what others say—help to clarify the situation and engender a sense of mutual ownership of the team's objective.

Any impulse to enter immediately into a solutions mode or make early judgements is best resisted. Often the stated situation, problem or concern is not the real one. Caution allows this to be discovered early although, with larger tasks, the mistaken assumption may only be clarified at the second stage of the task cycle. A team moving unchanged to a new and relatively uncomplicated project may only take ten minutes to find a sentence to capture its objective. For a more complex situation—the start of a marketing campaign or the adoption of a total quality programme—it may take several meetings to complete the process. Either way the definition will include the objective, the criteria for success and the actions required.

The objective

A good team affirms what it can accomplish. This may just mean tuning in to its assignment. All members agree on the team's goal and on their personal assignments. If any members have different or additional goals they say so at this point to ensure that the team is not blocked at a later stage. The team goal is clearly specified and quantifiable, attainable but challenging. To ensure clarity the goal is written down for all to see.

Criteria for success

An early decision on criteria for success brings immediate focus to the task. 'What would success look like?' is a question we always ask team members before launching into a team development programme. Creative teams speak in terms of design characteristics. Executive teams clarify the items they expect members to take back to the teams they lead. At this stage the criteria may be broad and sketchy but the more precise they are, the greater the impetus for the project. However, the first criteria are often formulated in a preliminary pilot for the decision stage which is reassessed later, by which time the team has further clarified its objective. The refined criteria then determine the best possible option for implementation.

Actions

The team may need to do some preliminary action planning to determine who will be doing what to move them on to stage 2 (understanding) of the team task cycle. If the team is still engaged in other projects, the only action may be simple verbal agreements that are noted by the recorder. Large projects, however, need a more formal preliminary planning session and major projects may need force-field analysis to chart a course before action planning starts.

SYSTEM FEEDBACK AND TEAM REGULATION

A CORE team aims for a high degree of self-regulation as early in its life as possible. However, optimal form will not be attained in the early stages of its development—this is a time of discovery. Instead, it discusses ways in which it can bring its process under control to enable it to perform consistently over time. Interpersonal skills can be the regulating factors for performance and, as such, need close scrutiny, maintenance and control if members are to perform effectively. This preliminary stage will highlight several apparently conflicting requirements. The team needs clear direction yet must explore its native opinions and perspectives. It needs to be receptive to the issue at the start but must clarify the task and eliminate ambiguities. It needs a shared objective but has to allow personal needs and motivation to be included in the big picture.

Consistent The first task is to establish a team membership that will include a wide range of potential qualities, facilitate the growth of relationships, model norms of communication, set out to discover the team's identity and provide clear direction. The team adopts warming up and warming down as norms and monitors the adoption of team roles. The entire process of team development, the acquisition of contactful communication norms and the discovery of its identity are tasks for the immediate future. Performance parameters for these and other meeting skills need to be set so that members can map their progress. The designated team leader can assume this function, if experienced, because the team is in task mode when discussing such parameters. However, the principle that facilitation is a separate role to leadership and cannot be combined is emphasized if the team chooses to bring in a facilitator at this stage.

Optimal Once performance has some consistency, it is possible to see how the team might improve. Task and process run in tandem. The team will gain enough insight to understand its own patterns—where it is out of control and how to differentiate between specific and common cause variations in its performance. It will then have a clearer picture of what it needs to do, using positive reinforcement of desirable patterns or negative reinforcement of limiting patterns, in order to hit its targets more consistently.

Robust Where possible, a team must improve its robustness *before* it is engaged in the task, not after. It must consider its vulnerability to obstacles over which it may have no control—including management pressures, resistance from other teams, interference of line management, inaccessibility of management, inadequate resources and lack of access to information. Internal sources of noise must also be identified. These might be a paucity of skills or knowledge and territorial conflicts. Though not the most optimistic of perspectives, this process acknowledges that teams which are innovative and challenge existing norms will inevitably encounter resistance. The more robust the team at the beginning, the better it will steer its course through the life cycle of the project.

Evolving   Although it is too early for a team to consider how it will evolve over the course of its project, it must now ensure that its processes and norms for increasing competency are in place. An early examination of corporate belief systems and thinking styles can identify possible supports and obstacles to exploration and creativity. But the ability to self-govern and steer will emerge over time as the team increases awareness, gains in experience and discovers its identity.

INSIGHT BARRIER

Clarity and direction are required to move from recognition (stage 1) to understanding (stage 2). The risk is that the team either wanders around at the first stage, having no clear idea of what needs to happen or jumps too rapidly from awareness to decision (stage 3). When a team is stuck at the 'insight barrier' confusion reigns. It may revisit the issue several times in the same meeting or at one meeting after the other, without ever moving on. This is usually because it does not know what to do or has not established a clear direction.

   Some symptoms of a team stuck at this barrier are:

- The team does not seem to recognize that a real issue exists or, if it does, no one is able to describe the issue properly.
- The issue is clear but it cannot be explored by using the methods the team has available. The team does not know how to proceed.
- The leader is not committed to working with the issue.
- Members are not convinced it is worth using the team's resources for this task.
- Members are ill at ease with the proposed project manager.
- The team has a valid issue but the time is not right to analyse or act.

- The team lacks a suitable budget.
- The team lacks authority.
- The team cannot agree.
- The team has no champion.
- Organizational boundaries for the work cannot be defined.
- Access to people, processes, systems and procedures is too difficult.
- The team lacks other resources it requires.
- The target for change is neither achievable nor measurable.
- Quantification of benefits is not possible.
- There is no shared vision and purpose.

Overcoming the insight barrier

Trust   Trust is the product of team development. If the project team is new, members will not yet have developed an unshakeable trust in each other. However, some basic *confidence* in the team's ability to understand and address the issue needs to be demonstrated. *Anxiety* about the nature of the operation or worries about certain team relationships may arise. The team needs to develop skills quickly that will enable it to regulate its process. The team's *credibility* may rest on the successful resolution of the issue. Members' willingness to pursue the task will grow as they demonstrate their skills and abilities to each other.

Congruence   All team members have conscious or semi-conscious expectations. These are a mixture of expectations of their own experience and for the team itself. The latter may include maintaining stability and making its mark in the organization. Making all such expectations explicit at this stage allows a reality check, lays a basis for common understanding and ensures an approach that will include as many personal goals as possible.

A good team finds levels of congruence between its purpose and goals and those of each member. As the team finds how to forward personal ambitions while achieving its objective, members come to derive a genuine satisfaction from their jobs that ensures the team's success. Establishing shared expectations at this initial stage provides a strong basis for reaching consensus at the decision stage of the task cycle.

Resistance   Although resistance may be experienced by many team members as a block to optimal performance, it points to a source of hidden energy in the system. The current expression of this energy may be viewed as an error state—an output which is other than the team's ideal output. However, since it indicates some aspect of team process that is not performing well and draws energy from the desired target, it also gives an opportunity to improve a process, structure, norm or set of behaviours—even when the precise way in which they detract from the team's performance has yet to be clearly identified.

Establishing congruence between individual and team goals makes some of the hidden agendas (potential obstacles to team performance) more explicit. Hidden agendas block the team from achieving increased capability, often emerging just as the team process appears to be under control and enhanced performance seems possible. In many ways they act as negative feedback mechanisms to maintain the team at the same level of performance. When it seems that a team may start to excel or even exceed its targets, these hidden agendas emerge to restore the old ways of working, to undercut new but delicate processes and to question emerging goals and aspirations. It is the underlying needs of team members who maintain hidden agendas that have to be addressed, not their surface positions. A team makes more progress by addressing restraining forces than by struggling to establish a new process. The harder one pushes, the harder the system pushes back.

Purpose To breach the insight barrier, the team leader needs to demonstrate a sense of direction, while showing concern for the anxiety and trust issues that other members may face. Taking sides in the conflicts that emerge now will destroy confidence that even-handedness will be the norm, as the team moves into the challenges ahead. The team needs time to explore its ambiguities in a structured way. Setting clear time boundaries, establishing and adhering to communication norms, maintaining other agreements as the team moves through this stage, will bring more clarity about the task and about the team itself. The team is then free to discover its strengths, its weaknesses, its values and its identity.

At this early stage, when the team's identity is still heavily veiled, the good leader avoids tinkering with membership, giving mixed messages, changing course unnecessarily, changing criteria for success or letting confusion leak through from outside the team's boundaries. Such behaviour undermines team development and slows the discovery of its identity, giving fuel to resistance, neurotic conflict, confusion and other more subtle forms of sabotage. As resistance and the underlying security needs of team members are addressed, the team can move forward with increasing clarity and determination.

OBJECTIVES OF THE RECOGNITION STAGE

Any attempt to lay a firm foundation for a successful project team requires:

- clear team membership, relationships, roles and responsibilities
- clear procedures, processes and norms of interaction within the team
- a champion who has resources, time and enthusiam to make the project a success
- background information, dominant ideas, assumptions and boundaries
- clear correlation between the task and the team's mission and values
- customers and customer requirements
- initial criteria for success
- if a large project, lines of authority and access to resources
- a decision on whether the situation (i) deals with a past problem, (ii) demands immediate action and/or (iii) requires future planning
- the team's objective, a clearly perceived need and a clearly defined target area
- goals for stage 2 (understanding), instead of jumping quickly to solutions.

16

Understanding

UNDERSTANDING THE SITUATION

Recognizing that a situation exists and truly understanding it are distinct phases of the task cycle. This second stage deepens knowledge and orders information in order to clarify the situation's history and the possibilities for action open to the team. There are three steps to take:

- Observation and data collection
- Systems analysis
- Recommendations for action.

Observation and data collection

The presenting issue re-examined

At stage 1 (recognition), the team listened to an initial description of the situation as perceived, clarified its nature and arrived at a preliminary statement. Team members now have to uncover as much additional data as possible and, if necessary, do a needs analysis to get a complete picture of the situation and the context in which it is set. This requires active listening (especially during the investigative steps), good speaking and questioning skills and dialogue where there are differences. This process provides a basis for setting priorities and establishing criteria at stage 3 (decision making).

System mapping is a valuable part of the data collection process, placing the situation in the context of the system of which it is part. It is not uncommon for the 'presenting' issue to be symptomatic of something more fundamental. This is frequently the case when the issue is internal. Each team member could have a different view of the task and it is often very difficult to know what is happening from inside the system. How far this is the case depends on how much time was taken to probe deeply at stage 1 before accepting the presenting issue at face value.

Very often the real issue, internal or external, is quite different to the one described to anyone who asked for help. This is not surprising since the person introducing the issue—team leader, champion or key stakeholder—often does not have the whole picture. A team leader who describes a 'problem player' or 'problem team' may be unaware that his or her leadership style is perceived as confrontative and dismissive, which is putting severe strain on other team members. We have been asked to motivate a team and found it to be highly motivated but intensely frustrated by the lack of clear direction. We have even been asked to help a team make a 'difficult transition', only to find that the team has already made the transition and is waiting for a new task to perform. In all cases the consulting team's job is to examine the presenting issue in detail and either confirm that it is the 'real' issue or find the 'real' issue that it hides.

Widen and deepen understanding

Teams need a systems perspective when clarifying a presenting issue, as the causes of a situation are often far removed in time and space from the symptoms. While the team may have an initial description or definition of their task, this is only the starting point. It needs further exploration. As the team continues to explore an issue, it needs to extract and clarify underlying patterns that may not appear on the surface. This process requires the *widening* and *deepening* of the perspective.

Widening

Widening requires the team to look out across the organization. This is a multi-functional, cross-functional and cross-departmental perspective. Where a team's focus is its own processes, widening may mean looking at where the team is situated in a process flow. Typically this involves the quality of its inputs from other teams or suppliers and the expectations for its outputs to teams further down the line—its customers. Placing the team in a context of inputs and outputs allows it to identify critical inputs or expectations from the larger system of which it is a part.

Deepening

Deepening requires the team to explore up or down the organizational hierarchy. A typical example is examining how authority and responsibility are structured and dispensed within the organization. It means, for example, looking for key mixed messages from management which say 'Go!' (i.e. perform this task) but communicate 'Stop!' (e.g. there are no resources or power to proceed). It may also mean exploring below the decision-making level and looking at production or delivery of products. This can show the obstacles that prevent the effective implementation of decisions or where there is always resistance on the way to change. Deepening will initially take the team away from the apparent task at hand but will move it closer to strong leverage points for intervention.

Research skills

Data collection for problem determination or confirmation requires analytical and diagnostic skills plus a range of other behaviours. Those doing the research need to see the wider picture into which the team's operation and the issue fits and develop a systems perspective on the team's process. They will have to separate fact from opinion, observations from interpretations. They will also have to set up and test hypotheses, explore possible alternatives and persist in discovering the underlying issue and correct facts.

Data collection tools

OBSERVATION *IN SITU*

If the task involves production, development or delivery resource, the team needs to tour the site in which the situation exists. If there is a problem to solve, then it visits the production's site. If the team is a product development team, benchmarking of other products would be valuable. If it is a process re-engineering team, then best practices need to be identified and observed in operation. Marketing teams would need to identify the main competitors and their products. On-site observation is essential.

PROCESS FLOW CHARTS

A process cannot be properly examined without making a flow chart. When a process improvement team is established, a process flow chart of the area to be improved plays a pivotal role in its understanding of 'what is'. Design and development teams may formulate a process flow chart for their development cycle. The same or a similar chart could be used to show lines of responsibility and communication that would help assess the current state of teamwork.

QUESTIONNAIRES

Questionnaires should be used with caution because: (i) they do not always measure what one thinks; and (ii) their data are not always as reliable or as 'hard' as their proponents suggest. Numbers are not the truth. Questionnaires should not be used as the primary source of data, though they may provide a back-up or starting point to observation and interviews. Systems dynamics even in relatively small teams are too sophisticated to be captured this way.

For a questionnaire to be beneficial, it should be developed in conjunction with the areas that are to be its subject. When identifying the voice of the customer, marketing and product development teams tend to go their separate ways and, as a result, the valuable information they each have, that could inform and influence the work of each other's team, is never shared. Vital details only emerge when the product is far down the developmental line at which point changes are costly. Internal customer surveys can help identify major arenas for change in organizational systems.

INTERVIEWS

Interviews with individuals or small groups provide a valuable addition to a needs analysis. They give an in-depth perspective on the issue and can often help structure the team's output in a way that serves the ultimate customer much better. Staff usually view such interviews as an opportunity for two-way communication with management and a chance to contribute to the design of the new approach.

Analytical tools

Every type of team has its own specific and useful tools for analysing data. These tools are used both in the collection of data and in subsequent analysis. Problem-solving teams use problem profiling, cause and effect diagrams and Pareto charts for data analysis but should also use them to structure the ways in which they collect those data. Strategic teams may use value analysis or resource audits to identify their strategic strengths in terms of the marketplace and their ability to produce products. Process re-engineering teams use flow charting to identify the steps that produce the most improvement for the least investment of resources. In the collection and analysis of data, each type of task team uses specific methodologies that are appropriate to their tasks. In addition to these macro approaches to collecting and organizing data, most employ the normal range of statistical and graphical tools, including Pareto charts, check sheets, histograms, cause and effect diagrams, spread sheets, pie charts, bar charts and normal distributions (Ishikawa 1982).

Systems analysis

Systems analysis sometimes suffers from a false perception of complexity. While these are no more complex than other approaches to data collection they do require a different approach to thinking. Systems analysis examines and maps circular and non-linear relationships between processes that are ordered but usually have a high degree of complexity. Identifying the impact of circular causality and systems behaviours will clarify confusing ambiguities in a system and highlight uncertainties that would otherwise be ignored. The most straightforward statement about the application of systems analysis is given by Morgan (1993: 254):

Conceptions of simple causality are just inadequate for understanding the dynamics of complex systems. As Anthony Wilden has noted, in complex systems there are always causes that cause causes to cause causes. By attempting to map system relations and identifying their principal tendencies, it is possible to acquire the appreciative understanding that Gregory Bateson has described as 'systemic wisdom' and to frame interventions that attempt to influence the pattern of relations defining a system, rather than attempting to manipulate artificial 'causes' and 'effects'. The best approach is often to (a) attempt to identify the principal subsystems or nests of loops that hang together, (b) modify their relations when necessary by reducing or increasing the strengths of existing linkages and adding or removing loops, and (c) give particular attention to the loops joining different subsystems. The latter are particularly important for understanding how local action can reverberate throughout the whole and how one can restrict or amplify those effects when necessary.

It is convenient to ignore systems behaviours and arrive at simple, mechanical cause and effect linkages between factors but this gives a false analysis. The world in which management lives is becoming more, not less, complex and more interactive by the day. Linear approaches to complex adaptive systems are increasingly limited in their applications. The 'one minute managers' have had their 20 minutes of fame. It is the big picture that now demands their attention if they are to get it right.

The judicial use of a mixed approach produces the best understanding of a situation. Mechanical and statistical approaches have their use providing a bedrock of data and identifying trends, but a systems approach comes into its own in the interaction between elements of the system. Nowhere is this more the case than when identifying primary causes for trends and planning interventions to introduce new processes, change old ones and anticipate future trends before they happen.

Systems behaviours

Growth trends through positive feedback

The team must look for emerging patterns that are assuming non-linear or exponential curves of growth or decay. These could be increasing costs, increasing failure rates, increasing employment or increasing delays. The trick here is neither to stop them if they are counterproductive nor enhance them if they are productive but to look into the system for balancing factors that will counteract them. In 1995, the first quarter profits for US auto manufacturers reflected massive sales to retail outlets and a huge burst in production but, by the second quarter, demand for new cars was cooling and dealers were sitting on huge stocks of automobiles 'sold' by the auto manufacturers (hence their huge first quarter profits) but not yet sold to the public. Consequently, on the heels of record profits, the manufacturers faced cutbacks in sales and production for the third and fourth quarters. Anticipation of counter trends and the modification of processes and goals in line with anticipated (but unrealized) trends would help to minimize the pain of cycles that are characteristic of these types of businesses.

'Negative' feedback and S curves

'Negative' feedback brings a system to some level of stability when it has strayed too far from target values for certain factors or has peaked at a certain level of performance. The question that needs to be asked is: 'Do I want more, less or the same level of "negative" feedback in the system?'

More 'negative' feedback is required when a system is overshooting its targets and the overshoot is counterproductive. 'Negative' feedback may then mean withholding resources further upstream or bringing other factors into operation to counter the impact. Reduction in 'negative feedback' is usually applied before a cycle has bottomed out or over-compensated. The delicate application of interest rate increases to the US economy during 1994 was an attempt to peak at the right stage of the growth cycle—slowly squeezing the increase of money supply but holding steady at a period before growth peaked so as not to over-counteract economic growth and plunge the country back into a recession. This 'don't intervene but keep a close eye on it' policy resulted in a 'soft landing'.

Delay

Delay is in the nature of the way systems work. The impact on a system of both 'positive' and 'negative' feedback can be delayed over time because inputs may be several stages removed from the area in which they have impact or, in large systems, because the growth of a factor in one area may need to reach a critical mass before it has an impact on another area. There was a 260-year delay between the discovery in 1601 that citrus fruits could prevent scurvy and their wide scale introduction in the merchant marine in 1865. This exceptionally long period reflected the culture's inability to transmit the data (Rogers 1983: 78). However, it also showed that until the practice of impressing sailors or prisoners was halted in Victorian times, the lives of the crew were not valued. When sailors died, their replacement cost little. Only when there was another restraining force—the lack of free labour—did the merchant marine begin to look seriously at ways to keep crew members alive over repeated voyages.

The initial Introductory Course of a major quality programme in which we were involved was constantly over-subscribed, whereas the subsequent Application Modules were regularly cancelled or run with minimal attendance. It took nearly two years before demand shifted and applications for the Application Modules began to outstrip the capacity to meet them, while the Introductory Course attendance levelled out and was filled by latecomers and new employees. Yet considerable resources had been spent on preparing for the delivery of the Application Modules well ahead of the time they were needed, rather than engaging in a simple system analysis that would have predicted the time-lag involved in building a critical mass of potential attendees.

Training budgets are usually among the first to be reduced to stem outgoings when a business has a period of contracting sales. The budgets are then renewed late in the subsequent upturn, at a time of rapid growth but this is too late for the acquisition of skills needed at the start of the upturn and is badly timed in terms of availability of company employees during a period of high production and overtime.

Oscillation

Oscillation is the product of continual over-shooting and over-correction of a system which seeks stability or homeostasis. Most systems find their target value for a critical factor and maintain it at a relatively constant level but often, when an intervention is based upon linear calculations rather than systems thinking, there is a tendency to ignore unidentified delay of outputs. Inventory control is perhaps the best example of how delays in the system work to produce oscillations in stock levels. Increasing demands for a product prompt increasing orders in component materials or parts but, if there is a delay in the delivery of the components, there may be increased pressure to order more components in anticipation of increased sales. If the season or cycle has turned by the time the components arrive, the company has excess raw materials and eventually excess stock. It therefore drastically curtails its orders from suppliers who, in turn, cut back on the production of their materials. A sudden upswing of demand then results in a rush order to the supplier and another delay as the supplier struggles to fill it.

This was typified by the sale of dehumidifers in the mid-west of the United States in the summer of 1995. Temperatures in the 90–105°F (35–45°C) range augmented by high humidity caused hundreds of deaths, particularly among the elderly, from breathing, heart and dehydration complications. The rush for portable dehumidifying units kept the industry in peak production but the stores were constantly out of stock due to time lags in availability of key components. When the temperatures finally dropped in the autumn, there was a massive sell off of dehumidifiers which had been unavailable during the peak of the hot spell.

Force-field analysis

When the initial data collection is complete, an assessment of driving and restraining forces likely to affect the achievement of change can be made with force-field analysis. This is a simpler but often useful form of systems analysis. Its advantage is that it identifies key forces affecting the balance of the system and allows a team to identify and target relatively quickly those forces that can be changed to shift the system towards a new, more desirable balance. Its potential disadvantage is that it may not map the dynamics sufficiently to see how the system is working and may then miss identifying key leverage points that are further removed from immediate symptoms.

Identify limiting factors

Good systems analysis identifies the limiting factors that keep a system at its current level of homeostasis. These are often the best sources of leverage for change even when they are removed in space and time from the presenting situation. A good analysis of limiting factors can anticipate the results that interventions will have further down the line before they are made. Indicators of the best leverage points to reduce the restraining force of limiting factors may be found in several places within the system.

Scarce resources

Scarce resources take a multitude of forms: they may be delays in access to resources, resulting in oscillations of system performance; they can be a lack of a particular commodity, which will maintain a cap on the growth potential of a team or department; or they may be a shared resource that has been over-utilized or plundered, as in the case of the cod banks in the North Atlantic by the mid-1990s and the fishing wars between the Canadians and the Spanish off the coasts of Newfoundland. This has been described among systems analysts as the 'Tragedy of the Commons'. These limiting factors may also be a scarcity of finance, production equipment, human resources, expertise or simply of a senior executive's time. The list is endless but scarce resources always act as 'negative' feedback to any system experiencing growth. Identifying them and the relationship they have to desired growth is an obvious and essential aspect of any analysis.

Organization

There are few more powerfully limiting factors to changing a system than inbred organizational culture and structure. It is discouragingly common for new initiatives to be crushed by a culture designed to control or limit deviations from established procedures. Identifying the underlying fears and concerns represented by an organizational culture will provide insight into the limiting factors built into the system.

Individuals

Specific individuals can operate as limiting factors in two main ways: either they are not capable of performing the function necessary to pursue the change or they are more interested in keeping the system the same or limiting change, thereby maintaining their power base. The latter are much more limiting than the former. Someone who does not have the capacity to deliver a particular service or product can be trained, circumvented, supported or even replaced by someone more skilled but an individual who knows how to use power and is able to play the bureaucratic political game is a more challenging hurdle, particularly when in a pivotal function or role.

Relationships

Key relationships can act as supportive powerhouses for positive synergies or deep black holes of conflict and territoriality which drain energy into prolonged error states and side-track any good initiative. At this understanding stage of the task cycle, team members may be interacting with a wide range of personnel. In a large project, the research and needs analysis team members meet many people a number of times. This helps them to identify key players, to see where positive or negative synergies exist and to discover the underlying concerns and interests of these key players. Good team leaders and effective systems interventionists look for such relationships and help to find positive synergies between the individuals involved.

One potential hazard is a lack of shared values between team members and their customers. Effective change agencies work with awareness of cultural differences between themselves and their clients, avoiding (a) communication difficulties that derive from 'being different' (b) the use of different language or (c) statements or references based upon false assumptions of shared experience.

Recommendations for action

Useful information

Accessibility

Information should be presented in a format that is readily comprehensible and comparable to data from other sources. Statistical analysis often gives reams of computer printout covered in figures: this may be comprehensive but is not very useful. The skill lies in picking the relevant numbers and relating them to the issue at hand. Data have to be standardized so that comparisons bring clarity.

Validity

Information is valid when it relates to the correct topic. Data that are accurate but irrelevant to a particular decision are invalid in that context. For instance, looking for a high-fibre loaf of bread in a supermarket, we may choose a brown 'Super Health Loaf' rather than a white 'Standard Loaf', believing it to contain more fibre. However, closer examination of the ingredients reveals that they offer identical amounts and the loaves are only different in colour and name.

Reliability

Information is reliable when it is accurate. Statistical process control (SPC) is now widely used in manufacturing to monitor ongoing processes and identify long-term patterns. This allows decisions to be made on reliable information, rather than on random or outlying samples. Not all situations or processes should be subjected to SPC but the principle that quality decisions can only be made with quality information still applies.

Report

Depending on the scope of the project, the next step in stage 2 is an analysis or report that could include the following:

- A brief description on how situation identification, research, needs analysis and change impact assessment were carried out.
- Identification of the prime limiting factors for change.
- A systems analysis which describes the current state, the major systems behaviours in operation, the driving and restraining forces affecting the possibility of change and how the current state might be shifted towards an improved situation.
- Conclusions and recommendations for possible courses of action.
- Details of the evidence to support conclusions and recommendations.
- Resources required, measures and costs.

TEAM REGULATION

By the time the team reaches this stage of its task cycle it has discovered a great deal more about itself. It will have collected data about itself and may have begun to establish the nature of its own system. This may have come from a long-term team development programme or from a more *ad hoc* refinement of the skills and relationships of team members. Failure to establish a good understanding between team members will mar the success of the team's project. Team members also need to be aware of their own interests in the project so that they can see where they may be in conflict or overly confluent with the team's goals and values.

Team consistency

By this time the team should have differentiated specific and common causes for variation and have eliminated or minimized the impact of the special causes. It is now attempting to maintain a consistent performance measured against key criteria it has established. Effective teams maintain clear structures, follow their processes and work towards maintaining relationships. Structures on which it will focus include regular well-managed team meetings that follow clear agendas. Within these meetings—usually during warming up—the team refers to and affirms its purpose and direction so that those who become confused or over-identified with a particular subteam or aspect of the project can reference back to the bigger picture. Inputs to team meetings should be related to attaining the team's overall purpose. Action plans with times, dates and responsibilities assigned to them will help maintain the connection between individual work and team work.

Warming up and warming down continue to shed light on the team's identity and strengthen team boundaries. The task aspect aligns the team with its purpose and ensures that all members know the direction they will pursue between meetings. Communication skills—descriptive feedback, speaking, questioning and listening—all keep the team process operating smoothly.

Process and maintenance checks allow members to maintain good contact under pressure. The sheer bulk of data can obscure purpose and direction, lending an air of confusion to the project. When members work individually or in pairs on different aspects of the project or at different sites, it is easy to become dispersed. Contact with others may be rare, each going about his or her business at different times, in different places and with different materials and interests. Process and maintenance checks are an opportunity to give the team system feedback—what works, what does not work, how they use their time, whether they understand the processes they are using, difficulties in relationships and their response to all this. Such feedback to the system allows the team to adjust its processes and procedures and to function with greater control.

If the team has not achieved the desired level of contact, communication and respect, then this can be due to one of a wide range of variations in its process, usually the result of inherent characteristics of developing teams. Team membership can change at an early stage of a project—the suitability of team members for a task is not always clear until after the project has begun. It may emerge that there is no need for a finance person at this stage or there may be a duplication of skills between two members that allows one of them to be released to another project. Consistent membership, attendance and participation allow continued team development; occasional lapses can evoke valuable process work; persistent deviation brings crisis or failure.

The challenge is for the team to expand its boundaries in order to include as much new material and ideas as it needs, without losing its focus or identity. This can make it difficult to maintain a sense of unity and belonging. Members may find that they have stronger resonance with the work area where they are conducting research or that they work extremely well in pairs or subteams but that full team meetings are ponderous and lack contact.

Team optimum

Teams improve by assessing their level of performance at a range of skills and behaviours and deciding which they need to enhance, which to maintain and which to change. They then establish new targets for those behaviours and pursue strategies that move them further forward.

If the team is new, there will still be many unknown factors affecting its performance. It will not yet have achieved a consistency that allows it to identify behaviours it wants to keep, increase or decrease. The team is still engaged in discovering its identity and establishing its positive norms. The optimum is not a reality at this stage (stage 2) but a target towards which the team can strive.

If, however, the team is revisiting a project or performing a familiar task, it can develop more quickly and begin to optimize its performance more easily. Communication skills, learned together, can be introduced at team meetings or refined if they have been applied before, making them less artificial and more timely. Roles that are already familiar can be adopted more easily and performed with a greater degree of skill. Resources can be managed more appropriately as the team will be better able to judge the timing and quantity required for a particular task. The team becomes more effective.

Team robustness

If a team has attained a degree of robustness, it will be able to include a wide range of ideas and information without losing its direction or purpose. It maintains the regularity of its team meetings and the consistency of its performance, even when pulled in a dozen different directions by research needs or management vicissitudes. Leadership itself is robust, minimizing the impact of limiting factors in the system and constantly aligning action to the team's vision.

At this stage the robust team is already able to hold and process diversity. While its structures and processes can be formal, the spread of its activity may be very broad. The team may now have to invite a wide range of visitors, guests or temporary members to join it, as it incorporates data and expertise from many sources. Only a relatively robust team can maintain its performance and processes as it expands and contracts with new people and specific tasks that come and go. A team leader must walk the tightrope between including information and input that may be valuable and preventing the team from having too wide a range or being diverted from its objective.

Conflict will disturb the team's ability to regulate its process and is to be expected as the team comes to grips with the nature of the situation and what it is able to do. As more data are discovered and members pursue specific areas of research or specialize in particular functions, there are usually more differences of opinion and purpose. These differences should be made explicit to enable the team to gain the full benefit of as wide a range of perspectives as possible. The shared understanding and clarity that comes from open dialogue at this stage allows the decision-making and implementation stages to be simpler and more effective.

A robust team holds to its initial vision and purpose. While it may expand or enhance that vision, it does not get distracted by intriguing side issues. Alignment operates as the key for discrimination among the huge jumble of input. Such a team has permeable boundaries at this stage to let in visitors and information, but it must have limitations to that permeability so that it does not dissolve into weakness or lack of discipline. It must also avoid losing sight of its own identity or getting subsumed under other teams in a way that compromises its autonomy.

Team evolution

At this stage, a team gathers momentum and develops basic competencies. Provided it maintains its focus throughout this process, it will lay the foundation for future evolution. Attention can easily stray from the present to the future as members anticipate the skills they will need to analyse data, anticipate the team's growth as it reaches the decision stage, anticipate their enhanced responsibility if the team is required to execute its decisions, anticipate the stresses and strains that the task may place on the team and identify the ways in which these can be minimized. So much is happening that the ability to engage and disengage becomes crucial, while making sure that the team remains robust to the strains placed on its identity, membership, process and purpose.

MOBILIZATION BARRIER

'He who desires but acts not, breeds pestilence'.

This barrier, which can be summed up in a line from William Blake's *Proverbs of Hell*, could be called the 'too much of a good thing' barrier. It is often the product of caution. Knowing how much is at stake, teams collect stacks of information, prepare, analyse and weigh every conceivable opportunity, forever putting off the day when they have to act. Teams that hit the mobilization barrier know what needs to be done but fail to take the plunge. They wait for just the right moment, when all their ducks are in a row or when they can make their pitch with the maximum opportunity for success. Such teams become bloated with information. In systems terms, they get input after input, collecting ever more energy but never releasing enough to push themselves over the edge and into the next stage. Even error states are never dramatic, appearing only as a leakage of energy.

This is the team that says 'we were just waiting to be given the go ahead'. Stuck at the mobilization barrier, it needs an outsider to prod it into action. It is more than willing to follow but does not feel it has the power to make a major decision alone. Yet if it persuades someone else—a sponsor, a new leader, a human resources representative or a consultant— to mobilize its energy, it may move on without having changed. This is a typical systems bind. The team and the intervenor are part of a larger system in which stability and initiative are divided. The team collects and holds energy and the intervenor initiates the release. They form a partnership in which the individual who sparks the team into action plays the hero or rescuer while the team just continues to collect data, waiting to be rescued. This is a co-dependency relationship within which neither party grows and the team remains stuck in its dependency on outside forces to initiate action.

Such teams need deadlines but if someone sets the deadline for them they will not feel responsible if it is missed and will claim they never really agreed. (Alternatively they retroflect, blaming themselves abjectly instead of doing something about it.) These teams need to produce their data regularly and if anything significant occurs they must report it at once. They cannot wait until the right moment arrives or until they are asked for it. Encouraging them is tempting, but nothing will help until they fully experience their 'stuckness', fully understand how they get themselves stuck as a system and appreciate themselves for doing it so well. They then discover other options and strategies, realizing perhaps how to design alternative courses of action to construct their own safety net.

OBJECTIVES OF THE UNDERSTANDING STAGE

At the understanding stage of the task cycle, the team identifies or confirms its task, puts forward recommendations for action and agrees on the basis for proceeding. The biggest risk in terms of project failure is that the information provided may be inadequate or falsely interpreted and that the proposal for action may not set out the team's commitments clearly. This would produce bad decisions or unrealistic objectives and mean that both resources and time scales would be inadequate. The main objectives for this stage are to:

- further the team development process, thereby increasing contact and trust;
- use appropriate techniques, quality tools and statistical methods to gather information and identify the 'real' issue;
- make certain that the initial objectives, established at the identification stage, are still operative and, where appropriate, refine them;
- keep the champion and sponsors informed and involved, particularly when approaching the decision stage;
- use descriptive feedback, process checks and team development exercises to further refine the team structure, process, norms and skills;
- improve the team and make it more robust to noise;
- reduce error states;
- map the ecology of which the team system is a part;
- maintain congruence of the team's values as the course of the project progresses;
- generate ideas, new processes, new solutions, root causes and key priorities;
- identify possible courses of action and, where required, begin to set priorities for the next stage: Decision.

17

Decision

Decision making, the pivotal stage in the task cycle, plays the central role in a team's performance. Decision making is itself a system, with inputs, outputs and a process. When making decisions a team is putting all of its information through a process, the output of which will indicate the optimal course of action. Following a systems approach, we can order the decision-making process into three progressive stages:

1 Identifying the inputs and desired outputs of the team system, including the criteria by which success will be judged.
2 Examining the team's internal structures, membership and expertise; establishing the best decision-making process to follow; and establishing both *systemic* criteria for success and *leverage* points for intervention.
3 Choosing the best course of action based upon the systems analysis and the prioritization methodology. Initiating appropriate actions and assessing them against both the success criteria and systemic criteria for successful implementation.

ESTABLISH THE INPUTS AND OUTPUTS OF THE SYSTEM

Inputs

The team has already received or generated data that form the primary input to the decision-making process. These data are organized in a way that is accessible, valid and reliable. The team also needs to recognize its biases and limitations so that its perspective is not distorted.

Context of information

Time

A decision required in five minutes is approached differently from one required in two months. Time constraints may influence the degree of urgency but not necessarily the quality of the decision.

Magnitude

Magnitude may be measured by the number of people affected, the amount of money involved, the geographical spread of the decision or by other considerations. The scale of potential consequences is also relevant. These factors will depend on the option eventually chosen but the question of magnitude moves both upstream and downstream of the decision itself. Magnitude defines the importance of the decision, yet may be independent of the quality of the eventual choice.

Reversibility

In some ways this is a subject of magnitude, as the scope for reversing the decision helps to determine its importance. Choosing to have major plastic surgery (irreversible without further major surgery) is very different to going on a diet and attending exercise classes (reversible), although both options can share the aim of improving one's appearance.

Nature of decision

It has been said that the average time devoted by managers to any given issue is about 15 minutes. Most of this time is not spent making the decision but in defining the issue. Shifting resources 'upstream' to the definition stage is therefore one way to increase the likelihood of an effective result. All decisions involve choice but different issues require decisions to be made in different ways. Once the approach is made, the decision-making process becomes increasingly difficult to change.

Selection decisions

Some issues require decisions based on known criteria. A typical example is filling a job vacancy from a range of candidates. The decision-making process is one of exclusion, potential candidates being eliminated as they fail to meet increasingly stringent demands.

Ranking decisions

Ranking issues are those where a range of choices must be prioritized. A government faced with a budget deficit and needing to make spending cuts is involved in this process. While established policies offer guidance, current political considerations usually mean that decisions are made on an *ad hoc* basis. Whether policies or expediency guide the process, some form of comparison is made between a number of options. Ranking decisions may lead to the development of criteria that are then used in a selection decision.

Where to decisions

These issues occur when the ultimate goal is poorly defined or unknown and the decision leads into unknown territory. In this case the decision-making process is one of prediction. Alternatives are considered on the basis of their probable consequences and the option that seems to offer the greatest benefit is chosen.

Conceptual biases

A team draws on the past to give structure and meaning to the present and to determine how it defines, seeks out and interprets information relevant to a decision. When a team prejudges a situation, its assumptions filter what it perceives so that its expectations appear to be met. Preconceptions become self-fulfilling, part of an iterative system: it becomes easier and less anxiety producing to use or modify an existing approach than to address a totally new challenge.

Unless a team is aware of its conceptual biases it is unable to define a decision-making situation in the most appropriate way. For example, transport planners have a conceptual bias: since their orientation induces them to lay the blame for motorway congestion on insufficient traffic lanes, they automatically identify the solution to be an increase in the number of lanes. Yet this has repeatedly been shown to draw more traffic into centres of population and eventually leads to even larger traffic jams.

Desired outputs

This is an area that depends on the nature of the team and its task. It could include outcomes, measures of success, return on investment, objectives and whatever else the team hopes will be the outcome of its efforts. The team's targets may be more, or less, quantitative or qualitative and reflect the vision and goals of the organization of which the team is a part. The essential thing to recognize is that these outcomes and their measures are *targets towards which the team is steering its process*. This steering or cybernetic process is not nearly as quantifiable or objective as the measures for successful team output. In terms of team development and competency, the process must be examined with the quite different set of measures discussed below.

Criteria for successful output

Setting criteria to make a considered and balanced decision is generally more effective than 'seat of the pants' intuition: the time for that comes at the end of the assessment processes. Criteria are usually used in a prioritization process. Some are highly analytical processes that weigh various courses of action against chosen criteria, thereby excluding the less desirable and the inappropriate options. Decision analysis and decision trees are examples of such processes. Others, like a SWOT analysis, focus on 'getting a feel' for the territory and options. Whatever the degree of 'hardness' in the analysis, comparison of alternatives against criteria is often at the core of decision making. However, even the most objective methodology should not commit a team irrevocably to a decision. Prioritization does not constitute decision making, it only sorts information into meaningful order, highlighting the main or best choices. The team will ultimately have to make the decision itself.

While decision making can be intuitive—a 'gut feeling' or a simple preference—some kind of analytical process usually leads to a more confident decision. Once the prioritization process is completed the team can still choose to follow a hunch, precisely because the criteria did not include factors that continue to weigh heavily. If nothing else, the process will have clarified what is really important. This further clarifies the key criteria for success, identified earlier, or highlights others that emerged subsequently. How criteria are set will be influenced by the decision-making methodology. Problem Analysis, Concerns Analysis, Failure Modes and Effects Analysis, Quality Function Deployment, Value Analysis and Critical Path Analysis all have different prioritization criteria. The choice of the most appropriate tool depends on the task and situation definition. The same situation, defined differently, may be amenable to quite a different decision methodology.

ESTABLISH A DECISION PROCESS

Re-examine team structure

At this stage, the team's structure and processes need to be re-examined. Team membership can change as some new experts may be required and others may no longer be essential or may be needed elsewhere. Finance people are often brought into the team at this juncture. If an experiment is to be run, the team may bring in someone familiar with experimental design. If the decisions affect a different department or a regional operation, representatives from these areas are brought in. If marketing has not been involved but the decision will clearly affect their operation, a marketing representative joins.

Decision making can test the team process, and there may be strong opinions as to the correct course of action. Different departments may have their positions staked out well in advance and emotions can run high. Yet, if a well-structured decision-making process is used and the team sticks to its positive norms, such conflict can be creative. How to play the different roles, starting times, warming up and warming down routines and the methodology all need to be established in advance. As the team moves from the wide-ranging 'understanding' stage to a more tightly focused 'decision' process, time for maintenance and process observations becomes essential.

When the pressure of contentious discussion is highest, maintenance and process interventions can be forgotten and the team leader is most inclined to bias the decision or adopt an autocratic style. Even a team on its second or third project—a team that has developed far and learned to share team roles—may opt to invite an outside facilitator. This allows the leader to focus on guiding the task methodology forward. When difficulties are foreseen, the leader might ask another member to remind the team periodically to step back from individual needs and tune in to its identity and vision—this being an aspect of the leadership role that he or she might easily forget.

Don't push the river: Identify leverage points for change

There is a fundamental problem with setting hard and fast objectives and measures for success: it leads to management establishing controls on output rather than creating opportunities to improve the team's process. This is an unthinking adoption of the old hierarchical, autocratic management style. Fixed structures and outcomes are appropriate for fixed, unchanging environments, but not for the contemporary world. The more structures are fixed, the less opportunity there is for a diversity of response. Today's teams excel as they tend to interpersonal relationships and become consistent, optimal and robust in a changing and unpredictable environment. Personal competencies are enhanced, so that a diversity of experience and a wide range of response is maintained. There is no longer one right answer: the systems law of *equifinality* states that a wide range of inputs to a system can all produce the same result. As Gareth Morgan (1993: 255) says:

An understanding of mutual causality in complex systems shows that it is extremely difficult to halt change, to eliminate all positive feedback or to preserve a given mode of organisation interminably. A more appropriate strategy is to learn to change with change, influencing and shaping the process when possible but being sensitive to the idea that in changing times new forms of system organisation must be allowed to emerge. This process often hinges on an ability to detect and avoid destructive system tendencies which often lie in the vicious circles created by positive-feedback relations, to create space in which learning and patterns of co-evolution can occur. In particular, attention needs to be given to the scope for collaborative action, to reduce the independent lines of activity that contribute to the complexity and turbulence of a system and thus to broaden the opportunities for learning and mutual adjustment.

Bearing all this in mind, several systems interventions may form the basis of the team's approach and help to identify its options. When combined with a more straightforward decision analysis, these help to inform or direct the course of action so that decisions can target a number of different obstacles to enhanced performance.

Add loops or break links

One of the most common problems with complex systems, i.e. most organizations, is that there are few reinforcing synergies between departments, functions and teams and too many that are counterproductive.

When we first visited British Petroleum in 1989 the traditional culture of the state-ownership era still seemed to have a lingering presence. Lunch was served at a T-shaped dining table, with the team leader at the top of the T, senior team members on either side and everyone else in descending seniority down the centre stem.

Yet chief executive and chairman Bob Horton was already destructuring at a furious pace. All parts of the organization were under review and all its previous norms were being questioned. Anyone could speak to anyone else and direct reporting lines were virtually gone. Departments with offices on the same floor, but whose members had had no interaction for years, suddenly found that they not only had permission to speak but were actively encouraged to seek each other out and establish contact. The result was a mix of excitement and angst. Power bases were eroded, contact between team members became intense and data coursed through the company as never before. However, there was also confusion and a loss of direction as everyone became involved with everything.

The disruption coincided with changes in the oil industry and a recession that undermined corporate profit margin. Bob Horton was asked to leave and David Simon was installed in his place. Simon had a different style, he was considered in his actions, financially cautious, astute in assessment, attentive in his questioning and superb at restructuring. After a harrowing period of reorganization BP emerged in 1994 as an efficient, competitive, learning organization. It also became an organization with internal lines of communication and firm bridges between its different divisions and departments. Horton's shotgun destructuring destroyed barriers between teams and decades of outdated hierarchical reporting chains, clearing the way for constructive interaction. Simon supported the best of these new links, continued to eliminate unnecessary loops and nudged the organization into a new, efficient and synergistic order.

Not all interventions are as radical as the four-year rebirth of BP but, in our work with numerous cross-functional teams in a wide range of organizations, one of the consistently most beneficial outcomes has been the self-regulating team and building of links between different functions.

The steps are usually simple: (1) create the opportunity, (2) minimize the obstacles and (3) build on the contact.

After the reorganization of Telia Respons, the operator services division of Telia Telecommunications in Sweden, there were very strong links between the business divisions providing the operator services but limited links between the divisions and the reformulated technical services department which held the majority of the engineers and technicians.

One of our jobs was to build links. This was done on a personal level by establishing areas of common interest and creating opportunities for these competing departments to talk to each other. Uptake was slow and initial meetings had to be structured and were often strained. Then, at a certain point, a critical mass was achieved and specific projects were targeted in the arena of business services and teleconferencing which required the expertise of the technical department but they were clearly business products in a growth area over which the business division would retain control. Building on the trust established from this single product link, a range of technically innovative opportunities for expanded services were identified. In the course of six months, the technical department went from being excluded with suspicion from business division's plans to being swamped with demands for their expertise. Links often build links, contact promotes contact. Loops that enhance relationships need to be added; links that keep people from relating must be broken.

Shorten delays

Delays make it difficult to identify cause and effect links between elements of a system, during the 'understanding' stage of the task cycle. Cutting these delays allows increased ability to plan and regulate performance.

One of our clients had three internal training offices for the delivery of its programmes. One was the site where courses were delivered, requests for attendance were collected, rooms were booked, resources were stored and the participants met. The second was the administrative office where decisions on the number of courses, the number of participants, the balance of different courses and yearly targets were made. The third site was the course tutors' offices. When a course was due to be delivered a decision had to be made—whether to run it or cancel. Had tutors been told that few people were enrolled, three to four weeks beforehand, they would have either phoned round to bolster numbers (they knew potential customers personally) or scheduled their time to be more productively involved in on-site consulting or supporting another course. Instead, there was a long delay between when the potential for a shortfall was identified at the delivery site and the time administrative offices were informed, with another long delay before the co-ordinator there passed on the message to the tutors. The co-ordinator was often out and procrastinated, hoping the course would fill so that a target could be met. The result was that the tutors only knew the situation a few days before the course was scheduled to run. It was then too late to get more participants and too late to arrange other useful work.

Shortening the delay in most situations is remarkably easy. The solution is simply to reframe the interaction between those concerned as a common problem, rather than a conflict. Communication can then become instantaneous and ongoing.

Expand growth

The most common of systems interventions simply increases something—be it resources, personnel, marketing, office space or sales—but it is often worth taking a step up, down or sideways in the hierarchy to see if there are other more effective points of leverage from which to work. Much more powerful and enduring results can often be obtained with less effort.

When one multinational client asked us to help identify why problem solving was not getting the desired results, we discovered that although seven figure sums had been spent sending employees on four- or five-day problem-solving courses, they were returning to desks so loaded with backlog that they had less time than ever to apply the methodologies, with the result that problems continued to go unsolved or unattended. At best, the methodology was applied (due to furious customer complaints) several months after the problem was first identified and then in such an abbreviated fashion that the root cause was frequently missed.

Clearly, the need was for an increased *application* of the methodology, not for more training. If no more than a quarter of the employees went on the four-day problem-solving programme course, they could spend up to twelve additional days a year solving problems. Since (a) rework time increased costs arithmetically, (b) stoppage time multiplied costs geometrically and (c) recall or warranty issues could escalate labour costs exponentially, the amount of time saved by finding the root causes of key problems (utilizing teams with dedicated time) eventually meant that any employee who wanted to attend a problem-solving programme could do so with no loss in production time.

Slow growth

From a systems perspective, there are two ways to slow the growth of a runaway or escalating process: move further upstream and interrupt the escalating process at a stage before it is out of control or increase a balancing or 'negative' feedback loop.

Moving resources upstream is a basic strategy of any quality initiative and optimizes resources. The opportunities are endless: giving more time to identify the voice of the customer, collaborating with marketing on the design of the product to meet emerging customer requirements, running experiments which anticipate a wide array of interactions before the product reaches the market and dedicating time to building cross-functional teams at the start of a project, rather than when they have gone wrong further down the line. Time and money invested on making any process more robust almost always pays.

Relieve limitations

Bottlenecks, resource restraints, lack of information, power-brokers, control freaks, bureaucratic backwaters, administrative checkpoints, financial ceilings and a hundred other limitations block both team and corporate development. These are ways the system maintains stability. Any new policy or course of action will evoke limitations that will keep the team from achieving its potential. The experienced team expects such a reaction, identifies such limitations early and uses the team development process to move ahead.

Establish a methodology

Once the team has identified the inputs to the decision-making process, it must clarify the nature of the decision and the methodology to be used. The methodology will depend on the type of team (problem-solving teams, for instance, will use one kind of process and creative teams will use another).

Prioritization

Most effective teams use some process to assess options against weighted criteria. Prioritization is a considered process. It requires time and energy to provide adequate information and then work with it with the full engagement of team members. It is difficult to conduct with a large group of people: either too many would be left out of the process or it would take too long. As stated previously, *prioritization does not make decisions*, it only sorts options into a meaningful order according to the team's chosen criteria. Unless the team is aware of this and members are invited to do more than supply strictly rational information, there will not be the emotional support necessary for successful implementation. Subjective reasons such as 'I like it' or 'it's new and exciting' are often excluded, even though they provide the emotional power base to support the decision. With these provisos in mind, prioritization is an excellent way to reduce a wide range of options to the most tenable. Here is a brief description of three such processes (see Table 17.1).

Decision-making matrix

This tool is typically used in selection situations, where a range of options can be compared to established criteria in order to produce a balanced choice that meets a specified end result. Two types of criteria are established: the first are *essential*, which means that any choices which fail

Table 17.1 Decision types and appropriate methodologies

Decision type	Methodology
Selection Working towards a defined end-result	Precedence chart for creation of criteria Decision matrix for best balanced choice

Where to?:
Faced with a go/no go choice and
  uncertain consequences
	Decision tree to assess probability and
	  outcome of alternatives

Ranking
Faced with the need to prioritize a
  range of alternative actions to meet a
  particular need
	Precedence chart if no criteria exist
	Decision matrix can also produce a
	  ranking if criteria can be established
	  and end result is defined

on these criteria are immediately excluded; the second are *desirable* and may be weighted according to their relative importance. Each option that meets all essential criteria is scored according to the degree to which it meets each of the desirable criteria. The final scores are calculated by multiplying the criteria weighting by the item score to produce a ranking of options.

Decision trees

Decision trees are often used for 'where to' decisions when alternative strings of consequence are taken into account. The initial decision may be limited to two options—for instance, we go or we do not go. Starting with one choice the possible outcomes are developed as branches of a tree. The cost of benefit of each outcome is noted and each in turn will have a range of further possible outcomes with their own costs and benefits. After a certain number of iterations it is possible to determine which path has the most favourable combination of probability and benefits. Decision trees can become highly mathematical, as the cumulative probabilities of a sequence of choices is calculated. However, such detailed calculations will not always be necessary or appropriate. If detailed probability statistics are not available then best guesses can be used and, if actual costs are not available, a simple positive or negative sign can show the likely effect of an outcome. The same process may be used in an intuitive, associative manner by visualizing the consequences of different choices.

Precedence charts

This is a way to prioritize a list of alternatives. It uses a matrix to make systematic comparisons. The end result is a precedence ranking that identifies the most powerful or effective steps, allowing resources to be channelled most effectively. Precedence charts fulfil a similar role to force-field analysis and could be combined with this process. Table 17.2 summarizes the attributes of prioritization and decision taking.

Generic vs unique solutions

One of the most awkward distinctions that all teams face is between situations that are so similar to previous situations that the same solutions may be applied and those that are genuinely new and for which past

Table 17.2 The attributes of prioritization and decision taking

Attribute	Use of prioritization in decision taking
Time required	Depends on availability of information. May be slow if many options to be considered and research to be done. Depends on availability of information, team effectiveness and kind of decision.
Application	Most decisions, especially those that require rational justification, i.e. major expenditure and policy. Moves the team on to next stage.
Degree of inclusion of team members	Primary role is to provide information, the system drives interaction. Depends on leadership and kind of decision process. Consensus totally inclusive.
Main benefit	May deliver a balanced choice and rational decision. May provide long-term perspective. Some methods make use of team synergy. May generate considerable support and commitment.
Main difficulty	Time consuming and complicated process requiring expertise and discipline. Depends on effective team interaction. May get bogged down or produce irrational decision.

approaches would be limited or outdated. Peter Drucker (1985: 103–5) suggests that there are only two categories: those that are generic and those that are unique, first-time events. Though somewhat over-simplified, this criterion can be very helpful. Drucker links this polar categorization to four categories of decisions.

1 The generic occurrence is one where the event exemplifies a category of situations. Generic situations are the most common types encountered by an executive team. They range from inventory control decisions to product design decisions and require the application of existing rules and guidelines, established through past experience. These decisions are taken quickly and effectively or immediately delegated, thereby saving the team's limited resources.
2 The second category involves events that are unique in the team's experience but which represent a generic category encountered by other teams. The team has to gain access to this experience and knowledge.

These principles and guidelines are not adopted wholesale and without question but are added to and contrasted with their own experience and perspective.

3 The third category is the unique event. It occurs rarely but requires fresh and innovative resolutions that can only be achieved through concentration, creativity and a dedicated amount of the team's time. The team may benefit from the first two stages of the creative team's task cycle, in which creative and lateral thinking approaches to generating options are more fully developed. The best teams relish the arrival of such events, as stimulating opportunities. These kinds of situations draw upon the team's ability to grow and evolve. They ask the team to explore new areas, develop new qualities and self-govern as they break old patterns of thought.

4 The last category of event is the one that appears to be unique but is actually the emergence of a situation that will become generic. Such events occur with increasing frequency and give the team an opportunity to demonstrate its ability to learn. The early identification of an emerging pattern of events allows the team to respond creatively, to build on its initiative and to actualize the organization's potential. This ability to recognize patterns releases the team from the constraints of its system, giving a metaperspective on both its process and its benefit to the company.

It is worth considering how the current situation differs from the past. The team can then often exploit crucial distinctions which support innovative approaches and anticipate what is emerging instead struggling to keep up. When identifying its chosen approach the team will consider:

- if it is comfortable with the approach
- if it would find itself in unknown territory if it did anything else
- if it does not have time to reflect on the situation more deeply
- if it needs to get some short-term results immediately
- if it does not know what else to do
- if it is jumping to conclusions
- if it is afraid of taking a risk
- if it is what it has always done before
- if it has to do something.

CHOOSING THE BEST COURSE OF ACTION

If the mind needs to prioritize, the heart must become involved in the act of decision. Whereas prioritization establishes the rational basis for decision making, implementation involves the whole person. A key element in this process is the degree to which the appointed leader includes or excludes the others in the team—whether the team is genuinely empowered or is operating under illusion.

There are four levels of power sharing—unilateral, polling, compromise and consensus—and each is reflected in a different decision-making process. Each has advantages and disadvantages but they become progressively more demanding on both the team and the designated team leader. The four levels are shown in Figure 17.1.

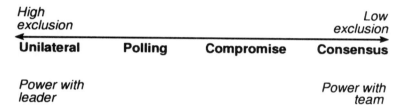

Figure 17.1   The four levels of power sharing.

Unilateral

Unilateral decision making involves one individual, usually the leader, making a decision based upon his or her personal criteria and objectives. It has its value, and when the leader has the necessary power and authority to carry it out, it can also be effective. Confusion or ambiguity often slows down processes or hamstrings action. Members might be avoiding difficult decisions for fear of being held responsible. There may in fact be only one or two individuals in an organization who have the knowledge, experience or insight to make the correct decision. In these cases unilateral decision making may be necessary.

Frequently, however, unilateral decision making is counterproductive. It may be that the decision makers do not know how to seek consensus or compromise or that they have always 'flown-by-the-seat-of-their-pants' and do not know how to make their prioritization process transparent. More often, it is used as a way to retain power and to disenfranchise other members of the team or organization.

The autocratic leader prefers this kind of decision making, occasionally not consulting team members throughout the entire process. Many businesses have attempted to moderate this management style with employee empowerment programmes, team development and consensus-seeking processes but autocratic decisions are still very much a part of many corporate cultures. Managers with this approach can undermine the confidence of other team members and destroy the sense of ownership essential to success. While being simple and widespread in its application, unilateral decision making does nothing to build team spirit or to use the potential of the team to its best effect.

Unfortunately this mode of decision making takes a long time to change. There is too much to lose. As Robert Swiggert, the former CEO of Kollmorgen Corporation, confesses:

In moving from the traditional authoritarian, hierarchical organisation to locally controlled organisation, the single greatest issue is control. Beyond money, beyond fame, what drives most executives of traditional organisations is power, the desire to be in control. Most would rather give up anything than control. (Senge 1990: 290)

Polling

The democratic process has a 2500-year-old tradition, although the process is not available to a large percentage of the Third World population. In fact, it is only in the past 130 years that black citizens of the United States have been entitled to vote. Women in Britain achieved emancipation less than 70 years ago and in Switzerland women gained the vote only after 1970!

Being enfranchised carries responsibility. When we vote we are seen to be taking part in the decision made by the organization or community at large and are therefore held accountable for these decisions. In teams, polling is used in an attempt to include everyone in the process of reaching a final decision. However, by its nature it excludes as well as includes. A majority of 1 will commit an entire team to a course of action that may not encompass the needs of the whole. In Britain, governments can gain large majorities in Parliament that are actually the product of a minority of the voting population. Ross Perot's 19 per cent of the popular vote in the 1992 USA elections allowed Bill Clinton to attain the presidency. Voting can disenfranchise or exclude as well as empower.

Voting preferences can be unpredictable and irrational: relying on a vote ignores the process by which individuals make their choice. Members may be swayed by peer pressure, personal bias, a desire for conformity or by misunderstanding the issue. Polling is more likely to be effective if, initially, all the options are discussed and understood by the whole team and if the team leader manages to guide the team away from polarization into opposing camps. Decision making by polling may also give the designated team leader a casting vote and therefore the balance of power.

Compromise

It is said that the camel is a horse created by a committee. Compromise is often the product of a team that has no clear leadership or where there are unclear lines of authority. Yet compromise is something in which we engage daily. Husbands, wives, partners, parents and children—any group of people living or working closely together—continually compromise.

Negotiations between union and management are by their nature attempts at compromise. Each party stakes out its positions well in advance and negotiation slowly leads to an acceptable point somewhere between the two. Compromise can resolve a deadlock, provided that team members are willing to concede some part of their position. At its best, compromise allows opposing subgroups to arrive at a decision that meets their underlying needs, which may not necessarily be the same as their starting position. Compromise can smooth over differences of opinion, and it is often used when operating under a time constraint.

This form of decision making allows many different positions to be included but the end result may be cumbersome. Compromise should not be mistaken for consensus. By its nature, it is less than ideal and is only used when there is no clear, shared way forward. As such, it is as likely to be half wrong as half right. In attempting to satisfy everyone it may excite no one and fail to produce an effective decision. A leader should know how far the wishes of individuals can be met without compromising the team's ultimate purpose. If the leader remains unattached to a particular point of view, he or she will have greater freedom as a broker.

Consensus

This is the most difficult of the decision-making processes because it is the most inclusive. To reach consensus, everyone contributes and discussion continues until everyone accepts the decision. In some cases this may take days but the end result mobilizes the energy of the team and ensures unanimous support. The leader agrees to do whatever the team decides, provided there is shared agreement. If one person disagrees or has reservations, discussion continues until agreement is reached. By involving the entire team, the search for consensus may lead to creative solutions outside the constraints of yes/no alternatives. A team with consensus moves ahead as a unit, committed to a shared purpose and course of action.

Consensus is often confused with compromise but is quite different. Consensus requires that all team members put aside divisive differences. It often means that some members give up their positions and commit to action that seems contrary to their own interests but which benefits the team as a whole.

Because concensus is difficult and time-consuming there is often the temptation to cut the process short and go for compromise. Apparent consensus may also hide unexpressed resentment that will later result in conscious or unconscious sabotage. The leader's role is to guide the process, ensuring that all views are heard and understood, that ideas are summarized and clarified and, eventually, that all members agree. Consensus is difficult to achieve but allows the team to act with high energy and great effect.

The productive and counter-productive aspects of the four levels of decision making are summarized in Table 17.3.

Proceed

The decision is the output. Once the team has agreed on the nature of the situation or concern and the priorities for action, it can decide how the recommendations will be implemented. A detailed proposed course of action, the result of considerable planning and commitment, would include:

- the final definition of the situation or concern, placing it in a wider context/system

Table 17.3 The four levels of decision making

Productive	Counterproductive
Unilateral	
Only one person involved	Team situation
Person making decision has the responsibility, authority and power	A number of people affected by decision
	Need support of others or team to implement
Need to cut through confusion	Does not build a sense of team identity
Polling	
Enfranchises	Small majority results in decision for all
Clear decisions	Decision may disempower many
Democratic	Not necessarily rational
Compromise	
With large groups	When needing clear decision
When at impasse	Simple solutions
In order to include as many positions as possible	Small teams
	Mobilizing full support
Consensus	
When entire team needs to get behind a project	For small or low priority projects
When conflict threatens to divide a team	Quick decisions
	Specific, technical decisions
For major policy decisions	

- a schedule of the work to be undertaken
- resources to be committed to the project, including direct and indirect costs
- team resources to be committed to the project
- time scale and milestones for planning and implementation
- deliverables
- an agreed 'vision' of success
- measures of success, as seen by the team, the organization and customers
- expected benefits (e.g. savings, increased revenue and cost reduction targets)
- how to meet internal and/or external customer requirements
- the benefits of positive quality
- the cost of negative quality.

Finally, decisions are seldom taken in isolation. They should be viewed in the context of relationships with others. A team decision is:

- an exchange between the team and the ongoing corporate social system
- a negotiation of an agreement for exchange of performance in the future
- dependent on an exchange of commitments to reduce potential uncertainty for both parties
- in need of management of interdependence
- representative of a co-operative strategy for exchange of influence
- supported by understanding and spoken or written agreements.

If the risks involved in the decision or choice were not considered earlier, now is the time. Once the risks are made explicit it becomes possible to prevent their occurrence by modifying the decision. This may require additional resources. If the risks are too great, it may be necessary to revisit alternative courses of action and choose a safer, if less effective, option. Even with preventative action already in place, it is worth adding safeguards to secure against the worst risks. Car design features such as traction control and anti-lock breaking are designed to prevent the occurrence of accidents while air-bags and side impact bars are designed to protect against injury should an accident occur, despite the presence of preventative features.

Feedback

Any decision will impact the future and also give feedback on the definition of the situation. The decision was *designed* to change or affect the situation. This may lead to redefining the situation, bringing new aspects into focus that also require action.

COMMITMENT BARRIER

Without commitment there is the chance to draw back but the team is stuck. One simple truth governs all acts of initiative (and creation), the ignorance of which kills countless splendid ideas. It is that the moment one definitely commits oneself, Providence moves too. All sorts of things occur to help that would never have happened otherwise. A stream of events springs from the moment the decision is made—all manner of unforeseen incidents and meetings and material assistance, that no team member could have predicted.

Whatever you can do,
or dream you can, begin it.
Boldness has genius,
power and magic in it.
          (Johann Wolfgang von Goethe)

Lack of commitment

The main obstacle to having an effective implementation process is lack of commitment. Team members may have complete agreement at the meeting but then forget the pledge they made. A team stuck at this barrier lacks the deep sense of commitment required to make the project work. This may be because it also lacks a genuine sense of its core values and operates superficially, sliding from one situation to the next. When a team is stuck at this barrier, it will not appear to be stuck. It will make many decisions in a flurry of activity; it will make high-profile statements about its intentions and objectives and will be noisily involved in its current project. It will be constantly on the move.

Narcissism

Continual movement with no progress may signal that the team is at this barrier, particularly if it never looks back to see what is happening in its wake and never returns to a decision with the same relish it had when it made it. A team stuck here makes each new situation the centre of its life and allows interest in the previous one to wane. Its main interest is the charge it gets from making a decision, not the outcome of its work.

Shift to risk

When considering a range of alternatives, a team will frequently choose a more extreme course of action with potentially higher rewards than an individual would if confronted with the same choices. Individuals tend to opt for a safer decision with moderate rewards. Studies have demonstrated this by asking individuals to make a choice alone and then meet together to take a group decision. Invariably the group decision represents a greater risk—in terms of money to be invested or acceptance of potential consequences—than that represented by an averaging of the individual decisions.

This is a form of synergy but the consequences may not always be favourable. There are explanations.

- Responsibility may be more diffused in a group with no one individual fearing the consequences.
- Risk acceptance may be an inherited team norm.
- Team members may prefer to take a view that appears slightly more adventurous than a 'middle of the road' course of action.
- Several members may want to appear slightly more adventurous than average but their sense of 'average' changes as they listen to each other.

The result is a decision that is a lot more risky than the one considered at the outset.

Taking risks has a certain glamour. Teams that remain stuck at the decision stage and are hesitant of commitment, or disinclined to engage personally in the support of implementation, will often be attracted to the spotlight of a glamorous position. The derivatives trader who goes astray can still make a fast tough decision but moves on, disinterested in the long-term impact. Such trading teams often find it difficult to spend time on long-term team objectives; they are at the centre of a whirlpool of action where tens of millions of dollars can be gained or lost in a momentary decision and commitment has to be totally on the issue of the moment. Teams stuck at the decision stage display the negative aspect of such aptitude, continuing to set short-term goals that are based upon increased profit, increased dividends and increased share value but are less concerned about the long-term direction of the company.

How to work with the commitment barrier

When team members are responsible for the implementation of their policies they are more conscious of the consequences of their decisions. Since responsibility for implementation evokes commitment, the barrier can be crossed by some team members working with the implementation team. In fact, teams which find themselves repeatedly at the commitment barrier need support to move from their busy decision-making schedules and should be encouraged to make regular visits to the sites and facilities that are having to implement their decisions.

Most teams meet to make decisions but few are aware of how they make them. A team that is continually stuck at the commitment barrier may profit by having an observer at its meetings who gives feedback on the team's decision-making patterns. Speediness is a virtue but so is its opposite, reflection, and a balance or easy shift between the two is healthy.

What exactly does each member do that results in the team taking a decision to which it is not really committed? As the team's awareness increases, so does interest and as each person speaks of his or her experience change becomes possible. As the team takes the first steps of the decision-making process more consciously, its commitment becomes more genuine. The question 'If we agree to this are we going to follow through?' needs to be asked at the start of the decision-making process. If team members cannot say a personal and emotional 'Yes' to this question, they should stop what they are doing, take a maintenance check and make the underlying issues explicit. It may then be possible to find something to which they *can* commit and are willing to follow through to completion.

OBJECTIVES OF THE DECISION STAGE

Decision making is an intricate process and any model is, at best, an approximation of what happens. Many decisions do not fit easily into neat categories and few situations present clear-cut options amenable to rational analysis. The real world and the people who inhabit it are unpredictable and complex and most choices have consequences that extend far beyond their initial scope. Despite the best efforts of mathematicians, decision-making remains more of an art than a science and perhaps the best way of utilizing such an art is through the synergistic efforts of a team equipped with the right information, skills and processes. As the main objectives of this stage, a team should:

- step back and see the big picture—how the particular situations fit into the larger system;
- focus on ways to eliminate problems, improve systems, design better products, plan for the future and make clear decisions;
- work out how the actions can be made robust in the larger system;

- find ways to balance clarity and purposefulness with inclusion and consensus;
- look for key leverage points with maximum returns for minimum effort;
- avoid getting caught in 'group think' or trapped by company norms;
- commit to the course of action and demonstrate that commitment.

18

Implementation

Albert Einstein is reputed to have said 'God is in the details'. The success of any project depends on the manner of its implementation. Each stage of the task cycle requires particular processes and methodologies, and implementation is no different. There are four steps within this stage: set-up, design, pilot and implement. Though this is not a rigid process and can be an organic progression, even small projects taken on by busy teams benefit from some reference being made to each step.

SET-UP

A typical set-up process might include the following:

- Completion of prerequisites. These should include: a clear presentation on the history of the process to date, the criteria for success established at the beginning and updated at the decision stage, relevant information gathered at the second stage (understanding), particularly process flow diagrams, benchmarks and, where appropriate, statistical analysis.
- Showing how the relevant decision-making priorities and criteria lead to this strategy.
- Checking the preliminary design requirements. They should be identified by now so there is no unnecessary time lag when the set-up is completed. (See 'The integration barrier'.)
- Reviewing the project definition. This is only necessary in large complex projects and is probably made by the project owner. It allows goals to be reaffirmed.
- Re-examining current team membership, to ensure that members with the right skills and knowledge are on the team. If, as is often the case in an

executive team, the project is now handed over to a subcommittee or a specific project team, this new team may need to take part in some team development. It may also need to redefine its project, which may now be a planning project, a process improvement project or even a problem-solving project. Either way, the project owner should play a major role in selecting the team.

- Checking the team members will be available to work on the project and getting their agreement on the time available for and the priority given to project work—especially when it becomes clear that implementation will require more time and effort than was originally allocated. Where a large or multi-disciplinary project team has been put together, a team development workshop, held before the design work is started, will enable the team to become more productive.
- Writing reports and recommending further actions.

DESIGN

Planning

Though the basic decision will have been made, it is often short on specifics. Each event, in order of occurrence, needs to be identified if the project is to be implemented successfully. A Critical Path Analysis ensures that no critical stages have been missed and the implementation is planned in an appropriate and logical sequence of steps. The plan may include the use of extant methodologies fitted to the project's particular needs, or it may be tailor made. The process expert or team leader makes recommendations for an appropriate design strategy. The team discusses these and agrees on a plan.

Simple projects can be planned informally but the team may allocate the work to specific members or, in the case of a large project, to a subteam. In projects where such tools as Critical Path Analysis are used, the team should either develop its own expertise or import it in the form of additional team members or external consultants. Anyone imported will be someone who knows the situation particularly well and is skilled in managing the kind of project involved. A reporting process has to be agreed. Even the design of a simple project has to be described to enable the next step to be taken.

Once the team has settled on a design strategy, an operational plan is developed. The project owner has to make a significant contribution. The facilitator at this meeting helps the project team members to remain aware of each other so that they may all contribute. A large project development will not only produce an operational system but may include preparation of training courses and the creation of system documentation and support.

System resistance to change

The processes or structures of teams or departments which influence the situation must be identified if the situation is to be better understood. Defensiveness is the biggest obstacle to implementing a new procedure and an implementation team will often find that its performance will be compared with that of other teams. This can create an impasse that an implementation team must consider in addition to the programme's technical difficulties.

Deflection of blame is endemic to organizational culture. Individuals, teams and departments protect themselves against criticism, real or imagined, rather than devote their energy to producing the ideal output— in this case the successful implementation of a complex change programme. Defensiveness is a mechanism that allows a team to maintain its identity and homeostasis.

At present, many decisions seem to lead to radical changes in the way people work. All the familiar structures, processes and culture are being re-engineered out from under them, while extra demands are made on their performance and their jobs are under constant threat. People are suspicious of change and efforts to shift them are bound to meet with serious obstacles.

Defensiveness and resistance are primary error states encountered in teams whose performance is based on a 'specification driven' evaluation of their behaviour: 'As long as we don't make any mistakes and meet our targets in line with the general targets of the company, we will be perceived as successful.' Meanwhile the rest of the team's energy and ability to excel, rather than just meet its specification, is channelled into defensiveness. The issue then becomes not the practicalities of application but fear of failure, on the part of the departments that have to produce results based on the new system. This has to be sorted out before attending to any quirks or bugs in the chosen procedure.

Both System Dynamics and the more simple Force Field Analysis can now help to identify how the organization may resist change. In a large project, System Dynamics will already have been used at the understanding stage, to provide options for choice that have a viable chance of being implemented. Alternatively, Force Field Analysis can be used as a support tool to identify the main restraining forces that have to be reduced if the objective is to be met. A number of forces within the system will try to keep things the same.

Synergies, negative and otherwise

Implementation strategies create winners and losers, causing changes that exclude as well as include. Some teams will get more resources while others will have their resources reduced; new plants will be built and old plants will be closed; new product lines will be developed as old product lines are phased out. The key to success is to watch for opportunities to challenge negative synergies. The people involved meet and, if necessary, can negotiate by using Fisher and Ury's approach (Fisher and Ury 1981). It is then possible to identify those areas in which it is not necessary to create losers, where it is possible to redirect energy or resources into other fruitful areas and where 'losers' are shown ways to support the new strategy that affirm their value to the team.

In one of our large project team exercises, all members are given two red cards, two yellow cards and two green cards, on which they write their name. They also, after deliberation, write the name of another team member on each card. The red cards are for people who, by doing their job well, actually make it more difficult for the writer to do his or her own job: they create negative synergies. The green cards are for people who, in the same way, help the writer's performance: they create positive synergies. The yellow cards indicate opportunities: they are for people who could create positive synergies with the writer through the way they work but that potential is not being achieved. All the cards are then given to the people concerned, without explanation. This done, all members look for the member who is named on their red card, the team splitting into pairs. Those who received the red cards can now ask for an explanation and the pair looks for ways in which both parties can adjust their behaviour to meet their needs. This is helped by following a structured dialogue process. The meetings continue until the team has dealt with all its red cards. It then introduces the yellow cards. The green cards represent affirmations and are equally important to voice, even though there may not be time during the exercise. Sometimes there can be surprises—as when the same pair discovers that one member has a red card to offer and the other a green.

We map these exchanges on a Metaplan board. This shows which members, while doing their job the way they thought best, may be creating obstacles or error states in the team's performance. Some people have negative synergies from all parts of the team, others from only one subgroup. One or two may have received no cards at all, suggesting their isolation. Others may have a lot of opportunities which are not being actualized. After clearing their individual relationships, the team can discuss how to reframe the patterns that have emerged, reducing their negative impact. The exercise avoids blame, while clearing obstacles to success that may have existed for years simply because they were not surfaced.

Maximize ease of adoption

Everett Rogers' criteria for 'adoption of innovation' can be useful, when looking at the implementation plan. A good plan will have details to meet the following criteria built into it:

- *Relative advantage* It should be possible to demonstrate the advantages of the decision to those who will be affected by it, particularly if they are seen to be achieved in a short amount of time and with minimal effort.
- *Compatibility* The new policy, actions and processes should be compatible with the existing values, beliefs, attitudes and practices. If the gap between the two is large, there will be a selling job to do.
- *Complexity* The simpler a solution, process or methodology, the more quickly it may be adopted. New products should be framed simply, at least initially.
- *Feasibility* The less time and resources customers and the team need to invest in implementation, the more rapidly the solution will be adopted. A complex solution may be introduced in smaller chunks.
- *Observability* If the observable advantage of the change is highly visible, it will be adopted by more people more quickly.
- *Availability* It should be easy for team members to gain access to a new methodology and to have the resources required to employ it.

Some further skills that the team will need to show might include:

- innovative ability to contribute to solution design
- analytical ability to assess a current situation and incorporate a new system
- a logical thinking process to plan implementation thoroughly
- interpersonal insight to understand the people issues involved in bringing about change and developing programmes to address those issues
- ability to lead meetings to get ideas, develop designs and prepare plans
- clear communication on technical matters, especially with regard to design
- selling ability to gain acceptance for a properly developed implementation plan.

PILOT

Once the design and development work has been completed, it can be tested on a small scale. This provides an opportunity to check that the system works to the standards agreed at the understanding and decision stages, before launching into a full-scale operation. If implementation is complex, involving a number of groups or stages or if the system is crucial, the project manager or process expert will recommend that implementation itself should be piloted. Should such a pilot be agreed, he or she will help to design it and ensure that criteria for success are established. The results of the pilot can then be evaluated against success criteria before full-scale implementation begins. Lessons learned can then be incorporated into the redesign of the system or implementation process.

The planning schedule should include enough time to (1) test the product or plan, (2) measure its performance, (3) evaluate the results and (4) correct for any shortcomings. For the launch of a major product, such as a cellular phone, a new drug or a new software package, there will be many iterations of this process and the product is continually refined.

IMPLEMENT

Project management

Once the preliminary work has been carried out (at the design and pilot steps) the process is transferred to site for implementation. Details are finalized, including the project's time scale. The initial broad times estimates will have been based upon the objectives of management, the realities of resources and time, the predictions of the Critical Path Analysis and the ongoing negotiation between those pushing for early implementation (management) and those holding back until everything is ready (planning). In fact, these timings are usually agreed and finalized in the earlier design and pilot stages.

While previous implementation stages involved planning, this one involves action. Resource distribution, cost analysis, progress reporting and project management will all need to be watched carefully. The team leader approves the plan, often informally, as much of it will have been prepared earlier or will be a modified version of a pilot that has already been run. The pilot is then put in the context of the whole organization.

When dealing with a large project, a team may be responsible for its entire implementation or operate in a variety of reduced relationships with a larger process. The team should know the extent of its responsibility in the project's management which ranges from modest to substantial involvement.

- As *project consultants*, the team (or certain of its members) acts as a consultant to the team responsible for the implementation of the project. It may be called in to help set up the project, to give support in designing the new system, to advise on implementation, to help develop training or to trouble shoot should something go wrong.
- The team can give additional *project support* by occasionally lending its members to the project team to help write reports, to be on hand for trials and pilots and to attend and facilitate meetings.
- *Project regulation* is a further support that gradually diminishes after the initial stages of implementation. Team members are frequently on site, schedule and run meetings, help set time schedules and provide resources for the project.
- *Project management* can include regulating the schedules of people who act as project resources, subcontracting other internal or external resources, scheduling and allocating resources and directing the project itself.

Obstacles to implementation

I once attended a presentation by a fellow consultant, at the relaunch of a major interactive information system. The system had been developed to deal with the complex issues of maintaining a global record of engineering changes taking place in an automotive design. It had run into problems. This was supposed to track *all* engineering changes in *all* models in *all* the major geographical regions of a major automotive manufacturer and to incorporate them in a gigantic database that was to be constantly updated. Engineers who wanted to make any design change could refer to this database to make certain that a similar change or idea had not already been specified or discarded for design failure reasons. They also had to add any engineering change they made to the database, down to the smallest nut, bolt and fastener. The system had been extremely difficult to develop, with countless bugs and crashes occurring along the way. The development team had spent nearly two years trying to identify all the failure modes and yet the system was still failing or was being ignored.

At an earlier seminar for the end users (the company's engineering departments) to identify why the system was not being implemented and why it had become so deeply resented, my fellow consultant attempted to induce the representatives from each major engineering area to identify obstacles to the system which *might* be internal to their own departments, rather than part of the system itself and which might hinder successful implementation. The participants seemed confused: they did not know of any internal obstacles in their departments to the system being introduced. What was the consultant trying to do? Get them to admit problems in their areas? To embarrass themselves in front of other competing departments? Of course, they all knew hundreds of reasons why such a programme was impossible to introduce and were willing to discuss all of its bugs at length but they made it clear that it was not due to any shortcomings in their own departments.

This is typical of the resistance organizations face when they attempt to introduce change. 'Re-engineers' tend to be better at explaining what should change than how it can be done willingly, productively and with enjoyment. Here are a few typical blocks to creating systemic change.

Ad hocism   Impromptu measures have their place but should usually be avoided at the implementation stage. In the short term, they can simplify the situation and support the more rapid implementation of a plan but, over the longer term, they will not be sustained or will contribute to more severe failures under pressure. Implementation will then stall, inviting another *ad hoc* intervention to shore up the plan. Eventually, the whole rackety system will founder and the consequences will be far worse than if the original plan had been adhered to.

Sabotage   Passive resistance is more effective than active resistance. Non-compliance needs attention. The assumption must be that there is a good (from someone's perspective) reason for it. This needs to be made explicit and acknowledged. A jointly developed compromise or alternative approach will help the plan to proceed with minimal obstruction. It may even result in new insight and an additional source of energy becoming available to support the plan's adoption.

Short-term fixes   Despite knowing better, it is easy to make a short-term decision and then move on. The implementation process needs monitoring since it is not uncommon for those people involved (but not part of the original team) to take shortcuts instead of following the actual implementation strategy.

Scarce resources   There are never enough resources when implementing a project. Yet it is also true that we have seen some organizations where resources were thrown at a long-delayed, over-budgeted project in an attempt to compensate for poor planning or poor project management. We have seen other teams get by on a wing and a prayer and produce outstanding products within remarkably short time spans through sheer willpower and personal commitment. From our perspective, resources need to be available to ensure proper upstream planning and the integration of customer requirements.

Power blocks   The power brokers and territorial watchdogs come into their own at the implementation stage. More projects are beached on the downstream shoals of line management scepticism and resistance, than are successfully launched. Downstream delivery or implementation facilities must be included in the initial stakeholders' analysis and consulted regularly throughout the project. This is the simplest and most effective way to avoid a fall at the last hurdle. When, in spite of all its efforts, the team encounters such resistance, internal negotiations to identify the interests concerned and ways in which they can be met are far more productive than pushing harder against the system. The system will usually find some way to push back and maintain its old homeostasis.

The team must identify interest, build bridges and cultivate personal alliances.

Patterns which maintain or reinforce resistance will only change when they are met with respect. The team should explore and make explicit how they are expressed throughout the hierarchy, avoiding head to head confrontation.

Skills

Some critical skills and competencies to support project implementation include:

- having a wider perspective of the organization and the situation or issue, giving an ability to foresee broad implications of implementation
- scheduling and organizing logistics and resources
- the ability to handle the detailed planning inherent in implementation
- management and leadership skills to run the implementation programme without necessarily having the authority to match the responsibility
- the ability to describe progress clearly and succinctly to the project champion
- the ability to support an ongoing methodology such as Critical Path Analysis
- leading without explicit authority
- persistence to complete the implementation, despite obstacles
- self-awareness to be able to leave the project when it is completed.

INTEGRATION BARRIER

This barrier, also known as the embodiment barrier, is one of the most difficult to understand, yet perhaps the easiest to observe. Implementation strategies are a part of initiatives for change. In order to introduce change successfully the team must integrate the principles, actions, methods and practices associated with the desired outcome of the project. Lack of integration of these qualities is the fourth barrier to success. The barrier stands until the team is consistent and 'walks its talk'. It is not enough to plan, organize, pilot and map out critical paths. The team's behaviour must change.

Teams blocked at the integration barrier do the same thing repeatedly. They insist that each stage of the plan is 100 per cent complete before moving on, that each gateway in the design process is fully ratified by all parties concerned before they continue. They get caught in bureaucratic detail while the programme languishes, customers wait and initiative withers on the vine. All this because they focus too much on details, imperfections and past errors—replaying them instead of relishing new found success. They mistake the plans and strategies for the final product. They mistake repetition of processes and procedures for change, never actually integrating the behaviours themselves. In the word of the Zen monk, they 'mistake the finger pointing to the moon for the moon itself'.

Integration is not just a matter of putting more procedures in place. The focus has to be on people's experience and the spirit of change. The greatest drawback of ISO 9000 is that it often leads to form being mistaken for substance—procedures mistaken for a work ethic, dutiful map reading for emotional engagement, the award of the 'standard' for a change in the hearts and minds of employees.

When a team is stuck at the integration barrier it can give an infinite number of reasons for not having finished, while ignoring that it is being left behind. It runs innumerable pilots but never gets into production. When it does, the joy and enthusiasm of the project are all gone: only boring, repetitive, antiseptic units of action are left. There will be nothing too large, nothing too fast, nothing too exciting, no surprises. Completion with teams at this barrier is forever postponed.

How to overcome the integration barrier

Teams stuck at this barrier lack passion. Although targets need to be met and plans need to be followed, they should not be the only focus. Nor should the team throw all of its planning cards in the air and become 'spontaneous'. If the team is to escape from its stuckness, without traces of resentment or defensiveness, it must either seek acknowledgement from outside or generate it within in the knowledge that appreciation rekindles enthusiasm.

Polarities inherent in the situation need to be explored. As members rediscover their enthusiasm, they become conscious of the death grip of the 'control freaks' in charge. This is a time for give and take. 'Take responsibility for that process and I'll let go of my authorization power.' 'I'll take some responsibility for this project if you will knock that shaky process into shape.' The ad-libbers and the control freaks can then move confidently to the completion stage together.

A team can get bogged down in all the expectations—of management, customers and suppliers—it is attempting to meet. These expectations need simplification, definition and agreement. Then the team can clarify its standards for performance, cut through the mass of detail and re-establish the direction and priorities of the project. Members no longer feel obliged to cover every possible angle.

Implementation involves cultivating relationships with people in a variety of situations and leading in a way that gets something done without the authority to do it. These situations involve a range of relationships, all of which require interpersonal skills. Teams that get stuck at the integration barrier may mistake their charts and reports for the work that has to be done and they need to interact with the people whose lives their plan will affect.

Implementation is time-intensive but time is precious. The desire to provide a perfect system is an admirable quality but can lead to project delay, eventually forcing the team to provide a less than ideal service. Accurate realistic timing plans and an ability to move a project along in line with those plans are both essential. The team has to ensure that its fascination with detail is not wasting time.

The implementation stage of the task cycle is characterized by the need to take responsibility for achieving an objective, without always having the requisite authority. This is difficult and places a premium on a team member's ability to influence, to build trust, to build on the ideas of others, to acknowledge other contributions and to understand other points of view.

OBJECTIVES OF THE IMPLEMENTATION STAGE

A project's success depends on how well it is run. It has to be supported at many levels—by expert knowledge, by the right mix of skills, by timetables, resource allocation and the scheduling of meetings. Responsibility for regulating these factors has to be determined and fulfilled.

Implementation transforms the preliminary work into reality. It is hard work that requires attention to detail and perseverance over time. It is here that all the system dynamics that push towards homeostasis begin to slow, block or diminish success. The preliminary stages of development and decision on a course of action can be exciting—the exploration of ideas, the brainstorming, the debate, the introduction of the unknown. During the implementation stage, however, team members are likely to perform a number of roles that demand perseverance, continuity, holding a clear line on the initial plans and not buckling under resistance to change in the system. This stage does require a special attention to detail.

This stage is completed when ownership of the implementation strategy is handed over to those who are engaged in the day-to-day operation of the system. They then run it without the team's involvement or support. The main objectives of implementation are:

- to give form and structure to the decisions made at stage 3
- to move forward in line with the initial objectives
- to update team membership and designate authority for action
- to provide a systematic plan for actualization
- to run experiments and pilots before final implementation
- to implement the plan with appropriate techniques and methodology
- to use systems mapping to ensure the plan is not obstructed by any systems barriers
- to empower those who will be responsible for supporting the decision with the appropriate skills and knowledge.

19

Completion

Completion is the Cinderella of the team task cycle. This is not because people do not complete but because they do not always do so consciously. Completion asks the team to withdraw its energy and hand over responsibility for maintenance of the change it has accomplished. Too many projects fail to come to fruition, either because they are never fully launched or because they are cast afloat without the initial attention they often need.

THE COMPLETION PROCESS

There are four steps to the completion stage of the task cycle. If these are followed, the right balance of support and independence will be provided. These are: refine the procedures, hand over, improve the system continuously and maintain change.

Refine the procedures

A set of procedures is needed to check conformance to standards of operation, to measure performance against agreed criteria and to monitor results against planned benefits—especially in cost savings. The measurement processes have to be agreed with the end users. It is at this stage, particularly with a large change, that the application of an agreed standard such as ISO 9000 is useful. Although this does not ensure quality, it is a standard against which the performance procedures may be measured.

Hand over

Once the team decision has been implemented and is operational, the ongoing maintenance of the process is handed over.

Resistance from those who are meant to adopt the policy or process is either a refusal to 'buy in' to the new approach or a lack of confidence in its operation or use. 'Buy in' problems need improved communication and management also needs to model the changes. Team members must still demonstrate their enthusiasm for the new system and use good interpersonal skills to tune into staff or user responses. The people taking over the project will be particularly sensitive to the level of commitment shown by the team that is handing over the project.

Cultural change, even on a small scale, requires a basic shift of attitudes, behaviours and beliefs as well as the acquisition of new knowledge and skills. If such changes are not addressed adequately at stage 4 (implementation), further energy may be required to help people downstream to discover new ways to think and feel. Although it will be more difficult at this stage to change behaviour or culture, human issues can no longer be ignored.

Sometimes the team is *still* reluctant to let go. Members may fear that the system is not fully developed or that it may contain some 'bugs' (this is the 'seeking for perfection' syndrome), or that the staff lack sufficient discrimination or cannot yet run the system without additional support.

A successful transition is likely to contain some or all of the following elements:

- The transfer of responsibility for maintenance of the programme and procedures.
- Successful completion of staff training prior to hand-over date for those due to operate the new process.
- Supervised practice after training.
- For a complex process, a phased transition—either by handing over the system part by part or by gradually increasing the degree of responsibility handled by the staff.
- Some simple measures to check that the new system is operating correctly.
- Involvement of the customer/recipient of change in designing the transition programme.
- Consensus achieved through good leadership and communication skills.
- A willingness on the part of the team leader to relinquish control.

- An acceptance by the team leader that achievement of perfection is not necessary.

Improve the system continuously

From a linear perspective, it is essential to ensure that a system continues to address the needs for which it was originally designed. There must be a process to review the system's *raison d'être* and the efficiency with which it performs its task—especially in the context of new ideas and technology. One is also needed to stimulate management action to make any necessary changes.

To support these processes, staff carry out their own continuous improvement reviews and have established channels for feeding back their ideas and eliciting management action. The team may need to arrange systems training for the operators and managers may also need training to understand the implications of empowerment and the way to derive the best results.

Recommendations are made to ensure that the ongoing application of technical and people skills is supported by necessary change in processes and procedures. This, too, is often ignored, although the benefits are self evident. When a major project has been completed, a process improvement team can be set up to follow their team task cycle.

- Errors will continue to be made unless the original faults are corrected.
- So much of the initial work has been done by now that, for a comparatively small outlay, process improvement methodology can be applied successfully.
- Applying process improvement at this stage will guarantee continual updating of structures and processes as required.
- Commitment to following up at this stage introduces the concept of continuous quality improvement to all members of the team.
- It empowers all team members to look for opportunities to improve processes.

Once there has been time to adopt the new process, the team carries out a review and reports back on the results:

- Is the process working properly and being operated correctly by staff?

- Have the staff taken mental ownership of the new process or do they have reservations about what they are doing?
- Is the process delivering the predicted results?
- Has the environment in which the process is operating changed and, if so, should a new process be developed?

The enhanced knowledge and expertise that results from the project should be shared with the rest of the company in the form of:

- best practice
- changes to ISO 9000 criteria
- benchmarking
- presentations on success
- case study material for future training
- other opportunities for continuous improvement.

Maintain change

In addition to the above support for the structural changes that have been implemented, there is value in continuing to support the change through systemic interventions—maintaining momentum and reaching for new target values. Corporate systems will evolve but it is our contention that this evolution can be steered towards unfolding new potential rather than an adaptive approach.

Purpose

One of the key requirements for systems to sustain change is constancy of purpose. Purpose is like the north pole to a team's compass. It helps align and mobilize the team's resources around a common goal. Should clarity of purpose be lost, the system will revert to a previous homeostasis (old ways of doing business or old levels of performance) because no force is being exerted on the system to sustain the growth of desirable factors or induce the reduction of undesirable factors, through negative feedback. Either way, the system will stabilize around some other level or target value but not around an optimal performance.

Auto-correction

Once a clear purpose is established, processes and procedures that ensure continuing momentum for change must be put in place. This is slightly different to the concept of equilibrium. Auto-correction is an aspect of the goal-seeking behaviour of the system. If the processes and procedures are in place to sustain a system's continuous movement towards a goal rather than simply maintaining a certain level of performance, it will bring itself back on target. However, this kind of auto-correction almost inevitably requires intervention by someone who has the skill, a sense of overall system and an idea where it is heading.

Most systems experience some oscillation. When they are targeted towards new values even the most effective change will be regularly out of alignment.

Seek critical mass

The introduction of innovations reaches a critical mass after a certain percentage of the population has adopted that innovation. The team targets its resources at the early adopters and opinion leaders, thereby reaching those people in the system who will adopt the change and present it in a way that is acceptable to their less adventurous colleagues. They become key allies for change and can act as valuable points of leverage.

Control escalation

Once a system begins to change, growth escalates. It is then the job of the team acting as a change agency to ensure that growth is maintained at a healthy level and that no runaway processes—such as the changes in BP's traditional culture mentioned above—cause distortion.

Variety equals success

This is a basic systems principle, not to be undervalued in the context of corporate change. The old days of one culture and one right way of doing things have passed. Diversity and flexibility are key attributes of successful organizations and successful teams. Ludwig von Bertalanffy makes this explicit (1968: 44):

At first systems are governed by dynamic interaction of their components; later on, fixed arrangements and conditions of constraints are established which render the system and its parts more efficient but also gradually diminish and eventually abolish its equi-potentiality. Thus dynamics is the broader aspect, since we can always arrive from general system laws to machinelike function by introducing suitable conditions of constraint but the opposite is not possible.

Continually enrich the new system

The team must now continue to widen and deepen the system by adding more loops where they reinforce emerging patterns, by breaking links which block or hinder change and by seeking out resistance so that it is able to build the concerns into the continuous improvements of its project.

INTERPERSONAL SKILLS

The interpersonal skills required at this stage relate to handling some of the issues that might arise during the post-project review, including:

- allowing the new owners to do the talking
- eliciting staff attitudes and personal agendas that may still be against change
- acknowledging team concerns and addressing the underlying needs
- good and appropriate questioning skills
- detachment, to evaluate the system during review
- persistence, to unearth any new concerns
- clear communication on technical matters
- clear communication on project issues with the project champion and the client
- ability to discover and agree on new procedures and monitoring processes.

WITHDRAWAL BARRIER

A team often becomes so identified and confluent with its output that it finds it difficult to let go. This reflects the self-absorption of being stuck at the withdrawal barrier. It continues to pursue the implementation of its policy long after its involvement is no longer appropriate. Such a team allows its identify to become so intertwined with its policy that the idea of letting go threatens a loss of purpose, self-image and identity. It clings on to the bitter end.

Attachment

It is difficult to leave a project and relationships that are working well. A particular feature of letting go in completion is the potential difficulty on the part of everyone involved in saying 'good-bye' to a person or group with whom there has been a very close working relationship over a significant period of time. The team must make a dispassionate judgement about when their customers are ready and willing to take over full responsibility. They need to be aware of their own emotions and attachments and not allow the customers to jeopardize a successful transfer of responsibility.

Organizational ownership

A new system will not continue successfully after implementation unless the management now responsible takes ownership. The operators of the system need to be empowered, as it is not sufficient merely to follow instructions. They, too, need to consider how the system might be improved, whether it is still appropriate to the current needs and whether there are any other areas in which the systems methodology might be applied. A continuous improvement process may satisfy an operator's reservations but operators who feel empowered can make more substantive, ongoing contributions to improve productivity. They can also greatly enhance organizational ownership of the system. When the organization integrates this sense of ownership, most teams are more than willing to withdraw from a project and hand it over to colleagues.

Group think

The phenomenon of groups clinging desperately to a failed strategy is termed 'group think'. It occurs when team members lose their sense of individual identity and become completely identified with the norms and culture of the team—an example of negative confluence. In so doing, members gain a false sense of invulnerability, a belief in the overriding morality of the team and lose touch with their ability to challenge or question their behaviour or the behaviour of others.

The group think phenomenon can be avoided by ongoing team development, where awareness of self and others is continually expanded and an effective team process with clear mechanisms for feedback is in place. A team suffocated by group think has lost such awareness if indeed it was ever present. Clear communication, the use of descriptive feedback and taking time to check out unspoken assumptions gives a metaperspective and allows the team to retain a more rigorous attitude to its own processes.

OBJECTIVES OF THE COMPLETION STAGE

The broad objectives for this final stage are:

1 Make certain that processes and procedures are in place to support the ongoing application of methodologies and skills in the workplace.
2 Hand over responsibility for maintaining the system after the team's involvement is over.
3 Set into place process improvement procedures so that, if the original situation was the result of failure at some stage, the process is improved to ensure that failure does not recur.
4 Set up a review procedure that will include checking that the new system is delivering the benefits for which it has been designed and installed.
5 Congratulate and reward team members and those who have supported the project during its lifetime.
6 Withdraw and move on.

Addendum:
The team audit

In our fifteen years of working with teams of all shapes and sizes—be they the small executive finance team at the head of a multinational organization or a professional Premier Division Football squad, a four-man Olympic Cycling team or the network of teams formed by a 20 000 plus engineering community—we have learned the importance of mapping the 'big picture'. Repeated experience shows that a preliminary assessment of the nature of the team system, the corporate ecology of which it is a part and the purpose or the team's existence will lay a foundation for effective team building and sustainable corporate change. What started as an informal preliminary 'audit' to minimize discrepancies between a manager's perceptions of a team and what the team members perceived as the 'real' team issues evolved into an appreciation of the richness of 'multiple realities' in team life and the doorway for introducing sustained team development into a corporate system.

A team audit provides the basis for a genuine assessment of team needs whether for an individual executive team or a number of teams in a department of thousands. Such an audit makes it possible to identify the major constraints on optimizing team performance, the team skills which need developing and the most time and cost effective points of leverage for change in the organizational system.

There are four levels at which a team audit can take place:

- Systems mapping
- Team development
- Team meetings
- Team task effectiveness.

SYSTEMS MAPPING

Systems mapping identifies how a team or teams operate within the organization:

- It maps the team system: its inputs, outputs, boundaries and membership.
- It identifies how to optimize basic team structures.
- It shows how to enhance a team's interface with other teams.
- It places the team in the context of the corporate culture and shows how it might expect to be supported or restrained by the organizational ecology in which it is embedded.

TEAM DEVELOPMENT

Opportunities for enhancing team performance are identified by observation of team meetings and through dialogue with team members. This clarifies:

- How to deal with the paradoxes of team life—contact and withdrawal, conflict and co-operation, resistance and change.
- The appropriateness of existing team norms, roles, skills and behaviours which shape the patterns of team life and identity.
- The relationship networks within the team, their positive and negative synergies and the unexploited opportunities for collaboration among team members.
- Ways to refine the internal processes which the team uses to transform its inputs and resources into ideal output.

TEAM MEETINGS

The team audit documents how teams regulate their time and resources during team meetings including:

- How they warm up or warm down—or fail to do so.
- How members communicate with each other during meetings.
- How the team members use feedback to regulate their process.
- How the team balances task, maintenance and process.

TEAM TASK EFFECTIVENESS

The team audit monitors how the key elements of task performance are managed by the team and where it excels or falters in the team task cycle:

- Does the team devote too much or too little time to one of the stages in the task cycle?
- Does the team get stuck on one or more of the transition barriers?
- Does the team utilize the most appropriate tools and techniques to move smoothly through the team task cycle?

Based upon a team audit, several options for team development are possible both at the team and the organizational level:

1 An individual team may proceed on a team development programme to build its identity, maximize its working relationships and cultivate its meeting skills.
2 An integrated programme to develop teams throughout the organization may be initiated to build shared norms and processes for optimal team performance.
3 The organization may target key system constraints to be reduced so that teams can benefit from their multiple team interfaces and function more effectively in the corporate ecology.
4 Team leaders can attend a leadership programme which enables them to manage their teams more effectively.

While we feel that the empowerment of teams must take place at the individual and team level, the opportunities for organizations to consciously reduce the systemic obstacles to successful performance are substantial and resource efficient. The complexity of organizational change requires an informed and systematically organized intervention to assure success. The possibilities provided by the audit allow such change to take place by creating clear direction for optimizing performance at the team and departmental level with minimal resource investment. Equally importantly it enhances both the personal power of the players in the organization and their sense of well being and meaning in their work life.

For information on Sporting Bodymind Ltd, conducting a team audit and team development programmes please contact:

Sporting Bodymind Ltd
28A Hampstead High Street
London, NW3 1QA
England

Telephone   0171 794 4066
Fax   0171 794 6700
E Mail   101360.1211@compuserve.com

References and bibliography

Baguley, Philip, *Managing Successful Projects: A Guide for Every Manager*, Pitman Publishing, London, 1995.

Ballé, Michael, *Managing with Systems Thinking*, McGraw-Hill, London, 1994.

Belbin, Meredith, *Team Roles at Work*, Butterworth Heinemann, Oxford, 1993.

Born, Gary, *Process Management to Quality Improvement: The Way to Document and Re-engineer Business Systems*, John Wiley & Sons, Chichester, 1994.

Brown, Judith R., *The 'I' in Science: Training to Utilize Subjectivity in Research*, Scandinavian University Press, Oslo, 1996.

Buchan, D. and Boddy, D., *The Expertise of the Change Agent: Public Performance and Backstage Activity*, Prentice Hall, Hemel Hempstead, 1992.

Callow, Simon, *Orson Welles: The Road to Xanadu*, Jonathan Cape, London, 1995.

Clarkson, Petrüska and Mackewn, Jennifer, *Fritz Perls*, Sage Publications, London, 1993.

Coombes, Alan, Connolly, Christopher, and Henshall, Ed, 'Engineering quality improvement programme', *World Class Design to Manufacture*, Vol. 2, No. 3, MCB University Press Ltd., Bradford, 1995.

Crosby, Philip, *Quality Without Tears*, McGraw-Hill, New York, 1984.

Csikszentmiyalsi, Mihaly, *Flow, the Psychology of Optimal Experience*, Harper Perennial, New York, 1990.

de Bono, Edward, *The Use of Lateral Thinking*, Penguin Books, Harmondsworth, Middlesex, 1982.

Deming, W. E., *Out of the Crisis*, Cambridge Univerisity Press, Cambridge, 1988.

Drucker, Peter, *The Effective Executive*, Butterworth Heinemann, Oxford, 1988.

Drucker, Peter F., *Innovation and Entrepreneurship*, Heinemann, London, 1985.

Fisher, Roger and Ury, William, *Getting to Yes*, Houghton Mifflin, Boston, 1981.

Forrester, Jay, *Industrial Dynamics*, MIT and Wiley, Cambridge, MA, 1961.

Frew, Jon E., 'The Functions and Patterns of Occurrence of Individual Contact Styles during the Developmental Phases of the Gestalt Group', *The Gestalt Journal*, Spring 1986, Vol. IX, No. 1.

Garfield, Charles A. and Bennett, Hal Zina, *Peak Performance: Mental Training Techniques of the World's Greatest Athletes*, Jeremy P. Tarcher Inc., Los Angeles, 1984.

Garfield, Charles, *Second to None*, Business One, Irwin, Illinois, 1992.

Gleick, James, *Chaos: Making a New Science*, Viking Penguin, New York, 1987.

Grafton, Sue, *J is for Judgment*, Henry Holt & Co., New York, 1993.

Harvey Jones, John, *Making it Happen*, Fontana, London, 1989.

Hillerman, Tony, *Talking God*, Penguin Books, Harmondsworth, Middlesex, 1993.

Howard, William G. Jr and Guile, Bruce R., *Profiting from Innovation*, The Free Press, New York, 1992.

Ishikawa, K., *Guide to Quality Control*, Asian Productivity Organization, Tokyo, Japan, 1982.

Ishiwata Junichi, *IE for the Shop Floor: Productivity through Process Analysis*, Productivity Press, Cambridge, Mass., 1991.

Johnson, Gerry and Scholes, Kevan, *Exploring Corporate Strategy: Text and Cases*, 3rd edn., Prentice Hall International (UK) Ltd, 1993.

Katzenbach, Jon R. and Smith, Douglas K., *The Wisdom of Teams*, Harvard Business School Press, Boston, Mass., 1993.

Kelley, George, *A Theory of Personality: The Psychology of Personal Constructs*, W. W. Norton & Co., London, 1963.

Korb, M., Gorrell, J. and Van De Riet, V., *Gestalt Therapy Practice and Theory*, 2nd edn, Allyn & Bacon, Mass., 1989.

Kuhn, Thomas, *The Structure of Scientific Revolutions*, University of Chicago, 1962.

Lewin, Kurt, *Field Theory in Social Science*, Harper & Brothers, New York, 1951.

Maslow, A., *Motivation and Personality*, Harper & Row, New York, 1954.

Maxwell Clark, James, *On Governors*, 1867.

May, Rollo, *Love and Will*, W. W. Norton & Co., London, 1969.

McKim, Robert H., *Experiences in Visual Thinking*, Brooks/Cole Publishing Co., California, 1980.

Merry, Uri and Brown, George I., *The Neurotic Behaviour of Organizations*, Gardner Press, New York, 1987.

Milgram, S., 'Some Conditions of Obedience and Disobedience to Authority', *Human Relations*, Vol. 18, 1965.

Miller, Michael Vincent, 'The Implications of Gestalt Therapy for Social and Political Change', *The Gestalt Journal*, Spring 1993, Vol. XVI, No. 1.

Mintz, Elizabeth, 'The Training of Gestalt Therapists: A Symposium', *The Gestalt Journal*, Fall 1987, Vol. X, No. 2.

Moody, Paul E., *Decision Making*, McGraw-Hill, New York, 1983.

Morgan, Gareth, *Images of Organization*, Sage Publications, London, 1993.

Moxey, Keith, *The Practice of Theory*, Cornell University Press, Ithaca and London, 1994.

Munro-Faure, Lesley and Munro-Faure, Malcolm, *Implementing Total Quality Management*, Pitman Publishing, London, 1992.

Naranjo, Claudio, 'The Techniques of Gestalt Therapy', *The Gestalt Journal*, Highland, New York, 1980.

Nevis, Ed. C., *Organisational Consulting: A Gestalt Approach*, Gardner Press, New York, 1987.

Oakley, E. and Krug, D., *Enlightened Leadership*, Simon & Schuster, New York, 1993.

Olins, Wally, *The Corporate Personality*, The Design Council, London, 1978.

Panosky, Erwin, *Meaning in the Visual Arts*, Doubleday, Garden City, 1995.

Pedersen, Paul, *A Handbook for Developing Multicultural Awareness*, American Association for Counselling and Development, Alexandria, Virginia, 1988.

Perls, F. S., *Gestalt Therapy Verbatim*, Bantam Books, New York, 1971.

Perls, F. S., Hefferline, R. F. and Goodman, P., *Gestalt Therapy*, Penguin Books, Harmondsworth, Middlesex, 1973.

Peters, Thomas and Waterman, Robert, *In Search of Excellence*, Harper & Row, New York, 1982.

Porter, Michael E., *Competitive Advantage*, The Free Press, New York, 1985.

Porter, Michael E., *Competitive Strategy, Techniques for Analyzing Industries and Competitors*, The Free Press, New York, 1980.

Rogers, Everett, *Diffusion of Innovations*, 3rd edn, The Free Press/Macmillan, New York, 1983.

Satir, Virginia, *Conjoint Family Therapy*, Souvenir Press, London, 1988.

Scherkenback, William W., *The Deming Route to Quality and Productivity*, Mercury Business Books, London, 1982.

Scholtes Peter, *The Team Handbook*, Joiner Associates, Wisconsin, 1990.

Schumacher, E. F., *Good Works*, Jonathan Cape, London, 1979. (Copyright Verena Schumacher.)

Senge, Peter, *The Fifth Discipline*, Doubleday/Currency, New York, 1990.

Siemens, Harry, 'Presentation on a Gestalt Approach in the Care of Persons with HIV', *The Gestalt Journal*, Spring 1993.

Smith, Kenwyn and Berg, David, *Paradoxes of Group Life*, Jossey-Bass, London, 1987.

Syer, John and Connolly, Christopher, *Think to Win*, Simon & Schuster, London, 1991.

Syer, John and Connolly, Christopher, *Sporting Body, Sporting Mind: An Athlete's Guide to Mental Training*, Cambridge University Press, Cambridge, 1984.

Syer, John, *Team Spirit, the Elusive Experience*, Kingswood Press (Heinemann), London, 1986.

Trist, Eric and Murray, Hugh, *The Social Engagement of Social Science, Vol. 1. The Socio-Psychological Perspective*, Free Association Books, London, 1990.

von Bertalanffy, Ludwig, *General System Theory, Foundation, Development, Applications*, George Braziller Inc., New York, 1968 (revised edition 1993).

von Neumann, J. and Morgenstern, O., *Theory of Games and Economic Behaviour*, Oxford University Press, 1953.

Waldrop, M. Mitchell, *Complexity: The Emerging Science at the Edge of Order and Chaos*, Viking Penguin, GB, 1993.

Watzlawick, Paul, Weakland, John and Fisch, Richard, *Change: Principles of Problem Formation and Problem Resolution*, W. W. Norton & Co. Inc., New York, 1974.

Weiner, Norbert, *Cybernetics: Or Control and Communication in the Animals and Machine*, MIT Press, London, 1948.

Weiner, Norbert, *The Human Use of Human Beings: Cybernetics and Society and Machine*, Free Association Books, London, 1989.

Wheelwright, Steven C. and Clark, Kim B., *Revolutionising Product Development*, The Free Press, New York, 1992.

Zinker, Joseph, *Creative Process in Gestalt Therapy*, First Vintage Press, New York, 1978.

Index

Absence, 152, 157
Acceptance/rejection, 68, 83
Acknowledgement role in maintenance, 188–9
Action/reaction, 72
Ad hocism, 362–3
Advice, 227
Affiliation, 131–2
Agenda:
  warming down, 284
  warming up, 174, 178–9
AIDS, 109
Answering techniques, 264–5
Anxiety, 116–18, 221, 311
Appreciation, 161, 293
  of differences, 89–90
Ardiles, Ossie, 236
Assimilation, 54
Attention switching, 67–8
Attentiveness, 165
Attitudes, 222–4
Attunement, 130–2, 165
  connotations, 130–1
Authority, undermining, 119
Auto-correction, 372
Autonomy, 131
Autotelic personalities, 42
Awareness, 54, 70, 77–90, 138, 140–1, 212
  and interest, 79
  Gestalt cycle of, 120
  of differences, 87–9
  of others, 84–7
Awareness Through Movement, 78

Behaviour:
  codes of, 36
  modelling, 143
  patterns, 71, 86
Belbin, Meredith, 85
Belbin model, 145
Belief system, 86
Bell Laboratories, 10
Belonging paradoxes, 68–9
Berg, David, 68, 89, 129, 144, 267
Boardman, Chris, 86
Body language, 86
  and listening skills, 273–5
  and speaking skills, 230
Boundaries, 152–8, 160, 244
  internal, 156–7
  permeable, 154–6
  redrawn, 157–8
  unclear, 153–4
Box, George, 3
Brainstorming, 30, 183
British Institute of Management, 142
British Petroleum, 337
Brown, George, 82, 84, 85, 140, 223, 226, 242, 258
Brown, Judith, 69, 88, 225, 232, 258, 270, 273, 293
Bulkin, Bernie, 125
Burkinshaw, Keith, 158
Bush, George, 133

Carlzon, Jan, 66
Cause and effect, 12
  diagrams, 318

Cause and effect, *cont.*
  distortions, 264
  relationships, 29
Change:
  counterbalancing forces, 121
  force for, 121
  inhibition, 69–70
  proposal for, 126
  resistance to, 121
  system resistance to, 357–8
Chaos, 42
Character assessment, 146
Chat vs. talk, 228–30
Circle check, 110
Circular causality, 11–13
Clarkson, P., 97, 274
Clemence, Ray, 100
Closed systems, 14
Closure, 59–61, 165, 287–8
Coaching, 159
Codes of behaviour, 36
Commitment, 58, 178, 240–1, 351–3
Communication, 102, 226
  verbal, 228, 274
Communication patterns, phases of, 87
Communication skills (*See* Listening
  skills; Questioning skills; Speaking
  skills)
Competency, 41–3
Competition, 111
Complementarity law, 15
Complex systems, 2, 8, 9, 337
Composition law, 14
Comprehension law, 14
Compromise, 24
Concentration, 79
Confidence, 311
Conflict, 100, 110–18, 129, 130, 187
  avoidance, 112–13
  denial, 114–16
  exploring, 111–12
  unresolved, 188
Confluence, 99–100
Confluent conversation, 229

Confusion, 79
Congruence, 311
Connolly, C., 234
Consensus, 24
Consistency, 30–2, 49
Constraints, 37, 40, 41
Consultants:
  help by not helping, 71
  role of, 191
Contact, 78, 156, 160, 161, 212, 214,
  226
  concept of, 54, 91–4
  interruptions of, 94–102
  quality of, 2
  warming up, 173
Contribution by team members, 2–3
Control relinquishment/gain, 70–1
CORE attributes, 49
CORE team, 27–44, 309
Creative competition, 111
Creative indifference, 86
Creative process, 79, 143, 226
Credibility, 311
Critical mass, 372
Critical Path Analysis, 183, 356
Crosby, Philip, 188, 238, 270
Csikszentmiyalsi, Mihaly, 41
Customer–supplier chain, 60
Cybernetics, 10
Cybernetics, 40
Cyberspace, 40

Dass, Ram, 80, 219
Data analysis, 50, 317–18
Data collection, 50
Data collection tools, 316
Data interpretation, 226
Day, Christopher, 167
Decision analysis, 183, 334
Decision making, 183, 331–54
  choosing the best course of action,
    344–51
  commitment barrier, 351–3
  compromise, 347

Decision making, *cont.*
　conceptual biases, 333
　consensus, 348
　counterproductive aspects, 345
　delays, 338–9
　feedback, 350–1
　generic vs. unique solutions, 342–4
　levels of, 345
　leverage points, 336
　limitations, 340
　magnitude, 332
　matrix, 341
　methodology, 341
　models, 47
　nature of decision, 332–3
　options for change, 336
　outputs, 334–5
　polling, 346–7
　process, 50–2, 149, 335–44
　productive aspects, 345
　proposed course of action, 349
　qualitative criteria, 335
　quantitative criteria, 334–5
　ranking issues, 333
　reversibility, 332
　selection issues, 332–3
　shift to risk, 352
　time constraints, 332
　unilateral, 345
　'Where to?' issues, 333
Decision trees, 334, 342
Decomposition law, 14–15
Deflection, 100–2, 269
Deletion, 262–3
Demands, 292–3
Deming cycle, 185
Denial pattern, 140
Descriptive feedback, 39, 141, 142, 206–14, 231
　basic functions, 28–9
　focusing on physical presence, 209
　focusing on speech, 208–9
　stating the obvious, 207–8
Design strategy, 356–60

Design team, 35
Dialogue, 24
Differences:
　appreciation of, 89–90
　awareness of, 87–9
Differentiation, 24
Disclosure, 68–9
Discovery, 128–30
Distortion, 263–4
Double binds, 140–1
Dover, Bob, 168
Drucker, Peter, 343
Dynamic system, 42
Dynamics, 37

Einstein, Albert, 355
Embarrassment, 79, 216
Embodiment barrier, 364–6
Emerson, Ralph Waldo, 78
Empowerment 41, 378
Encouragement, 41
Energy mobilization, 54
Energy transfer, 15
Engagement, 102
　paradoxes, 69
Equipotentiality, 39, 42, 43
Error states, 37, 39, 50
European TOPS (Team Oriented
　　　Problem Solving) programme, 242
Evaluative feedback, 206
Evolving team, 37–43
　key aspects, 38
Exploration, 42–3
External noise factors, 35–6

Facilitation, 143
Facilitation skills, 112
Facilitator, 156, 161, 233, 235, 273
　role of, 191, 200–3, 220
Failure modes and effect analysis, 183
Feedback, 21–5, 39, 40, 55
　as control mechanism, 10
　decision-making, 350–1
　mechanisms, 10

Feedback, *cont.*
 performance, 205–27
 team meetings, 25
 team regulation through, 27–30
 (*see also* Descriptive feedback;
  Evaluative feedback; Negative
  feedback; Positive feedback;
  System feedback)
Feelings, 190–5, 215–18
 and performance, 218
 and thoughts, 216
 contribution of, 217
 personal, 217
 physical and emotional, 217
 pseudo, 216
Feldenkrais, Moshe, 78
Findhorn Foundation, 130, 150, 151,
 198
Fisher, R., 358
Flow, 41–2, 151
Followership, 144–5
Force-field analysis, 322
Ford, Henry, 27
Ford Motor Company, 19, 73, 129, 135,
 166, 181, 182
Ford Technical Education Programme,
 70
Forrester, Alan, 70
Frankl, Victor, 82, 293
Freud, Sigmund, 109
Frozen process, 17–18
Fuller, Buckminster, 106

Gantt charts, 183
Garfield, Charles, 93
General systems theory, 10–11
General Systems Theory, 11
Generalizations, 241–2, 263
Generic situations, 342–4
Gestalt approach, 69, 124
Gestalt cycle, 54–5
Gestalt cycle of awareness, 120
Gestalt dialogue exercise, 234
Gestalt questions, 257–8

Gestalt therapy, 225
Gibson, William, 40
Goals, 135–6
Good-bye, 289–90
Goodman, Paul, 54
Gossip, 234
Governability, 38–9
Group think, 374–5

Hampton, Christopher, 90
Hanafin, Jonno, 289
Harman, 92
Headlines, 243
Hillerman, Tony, 128
Homeostasis, 23–4
Horton, Bob, 337, 338
Human resources representative, 142
Hypersensitivity, 95

Ikelani, Masanari, 66
Image, 139–41
Individual peculiarities, 120
Individuals:
 and affiliation, 131–2
 as limiting factors, 323
Information:
 accessibility, 324
 exchange, 29
 reliability, 324
 validity, 324
Innovation decision process, 55
Inputs, 15, 36
 project teams, 306–7, 331–3
Insight as transition barrier, 57–8
Insight barrier, project teams, 310–13
Integration as transition barrier, 58
Integration barrier, 364–6
 project teams, 364–6
Internal noise, 36
Interpretations, 224–6
Interrelationship diagrams, 183
Interviews, 317
Introjection, 97–8
Involvement, 178

ISO 9000, 365
Isolation, 119, 154

Jaguar Cars, 168
Johari window, 80

Kaizen approach to quality, 169
Katzenbach, J. R., 104, 107, 132, 145,
    187, 188
Key points, 244
Klein, D., 121
Knowledge, project teams, 305
Knowledge requirements, 55
Korb, Margaret, 239
Krug, D., 131

Labelling, 146
Leadership (*See* Project teams; Team
    leaders)
Linear causality, 12
Links, 244, 337–8
Listening circle, 276–82
    adaptation, 282
    likes, 279–80
    proposal, 277–8
    restatement, 278–9, 282
    wishes, 280–2
Listening skills, 266–82
    being out of touch, 272
    body language in, 273–5
    good listening, 272–5
    inattention, 267–8
    listening to the sound of the voice,
        273
    making contact, 272–3
    not hearing, 269–71
    poor listening, 267–72
    quality of listening, 275
    selective attention, 268–9
    synergistic listening, 275–82
Lloyd, John Bailey, 45
Lloyd Webber, Andrew, 90
Loops, 337–8
Luff, Bill, 66

McGeecham, Ian, 107
Maintenance, 187–95
    acknowledgement role in, 188–9
    and personal response, 190–1
    breaking down, 187–8
    difficulty with feelings, 192
    disclosure of feelings in, 191–2
    informal encounters, 189–90
    integrating feelings, 193–5
    physical and emotional feelings,
        192–3
    relationship with task and process,
        198–9
    review, 294
    warming down, 286
Males, Jonathan, 222
Marcus, Steve, 264
Marketing team, 35
Maslow, Abraham, 40
Mason, Jessica, 219
Maxwell, James Clark, 10, 18
Meetings, 142
Mental training, 110, 159
Mentoring, 159
Metaperspective, 15
Metaphors in speaking skills, 243
Metaplan board, 88, 138, 359
Metaposition, 79, 82
Middle zone, 72, 73
Milgram experiments, 17
Milhone, Kinsey, 84
Miller, M.V., 92
Mind reading distortions, 264
Mintz, Betsy, 86
Mirroring, 210
Mission statement, 133
Mobilization barrier, 58, 329
Modelling, 147, 210–11
Monitoring, 28, 32, 34, 47
Moody preference charts, 183
Morgan, Gareth, 318, 336
Multicultural awareness, 86
Multiple-choice questions, 255
Multiple realities, 129

Myers–Briggs, 145

Narcissism, 351
Negative feedback, 21–3, 40, 319–20, 340
  continuous, 23
Negative projection, 96
Negative reinforcement, 17
Networks, project teams, 305
Neuromancer, 40
Neurotic competition, 111
Nevis, Ed, 92, 114, 118, 120, 219
Noise factors, 35–6, 37, 49
Normalization, 263–4
Norms, 136–41
  focus switching, 152
  of unacceptable behaviour, 137
  old-fashioned human values, 136
  re-evaluation, 137

Oakley, E., 131, 133, 143
Objections, 119–20
Off-handedness, 240
Onassis, Jacqueline Kennedy, 109
One-on-one relationships, 174
Open systems, 14
Optimal performance, 42, 327
Optimal team, 32–4
  concept of, 33–4
  consistency of performance, 33–4
Outputs, 16, 36, 39
  project teams, 307–8

Pair relationships, 160
Pairs fantasy, 87–8, 100
Paradox of intimacy, 267
Paradoxical intervention, 211
Pareto charts, 318
Past–Present–Future approach, 181–4
Pederson, Paul, 86
Performance, 4
  consistency of, 33–4
  feedback, 205–27
  improvement, 8

maximization, 2
measurements, 7–8
potential, 120
regulation, 29
variation, 30–2
  common causes, 31–2
  specific causes, 31
Perls, Fritz, 54, 70, 221, 227, 230, 240, 257, 274, 289
Perls, Laura, 79
Perryman, Steve, 66–7
Personal differences, 129
Personal names, 232–3
Personal response, 212–14
  and maintenance, 190–1
  interrupting, 220
Personality models, 27
Personality profiling, 146
Persuasion, 55
PERT charts, 183
Peters, Tom, 70, 130, 141, 167, 303
Pilot scale, 360
Plan–Do–Study–Act (PDSA) cycle, 185–6
Planning tools, 183–4
Polarities, 72–6
Polarization, 187
Positive feedback, 21, 22, 40, 319
Power blocks, 363–4
Power sharing, 345
Precedence charts, 342
Prioritization, 183, 334, 341–2, 345, 350
Problem prevention, 150
Problem profiling, 318
Problem relationships, 72
Problem-solving, 48, 149, 339
  application of methodology, 339
  methodology, 182–3
  models, 47
Problem-solving teams, 35, 154, 318
Process benchmark, 47
Process flow charts, 317
Process improvement, models, 47
Process observation, 32

Process orientation, 18
Project management, 52, 360–1
  schedule, 184
Project planning, 356–60
Project teams, 299
  action planning, 308
  adoption criteria, 359–60
  autonomous teams, 302
  boundaries, 305
  communication, 305–6
  completion process, 368–75
  consistency, 325–7
  contact, 305
  continuous system improvement,
    370–1
  criteria for success, 308
  data collection, 314–18
  decision-making stage, 331–54
  evolution, 310, 328
  executive teams, 302
  formalization, 304
  formation, 303–6
  functional teams, 300
  hand-over, 369–70
  heavyweight teams, 301–2
  identity, 305
  implementation, 335–67
  implementation skills, 364
  implementation strategies, 358–9
  inputs, 306–7, 331–3
  insight barrier, 310–13
  integration barrier, 364–6
  interpersonal skills, 373
  knowledge, 305
  leadership, 306
  lightweight teams, 301
  members, 299
  mobilization barrier, 329
  networks, 305
  objectives, 308
    completion stage, 375
    decision stage, 353–4
    implementation stage, 366–7
    recognition stage, 313

    understanding stage, 330
  observation, 314–18
  obstacles to implementation, 362–4
  organizational ownership, 374
  outputs, 307–8
  performance optimum, 327
  pilot scale, 360
  presenting issue re-examination,
    314–15
  process, 305–6, 335
  purpose, 312
  recognition stage, 299–313
  recommendations for action, 324–5
  refining the procedures, 368
  regulation, 309–10, 325–8
  reporting, 325
  reporting format, 299
  resources, 307
  robustness, 327–8
  roles, 304
  size, 304
  skunk works, 303
  small operations teams, 302–3
  structural changes in system, 371–3
  structure, 304–5, 335
  structure, processes and identity, 300
  system feedback, 309–10
  understanding stage, 314–30
  understanding the situation, 314–25
  widening and deepening
    understanding, 315–16
  withdrawal barriers, 373–4
Projection, 94–7, 159
Psychoanalysis, 225
Psychometrics, 27
Pugh concept selection techniques, 183

Quality, *kaizen* approach to, 169
Quality team, 119
Questioning skills, 246–65
  expression, 252
  Gestalt questions, 257–8
  'how?' questions, 258–9, 259–60
  structure, 252

Questioning skills, *cont.*
  supportive questioning, 255–64
  unsupportive questioning, 246–55
  vocabulary, 251
  'what?' questions, 256–7, 259–60
  'where?' questions, 258–60
Questionnaires, 317
Questions:
  and statements, 237–8
  asking for advice, 247–8
  biased, 250–5
  clarification, 262–4
  closed, 252–3, 260
  deflective, 248–9
  dichotomous, 254–5
  multiple-choice, 255
  open, 252–3, 260–2
  task development, 250–5, 259–64
  team development, 246–50, 256–9
  'why?' questions, 249
  with hidden subtext, 246–7, 250–5
  yes/no, 253–4

Reaction (*See* Action/reaction)
Recorder, 203
References, 148
Regulation, 39, 50
  project teams, 309–10, 325–8
  through feedback loops, 27–30
Reification, 240
Rejection (*See* Acceptance/rejection)
Relationships, 21, 72, 95, 147
  as limiting factors, 323–4
  between team members, 1–3, 8, 84–7,
    151
  with team leaders, 96
Reporting, project teams, 299, 325
Research skills, 316
Resentments, 290–2
Resistance, 109–26, 158–9, 311–12
  as healthy defence, 118–24
  as need in another direction, 120
  as strength, 123–4
  exploring, 125–6

  forms of, 109
  supporting, 124–6
  (*See also* Change)
Respect, 102
Response, 68–9
Responsibility, 71, 86, 239, 241, 374
Retroflection, 99
Risk:
  in decision-making, 352
  priority numbers, 183
Risk-taking, 105
Ritual, 132
Robust team, 35–7
Rogers, Everett, 55, 359
Rushforth, Winifred, 221

S curves, 319–20
Sabotage, 363
Sapir, Edmund, 230
Satir, Virginia, 225
Scapegoating, 154
Scarce resources, 363
Schumacher, Fritz, 42
Scribe, 203
'See...imagine...feel...exercise', 231
Selection criteria, 148–9
Self-acceptance, 83
Self-actualization, 41, 42
Self-appreciation, 82–3
Self-awareness, 41, 71, 78–82, 97, 126,
    257
Self-image, 80, 139, 141, 147
Self-regulation, 39, 138, 205, 309
Self-steering, 40, 42
Self-support, 227
Semler, Ricardo, 143
Senge, Peter, 56
Set-up process, 335–6
Shewart cycle, 185
Short-term fixes, 363
Siemens, H., 82
Signposts, 243
Simon, David, 337
Skunk works, 303

Smith, D.K., 104, 107, 132, 145, 187, 188
Smith, Kenwyn, 17, 68, 89, 129, 144, 267
Speaking/acting paradoxes, 69
Speaking directly to other team members, 233–4
Speaking skills, 228–45
  and body language, 230
  commitment, 240–1
  'either-or' statements, 241
  generalizations, 241–2
  'I' statements and responsibility, 239
  'I won't' vs. 'I can't', 239–40
  metaphors in, 243
  negative effect of 'but', 238–9
  off-handedness, 240
  reframing problems, 242
  use of first person, 235–7
  use of 'really', 242–3
Sporting Bodymind Ltd, 379
Sports team, 35
Statements and questions, 237–8
Statistical process control (SPC), 324
Steering, 40
Step-down process, 56
Strategic planning, 52
Stratford, Claire, 256
Stress effects, 147
Structural patterns, 7
'Stuckness' (being stuck), 72–6, 110
Subliminal clues, 86
Success, 123
Suggestion boxes, 169
Swiggert, Robert, 346
SWOT analysis, 48, 183, 334
Syer, John, 105, 234
Symbols, 132
Symptom prescription, 293
Synergy, 14, 106–8, 113, 129–30, 151
System boundaries, 14, 18–21
System dynamics, 56, 357–8
System elements, 15
System feedback, project teams, 309–10

System resistance to change, 357–8
System stability, 23–4
Systems analysis, 318–24
  limiting factors, 322–4
Systems approach, 50
Systems behaviour, 319–21
  delay, 320–1
  oscillation, 321
Systems interventions, 339
Systems laws, 14–15
Systems mapping, 377
Systems theory, 9–18
  basic concepts, 11–18
  origins, 10–11
Systems thinking, 10–11

Talk vs. chat, 228–30
Task, 180–7
  definition, 180
  development, questions, 250–5, 259–64
  effectiveness, 378
  optimizing effectiveness, 186–7
  Past–Present–Future approach, 181–4
    analysis stage, 181–2
    decision making, 183
    planning, 183–4
    problem-solving methodology, 182–3
  Plan–Do–Study–Act (PDSA) cycle, 185–6
  relationship with maintenance and process, 198–9
  responsibility, 52
Task life cycle, 7, 45–61, 186
  closure stage, 59–61
  five-stage model, 46–54
  potential pitfalls, 59–61
  Stage 1: Recognition, 48–9
  Stage 2: Understanding, 49–50
  Stage 3: Decision making, 50–2
  Stage 4: Implementation, 52–3
  Stage 5: Completion, 53–4

Team audit, 32, 376
  levels of, 376
Team behaviour, 29
  current patterns, 134–5
Team boundaries, 18–21
Team building, 36
Team development, 32, 77–108, 303–4, 377, 378
  model, 7
  points of focus, 180
  questions, 246–50, 256–9
  systems approach, 9
  workshops, 117, 121, 125, 131, 137
Team effectiveness, 4, 25, 40, 61, 149
Team experience, 65–76
Team identity, 21, 65–6, 127–61
  alignment with, 131
  and absence, 152
  new, 150
  past, present and future, 127
  reflections, 145
  warming up, 175–6
Team leader, 60, 141–5
  change of, 144
  conflict, 100
  control relinquishment/gain, 70–1
  heavy-handed, 120
  help by not helping, 71
  relationships between team members and, 96
  responses and relationships, 84–7
  role of, 199–200
  self-appointed, 119
  trust, 103
Team life, 21
Team meetings, 34, 377
  agenda, 178–9
  combining roles, 204
  feedback loops, 25
  furniture arrangement, 168–9
  location of venue, 167–70
  non-habitual environments, 168
  purpose of, 176–8
  roles in, 199–204

warming up (*See* Warming up)
  (*See also* Maintenance; Task; Team process)
Team members, 20, 49, 65–6
  newcomers, 138–9, 150
  paradox of, 131
  qualities and skills, 145–7
  recalcitrant, 122
  relationships between, 147
Team norms, 72–3, 191, 196
Team performance (*See* Performance)
Team process, 3, 8–9, 16–18, 195–8
  characteristics, 29–30
  completion stage, 53–4
  decision stage, 51–2
  definition, 17
  focus on, 34
  implementation stage, 53
  interventions, 196–8
  maximizing, 29
  project teams, 305–6, 335
  recognition stage, 49
  relationship with task and maintenance, 198–9
  understanding stage, 50
Team respect, 226
Team roles, 96
Team size, 150–2, 155
Team skills, 32
Team spirit, 78, 102–8, 155, 214
  experience of, 105–6
Team structure, 16–18
Team system, 2, 7–26, 36, 49, 159–61
  continuity, 21
Team task (*See* Task)
Telia Respons, 338
Threats, 170
Time manager, 203
Tomlins, Lily, 107
Tone of voice, 86
Traits, 71
Transition barriers, 56–9
  commitment, 58
  insight, 57–8

Transition barriers, *cont.*
  integration, 58
  mobilization, 58
  withdrawal, 58
Trust, 103, 311
Turner, Ted, 82
Tynan, Kenneth, 83

Unfinished business, 219
Unique events, 342–3
Unsolicited advice, 71
Ury, W., 358
Ury–Fisher negotiation model, 89

Value judgement distortions, 264
Verbal communication, 228, 274
Vision, 133–6, 143
von Bertalanffy, Ludwig, 11

Warming down, 165, 283–95
  agenda, 284
  good-bye, 289–90
  maintenance, 286
  oneself, 294–5
  purpose, 285–6
  review questions, 286–7
  unfinished business, 290
Warming up, 139, 165–79
  agenda, 174, 178–9

background factors, 167
contact role, 173
late arrivals, 174
maintenance, 175–6
need for, 165
personal routines, 171–2
programmed, 174
purpose of meeting, 176–8
stages of, 166
structure, 167–79
team identity, 175–6
timing, 165–6
Waterman, R., 303
Weiner, Norbert, 10, 40
Welles, Orson, 83
Wilder, Billy, 90
Withdrawal, 54–5, 66
  as transition barrier, 58–9
Withdrawal barriers, 373–4
  project teams, 373–4
Wordsworth, William, 91
Working group, concept of, 107
Workshops, team development, 117, 121, 125, 131, 137

Zinker, Joseph, 95, 97, 229
Zuckerman, Janet, 223